SEX IN ADVERTISING

LEA's COMMUNICATION SERIES
Jennings Bryant and Dolf Zillmann, General Editors

Selected titles include:

Berger • *Planning Strategic Interaction: Attaining Goals Through Communicative Action*

Bryant/Zillmann • *Media Effects: Advances and Theory in Research, Second Edition*

Ellis • *Crafting Society: Ethnicity, Class, and Communication Theory*

Greene • *Message Production: Advances in Communication Theory*

Shepherd/Rothenbuhler • *Communication and Community*

Singhal/Rogers • *Entertainment Education: A Communication Strategy for Social Change*

Zillmann/Vorderer • *Media Entertainment: The Psychology of Its Appeal*

For a complete list of titles in LEA's Communication Series, please contact Lawrence Erlbaum Associates, Publishers at www.erlbaum.com

SEX IN ADVERTISING

Perspectives
on the Erotic Appeal

I 6 02 0I

Edited by

Tom Reichert
University of Alabama

Jacqueline Lambiase
University of North Texas

LAWRENCE ERLBAUM ASSOCIATES, PUBLISHERS
2003   Mahwah, New Jersey   London

Credits

Chapter 9: Advertising and Disconnection by Jean Kilbourne. Reprinted with the permission of The Free Press, a Division of Simon & Schuster, Inc. from CAN'T BUY MY LOVE: How Advertising Changes the Way We Think and Feel (originally published in hardcover entitled DEADLY PERSUASION) by Jean Kilbourne. Copyright © 1999 by Jean Kilbourne.

Chapter 10: Adcult and Gender by James B. Twitchell. From *Adcult USA* (1996). New York: Columbia University Press; pp. 142–160. Reprinted with the permission of the publisher, Columbia University Press, and James B. Twitchell, Department of English, University of Florida, P.O. Box 117310, Gainesville, FL 32611-7310.

Chapter 11: Subliminal Sexuality: The Fountainhead for America's Obsession by Wilson Bryan Key. Printed with the permission of Dr. Wilson Bryan Key. Copyright © 2002 by Mediaprobe, Inc.

Cover design concept by Susan Daria. Image used courtesy of Bisou-Bisou.

Lawrence Erlbaum Associates, Inc., Publishers
10 Industrial Avenue
Mahwah, NJ 07430

Library of Congress Cataloging-in-Publication Data

Sex in advertising : perspectives on the erotic appeal / edited by
 Tom Reichert, Jacqueline Lambiase.
  p. cm. — (LEA's communication series)
Includes bibliographical references and index.
ISBN 0-8058-4117-2 (cloth : alk. paper)
ISBN 0-8058-4118-0 (pbk. : alk. paper)
1. Sex in advertising.   I. Reichert, Tom.   II. Lambiase, Jacqueline.
 III. Series
HF5827.85 .S494 2002
306.7—dc21   2002023530
                                                                CIP

Books published by Lawrence Erlbaum Associates are printed on acid-free paper, and their bindings are chosen for strength and durability.

Printed in the United States of America
10 9 8 7 6 5 4 3 2

Contents

Preface   ix

1   One Phenomenon, Multiple Lenses: Bridging   1
Perspectives to Examine Sex in Advertising
Tom Reichert and Jacqueline J. Lambiase

Part I: Research Approaches to Sex in Advertising

2   What Is Sex in Advertising? Perspectives From   11
Consumer Behavior and Social Science Research
Tom Reichert

3   Historical and Psychological Perspectives of the Erotic   39
Appeal in Advertising
Juliann Sivulka

4   Dark Desires: Fetishism, Ontology, and Representation   65
in Contemporary Advertising
Jonathan E. Schroeder and Janet L. Borgerson

Part II: Consumer Responses to Sex in Advertising

5 Nudity and Sexual Appeals: Understanding   91
       the Arousal Process and Advertising Response
       Michael S. LaTour and Tony L. Henthorne

6 The Effects of Sexual Appeals on Physiological,   107
       Cognitive, Emotional, and Attitudinal Responses
       for Product and Alcohol Billboard Advertising
       Annie Lang, Kevin Wise, Seungwhan Lee, and Xiaomei Cai

7 Sex(haustion) Sells: Marketing in a Saturated   133
       Mediascape
       Collin Gifford Brooke

8 Toward a Theory of Advertising Lovemaps in Marketing   151
       Communications: Overdetermination, Postmodern
       Thought and the Advertising Hermeneutic Circle
       Stephen J. Gould

Part III: Cultural Impact and Interpretation

9   Advertising and Disconnection   173
        Jean Kilbourne

10 Adcult and Gender   181
        James B. Twitchell

11 Subliminal Sexuality: The Fountainhead   195
        for America's Obsession
        . Wilson Bryan Key

Part IV: Contexts and Audiences

12   Masculinism(s) and the Male Image: 215
        What Does It Mean To Be a Man?
        Barbara B. Stern

13   Media at the Margins: Homoerotic Appeals   229
        to the Gay and Lesbian Community
        Gary R. Hicks

14   Sex—Online and in Internet Advertising   247
        Jacqueline J. Lambiase

Part V: Conclusion

15   Future Questions and Challenges: Advertising Research   273
        in the Midst of Sex Noise
        Jacqueline Lambiase and Tom Reichert

        About the Contributors   279

        Author Index   283

        Subject Index   289

Preface

Despite the presence of sexual information in mainstream advertising, either in the form of sexual behavior, nudity, attractive models, fetishism, or promises of sexual fulfillment and intimacy, few sources are available to those interested in studying this multifaceted phenomenon. Although sexual appeals are used to sell more products—and to boost popularity of media products such as television programming, films, magazines, music, and Web sites—many scholars and consumers are still unable to describe "if" and "how" sex sells. In our minds, it was time for a book devoted to reviewing and advancing understanding of the interpretations, functions, and effects of sex in advertising.

Sex in Advertising: Perspectives on the Erotic Appeal addresses these concerns by bringing together writers, thinkers, and researchers from several areas to examine what sex "is" in advertising, how it works, and how it may affect consumers and society. Nearly all of the contributors have written extensively about sex in advertising, whereas others apply theory in new ways to reexamine representations of sexuality in advertising. As a result, this book contains a variety of perspectives focused on a singular theme, to offer readers a definitive source that spans quantitative and qualitative perspectives to document past research, report ground-breaking research, and provide clear directions for future research. In addition, this book helps those interested in the nature and nuances of erotic appeals to navigate the disparate information available within disciplinary boundaries, but perhaps not well known beyond those boundaries.

That there was a need for this book became clear to us while conducting our own research. In the process of familiarizing ourselves with sexual appeal research in our respective areas, we became aware of important viewpoints in other disciplines during literature searches and attendance at conference sessions. Yet, except for these chance meetings, there was little cross-fertilization of ideas among these multiple camps.

As relationships were established with people working in this area, including theorists, popular authors, and researchers, it became clear that a book combining perspectives was needed. Researchers were contacted and asked to outline new ideas, to summarize their work, or to apply new concepts. As a result, this book includes work by James Twitchell, currently a leading voice on advertising, especially after the publication of his book *Adcult* in 1996. Similarly, Jean Kilbourne, renowned for her lectures and video presentations on the harmful effects of ad images on women and relationships, added her perspective. Kilbourne's popular documentary series, *Killing Us Softly*, has influenced thousands of students around the country. This book also includes original work by Wilson Key, one of the most prolific (and widely read) writers on the issue of sexual embeds in advertising and media. Key's writings, *Subliminal Seduction* and *Clam-plate Orgy*, have sold millions and influenced not only a generation, but sparked considerable controversy as well. Key agreed to express his views on the cumulative effects of years of corporate media subliminal sexualization on society.

The book also contains work from a mix of academic contributors in advertising, marketing, mass communication, telecommunications, humanities, and journalism. They include Janet Borgerson, Collin Brooke, Xiaomei Cai, Stephen Gould, Tony Henthorne, Gary Hicks, Annie Lang, Michael LaTour, Seungwhan Lee, Jonathan Schroeder, Juliann Sivulka, Barbara Stern, and Kevin Wise. These writers supply another essential characteristic of this book by providing the many lenses through which issues relevant to sex in advertising may be viewed. For example, Gary Hicks discusses the development of the homosexual press and how its evolution gave rise to sexual expression in gay and lesbian magazine ads. Barbara Stern outlines how men and the ideals of masculinity have been portrayed and imagined over time. Her views are important in the context of this collection, especially because the editors' own research has shown men to be increasingly portrayed sexually in advertising, even while images of women still provide the content for most sex-tinged appeals. Juliann Sivulka traces advertising's history of sexual appeals in the 20th century, while Collin Brooke explores the notion of *(sex)haustion* in the cluttered mediascape of late capitalism. To address visual consumption in an image economy, Jonathan Schroeder and Janet Borgerson study fetishistic depictions in advertising. Stephen Gould introduces theory from sex research to describe how people's lovemaps, which are personal guides to how people think and feel about their own sexuality, influence their responses to sex in advertising. The flexibility of these lovemaps is shown in his discussion of the inroads of Tantric sex into Western culture and practice. Annie Lang and her colleagues test consumers' emotional and cognitive responses to sexual appeals in billboard ads, while Michael LaTour and Tony Henthorne create links among sex in advertising research on psychophysiological response, ethical consequences, and feminist issues. In separate chapters, the editors themselves reflect on the past and speculate on the future, by outlining the ways that sex in advertising has been studied by consumer behavior scholars and by beginning to chart the use of such appeals online. Many chapters contain recommendations for future research on this topic.

Another goal of this book is to provide a range of perspectives. Instead of speaking about sexual appeals in advertising by way of dichotomy, this collection approaches the subject by way of a continuum in order to emphasize the richness of studies in that middle ground between qualitative and quantitative research. Because scholars from both the sciences and humanities have been discussing sexual appeals inside disciplinary boundaries, this collection allows dialogue to occur across those boundaries to create synergy among these varied perspectives.

Quantitative perspectives include studies of audience effects and individual difference variables, integrative reviews of past research, and new studies building on past research using social science theories not yet applied to understanding the effects of sexual appeals. Definitional issues are addressed, as well as directions for future research. The qualitative perspectives explore past and current theories, propose new theories with a basis in qualitative studies, and use the tools of these varied disciplines to scrutinize and understand sexually oriented content in advertising and new media.

ACKNOWLEDGMENTS

Although we are responsible for organizing and compiling the work within this volume, much credit goes to the people at Lawrence Erlbaum Associates who saw the value of this book. Specifically, Linda Bathgate, the editorial board, and the series editor Jennings Bryant deserve credit for recognizing the need for a contributed collection in this area. With their guidance and constructive suggestions, and those of the anonymous reviewers, this book is better organized and accessible to readers. In addition, help from Karin Wittig Bates, Linda Eisenberg, and LEA's marketing team has been especially important.

As deserving of special recognition are the valuable and meaningful projects from the contributors themselves. Special thanks to Janet Borgerson, Collin Brooke, Stephen Gould, Tony Henthorne, Gary Hicks, Wilson Key, Jean Kilbourne, Annie Lang, Michael LaTour, Jonathan Schroeder, Juliann Sivulka, Barbara Stern, and James Twitchell. All contributed groundbreaking work that was substantive, easy to read, and most important, easy to edit. We sincerely appreciate your attention to deadlines and special requirements. It was a pleasure to work with all of you.

In addition, this work would not have been possible without help and support from our departmental colleagues, as well as the Department of Journalism at the University of North Texas and the Department of Advertising and Public Relations at the University of Alabama. Both of our departments buoyed us with resources and encouragement. The following students also were helpful with compiling information: Joshua Buckman, Kenna Sloan, and Thomas Kidenda. Other supporters along the way include Susan Heckler, Sally Jackson, Chris Puto, David Williams, Kay Colley, Nancy Durr, Stacy Anderson, Jennifer Crowder, Melissa Handley, Vicki Dutcher, and Chrissie Schroyer.

Finally, our families deserve much gratitude. For Tom, his wife Jill and his Grandmother Christamae were steadying forces. And from Jacqueline, much love goes to her spouse, Tom Lambiase, and daughters, Tacy and Emma, as well as to her parents, Rosalyn and Jim Johnson.

—Tom Reichert
—Jacqueline Lambiase

REFERENCES

Key, W. B. (1973). *Subliminal seduction: Ad media's manipulation of a not so innocent America.* New York: Signet.

Key, W. B. (1986). *The clam-plate orgy and other subliminal techniques for manipulating your behavior.* New York: Signet.

Kilbourne, J. (Writer/Creator), & Jhally, S. (Producer/Director). (2000). Killing us softly 3: Advertising's image of women [Motion picture]. (Available from Media Education Foundation, 26 Center Street, Northhampton, Massachusetts 01060)

Twitchell, J. (1996). *Adcult USA: The triumph of advertising in American culture.* New York: Columbia University Press

One Phenomenon, Multiple Lenses: Bridging Perspectives to Examine Sex in Advertising

Tom Reichert
University of Alabama

Jacqueline J. Lambiase
University of North Texas

Although most Americans report being turned off by sexy ads and feeling less likely to purchase products that feature sexual imagery in ads (Fetto, 2001), marketers continue to use more sex in advertising for a greater range of products. For example, a recent ad in *Linux Journal* for computer hardware products featured the face of an attractive woman and this headline: "Don't feel bad, our servers won't go down on you either." Although the ad is tasteless and sexist, it represents a use of sexual imagery and double entendre used to sell a brand not traditionally linked to sex. At the same time, brands traditionally associated with sex appeals—designer clothing and accessories, alcohol, and "better sex" videos—appear to be featuring sexual imagery that is increasingly explicit (Reichert, Lambiase, Morgan, Carstarphen, & Zavoina, 1999; Shapiro, 1993; Soley & Reid, 1988).

Despite the perpetual encroachment of sexual appeals into mainstream advertising, academic research has failed to keep up. According to Michael Ross, president of the Society for the Scientific Study of Sexuality, "Health and science professionals are among the last groups who are comfortable with sexuality" (2001, p. 2). Ross argued that media coverage of sexual issues such as the advent and subsequent promotion of Viagra, along with the sensationalism of the Clinton–Lewinsky affair, has resulted in an American public better able to handle sexual issues than ever before. The academy, however, remains somewhat conservative regarding issues and research about sexuality (Bullough, 1994). Researchers who pursue sexual

1

research risk scrutiny and aspersions from colleagues and administrators, even from those outside academe (see LaTour & Henthorne, chap. 5, this volume.) This may be one reason that appeals using fear and humor—strategies arguably as common as sexual appeals—receive more research attention and are better understood than sexual appeals. Researchers who eschew institutional pressures and ignore raised eyebrows, at least regarding sexuality in advertising, are brought together in this book.

Another factor that may be limiting the development of sex-appeal research is the cloaking of such knowledge within disciplinary boundaries or methodological schools of thought. These boundaries prevent scholars and students new to the study of this phenomenon from easy access to existing scholarship. Even within the chapters of this book, there is little cross-pollination among disciplines. Note, for example, that the chapter by Sivulka, an advertising historian, contains only one reference to work by advertising effect researchers or interpreters. Similarly, work by quantitative researchers LaTour and Henthorne contains no references of work by cultural theorists. Marketers assess reactions to sexual information, whereas scholars in the humanities are more interested in interpretations of the meaning of sexuality in advertising, and what it reflects about contemporary culture. Although scholars are talking about the same representations, they see them in different ways for different reasons.

MULTIPLE PERSPECTIVES

Sexuality is a fundamental characteristic of people that influences their thoughts and behaviors, their orientations toward others, and life in general. Freud may have overstated his claim that everything people do can be linked to sexual motivations, but his ideas have had profound impact in the development of theories and research models about sex and consumption patterns, influencing studies about what people drive, what they wear, and what fragrances they use. Scholars from different research traditions vary in terms of the levels of meaning they analyze and the concerns they address with regard to sex in advertising. For example, marketers are primarily concerned with micro-level effects; they want to know how sexual information evokes reactions within viewers, and how those reactions influence consumer behavior. Important variables include attention, feelings about the ad and about the brand, memory, and intentions to purchase the advertised product. In this context, marketing research on sexual appeals is not only concerned with understanding how sex affects processing and purchasing, but also with providing useful generalizations to help practicing professionals make decisions about using these appeals. Research in this area rarely attempts to assess the implications of sexual appeals beyond negative reactions and damage to the brand's image and reputation (for exceptions to this pattern, see LaTour & Henthorne, and Gould, chaps. 5 and 8 respectively, this volume). For example, Courtney and Whipple (1983) reviewed the sex in advertising effects literature and concluded, "advertisers would be well advised to ... avoid overtly seductive, nude, or partially clad models" (p. 118). Their recommendation was based on findings suggesting that sex in advertising could be offensive and distracting. More important, their caveat illustrates the concern for protecting advertisers' interests.

Humanities research sees sexual stimuli from wholly different perspectives, usually at a macro level. These scholars are interested in what sex-tinged advertising says about cultural myths, power, iconographies, relationships, development of gender identities and stereotypes, people's fantasies, ethics, and shared grammars of the body as commodity. In this book, several authors approach their topics by writing histories of cultural movements and using these histories as places from which to address sexual appeals. Their projects, from many perspectives, chip away at the notion of an Advertising History that features big men and big campaigns. Stern, a marketing scholar, provides a history of masculine poses and stereotypes, whereas historian Sivulka documents the ways that culture and advertising reinforced long-standing images of sex roles. In another cultural history, Twitchell, an English professor, credits the feminist movement with power enough to critique the use of women's images in advertising. Hicks outlines the development of sexual advertising for gays and lesbians, including the history of the gay and lesbian press as a forum for such advertising. When considering online sexual appeals, Lambiase recounts the growth of the Internet and its continued reliance on pornography Web sites, which have influenced technological innovation and new media culture in general.

Sex also means different things to different sets of scholars, be they from the humanities or social sciences. Marketers, sex researchers, and social psychologists view sexual information as stimuli with ascribed sexual meaning. They are interested in describing responses that viewers experience when exposed to sexual information (e.g., thoughts, feelings, and arousal; see Lang et al., chap. 6, this volume). Alternately, when some hear the term *sex in advertising* they think about gender. One of the authors remembers that every time sex in advertising was mentioned, a colleague thought it referred to sex differences: individual differences regarding women and men, with no sexual meaning at all. Still others consider sex as inseparable from conceptions of social power, and this perspective is discussed eloquently by Kilbourne, who makes the argument that sexualized images of women maintain unequal gender roles through objectification, dismemberment, and disconnection.

Because scholars from both the sciences and humanities have been discussing sexual appeals inside disciplinary boundaries, this collection allows dialogue to occur across those boundaries to create synergy among these varied perspectives. In addition, because sex is wrapped up in issues of power, sexuality, gender, and culture, it is important to talk about these appeals from multiple perspectives. Assessing the marketing perspective, for example, would only provide a very narrow outlook with regard to sex in advertising. Combining perspectives allows for diversity of perspectives to be represented in one area. As a result, anyone, no matter what her or his methodological predilection or specialty, may find familiar and useful views represented. More important, readers are likely to be exposed to new ideas from other viewpoints that can stimulate robust research questions in their own areas of expertise.

A benefit of this book is that it does not focus on only quantitative *or* qualitative research, but presents both research approaches. It includes chapters across disciplines from scholars who explore erotic appeals through a range of methods including empiricism, theory, interpretive analysis, and some of what lies among these perspectives. The more quantitative perspectives include studies of audience effects and individual difference variables, integrative reviews of past research, and new studies that build on past research using theory not yet applied to understanding the effects of these appeals. Definitional issues are addressed, as well as directions for future research. Qualitative perspectives include studies by scholars working in visual persuasion, rhetoric, cultural studies, media studies, gender studies, and others.

OUTLINE OF THE BOOK

Part I contains a collection of chapters that represents a variety of approaches to the examination of sexual appeals in advertising. These chapters use tools from a variety of disciplines including consumer behavior, historical, epistemological, rhetorical, and postmodern perspectives. The section is valuable because it provides coherence regarding the different ways scholars and professionals have studied and described sexual appeals in the past. In addition, the material in these chapters should be valuable for those initiating research in this area, as well as for those searching for new research questions to pursue.

In chapter 2, Tom Reichert provides a review of the ways sexual content has been analyzed in the advertising and mass communication literatures (e.g., nudity, suggestiveness, physical attractiveness), including a brief summary of the ways the effects of sexual appeals have been studied. It is argued that past research often tested sexual appeals that contained a blend of sexual content, despite attempting to isolate sexual content. Suggestions to improve on and extend past research are provided.

Juliann Sivulka in chapter 3 uses landmark advertising campaigns, coupled with insights on psychological theory and cultural trends, to illustrate the use of sexual appeals in images and text throughout the 20th century. Included in her historical study are quaintly sexual advertisements from that century's first decades, followed in the 1930s by some of the first nude photos of women used to sell products to women, both from Woodbury's Soap. Springs Cotton Mills also successfully used provocative images and double entendre in the 1940s and 1950s, but under certain conditions that kept jaded readers in mind. From there, the chapter covers the use of super-sexed ads for blue jeans and cologne from the 1980s and 1990s.

Chapter 4 at first narrowly focuses on two representative Absolut Vodka ads from the 1990s, then telescopes to a much broader discussion of fetishistic images used in contemporary advertising. Jonathan Schroeder and Janet Borgerson explore how advertisers create powerful and positive images for their products via fetishistic themes, in order to build theory about the ways such images create cultural meaning.

In Part II, four chapters focus a spotlight on sex in advertising in the consumer context, by examining responses at both an individual and cultural level. One reviews the arousal construct and its effect on consumer advertising processing, while another on sex and alcohol uses cognitive theory to explain how arousal influences consumer responses to sexual billboard images. The third essay in this section examines new media interactivity and advertising from a rhetorical and critical theory perspective while the last chapter in this section explicates a theory of advertising lovemaps to link media images with personal experiences of sexual pleasure. Altogether, these chapters provide reviews, theoretical perspectives, rhetorical structures, and lessons for advertising professionals and researchers.

Michael LaTour and Tony Henthorne provide an overview in chapter 5 of their research as it pertains to arousal responses to sexual appeals. These researchers have been influential through their work because they bridge the gap between information processing investigations and emotional responses to sexual information. LaTour and Henthorne synthesize their research by providing a summary of their findings, especially as it relates to feminist and ethical evaluations. Last, the researchers provide a strong warning, as well as recommendations, to professionals and researchers alike for constructing sexual appeals.

Chapter 6 by Annie Lang, Kevin Wise, Seungwhan Lee, and Zaiomei Cai examines the influence of sexual appeals on alcohol billboard advertising. Lang et al.'s chapter is important because the limited processing model of message processing is used to explain how sexual information evokes attention, affect, and arousal, and how these emotional responses influence respondents' processing of the ad. The model, developed by Lang, is described in the chapter and related research is cited within the chapter, with a useful review of the literature that explains how emotional information affects message processing. In addition, the chapter describes the use of procedures to test processing and outcome variables such as heart rate, skin conductance, facial electromyography, and speed recognition tests. These researchers employed methods, sometimes using multiple computers, to simulate naturalistic viewing of outdoor advertising.

Chapter 7's rhetorical essay understands the use of sex in advertising as a species of broader dependence on "spectacle." In it, Collin Brooke argues that sexually charged advertisements rely on a version of what Benjamin (1968) described as the "aura" of a work, and that this aura has waned in recent years. Evidence for this trend is located in commercials typified by Pepsi's "Two Kids," featuring supermodel Cindy Crawford and a storyline that completes the marketing–consumption circle, thereby blunting the decision-making process for consumers. This strategy is one that ultimately fails in a broadcast medium such as television, but has been deployed with great success online, through the proliferation of information agents. This latter strategy, promotion in the guise of providing information, may prove to be especially successful in a time characterized by information overload and image saturation.

In chapter 8, Stephen Gould goes beyond traditional marketing thought and practice to offer new ways to think about and conceptualize sexual appeals in advertising. He offers his theory of *advertising lovemaps* as a starting point for understanding the interplay between sexual meaning in ads and sexual experience in people's lives. Gould outlines and describes the four dimensions of the advertising lovemap: differences related to individuals, products, culture, and advertising. For those interested in pursuing postmodern or interpretive consumer research on sex in advertising, his article provides a fine starting point.

Part III contains chapters written by popular scholars and authors who have addressed the impact of sexual appeals on culture. For example, James Twitchell talks about how we are all a part of advertising culture, which diminishes advertising's effect on people and institutions. His point of view is countered by Jean Kilbourne, who talks about how sexual images pollute relationships, as well as individual and cultural identities. Wilson Key has written an original chapter for this book. In it, he describes the harmful social effects of subliminal sexual embeds in advertising and society's complacency about such manipulation.

In chapter 9, James Twitchell works on the theory that myths about beauty or sexuality cannot be unwillingly imposed on culture through its advertising messages. In a reprint from his book *Adcult USA: The Triumph of Advertising in American Culture* (1996), he asserts sexual images work in advertisements because these myths still have resonance with their audience. Yet he doesn't discount the importance of addressing why advertising, in its "reflecting (and shaping)" role, depicts women in demeaning ways.

Jean Kilbourne in chapter 10 attacks the pseudo-sexuality sold in contemporary advertising, in an excerpt from her book *Can't Buy My Love: How Advertising Changes the Way We Think and Feel* (1999). Almost all of these images portray passively sexualized women who are "young, thin, carefully polished and groomed, made up, depilated, sprayed, and scented," a condition that Kilbourne calls "quite unerotic." Those who are homosexual, middle-aged or old, disabled, or deemed "imperfect" by this impossible standard are never shown as sexually desirable, Kilbourne asserts, and this translates into larger societal judgments about how sexuality should work inside relationships.

Wilson Key is "the" most prolific writer, lecturer, and believer in the use of subliminal appeals, as well as the most controversial authority. He has sold more than 8.5 million copies of books, with *Subliminal Seduction* (1973) a major seller. In chapter 11, Key provides an overview of his argument along with his classic examples of subliminal techniques for Kanon cologne. Key also provides recent examples by discussing the word "RATS" appearing in a political presidential ad as well as the cover of *Time* featuring George W. Bush. In addition, Key describes his method of subliminal reading. He speculates about the effect on society and culture of the continual bombardment of hidden sexual messages, and provides an area for future research in this area.

Chapters in Part IV represent areas in which researchers are advancing the debate about sexual advertising appeals. One scholar here discusses sexual appeals used by mainstream brands to appeal to gay and lesbian audiences, whereas another discusses how images of men have become sexualized and have been tied to both accepted and contested stereotypes of gender roles. In another chapter in this section, the use of sexual appeals in online environments is described and contrasted with off-line strategies, as well as compared to pornographic content on the Web.

In this section, Barbara Stern traces the history of masculinity in its various forms into present day sexualized images of men in advertising in chapter 12. She juxtaposes masculinism with feminism, especially as she discusses how the "female gaze" gives women power to view men. Among her descriptions of the idealized male form as it exists today, Stern asks provocative questions, such as, "What are the effects of men's images? What is the ideal men's image? Who consumes it and with what effect?" In so doing, Stern provides a foundation for understanding the increased prevalence of men as objects in sex in advertising.

In chapter 13, Gary Hicks addresses a recent phenomenon in the use of sexual appeals—the targeting of sexual appeals to gay and lesbian audiences. In addition to providing a valuable review of past research in this area, Hicks describes recent appeals by mainstream advertisers such as Coors and Budweiser that use same-sex sexual themes in advertisements in gay media. Ads featuring lesbian-chic images are also discussed. Hicks' chapter provides an important perspective with regard to targeted sexual appeals to populations with sexual orientations different from "mainstream" notions of sex in advertising. As such, Hicks asks and answers the question: "Are sexual ads targeted toward homosexuals similar to those targeted toward heterosexual audiences?"

Jacqueline Lambiase in chapter 14 identifies reigning rhetorical structures that provide safe haven for sexual images on the Web, in advertising and in entire web environments. Sites such as Maximonline.com and IGN.com, a gaming site, feature both sexually oriented appeals and editorial content matching a macho sensibility. Conversely, mainstream sites such as Yahoo.com have tread more carefully after being chastised by users for including sexual content. The chapter explores sexual persuasion through virtual models, user profiling and surfing habits, and technology development and culture, followed by recommendations for future studies, because no published research exists in this area.

In the final chapter, the editors weave together similarities and locate dissonances within the chapters to provide questions for future research and challenges to existing research. The chapter identifies additional areas regarding sexual appeals that are in need of further discussion, such as the issue of sex noise and the "disappearance" of sexual appeals from culture's field of vision.

Although across this book contributors vary in their approaches, each examines how sexual appeals function in today's advertising environment. At its heart, the book is envisioned by the editors as a source book on sex in advertising that spans quantitative and qualitative perspectives, documents past research, reports new research, and provides clear directions for future research.

REFERENCES

Benjamin, W. (1968). The work of art in the age of mechanical reproduction. In H. Arendt (Ed.), H. Zohn (Trans.), *Illuminations: Essays and reflections* (pp. 217–242). New York: Shocken.

Bullough, V. L. (1994). *Science in the bedroom: A history of sex research.* New York: Basic Books.

Courtney, A. E., & Whipple, T. W. (1983). *Sex, stereotyping and advertising.* Lexington MA: D.C. Heath.

Fetto, J. (2001). Where's the lovin'? *American Demographics, 23*(2), 10–11.

Key, W. B. (1973). *Subliminal seduction: Ad media's manipulation of a not so innocent America.* New York: Signet.

Kilbourne, J. (1999). *Can't buy my love: How advertising changes the way we think and feel.* New York: The Free Press.

Reichert, T., Lambiase, J., Morgan, S., Carstarphen, M., & Zavoina, S. (1999). Beefcake or cheesecake? No matter how you slice it, sexual explicitness in advertising continues to increase. *Journalism & Mass Communication Quarterly, 76*(1), 7–20.

Ross, M. W. (2001, Winter). From the president. *Sexual Science, 42*(1), 2.

Shapiro, E. (1993, December 3). In the safe-sex society, advertisers lose inhibitions about how much sex is safe. *Wall Street Journal*, B1.

Soley, L., & Reid, L. (1988). Taking it off: Are models in magazine ads wearing less? *Journalism & Mass Communication Quarterly, 65*(Winter), 960–966.

Twitchell, J. (1996). *Adcult USA: The triumph of advertising in American culture.* New York: Columbia University Press.

PART I

Research Approaches
to Sex in Advertising

What Is Sex in Advertising? Perspectives From Consumer Behavior and Social Science Research

Tom Reichert

University of Alabama

While speaking to a group of advertising executives in 1968, Thomas Shepard, publisher of *Look* magazine, went on record as saying that the days of scantily clad models in advertising were numbered. He foretold of a day in the not-so-distant future when advertisers would resort to putting clothing *on* models to grab consumer attention, instead of taking it off ("Nudity is Ad Fad," 1968). Shepard was referring to advertising's reflection of the sexual revolution in the mid- to late-1960s, but by most indications his prediction was in the wrong direction. A recent *Adweek* poll revealed that more than 70% of respondents think there is too much sexual imagery in advertising (Dolliver, 1999), and advertising analyses suggest ads are more sexual than ever before (Lin, 1998; Reichert, Lambiase, Morgan, Carstarphen, & Zavoina, 1999; Soley & Reid, 1988).

Although Shepard was referring to nudity, he was probably aware that other forms of sexual information are woven into ads. For example, a recent Revelstoke whiskey ad depicts a man getting a lap dance in a gentlemen's club. Women in Clairol Herbal Essences commercials exclaim "Yes! Yes! Yes!" as they wash their hair in service station restrooms and airplane lavatories. And print ads for Christian Dior feature female models in unmistakably sexual embraces. These ads are all examples of sex in advertising, but they involve more than just scantily clad models. Because sexual content can vary in form and meaning, it is important to provide an overview of recurring representations of sex in advertising. As such, this chapter reviews sex in advertising research with the purpose of identifying common types of sexual information.

The lion's share of academic research pertaining to sex in advertising exists in the consumer behavior domain. Advertising and marketing researchers have studied this topic since the 1960s, and it is easy to understand why. Their investigations are concerned with understanding consumer responses to sexually oriented marketing communications in an effort to increase the practicality of effects.

Most studies examine the effects of sexual ads from the information processing (McGuire, 1968, 1972) and hierarchy of effects perspectives (Barry, 1987; Stewart, Pechmann, Ratneshwar, Stroud, & Bryant, 1985). These approaches assume persuasion occurs in a linear manner. Information must first be noticed and encoded before receivers become receptive to it, yield to it, and ultimately act in accordance with the recommendation. Important dependent variables include attention, cognition, recognition, recall, and purchase intention. Brand-name recall, unaided memory of the brand name, is an important outcome in this research because it assesses whether brand information is encoded or not. For example, Reid and Soley (1983) examined the effect of decorative female models on ad attention and message processing. In a seminal study, Steadman (1969) examined the impact of nude women in magazine ads on brand-name recall. The results of these studies (for review, see Belch, Belch, & Villarreal, 1987; Percy & Rossiter, 1992; Reichert, in press) lend tentative support to the generalization that attention and processing resources are directed toward the sexual information in ads, resulting in fewer resources available to process brand information.

Recently, researchers have examined the impact of emotion (affect and arousal) evoked by sexual information on evaluations of the ad and the brand (Jones, Stanaland, & Gelb, 1998; LaTour, 1990; LaTour & Henthorne, 1993). Investigations of emotional effects center on the concept of attitude-toward-the-ad (MacKenzie, Lutz, & Belch, 1986; Muehling & McCann, 1993). Findings from these studies suggest that the relationship between evaluations and sexual imagery are complex and depend on several contextual and individual difference variables. For example, evaluations can be influenced by sex of the respondent, sex of the model/actor (LaTour, 1990), level of explicitness (LaTour & Henthorne, 1994), and relevance to the brand (Peterson & Kerin, 1977; Simpson, Horton, & Brown, 1996). The processing approaches were the first to be used to understand how sex influences advertising effectiveness. As a result, most of what is known about sex appeals is limited to processing effects, with attitude research providing additional insight. To fully understand the effects of sexual information in ads, however, it is important to consider the types of sexual content that have been tested.

WHAT IS SEX IN ADVERTISING?

Former U.S. Supreme Court Justice Potter Stewart stated that, at least for him, pornography was easy to identify: "I know it when I see it" (*Jacobellis v. Ohio*, 1964, p. 804). When conceptualizing sex in advertising, it is important to move beyond individual-level interpretations to conceptions that are more useful. Fortunately, there are types of stimuli that groups of people predictably recognize and consider as sex in advertising.

As a basic working definition, an instance of sex in advertising can be thought of as a sexual appeal. By its very nature, advertising is an applied form of persuasion that attempts to inform, position, convince, reinforce, differentiate, and ultimately sell products and services. As such, sexual appeals are persuasive appeals that contain sexual information integrated within the overall message (Reichert, Heckler, & Jackson, 2001). Sexual information, defined by Harris (1994) as "any representation that portrays or implies sexual interest, behavior, or motivation" (p. 206), is often integrated within the advertisement as images, verbal elements, or both. For example, ads can contain images of attractive people clothed in revealing or tight-fitting clothing, or contain verbal elements such as double-entendres and sexually suggestive words and phrases. Often, both elements coalesce to create sexual meaning in ads.

Aside from simply containing sexual content, sexual information in ads can be integrated within the message to greater or lesser degrees. For example, some ads contain images of blatant nudity or models engaged in erotic liaisons. On the other hand, some ads contain only a hint of sexual suggestion, perhaps a subtle innuendo or play on words. In many cases, people consider images of fully clothed, physically attractive women and men to be sexually attractive, and thus, a subtle instance of sex in advertising.

What follows is a review of common types of sexual stimuli researched in advertising, and to a lesser degree, mass communication research. The following categories also provide a framework for conceptions of sex in advertising as they are presented in the chapters contained in this book (see Table 2.1).

Types of Sexual Information in Advertising

Nudity.   It almost goes without saying that people, and revealing displays of their bodies, constitute an essential source of sexual information. In a recent study, participants were asked to think of a sexual ad, and then to identify the characteristics of that ad that made it sexual to them (Reichert & Ramirez, 2000). Without exception, physical aspects of the people in ads—physiques and revealing clothing—were mentioned most often. Common responses referred to chiseled chests, short skirts, tight

TABLE 2.1
Types of Sexual Content Identified in Advertising Research.

Type	Description
Nudity/Dress	Amount and style of clothing worn by models. Examples include revealing displays of the body, ranging from tight-fitting clothing, to underwear and lingerie, to nudity.
Sexual Behavior	Individual and interpersonal sexual behavior. Includes flirting, eye contact, posturing, and movement (body language, nonverbal and verbal communication). Sexual interaction between two or more people typically includes hugging, kissing, voyeurism, and more intimate forms of sexual behavior.
Physical Attractiveness	General level of model's physical beauty. Often incorporates facial beauty, complexion, hair, and physique.
Sexual Referents	Allusions and references to objects and events that have sexual meaning by means of double entendre and innuendo. Also includes facilitating factors that enhance or contribute to sexual meaning, such as setting, music, lighting, design elements, camera techniques, and editing.
Sexual Embeds	Content interpreted as sexual at the subconscious level. Includes words like sex, nonsexual perceptible objects that can connote sexual body parts and sexual actions, and small images of genitalia, body parts, and people.

tops, muscular arms, breasts, bikinis, bare midriffs, and lingerie (see Fig. 2.1). Given that other forms of sexual content (e.g., erotica and pornography in magazines, romance novels, videos; Brown & Bryant, 1989) depict people, typically in various stages of undress, it is reasonable to assume that models in various stages of undress represent a fundamental type of sex in advertising.

Indeed, nearly all sex in advertising studies have examined levels of nudity as a form of sexual content. For example, advertising content analyses have assessed nudity and body display in magazine ads and commercials (Lin, 1998; Soley & Reid, 1988). Similarly, nudity has been assessed in main-

THE POLO SPORT BEACH TOWEL

THE POLO SPORT BEACH TOWEL IS YOUR GIFT WITH
ANY $35.00 POLO SPORT MEN'S FRAGRANCE PURCHASE

Fig. 2.1. Revealing displays of the body are considered sexual by most people.

stream mass communication analyses of primetime television programming (Sapolsky & Tabarlet, 1991), music videos (Seidman, 1992), film (Dempsey & Reichert, 2000; Greenberg et al., 1993), and network promotional messages (Walker, 2000).

The term *nudity* does not imply that models are completely unclothed. In this research, the term generally refers to the amount and style of clothing worn by models. In a typical study, images of female models in progressive stages of undress (e.g., suggestive, partially revealing, and nude; Soley & Reid, 1988) are integrated into ads representing different levels of nudity. Suggestive dress is often represented by open blouses with partially exposed cleavage, tight-fitting clothing that accentuates the body, and mini-skirts. Partially clad models wear underwear or bathing suits. Nudity ranges from implications that models are not wearing clothing to full-frontal nudity. Because complete nudity is extremely rare in mainstream advertising, nudity is often represented by side and back shots of the model, tub and shower scenes, and in some cases, frontal nudity from the waist up (see Fig. 2.2).

Experimental studies test the effects of nudity levels on advertising processes and outcomes. Investigators compare responses to ads with sexually dressed models to ads with either demurely dressed models or no model at all (i.e., pastoral scenes; for example, see LaTour, 1990). Common dependent variables include attention, attitude-toward-the-ad, cognitions about the ad and/or brand, and ad/brand recognition and recall (Alexander & Judd, 1978; Belch, Holgerson, Belch, & Koppman, 1981; Jones et al., 1998; Judd & Alexander, 1983; LaTour, 1990; LaTour & Henthorne, 1993; Peterson & Kerin, 1977; Sciglimpaglia, Belch, & Cain, 1978; Severn, Belch, & Belch, 1990; P. Simpson et al., 1996; Steadman, 1969). Consequently, most of what is known about the effects of sexual ads pertains to the effects of people (i.e., women) in various stages of undress.

An assumption in these studies is that sex is synonymous with nudity, and that risqué clothing, or lack thereof, is the primary determinant of sexual response. In actuality, other aspects of partially clothed models (e.g., physical attractiveness, facial expression, eye contact with viewer) also contribute to sexual perceptions. Researchers assume that a linear relationship exists between progressive levels of undress and sexual arousal (e.g., the less clothing someone is wearing, the sexier he/she is). Although true in most cases, there are situations in which nude models are not sexually appealing, while fully clothed models are. Revealing displays of the body are an important component of sexual interest and sexual attraction, but limiting sex in advertising to nudity neglects other, often more important determinants of sexual attraction such as behavior, physical interaction, and sexual contexts.

Sexual Behavior.   Pornography can be defined as "the visual (and sometimes aural) representation of living, moving bodies engaged in explicit ... sex acts" (Williams, 1989, p. 30). Although sexual content in mainstream advertising omits the sex act, it does include sexually provocative

Fig. 2.2. Full nudity in advertising is often represented by implied nudity or side shots.

behavioral displays. Models are filmed and photographed in enticing poses and positions—sometimes with other models, sometimes alone. In an analysis of magazine ads from 1993, more than half of ads that contained both men and women portrayed the couples engaging in sexual contact (Reichert et al., 1999).

Sexual behavior can be woven into ads in two ways, as individual behavior or interpersonal interaction. Models behave sexually in ads by making eye contact with the viewer, flirting, and moving provocatively. In these ways, models can communicate sexual interest with the viewer or simply attempt to elicit sexual arousal. In the Reichert and Ramirez (2000) study, sexual behavior was mentioned by about 40% of respondents. Respondents referred to the model's behavior (e.g., pose, walk, hip movement), the model's demeanor (e.g., sultry), and the model's words and tone of voice. Behavioral characteristics of models in sexual ads are similar to those of people enacting flirting behavior (Simpson, Gangestad, & Nations, 1996), including eye contact, open postures, bedroom eyes, and inviting smiles. For example, the model in the Pepe Jeans magazine ad in Fig. 2.3 communicates sexual interest with her pose, facial expression, and eye contact with the viewer. Similarly, the model in the *Maxim* promotional ad is physically attractive, but it is her expression that is designed to elicit a sexual response (see Fig. 2.4).

Audiovisual characteristics of television commercials can accentuate sexual behavior by showing models moving and talking seductively. Bello, Pitts, and Etzel (1983) analyzed the effects of a commercial containing sexual behavior when they compared the communication effectiveness of the infamous Calvin Klein jeans commercial featuring Brooke Shields to a less provocative version of the commercial. In the ad, Shields sits on the floor in an open position while the camera pans slowly from her foot to her body. Shields looks at the camera and says, "Do you know what comes between me and my Calvins? Nothing." Double entendre and other sexual elements were certainly at play, but Shields' body positioning and vocalics contributed to the construction of sexiness in the ad. Lin (1998) attempted to capture sexual behavior in commercials by creating a simple coding protocol that measured sexual appeal in primetime commercials. The coding scheme assessed the model's persona as conveyed by verbal and nonverbal behavior.

A second form of behavior in sexual ads involves two models—sometimes more—shown engaging in sexual contact. The degree of explicitness and progressiveness of the encounter can vary from portrayals of voyeurism, to simple displays of affection, to inferred intercourse (see Fig. 2.5). In advertising, Soley and Kurzbard (1986) used a four-level ordinal scale to analyze physical contact between models. Any time a heterosexual couple appeared in an ad, physical contact was coded as not touching, displaying

Fig. 2.3. The woman in the Pepe Jeans ad communicates sexual interest with her facial expressions and behavior.

Fig. 2.4. The female model's facial expression and mussed hair in the Maxim promotional ad contribute to viewers' sexual perceptions.

The human body has over
45 miles of nerves.

Enjoy the ride.

Set yourself free. In a new Durex® condom.

Feel what you've been missing. With the most exciting condoms ever made.
New **Durex** condoms for ultimate sensitivity. Now safe sex doesn't have
to feel that way. Free sample at www.durex.com.

Fig. 2.5. Models engaging in sexual behavior (together) is another form of sex in advertising.

simple contact (e.g., holding hands), more intimate contact (e.g., kissing, embracing, playful wrestling), or depictions of intercourse (e.g., implied, suggestion of). For example, the couple in the Durex condom ad would be categorized at the most intimate level.

The effects of suggestive behavior have been tested several ways. For example, Belch et al. (1981) and Sciglimpaglia et al. (1978) tested responses to images of heterosexual couples in various degrees of physical contact. Reichert, Heckler, and Jackson (2001) tested ad pairs for 13 social marketing topics containing images of sexual or nonsexual depictions of couples. Similarly, LaTour and Henthorne (1994) compared two print ads with images of couples at two different stages of sexual interaction. In the moderately sexual ad, the heterosexual couple was holding hands, whereas the couple in the highly sexual ad was positioned in a sexually suggestive embrace with the woman's naked breasts and abdomen covered by the man's arm as they kissed passionately. In addition, Severn et al. (1990) compared two visuals for Fox sports shoes. Consider the researchers' description of one of the visuals

> The ... advertisement showed a side profile of two adults from the chest down—one male and one female—completely nude except for the advertised sports shoes and matching socks. The models were shown in a position clearly suggesting sexual intercourse. (pp. 16–17)

Sexual behavior is a central variable in analyses of sexual media content. In television programming, behavior is analyzed by explicitness and arrayed according to levels of sexual intimacy (e.g., hugging, kissing, petting, oral sex, intercourse; Sapolsky & Tabarlet, 1991), as well as categories of implied and explicit sexual behavior: rape, homosexual acts, intercourse, prostitution, petting, and miscellaneous (Greenberg, Graef, Fernandez-Collado, Korzenny, & Atkin, 1980). Intercourse (implied and references to) and petting are reflective of advertising content.

Physical Attractiveness. According to psychologist David Buss (1994), physical attractiveness among humans is a trait that is central for predicting interpersonal attraction and mate selection. In his cross-cultural study, Buss argued that features of physical appearance, including facial beauty and complexion, play a central role in sexual interest and desire. There is little doubt a link exists between physical attractiveness and sexual interest. For this reason, physically attractive models in advertising can be—and often are—considered examples of sex in advertising.

In marketing and advertising studies, physical attractiveness is often operationalized by having members of the respondent pool rate photographs of people (e.g., Baker & Churchill, 1977; Caballero, Lumpkin, & Madden, 1989; Caballero & Pride, 1984). Determination of attractiveness levels (high, moderate, low) is made by comparing mean ratings. As Joseph (1982) pointed out, there is little discussion of what constitutes physical attractiveness in the photos, but most likely it is linked to facial features. More recent studies, however, ask respondents to consider the model's hair, face, complexion, eye contact, dress, physique, and behavior when rating attractiveness (Brumbaugh, 1993; Englis, Solomon, & Ashmore, 1994).

Work by Solomon and colleagues has identified types of physical beauty represented by female models in advertising. For example, Solomon, Ashmore, and Longo (1992) differentiated between six types of physical attractiveness: classic beauty, cuteness, sex kitten, sensuality, girl-next-door, and trendy. In a related study, it was determined that viewers are able to differentiate between sexual, cute, and trendy images of female physical attractiveness (Ashmore, Solomon, & Longo, 1996). These studies suggest that physical attractiveness is not one-dimensional, and research that simply compares general levels of attractiveness neglects factors such as inferred personality attributes about the models that can affect responses (Brumbaugh, 1993).

Agreement is mixed regarding how physical attractiveness works in advertising. Advertising researchers agree that attractive models draw attention to ads (Joseph, 1982). Researchers also agree that physical attractiveness can influence evaluations of ads (Baker & Churchill, 1977), but contributes little or no effect on behavior and purchase intention (Caballero et al., 1989). There is weak evidence that purchase behavior is higher when ads contain images of physically attractive people, but only for romantically linked products such as fragrances (Baker & Churchill, 1977). It has also been argued that attractive models serve as implicit arguments for the brand: Good-looking people use the brand, so the brand will make you better looking (Kahle & Homer, 1985). The effect of physical attractiveness may be greater for low-risk purchases or when consumers have limited ability, motivation, or opportunity to process marketing communication.

Joseph (1982) argued that research should differentiate between models who are pleasing in appearance and models who are sexy. Work on beauty types may provide information in that area, as it is obvious that not all attractive models elicit a sexual response. As an integral component of interpersonal attraction, physical attractiveness is an important ingredient in representations of sex in advertising.

Sexual Referents. Images and words that subtly refer to sex or that trigger sexual thoughts can also be considered examples of sex in advertising. These suggestive images are less tangible and are more oblique than graphic depictions of nudity or erotic behavior. Researchers have referred to sexual referents as "implicit" (Bello et al., 1983), because references to sex are implied or subtle (e.g., innuendo, double entendre).

In advertising, sexual referents can be defined as message elements (visual or verbal) that serve to elicit or educe sexual thoughts. Although this definition can encompass any type of sexual information, it is meant to refer to instances of sexual innuendo and allusion. Sexual content takes form in the viewer's mind not in the ad. For example, Belch et al. (1981) quoted Freud when defining sexually suggestive content as "a command or piece of information that triggers or arouses an idea in a person's mind" (as cited in Belch et al., p. 424). Similarly, Richmond and Hartman (1982) labeled referents as *fantasy*, and defined it as "an appeal that links the product to imaginative wish fulfillment, implicitly promising fantasy gratification of sexual motives" (Tinkham & Reid, 1988, p. 118). The example was an ad for J&B Scotch featuring a close-up image of a smiling woman looking up and off the page with a man's hand on either side of her face. The caption read, "Whatever you've got going ... keep it going with J&B."

Sexual referents are different from other forms of sexual information because they depend on the receiver to interpret the message in the intended way. In this manner, referents work at a cognitive level by having viewers generate sexual thoughts, as opposed to making the sexual information explicit. Consider the sexual innuendo in the E-greetings ad in Fig. 2.6. The e-mail message has sexual meaning when accompanied by images that serve to trigger sexual thoughts. The ad supplies symbols that only have sexual meaning within the context of the message, and viewers have to put the pieces together by thinking about the connection between the message and the objects in the image. Sexual cognitions are a form of sexual response (Fisher, 1986), and in this context serve to stimulate cognitions instead of using graphic images that evoke visceral responses.

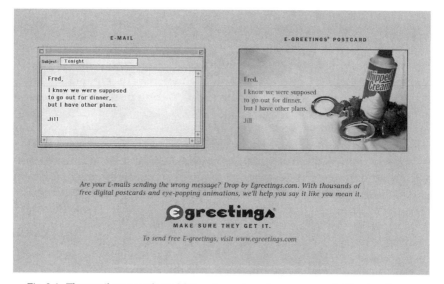

Fig. 2.6. The email message has additional meaning when accompanied by visual props.

Somewhat related to referents, elements of the ad apart from models can contribute to sexual meaning. The way commercials are filmed, along with design elements, camera effects, music, and lighting, can contribute to the construction of sexual meaning. In the Reichert and Ramirez (2000) study, 25% of respondents identified things about the ad other than models that contributed to sexual perceptions. For example, where the commercial was filmed (bedroom, exotic local) played a role in making an ad sexy. Often, these factors were mentioned in conjunction with references to physical aspects of models and their behavior. In this way, referents and objects other than the model serve to facilitate and enhance sexual interpretations.

Sexual Embeds. Although sex in advertising is a controversial topic in and of itself (see Gould, 1994), nothing in this area raises more debate than the supposed use of sexual embeds. Often referred to as subliminal advertising, *sexual embeds* are defined as referents or forms of sexual representation designed to be perceived subconsciously (Theus, 1994). Common types of embeds include: the word *sex*; objects that are shaped or positioned like genitalia and sexual acts; and small, hidden images of naked people, body parts, and genitalia. Sexual embeds are integrated into images by ad creators and are intended to go undetected by those viewing the ad. The use of embeds in advertising was popularized by Key in the 1970s and 1980s with the publication of his books *Subliminal Seduction* (1973) and *The Clam-Plate Orgy* (1986). Controversy pertains to the existence and supposed effects of sexual embeds.

Sexual embeds represent a type of sex in advertising because they consist of sexual information—albeit small and imperceptible. One class of sexual embed refers to sexual symbolism, which includes representations of objects that connote either genitalia or sexual acts (for review, see Ruth, Mosatche, & Kramer, 1989; Theus, 1994). For example, a receiver could subconsciously interpret an image of a cylindrical cologne bottle positioned at a 45-degree angle as an erect penis. Similarly, the image of a key inserted into a lock could represent intercourse. Consider the Baileys ad in Fig. 2.7. An advocate of embeds might argue that the positioning of the woman's finger in her open mouth would register as fellatio in the viewer's subconscious.

A second type of sexual embed is often characterized by hidden sexual images and words (for review, see Rosen & Singh, 1992). For example, these embeds are often represented by words and images of people and body parts (i.e., genitalia, breasts). The difference between the two types of embeds is that one consists of readily perceptible images of nonsexual objects, whereas the other consists of imperceptible sexual words and images. Both are similar because sexual content is perceived below conscious detection, and both are explained by the same operating premise. As embeds trigger unconscious recognition, they stimulate sexual arousal and motivation. Ultimately, ob-

Fig. 2.7. Sexual embed advocates might argue the image in the Baileys' ad subconsciously represents fellatio.

servers are motivated toward goal-directed behavior (e.g., movement toward the stimulus). When embeds are consciously detected their power diminishes because viewers' defense mechanisms are stimulated.

The following two studies exemplify the controversy over embed effects. In one study, Ruth et al. (1989) examined the effect of images connoting genitalia in liquor ads on purchase intention. Using Freudian symbolism theory as a framework, the researchers hypothesized that embeds trigger unconscious recognition and motivation toward the stimulus (purchase intention). The results were such that respondents reported more intention to buy the advertised liquor after viewing ads with embeds (i.e., genital symbolism) compared to ads without embeds. Although the study involved a comparison of seven similar (i.e., type of liquor) pairs of ads (with embed/without), the commercially produced ads used in the study varied in ways other than the variable of interest, thereby weakening support for the findings.

Efforts at tightly controlled studies typically yield no effects. For example, Rosen and Singh (1992) assessed the impact of three types of embeds (sex, death, and nudity) in ads for two products (cologne and liquor). The embeds were small (the word *sex*, the word *death* with skulls, and a naked woman with phallic symbols), and integrated within the ads to inhibit detection. The researchers found no effects for either type of embed on any processing or outcome variable.

These two studies represent the dilemma with regard to influence of sexual embeds. Although Rosen and Singh's (1992) study was carefully controlled, it lacked realism. On the other hand, the findings of the other investigation were open to alternative explanations. Many researchers and advertising professionals consider embeds to be a hoax because controlled research has not substantiated their effects, and they doubt that media professionals intentionally use embeds. A comprehensive study combining the best of both approaches (e.g., replicated message design, Jackson, O'Keefe, & Brashers, 1992) is warranted, and might provide definitive results. At this point, however, interested readers are encouraged to review work in sexual embed research to reach their own conclusions.

CHALLENGES AND OPPORTUNITIES FOR FUTURE RESEARCH

A number of opportunities exist to extend what is known about the effects of sexual information in advertising. Research that can unify the sometimes idiosyncratic findings pertaining to sexual appeals would be especially useful. Following are considerations and suggestions for rethinking ways to conceptualize and test sex effects, as well as specific research concerns that can strengthen conclusions and generalizations.

Sexual Explicitness and Intensity

Despite efforts to identify and test different types of sexual information, past research has frequently intermingled the types of sexual content when assessing sexual meaning in advertising. Physically attractive models in ads can be, and often are, explicitly dressed and move or speak seductively. Similarly, ads can contain images of relatively demure models with head-lines or body copy that allude to sexual behavior. In reality, variations of these images, as well as combinations of types of sexual information, are in-finite. As such, attempts to isolate and test specific types of sexual content offer conclusions that not only are confusing, but so narrowly focused as to be unrepresentative of real-world content effects.

One way to address both the range and blending of sexual content in ad-vertising is to array representations according to explicitness and intensity. Both dimensions could range from low to high, and sexual content that var-ies along each dimension could be located relative to other types of sexual information. Such an approach would be helpful because it is likely that two different content types (e.g., physical attractiveness and suggestive clothing) evoke similar levels of sexual response. Researchers have been combining types of sexual content all along. For example, it is likely that the female model in LaTour's (1990) investigation of nudity was also physi-cally attractive. Similarly, Englis et al. (1994) determination of physical at-tractiveness types was based on behavior, physique, facial expression, and clothing—in addition to ratings of beauty. Arraying sexual content along dimensions might allow future research to make generalizations about sex in advertising that are more robust.

Explicitness of the appeal refers to the graphic nature of the sexual infor-mation in the ad. Images featuring nude models and intimate sexual behav-ior would represent high explicitness, whereas subtle innuendo and demurely dressed models would be characterized as implicit. For example, the Durex condom ad in Fig. 2.5 contains a highly explicit image. On the other hand, the message and images in the ad for E-greetings (Fig. 2.6) are implicit because the sexual reference is inferred by the viewer.

Sexual content can also vary in degree of intensity. For example, two un-clothed models can easily represent different levels of intensity. A model portrayed in an "in-your-face" posture is likely to represent high sexual in-tensity, whereas another model, perhaps in a classic pose, might represent low intensity. Burgoon (1989, p. 151) defined intensity as "the degree to which a persuasive message deviates from neutrality." Although Burgoon was writing about language and verbal variables, he argued that sexual metaphors can be manipulated within sentences to represent different vari-ations in language intensity. Similarly, sexual imagery can be represented in a manner that varies in terms of how sexually charged the information is.

For example, Grazer and Keesling (1995) tested sexual ad appeals that represented high, moderate, and low levels of sexual intensity. Similarly, LaTour and Henthorne (1994) examined responses to two ads representing either moderate or high sexual content. The ads differed in regard to explicitness and intensity levels.

In the case of sexual information, appeals that represent high intensity and explicitness could be described as graphic, leaving little to the imagination, and visually characterized by nude or scantily clad people. As such, ads that stoutly sexualize or emphasize physical, behavioral, or relational aspects of models are likely to represent high-intensity appeals in this quadrant. Similarly, images of models engaged in simulated sex acts exemplify powerful images. High-intensity verbal appeals that make very straightforward or egregious references to sex would be located at this level as well.

On the other hand, sexual information low on both dimensions is subtle and implicit. Sexual appeals in this quadrant are manifested in visuals that are less obtrusive and more veiled than more explicit forms. For instance, images might consist of couples that are playful and flirtatious instead of engaged in a passionate embrace. The same would be true for verbal appeals. Subtle innuendos and double-entendres are more ambiguous with regard to sexual meaning and more apt to be implied.

Explicitness and intensity are important to consider because they may correspond with the type of responses people have to sexual information and how those responses influence processing. Appeals that represent high intensity and explicitness are likely to be visual in nature and apt to evoke emotionally charged reactions. On the other hand, information represented as low on both dimensions is less apt to elicit strong reactions and may depend on the viewer to think about the implied sexual message. In addition, highly intense messages are more likely to be offensive, whereas low-intensity messages will elicit less intense reactions.

In addition, the type of sexual content in the ad may influence distraction. Sex research has shown that arousal can be inhibited if respondents are given distractive tasks while listening to erotic stories or being asked to imagine erotic imagery (Przybyla & Byrne, 1984). On the other hand, distractive tasks had no effect if respondents were viewing erotic images. When considering sex in advertising, explicit sexual information affects people at a visceral level, and should be able to be processed instantaneously with little opportunity for distraction. Alternately, more creative approaches involving sex that invite the viewer to piece together the story (implicit/low-intensity appeals) may be affected by normal ad viewing distractions such as flipping pages, driving, or conversing. Assessing explicitness and intensity provides a Gestalt approach to testing sexual information that may be more informative than testing isolated types of sexual content.

Sexual Brand Benefits

Most research questions have sought to determine how sexual information influences processing and emotional responses. More interesting, there is little discussion of one of the primary reasons sexual appeals are used in ads—as a benefit or outcome of using the brand. Many sexual appeals argue that sex-related benefits accrue to brand users. Past research assumes that sexual elements in ads are creative execution devices that only serve to grab attention. In actuality, sexual information is incorporated into ads to demonstrate that brands can make consumers more sexually attractive and more sexually active. In this way, sexual models and sexual scenes are arguments for buying the brand, while also serving as attention-getting devices. To neglect the former prevents us from fully knowing *how* sexual appeals operate in advertising.

In their exploratory study, Richmond and Hartman (1982; see also, Tinkham & Reid, 1988) identified a type of sexual ad that featured brand promises linked to sexual wish fulfillment. The sexual ad attempted to position the product, with either implicit or explicit reasons, for buying the brand. Work by Lambiase and Reichert (in press) revealed three promises common in sexual advertising appeals: (a) sexual attractiveness for the consumer, (b) likely engagement in sexual behavior (and more enjoyment from these encounters), and (c) feelings of being sexy or sensual (sex-esteem). In these types of ads, there is a quid-pro-quo promise: "Buy this product, use it as directed, and you'll end up in a situation like the one pictured in this ad."

Consider the argument made in the Jovan Musk ad in Fig. 2.8. The headline reads, "What attracts? This is what attracts." When combined with the visual image of a couple engaged in sexual behavior, the argument is that wearing Jovan Musk will either make you more attractive to the opposite sex, or that you are more likely to increase your opportunities for being in a similar situation as the one depicted in the ad. As such, the utility of the brand is that it enhances sexual prowess. To fully understand how sexual appeals operate to stimulate transactions, it's imperative to consider the promises and pledges made by advertisers for brands. Research that demonstrates the effectiveness of sex-related benefits in advertising will provide important insight into understanding how sex works in advertising.

Other Considerations

Despite the number of studies that have investigated the effects of sex in advertising, most have only assessed male responses to female sexual imagery (i.e., scantily clad women). Although there are exceptions, it is important for future studies to assess women's responses to sexual content

Fig. 2.8. Sex in advertising often offers sexual benefits as an outcome of buying and using the brand. Consider the brand promise made in the Jovan fragrance ad.

in advertising. One reason for the emphasis on male response is that historically, images of women represent most sexual information in advertising. Times are changing, however, as research shows that beefcake imagery is on the rise (Kervin, 1990). Although some male images are directed toward men, for the same reasons decorative female images are directed to women, sexualized male images are appearing in media directed toward women. Because men and women may respond to these images differently (men to female images, and women to male images), it is important to provide a better understanding of women's responses to sexual advertising content.

Another limitation of sex in advertising research is the difference between naturalistic and forced exposure to advertising. Most of what is known about sexual ad appeals is derived from testing respondents in lab settings after one exposure to the ad. Unfortunately, the practice of carefully controlled scientific research does not always simulate naturalistic viewing experiences. As a result, a credibility gap exists between academic research conclusions and what resonates as meaningful for advertising professionals. For example, Courtney and Whipple's (1983) review of the sexual appeal literature led them to recommend that "advertisers would be well advised to ... avoid overtly seductive, nude, or partially clad models" (p. 118). There is little evidence to suggest that advertisers paid heed to Courtney and Whipple's caveat. In fact, some major brands have successfully positioned themselves by relying exclusively on images of scantily clad models. Similarly, although it is generally regarded that sexual appeals distract viewers from processing brand information, in real-life situations, consumers view ads many times, affording them the opportunity to learn information about the brand over time. Naturalistic research is expensive and difficult to implement, but unless research can approximate naturalistic exposure to advertising, the credibility gap with ad professionals will continue.

An additional challenge for sexual appeal research is its dependence on inadequate message designs. Most sex-effects studies utilize single-message designs—designs that compare one message category to another using only a single ad to represent each condition. For example, a single-message design might attempt to test the effect of nudity by comparing two images of the same model portrayed as nude and fully dressed. Although models and meaning in ads vary in an infinite number of ways, generalizations are often made about the effectiveness of nudity based on the one comparison. A number of communication researchers have argued that the use of single concrete messages to represent abstract message categories fails to offer the type of generalizations researchers seek to make (Jackson 1992; Jackson, O'Keefe, & Brashers 1995). Even carefully controlled, single-message designs fail to guard against rival hypotheses by not representing the variation inherent in messages. Interested researchers are encouraged to review the arguments for replicated message designs when testing sexual ad effects (see Jackson, 1992).

Last, an opportunity exists to make use of persuasion and marketing theory to understand how sexual information operates in advertising. At an advertising conference in late 1970s, Wilson and Moore (1979) argued that theoretical development was needed in this area: "Little thought seems to have been given to those theoretical concepts which may be useful in understanding the effectiveness of sexually oriented ads" (p. 55). Although investigations in this area utilize information processing and attitude-toward-the-ad concepts, there are other approaches that have proved useful for explaining effects.

Interested researchers could apply concepts related to emotion-evoking message research to better understand the effects of sex in advertising. Recent work in communication and persuasion research pertaining to emotional content in messages is promising (Dillard & Meijnders, 2002; Dillard & Wilson, 1993). Messages that evoke emotional reactions can influence persuasion in several predictable ways. Because sexual responses to sexual information are often characterized as consisting of affect and arousal, appeals containing sexual information appear to be central to that type of research. In addition, process theories such as the *Elaboration Likelihood Model* can provide additional insight. It is possible that sexual information can serve as both peripheral cues and central arguments. For example, sexual content could serve as a peripheral cue in low-involvement situations, having little effect in high-involvement situations. On the other hand, sexual information may serve as an argument for using the brand if it is analyzed in terms of sexual promises and benefits. As such, sex could influence persuasion through central-route processing by serving as a compelling reason for buying and using the brand. An enterprising researcher could contribute to the body of sexual appeal research by applying persuasion theory to advance meaningful generalizations regarding the effects of sex in advertising.

CONCLUSION

Despite Shepard's prognostication in 1968, there is little doubt that nude models and other forms of sexual advertising content are here to stay. Sexual appeals that feature a range of sexual information (nudity, behavior, referents, and physical attractiveness) are commonplace and used to promote an increasingly wider range of mainstream products and services. Advertisers not only use sexual appeals to attract attention to their ads, but to position their brands as sexual, and to suggest that sex-related benefits can accrue to the brand purchasers. Future research that takes a more unifying view of sex in advertising, while employing research strategies that consider naturalistic viewing and natural message variation, is likely to extend past research by further illuminating how sexual appeals affect advertising responses. Findings of such research will be meaningful to professionals, as well as to researchers.

REFERENCES

Alexander, M. W., & Judd, B. B. (1978). Do nudes in ads enhance brand recall? *Journal of Advertising Research, 18*(1), 47–50.

Ashmore, R. D., Solomon, M. R., & Longo, L. C. (1996). Thinking about fashion models' looks: A multidimensional approach to the structure of perceived physical attractiveness. *Personality & Social Psychology Bulletin, 22*, 1083–2005.

Baker, M. J., & Churchill, G. A. (1977). The impact of physically attractive models on advertising evaluations. *Journal of Marketing Research, 24*, 538–555.

Barry, T. (1987). The development of the hierarchy of effects: An historical approach. In J. H. Leigh & C. R. Martin (Eds.), *Current issues and research in advertising* (Vol. 10, pp. 251–295). Ann Arbor, MI: University of Michigan.

Belch, G. E., Belch, M. A., & Villarreal, A. (1987). Effects of advertising communications: Review of research. In J. Sheth (Ed.), *Research in marketing* (Vol. 9, pp. 59–117). New York: JAI Press.

Belch, M. A., Holgerson, B. E., Belch, G. E., & Koppman J. (1981). Psychophysical and cognitive responses to sex in advertising. In A. A. Mitchell (Ed.), *Advances in consumer research* (Vol. 9, pp. 424–427). Ann Arbor, MI: Association for Consumer Research.

Bello, D. C., Pitts, P. E., & Etzel, M. J. (1983). The communication effects of controversial sexual content in television programs and commercials. *Journal of Advertising, 12*(3), 32–42.

Brown, D., & Bryant, J. (1989). The manifest content of pornography. In D. Zillmann & J. Bryant (Eds.), *Pornography: Research advances and policy considerations* (pp. 3–24). Hillsdale, NJ: Lawrence Erlbaum Associates.

Brumbaugh, A. M. (1993). Physical attractiveness and personality in advertising: More than just a pretty face? In L. McAlister & M. L. Rothschild (Eds.), *Advances in consumer research* (Vol. 20, pp. 159–164). Provo, UT: Association for Consumer Research.

Burgoon, M. (1989). Messages and persuasive effects. In J. J. Bradac (Ed.), *Messages effects in communication science* (pp. 129–164). Newbury Park, CA: Sage.

Buss, D. M. (1994). *The evolution of desire*. New York: Basic Books.

Caballero, M. J., Lumpkin, J. R., & Madden, C. S. (1989). Using physical attractiveness as an advertising tool: An empirical test of the attraction phenomenon. *Journal of Advertising Research, 29*, 16–22.

Caballero, M. J., & Pride, W. M. (1984). Selected effects of salesperson sex and attractiveness in direct mail advertisements. *Journal of Marketing, 48*, 94–100.

Courtney, A. E., & Whipple, T. W. (1983). *Sex, stereotyping and advertising*. Lexington, MA: Heath.

Dempsey, J. M., & Reichert, T. (2000). Portrayal of married sex in the movies. *Sexuality & Culture, 4*(3), 23–38.

Dillard, J. P., & Meijnders, A. (2002). Persuasion and the structure of affect. In J. P. Dillard & M. W. Phau (Eds.), *The persuasion handbook: Developments in theory and practice* (pp. 309–328). Thousand Oaks, CA: Sage.

Dillard, J. P., & Wilson, B. J. (1993). Communication and affect: Thoughts, feelings, and issues for the future. *Communication Research, 20*, 637–646.

Dolliver, M. (1999). Is there too much sexual imagery in advertising? *Adweek, 21*, 22.

Englis, B. G., Solomon, M. R., & Ashmore, R. D. (1994). Beauty before the eyes of beholders: The cultural encoding of beauty types in magazine advertising and music television. *Journal of Advertising, 23*(2), 49–64.

Fetto, J. (2001). Where's the lovin'? *American Demographics, 23*(2), 10–11.

Fisher, W. A. (1986). A psychological approach to human sexuality: The sexual behavior sequence. In D. Byrne & K. Kelley (Eds.), *Alternative approaches to the study of sexual behavior* (131–171). Hillsdale, NJ: Lawrence Erlbaum Associates.

Gould, S. J. (1994). Sexuality and ethics in advertising: A research agenda and policy guideline perspective. *Journal of Advertising, 23*(3), 73–80.

Grazer, W. F., & Keesling, G. (1995). The effect of print advertising's use of sexual themes on brand recall and purchase intention: A product specific investigation of male responses. *Journal of Applied Business Research, 11*(3), 47–58.

Greenberg, B. S., Graef, D., Fernandez-Collado, C., Korzenny, F., & Atkin, C. (1980). Sexual intimacy on commercial TV during prime-time. *Journalism Quarterly, 57*, 211–215.

Greenberg, B. S., Siemicki, M., Dorfman, S., Heeter, C., Stanley, C., Soderman, A., & Linsangan, R. (1993). Sex content in R-rated films viewed by adolescents. In B. S. Greenberg, J. D. Brown, & N. L. Buerkel-Rothfuss (Eds.), *Media, sex and the adolescent* (pp. 45–58). Cresskill, NJ: Hampton Press.

Harris, R. J. (1994). The impact of sexually explicit media. In J. Bryant & D. Zillman (Eds.), *Media effects: Advances in theory and research* (pp. 247–272). Hillsdale, NJ: Lawrence Erlbaum Associates.

Jackson, S. (1992). *Message effects research: Principles of design and analysis.* New York: Guilford.

Jackson, S., O'Keefe, D. J., & Brashers, D. E. (1995). The messages replication factor: Methods tailored to messages as objects of study. *Journalism Quarterly, 71*, 984–996.

Jacobellis v. Ohio, 378 US 184, 12 L ed 2d 793, 84 S Ct 1676 (1964).

Jones, M. Y., Stanaland, A., & Gelb, B. D. (1998). Beefcake and cheesecake: Insights for advertisers. *Journal of Advertising, 27*(2), 33–51.

Joseph, W. B. (1982). The credibility of physically attractive communicators: A review. *Journal of advertising, 11*(3), 15–24.

Judd, B. B., Alexander, M. W. (1983). On the reduced effectiveness of some sexually suggestive ads. *Journal of the Academy of Marketing Science, 11*(2), 156–168.

Kahle, L. R., & Homer, P. M. (1985). Physical attractiveness of the celebrity endorser: A social adaptation perspective. *Journal of Consumer Research, 11*, 954–961.

Kervin, D. (1990). Advertising masculinity: The representation of males in *Esquire* advertisements. *Journal of Communication Inquiry, 14*(2), 51–69.

Key, W. B. (1973). *Subliminal seduction: Ad media's manipulation of a not so innocent America*. New York: Signet.

Key, W. B. (1986). *The clam-plate orgy and other subliminal techniques for manipulation your behavior*. New York: Signet.

Lambiase, J., & Reichert, T. (in press). Promises, promises: Exploring erotic rhetoric in sexually oriented advertising. In L. Scott & R. Batra (Eds.), *Persuasive imagery: A consumer perspective*. Mahwah, NJ: Lawrence Erlbaum Associates.

LaTour, M. S. (1990). Female nudity in print advertising: An analysis of gender differences in arousal and ad response. *Psychology & Marketing, 7*(1), 65–81.

LaTour, M. S., & Henthorne, T. L. (1993). Female nudity: Attitudes toward the ad and the brand, and implications for advertising strategy. *Journal of Consumer Marketing, 10*(3), 25–32.

LaTour, M. S., & Henthorne, T. L. (1994). Ethical judgments of sexual appeals in print advertising. *Journal of Advertising, 23*(3), 81–90.

Lin, C. A. (1998). Uses of sexual appeals in prime-time television commercials. *Sex Roles, 38*(5/6), 461–475.

MacKenzie, S. B., Lutz, R. J., Belch, G. E. (1986). The role of attitude toward the ad as a mediator of advertising effectiveness: A test of competing explanations. *Journal of Marketing Research, 23*, 130–143.

McGuire, W. J. (1968). Personality and attitude change: An information-processing theory. In A. G. Greenwald, T. C., Brock, & T. M. Ostrom (Eds.), *Psychological foundations of attitudes* (pp. 171–196). San Diego, CA: Academic Press.

McGuire, W. J. (1972). Attitude change: The information-processing paradigm. In C. G. McClintock (Ed.), Experimental social psychology (pp. 108–141). New York: Holt, Rinehart, and Winston.

Muehling, D. D., McCann, M. (1993). Attitude toward the ad: A review. *Journal of Current Issues and Research in Advertising, 15*(2), 25–58.

Nudity is ad fad, not trend, four A's told (1968, October 28). *Advertising Age*, pp. 1, 88.

Percy, L., & Rossiter, J. R. (1992). Advertising stimulus effects: A review. *Journal of Current Issues and Research in Advertising, 14*(1), 75–90.

Peterson, R. A., & Kerin, R. A. (1977). The female role in advertisements: Some experimental evidence. *Journal of Marketing, 41*, 59–63.

Przybyla, D. P., & Byrne, D. (1984). The mediating role of cognitive processes in self-reported sexual arousal. *Journal of Research in Personality, 18*(1), 54–63.

Reichert, T. (in press). Sex in advertising research: A review of content, effects, and functions of sexual information in consumer advertising. In J. Heiman (Ed.), *Annual review of sex research, Vol. 13*. Mount Vernon, IA: The Society for the Scientific Study of Sexuality.

Reichert, T., Heckler, S. E., & Jackson, S. (2001). The effects of sexual social marketing appeals on cognitive processing and persuasion. *Journal of Advertising, 30*(1), 13–27.

Reichert, T., Lambiase, J., Morgan, S., Carstarphen, M., & Zavoina, S. (1999). Beefcake or cheesecake? No matter how you slice it, sexual explicitness in advertising continues to increase. *Journalism & Mass Communication Quarterly, 76*(1), 7–20.

Reichert, T., & Ramirez, A. (2000). Defining sexually oriented appeals in advertising: A grounded theory investigation. In S. J. Hoch & R. J. Meyer (Eds.), *Advances in Consumer Research* (Vol. 27, pp. 267–273). Provo, UT: Association for Consumer Research.

Reid, L. N., & Soley, L. C. (1983). Decorative models and the readership of magazine ads. *Journal of Advertising Research, 23*(2), 27–32.

Richmond, D., & Hartman, T. P. (1982). Sex appeal in advertising. *Journal of Advertising Research, 22*(5), 53–61.

Rosen, D. L., & Singh, S. N. (1992). An investigation of subliminal embed effect on multiple measures of advertising effectiveness. *Psychology & Marketing, 9*(2), 157–173.

Ruth, W. J., Mosatche, H. S., & Kramer, A. (1989). Freudian sexual symbolism: Theoretical considerations and an empirical test in advertising. *Psychological Reports, 64*, 1131–1139.

Sapolsky, B. S., & Tabarlet, J. O. (1991). Sex in primetime television: 1979 versus 1989. *Journal of Broadcasting & Electronic Media, 35*(4) 505–516.

Sciglimpaglia, D., Belch, M. A., & Cain, R. F. (1978). Demographic and cognitive factors influencing viewers' evaluations of "sexy" advertisements. In W. L. Wilke (Ed.), *Advances in Consumer Research* (Vol. 6, pp. 62–66). Ann Arbor, MI: Association for Consumer Research.

Seidman, S. A. (1992). An investigation of sex-role stereotyping in music videos. *Journal of Broadcasting & Electronic Media, 36*(2), 209–216.

Severn, J., Belch, G. E., & Belch, M. A. (1990). The effects of sexual and non-sexual advertising appeals and information level on cognitive processing and communication effectiveness. *Journal of Advertising, 19*(1), 14–22.

Simpson, J. A., Gangestad, S. W., & Nations, C. (1996). Sociosexuality and relationship initiation: An ethological perspective of nonverbal behavior. In G. J. Fletcher & J. Fitness (Eds.), *Knowledge structures in close relationships: A social psychological approach* (pp. 121–148). Mahwah, NJ: Lawrence Erlbaum Associates.

Simpson, P., Horton, S., & Brown, G. (1996). Male nudity in advertisements: A modified replication and extension of gender and product effects. *Journal of the Academy of Marketing Sciences, 24*(3), 257–262.

Soley, L., & Kurzbard, G. (1986). Sex in advertising: A comparison of 1964 and 1984 magazine advertisements. *Journal of Advertising, 15*(3), 46–54, 64.

Soley, L., & Reid, L. (1988). Taking it off: Are models in magazine ads wearing less? *Journalism and Mass Communication Quarterly, 65*, 960–966.

Solomon, M. R., Ashmore, R. D., & Longo, L. C. (1992). The beauty match-up hypothesis: Congruence between types of beauty and product images in advertising. *Journal of Advertising, 21*(4), 23–34.

Steadman, M. (1969). How sexy illustrations affect brand recall. *Journal of Advertising Research, 9*(1), 15–19.

Stewart, D. W., Pechmann, C., Ratneshwar, S., Stroud, J., & Bryant, B. (1985). Methodological and theoretical foundations of advertising copywriting: A review. In J. H. Leigh & C. R. Martin (Eds.), *Current Issues and Research in Advertising,* (Vol. 2, pp. 1–74). Ann Arbor, MI: University of Michigan.

Theus, K. T. (1994). Subliminal advertising and the psychology of processing unconscious stimuli: A review of research. *Psychology & Marketing, 11*(3), 271–290.

Tinkham, S. F., & Reid, L. N. (1988). Sex appeal in advertising revisited: Validation of a typology. In J. D. Leckenby (Ed.), *Proceedings of the 1988 conference of Ameri-*

can academy of advertising (pp. 118–123). Austin, TX: American Academy of Advertising.

Walker, J. R. (2000). Sex and violence in program promotion. In S. T. Eastman (Ed.), *Research in media promotion* (pp. 101–126). Mahwah, NJ: Lawrence Erlbaum Associates.

Williams, L. (1989). *Hardcore: Power, pleasure, and the "frenzy of the visible"*. Berkeley, CA: University of California Press.

Wilson, R. D., & Moore, N. K. (1979). The role of sexually-oriented stimuli in advertising: Theory and literature review. In W. L. Wilkie (Ed.), *Advances in consumer research*, (Vol. 6, pp. 55–61). Ann Arbor, MI: Association for Consumer Research.

Chapter 3

Historical and Psychological Perspectives of the Erotic Appeal in Advertising

Juliann Sivulka
University of South Carolina

One area of advertising that has to be continually relearned is how to use sex in advertising, because what is permitted this year is taboo in the next one, and vice versa. Prior to World War I, for example, it took only an armpit or a glimpse of stocking to bring readers to a full halt. Consider the advertisement for R & G Corsets, which is reproduced here (see Fig. 3.1). In 1898, the picture was one that *The Ladies' Home Journal* refused to print, because it was held to be immodest ("Editorial," 1899)—a far cry from the sexually explicit ads of Calvin Klein today. The corset ad is also revealing of a dramatic change in erotic appeals over the 20th century, which can be described as a continuum of escalation, an escalation of eroticism.

A number of factors have accounted for the significant changes in the erotic appeal in advertising and sexual norms. Little in American culture has been left untouched by the cycles of economic boom and bust, by sweeping political realignments, and by the social fads including the youth craze, clothes, leisure, and sexuality. When scholars have explained the changing nature of sex in advertising, they have often viewed this shift as an evolution from a relatively innocent representation of a sexually alluring woman to a new type of image, in which sex is explicit. A model once may have revealed a full bosom for men's pleasure, whereas today she might be fondling herself with undisguised pleasure. This has been a development over the past century whereby not only women but men also have shed their clothes and inhibitions. Even so, advertisements constituted a major source of popular sexuality well into the 1940s, when pinups and the movie industry's sexual interludes provided stiff competition. The sheer volume of sex in advertising reflects our continuing fascination with one of the more engaging aspects of life.

FIG. 3.1. Advertisement for R & G Corsets, 1898.

I would like to suggest, however, that there are four directions under which a majority of the ads can be subsumed:

1. The appeal to idealization or the motive to emulate is effective when the reader seeks to either model after or associate with the "beautiful people."

2. The sexually evocative advertisement may also function as an erotic fantasy, by which the viewer safely looks for a fantasy mate who may function as a personally acceptable diversion.

3. The other general class of images has been objectionable to the feminist movement. It has presented women exclusively as sex objects. Actresses and dancing girls, as well as burlesque queens, show girls, chorus girls, and movie starlets came to represent the promiscuous image of women, relished mainly by men.

4. A similar form of erotic stimulation for women is emerging today, which portrays men as sex objects in the same negative way women had been featured for years. A common (and it could be argued, sexist) mistake is to assume that men are interested in sex and women are not. In truth, the publications that carry the sexiest advertising have been women's publications.

Magazine advertising provides one way of tracking this shift, for it provides a way to examine the images and ideals that seemed to appeal to Americans. In fact, the most artful and daring examples appear in magazines. Unlike other media, magazines issue little in the way of blanket prohibitions. They tend to accept advertising on the basis of its congruence with the publication's editorial policy and the appropriateness for its particular audience. Even so, nudity has become almost commonplace in upscale fashion magazines, the controversial specifics masked by artfully placed underthings, towels, and other props. But how did we come to expect to find sex in an ad? In this chapter, I examine the antecedents of how the ever-present use of sex began in advertising. Although the rules by which advertisers play in this field continually change, the psychological insights in this complex subject seem to have held up during the 20th century. One thing is clear. It's not that there is so much more sex in ads than in the past, it's simply that the sexual content is more explicitly defined.

PRIOR TO WORLD WAR I, SOFT SELL AND PRETTY GIRLS

The development of sex appeal in American advertising can be traced to the earliest known print forms. Images of pretty women as ornate accessories have long enhanced magazine advertisements and posters to sell products. In the 1850s, for instance, admakers used the heads of beautiful women, and after the Civil War the heads acquired bodies. Strangely enough, circus ads featured women clothed in tights that could be quite revealing, whereas patent medicine ads often emphasized low-cut bodices, a common practice during the reign of Napoleon (1804–1821). But in the 1880s, the fashionable shirtwaist took cloth right up to the chin, and floor-sweeping skirts covered everything but the tips of the shoes. "At last the advertisers had a target of titillation: a peek at the forbidden," notes Charles Goodrum (Goodrum & Dalrymple, 1990, p. 71).

Until World War I, the artist's wind gust could lift the hemline as high as the ankle, and readers could be brought to a full stop (Goodrum & Dalrymple, 1990, p. 71). Because the concealed is so exciting, the long skirts also provided an almost endless game of trying to glimpse at naked delights. Although the outer clothes reached to the ground, the hems could in some way be rumpled, or caught up, or lifted by a gust of wind, in the dance, or in a spill. In any event, the influence of burlesque then, and its discovery of calves and other carefully exposed parts of women's bodies, is not to be underestimated in its effect on a fairly puritanical culture. As a result, the exploitation of the female figure steadily increased, showing "spicy" illustrations of legs, tights, and lingerie.

During the 1890s, the new ability to print high-quality illustrations further popularized "pretty girl" pictures as a new generation of magazines appeared as advertising vehicles. Their styles ranged from the *Ladies' Home Journal* to the reformist *McClure's Magazine* and the impassioned *Munsey's.* Although they varied in content, these magazines had one thing in common: They depended on a new class of subscribers, the middle-class readers who were ready to buy consumer goods advertised in an appropriate fashion. Yet it was the women's service magazines known as the Seven Sisters—*The Ladies' Home Journal, Good Housekeeping, Better Homes and Gardens, McCall's, Woman's Day, Redbook,* and *Family Circle*—that reigned over the women's market with articles on recipes, child-rearing, health, and home decoration, all aimed at married women with children. In this way, these new magazines created new opportunities for national advertisers.

In addition to new mass communication vehicles, the increase in sex in advertising was due in part to better methods of reproducing illustrations and to more numerous drawings and paintings available for commercial purposes. Admakers reproduced original oil paintings, delicate oil-and-water drawings, and sketches. The ads sought to combine style, design, and tone to create "picture magic" (Miller, 1982). Placement of the all-important product name and identifying symbols, trademarks, and slogans also became an important part of the advertisement.

Another result of the new lifelike advertising was the expanded use of the printing medium to achieve convincing real images. Pictures of burlesque actresses, dancers, and singers, dressed in tights or short pants or low-cut dresses, appeared on playing cards, postcards, cigarette cards, plug tobacco cards, calendars, magazines, and outdoor signs. Thus, the use of alluring women in advertising evolved as a concept from many different sources. Whether from prints, magazines, or other printed ephemera, the earliest "pretty girls" images were almost all tied to sex in advertising, promoting commercial products, stories, and professions. Unlike the pinup, the presentation of the body was not only for the visual delectation of the onlooker, but functioned in his or her own world to sell a product, service, or an idea. Be she on a poster on the wall of a bachelor's apartment, on a girlie calendar in a barbershop displaying the sponsor's name, or on the magazine pages read by a married adult bored with domestic humdrum, the pretty girl pictures allowed the reader to escape into a private and gratifying world through vicarious eroticism, promiscuity, or other lifestyles. But the essential erotic appeal, characteristic of modern advertising, did not suddenly appear. Rather, it slowly evolved from a subtle approach to more explicit presentations as psychological theorists began to develop new perspectives on the underlying drives that established emotional ties with consumers and contributed to buying actions.

Academic psychology first became involved in advertising at the beginning of the 20th century. As early as 1908, Walter Dill Scott (1869–1955) published his famous book, *The Psychology of Advertising in Theory and in Practice*. This book, which contained almost 300 pages, was respectfully dedicated to "That increasing number of AMERICAN BUSINESSMEN who successfully apply science where predecessors were confined to customs" (Scott, 1908). After stressing the benefits of experimental research, Scott discussed a broad spectrum of psychological topics such as perception, attention, memory, volition, emotion, suggestion, and habits to assess the efficiency of advertisements to induce a sale. Thus, Scott challenged admakers to associate the advertised product with emotive suggestions to make an impression:

> How many advertisers describe a piano so vividly that the reader can hear it?
> How many food products are so described that the reader can taste the food?
> How many advertisements describe a perfume so that the reader can smell it?
> How many describe an undergarment so the reader can feel the pleasant contact with his body? (quoted in Presbrey, 1929, p. 442–443)

Still, the idea of studying people's wants and buying behavior was just beginning to take root.

A successful ad works because it creates a connection between the product being advertised and some need or desire that the audience perceives. These links, called *appeals*, generally fit into one of two categories: (a) logical or rational, and (b) emotional. The underlying content of logical or rational appeals focuses on the consumer's practical, functional, or utilitarian need for the product or service. In contrast, emotional appeals base the selling argument on emphasizing the satisfaction that comes from purchasing the product and then owning it or making a gift of it. An extremely strong emotive appeal tells the consumer: "This is *the* product that will meet your needs or fulfill your desires." Although fundamental to advertising today, these concepts seemed novel and revolutionary in the early 20th century, especially the idea that the skillful use of emotional appeals could move products faster than any other approach.

At this point Helen J. Lansdowne Resor, a copywriter for J. Walter Thompson, added the essential emotional appeal to the logical or rational sales argument when her celebrated ad for Woodbury's Facial Soap first appeared in 1911 (see Fig. 3.2). Moreover, the landmark campaign tapped into a basic human interest: sex. The ad featured a painting of an attractive couple in an embrace and the provocative headline "A skin you love to touch." This line embodied a strong emotional appeal to women's desire to be beautiful and charming, to have a smooth, clear, attractive skin. The ad copy featured a skin-care regimen and closed with an offer for a week's supply of soap, plus the art from the advertisement. Later ads in the series appeared with different illustrations but kept the same headline with its muted sexuality. The advertising initially appeared exclusively in the important women's magazines with large national circulation, such as *The Ladies' Home Journal*, to reach a female, middle-class audience (J. Walter Thompson advertising collection, 1926; see also JWT collection, no date).

Certainly, the women's viewpoint was apparent in the choice of media and copy appeals for the Woodbury's campaign. What the Woodbury ad campaign undertook was to educate women about the nature and working of their skin, the cause of common skin problems, and the way in which these defects could be overcome by the right cleansing method with the advertised product. But the words and visuals of the advertisement also embraced women's hopes, fears, desires, and dreams regardless of what they did in their daily lives. "I added the feminine point of view," explained Helen Lansdowne Resor. "I watched the advertising to see that the idea, the wording, and the illustrating were effective for women" (quoted in Fox, 1983, p. 81). Thus, the campaign transformed an unpleasantly stinging soap into a wildly popular beauty aid by dramatizing the product itself, describing it with so much feeling that it seemed attractive and desirable (Peiss, 1999, p. 122). In the next 5 years, sales of the Woodbury line skyrocketed, from $515,000 in 1915 to $2.58 million in 1920 ("The Story of Woodbury's Facial Soap," 1930). Indeed, sex could sell a lot of soap.

Previous ads had exploited sex and pretty women, but none with the effectiveness and persistence of the Woodbury's campaign. What made this

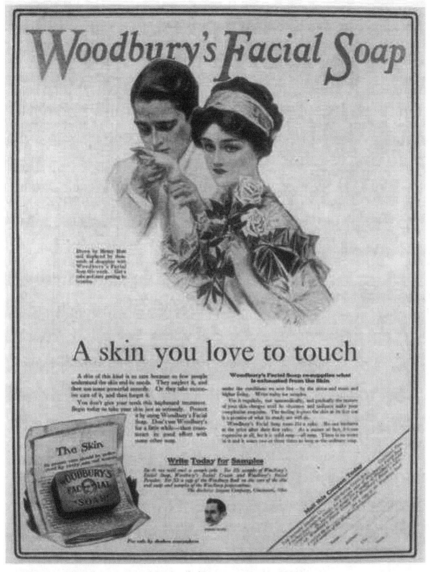

FIG. 3.2. Woodbury's Facial Soap ad, first appearing in 1911.

campaign so successful? Edith Lewis, a Thompson agency copywriter, later explained that where a product faced great resistance, or where it had strong competition, the admaker sometimes draws on outside sources in order to reinforce the emotional quality. That is, one "has to invent a situation or create an interest outside the product itself or its uses, in order to awaken an emotional response." In the case of the Woodbury campaign, Resor powerfully brought before the reader's imagination not only the social disadvantages of a bad complexion, but also the admaker presented the social incentives for a good one—you, too, could find romance or secure a personal relationship by using the advertised product. Nevertheless, the omnipresence of sex in selling had not reached the point where admakers were selling sex to get the reader's attention. Although the Woodbury's campaign used sex in the copy, it was barely hinted at in the artwork.

SEX AND CONSUMPTION

The spirit of the "Roaring Twenties" represented liberation from Victorian constraints. The era was a source of delight to some and of horror to others. Young working women also made it clear in many ways that they wanted the same freedoms men had. The flapper emerged as the symbol of this spirit of liberation; in 1915, H. L. Mencken coined the term *flapper* for the new American woman (Ostrander, 1958, p. 335). Women threw away their corsets, bound their breasts for a flat-chested look, raised their skirts to the knee, replaced their cotton underwear with rayon and silk, bobbed their hair, plucked their eyebrows, and painted their lips; some also used shocking words, drank on occasion, and publicly smoked. About these trends in 1922, the *Pittsburgh Observer* reported "a change for the worse during the past year in feminine dress, dancing, manners, and general moral standards" (Daniel, 1989, p. 60).

The role of advertising in this revolution in American values cannot be exaggerated. It was both cause and effect. Just as advertising originated in the need to persuade more and more purchasers to acquire more and more material goods, it also provided women with a version of reality that reflected the changing values and beliefs of consumers. The pages of popular women's magazines, such as *Ladies' Home Journal, Good Housekeeping,* and *True Story,* and general periodicals like *Saturday Evening Post,* vividly set forth the vision of the "good life" and changing sexual norms.

A common theme in advertising in this era revolved around issues of lifestyle and image. Consumers were encouraged to buy the "right" bread, the "right" vacuum, and the "right" car. But ads didn't stop there. Consumers also discovered that, to be socially acceptable, they had to look and smell a certain way, had to maintain spotless homes, and even had to wear silk hosiery. And the prime targets of all this promotion were women. From the very start, the advertising world made women the prime target of their efforts, because women read more ads and purchased more products than men. According to *The Ladies' Home Journal,* women controlled an estimated 80% to 85% of household spending in 1929 (1929, p. 35). Admakers also drew on a long tradition that assumed a woman's place was in the home, believing that women were only concerned with "their desire to look young and sexually appealing" (Fishburn, 1982, p. 163).

A case in point: The imaginative ads for silk hosiery that appeared in all of the major women's magazines pushed the line of acceptability in the 1920s. After World War I, silk stockings, which had been limited to the rich until the war arrived for ordinary people to replace the black cotton stockings, and hemlines shot up. But the flapper's short skirt was specifically raised to show off the newly available silk stockings, claims sociologist Robert Atwan. That is, the "democratization of silk was largely responsible for the 'invention' of legs as a sexual appendage in the years immediately preceding World War I." Other sociologists believe that it was the iconoclasm of the Jazz Twenties that lifted the hems, and the silk stockings were needed to cover the unattractive bare skin of the legs.

In any event, the advertiser had to learn an entirely new set of rules. By 1915, admakers could reveal a good 18 inches of stocking without being accused of bad taste (Goodrum & Dalrymple, 1990). As hemlines rose, the first uncovered kneecaps in advertisements appear in the early 1920s.

Working between World War I and the late 1920s, the well-known illustrator Coles Phillips drew dozens of ads for hosiery. Phillips, whose ads appeared in all the major magazines, pushed the line of what was acceptable further and faster than any of his contemporaries. In fact, some social historians credit Phillips with the invention of the pinup girl. At this time, his advertisements for Holeproof Hosiery were considered very daring for the time. For example, one 1921 ad for Holeproof Hosiery pictured a beautiful woman in a carefully designed geometric frame showing off the newly available stockings. The copy read: "Trim ankles, demurely alluring. How they fascinate, captivate. And well she knows glove-fitting Holeproof Hosiery makes them so" (Goodrum & Dalrymple, 1990, p. 72). Still, display of the backs of the knees was forbidden. Up to this point, this presentation was considered as firm a taboo as the depiction of pubic hair as of this writing. In 1925, however, the first ad thought to show the back of the knee appeared for Allen Hosiery with the headline "For Your Easter Hosiery, Madame." It was considered far beyond the line of acceptability even in the Roaring Twenties. Full female nudity in ads would not appear until the mid-1930s.

Nevertheless, male nudity was permitted, but again it was used on products bought primarily by women such as soap and underwear. Notably, Ivory Soap showed pictures of nude youths cooling off in a stream, and men showering in the locker room, while meeting the requirements of contemporary good taste in 1916 (Goodrum & Dalrymple, 1990, p. 53). At this point, the ideas of applied psychology and campaigns aimed at the unconscious mind of the buying public were just beginning to take root.

FROM COQUETTISH SUGGESTIONS TO FULL NUDITY

The science of psychology held a great interest for two reasons. First, it provided information about the instincts, drives, and wants of people. Second, it suggested new ways in which they might be controlled (Vinikas, 1992, p. 14). "Out of this change," wrote Abram Lipsky in 1925, "has sprung the universal interest in psychoanalysis, mob psychology, salesmanship—all connoting a technique with which one may control the minds of others" (quoted in Ostrander, 1968, p. 340). As for advertising, the study of psychology offered a key to overcoming consumers' objections to purchasing the promoted product. Instead of accepting people as rational beings who knew what they wanted, admakers began to examine what triggered people to make choices such as to buy or not buy a bathroom sink or to choose one brand of soap over another. Armed with this information, advertisers could make the their products more appealing. In any case, one industry analyst exhorted advertisers "to stir up the heart, and the head will blind obey" (*Printer's Ink*, 1919, p. 86).

Not surprisingly, then, sex was neatly woven into an increasing number of advertisements from the 1920s through the 1950s. Admakers had recognized that the desire to attract a romantic partner, a direct appeal to the sex instinct, appeared to be more effective than a technical discourse on the nonirritant qualities of the soap or the features of rustless steel in corsets (*Printer's Ink*, 1919, p. 86). Thus, advertisers experimented with the full range of erotic appeals, creating ads that incorporated subtle hints to blatant displays of skin, the romance formula, and in the language of advertising, buried sexual allusions, puns, innuendo, double entendres, and what advertisers call *near words*. The impetus for much of the sexual energy associated with products continued to come from psychological advice advertisers acquired over the years.

By the early 1920s, admakers had adapted some of Sigmund Freud's ideas to the field of buyer behavior. Unlike Scott's work, these perspectives were qualitative in the sense that they were largely based on an analyst's interpretations of a patient's accounts of dreams, traumas, sexual experiences, and so on. In particular, Freud's theories highlighted the potential importance of unconscious motives underlying purchases. The implication was that consumers could not necessarily express their true motivation for choosing a product, even if the researcher devised a sensitive way to ask them directly. The Freudian perspective also hinted that people might channel their desire to gratify their needs into outlets acceptable to the outside world by using products that signify their underlying desires. As Dr. Albert T. Poffenberger later advised in his 1925 book, *Psychology in Advertising*, people may frequently respond to the sex appeal in sublimated form. "Not only persons of the opposite sex, but objects, pictures, statements, ideas may arouse these desires that may manifest themselves in the purchase of handsome garments, jewelry, books, face powder, automobiles, furniture, and decorations." In fact, this desire is so strong that it may, under skillful hands, "be made to furnish the drive toward the purchase of almost any kind of object" (Poffenberger, 1925, p. 57).

Once admakers then recognized that their audience was overwhelmingly female, strategies for copy content and selling appeal seemed evident. Admakers, who considered women to be more emotionally vulnerable than men, often tried to manipulate women's supposed and "hidden" desires to be sought after and well liked and to join the successful middle class. Although more Americans had more money to spend than ever before, they also spent more time worrying about social acceptance and approval. "The advertising culture, more than the culture at large, acknowledged that one of the things that linked women was a persuasive discontent," wrote Jennifer Scanlon. "Women found their inarticulate longings for sensuality, financial independence, and emotional fulfillment channeled through what Jackson Lears calls an 'unconscious collaboration,' rather than a conspiracy" (Scanlon, 1995, p. 225).

In linking those "inarticulate longings" to consumption, emotive advertising campaigns appealed to yearnings for social acceptance that coincided with an American society geared to social mobility and liberation from Victorian restraints. Ads of the time were quite explicit about how products and activities helped to define different social and gender roles. Individuals' clothing, jewelry, furniture, cars, and so on helped to determine how people perceived themselves, as well as how they imagined others perceived them. Other ads suggested avenues for romance, personal fulfillment, and even escape. Just as individuals contribute symbols to advertising, so advertising adds meanings back to people's lives. The symbolic self-completion theory lends support to this point, by suggesting that people complete their identities by acquiring and displaying symbols from their culture that they find meaningful (Wicklund & Gollwitzer, 1982).

Advertising also acknowledged the new mass media that was shaping the values of a younger generation, including movies, radio, glossy magazines, and tabloid newspapers. Hollywood film stars usually embodied the ideal, which was presented to the nation through the movies and reinforced by magazine photographs and articles and advertisements, featuring models and pinup girls.

In particular, two popular culture phenomena provided admakers with new insights into a large part of the female market: tabloid newspapers and confession magazines. Following publication of the *Illustrated Daily News* in 1919, the concept of "tabloid copy for tabloid minds" gained credibility as the tabloid newspapers quickly gained widespread circulation (Marchand, 1985, p. 52). Like the tabloids, cheap confession magazines also attracted a vast audience. The confession magazine featured first-person stories aimed at young working women, offering dramatic personal accounts of tragic adventures, temptations, and romantic triangles such as "The Primitive Lover," "Her Life Secret," and "How to Keep the Thrill in Marriage." By 1926, one such magazine, *True Story*, achieved a circulation of almost 2 million, a remarkable achievement considering that the mainstream *Saturday Evening Post* enjoyed a circulation of about 3 million in the mid-1930s (Janello & Jones, 1991). Along with the tabloids and confession magazines, Hollywood also attracted a vast new audience. At this time, motion pictures reflected the national preoccupation with sheiks, vamps, and sex goddesses. Movies with titles such as *Cheap Kisses*, *Soiled*, and *Sinners in Silk* attracted large numbers of patrons (Printer's Ink, 1938).

Madison Avenue began to recognize that the female readers of the new mass media—tabloids, confession magazines, and film—offered new opportunities for advertisers. The new publications had fashioned, in effect, a female market that had plenty of money to spend for products like clothing, cosmetics, and soap. Poor, working class, and black women, largely ignored by national advertisers and magazines, joined the affluent in the market for beauty and fashion. American women spared little effort or expense trying to make themselves over according to the ideals set forth in the national media. By 1929, expenditures on perfumes, makeup, and toiletries were more than 10 times the amount spent per capita 20 years earlier (National Markets and National Advertising, 1929).

To reach this tabloid audience, admakers experimented with a wide range of selling formulas that promoted romantic love, nudity, and the high-class tease, while crafting sexual messages that invited the reader's vicarious participation.

THE ART OF ROMANCE

In the case of the romance formula, the crucial defining characteristic was not that it starred a woman, but that the organizing action involved the advertised product bringing two potential lovers together in a deeper, more secure relationship. The Woodbury's Facial Soap campaign "A skin you love to touch" had already demonstrated that sex could sell a lot of soap. The advertisements featured three essential elements: (a) a romantic man-and-woman situation; (b) a dominant sex appeal, focused on "the skin you love to touch" as key to desirable charm; and (c) the famous Woodbury treatment for overcoming skin problems. Thus, the advertisements made it quite clear that the primary responsibility of women was to be sexually attractive.

Instead of merely selling soap, the Woodbury campaign had discussed the benefits of using the product, suggesting softness, sex appeal, and even romance. These advertisements also employed fantasy appeals, which allowed women to extend their vision of themselves by permitting them to escape from problems in the real world and "try on" interesting or provocative roles. Emulating the Woodbury approach, Palmolive launched a campaign that focused on the romance formula. To differentiate soap from Woodbury's Facial Soap, when both personal soaps were so much alike, the copy emphasized aging: "Keep that schoolgirl complexion." Ads featured the modern women staying young with her husband at 18, at 30, and at 50, with exactly the same face as in her youth ("Milestones," 1928). The beauty appeal also reinforced the notion that all women shared identical desires—to remain magically young forever—so that they could not only capture a man, but also keep him by staying attractive. In this way, the ads showed women how the Palmolive "simple beauty ritual" could help them retain their freshness of youth. The suggestion of romance is implicit in one August 1928 ad from *The Ladies Home Journal* with the headline "He remembered"; it was left to the imagination of the viewer what inexplicable thing brought about the note and bouquet of fragrant roses for the woman in the illustration (Palmolive, 1928).

Did sex sell? Although the use of sex appeal did appear to draw attention to an ad, sometimes its use also may have been counterproductive for the admaker. Ironically, a provocative picture could be too effective if it attracted so much attention that it hindered the consumer's processing and recall of the ad's content. Sexual appeals appeared to be ineffective when used as a "trick" to grab attention. They appeared to work, however, when the product itself was related to sex (LaTour & Henthorne, 1994).

In the case of Woodbury and Palmolive, the ads convinced women that the advertised soaps could beautify and soften the skin, and thus persuaded them that they would become more attractive to the opposite sex. Still, the Woodbury and Palmolive campaigns only hinted at sex in the artwork and copy. The themes had been "you can keep your man if you keep your skin as attractive as it was when you captured him," "The skin you love to touch" and "Keep that school girl complexion" (J. Walter Thompson advertising collection, 1938).

What is important here is that the romance formula offered a pliable advertising concept to reach both the women of the smart salon trade and working women from the factory. The advertising invoked the mythic expectation of romantic love. According to one version of the romantic love myth, for each individual there is one perfect partner who, once found, will make life complete; the logical extension is the myth of the nuclear family. That is, the continued use of the advertised product will not only bring romance, but also will lead to marriage replete with children and a well-appointed home. Thus, the Woodbury, Palmolive, and hosiery campaigns, among others, continued to repackage 19th-century ideals and gender roles. In this view, a woman's place was in the home, and her beauty, not her accomplishments, measured her worth. "Through beauty woman can enter into her kingdom—woman's kingdom—where, as friend, sweetheart, wife, mother, she reigns in serene majesty and infinite power," explained one Palmolive ad. Certainly the romance formula in advertising further legitimated women's pursuit of beauty.

In any event, the sexual content of advertising continued to become more explicit decade after decade. The introduction of female nudity is thanks to admakers in the mid-1930s, when again they pushed the line of accepted taste to the limit.

THE ART OF THE NUDE

In the 1930s, photography in advertising had progressed gradually, from quite commonplace reproductions to dramatic realism. In this era photographic compositions differed markedly from the earlier pictures, in which actors posed stiffly in unreal situations and in obviously superficial sets. Following the success of the tabloid newspapers, picture-filled magazines emerged. *Life* debuted in 1935, featuring a dramatic photograph on the cover and dozens of pictures inside chronicling current events and entertainment news; photo-filled *Look* came out 2 years later. Some of the photos seemed almost clipped from a reel of movie film, with a new sense of beauty, realism, and drama.

In this era, however, admakers began to offer new visions of women's beauty that challenged what had seemed to be fixed and unshakable codes in the early 20th century. The line between fine art and risqué illustrations blurred more and more. Although sex had been used in copy before, illustrations had barely hinted at it. Scantily clad women, formerly encountered mostly in lingerie ads, sold household products from towels to soap. In the trade magazines, advertisers often used images of nude women to sell male-oriented or industrial products, because there they could be reasonably certain the viewers would be men.

What was new in the mid-1930s, however, was the use of such an image in popular magazines addressed to middle- and upper-class women who read fashion magazines. A new Cannon Mills towel campaign introduced the approach in 1936. Initially Charles Coiner, art director at the N. W. Ayer agency, commissioned the fine art photographer Edward Steichen to develop a series of nude studies. The models were shown relaxing after the bath or attending to their personal grooming with towels placed in their usual setting. The images were printed in sepia tones, yielding a softer look than the more obvious photographic black-and-white. They also tacitly affirmed that Steichen's photographs were fine art. The advertising trade press hailed the Cannon ads a success, arguing that good art attracted readers' attention. Yet

Steichen's nude studies were only one element of the overall advertising strategy of the Cannon campaign. The appearance of Steichen's nudes for Cannon towels in *Vogue* and *Harper's Bazaar* underscored the admakers' goal of targeting middle-class women, whereas *The Ladies' Home Journal* advertisements pictured attractive but fully-clothed housewives.

Using women's nude bodies to attract attention and market products appears to have been the hot new idea for 1936. Woodbury's Facial Soap and Camay Soap followed Cannon Mills with a similar series of nude studies. Through the Lennen and Mitchell agency, however, Woodbury hired Steichen to give its advertising the veneer of fine art.

In the Woodbury nude series photographed by Steichen, an unclothed model wearing only sandals and lounging near a swimming pool emerged as the most prominent image in the campaign (see Fig. 3.3). Soap in a swim-

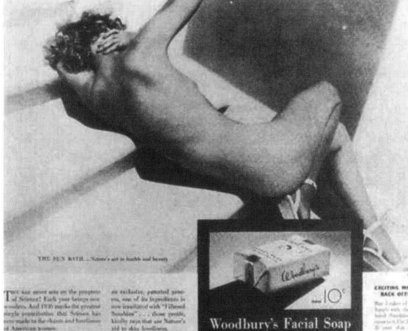

FIG. 3.3. Edward Steichen's Woodbury nude series, mid-1930s.

ming pool? Sunbathing in ankle-strap sandals? However, the copy provided an explanation of how this soap packed "Filtered Sunshine" into every bar to give the consumer "all the benefits of a sun bath." The other images in the campaign referenced classical nude studies. In one a sundial on a classical column partially obscured the model; and in another, a woman shown from the back from the waist up was draped over a large urn. Nevertheless, it appeared that the woman's body was there mainly to attract attention. Whereas Steichen's Woodbury ads seemed overworked, a series of Cashmere Bouquet soap ads by an unknown photographer presented a woman's body in more natural ways attending to the bath or her personal grooming.

Given the magazines where the ads were placed, the implication was that the nude female body no longer shocked and offended when it appeared in a commercial context. The Woodbury ads appeared in magazines such as *Good Housekeeping, Ladies' Home Journal*, and *True Story*, all aimed at a middle- and even working-class audience, both proper housewives and shopgirls. By the mid-1930s, one could run nude studies inside a magazine if not on the cover, observed historian Patricia Johnston. "What seems new in the advertising agencies' strategies for Cannon and Woodbury was their commissioning a well-known photographer to design photographs of female nudes that clearly referred to the history of Western art and appealed to the upright middle-class consumer" (Johnston, 1997, p. 217).

At the same time, advertisers were using sex to attract male customers to sell "male products," but in a different way. In the trade magazines, for example, advertisers often used images of nude women to get the reader's attention, because there they could be reasonably certain the viewer would be male. But nudity also now appeared in general magazines such as *Life* magazine. For example, a 1937 issue carried a Simoniz car wax ad portraying an unclad woman with the headline "Your car is no nudist." In other ads, women leaned on cars, women with blowing hair drove speedboats, and elegantly dressed women accompanied men in three-piece suits. The difference was that the woman was used less to arrest the reader's attention than to present a situation and imply a syllogism: If I buy a car just like it, then I, too, can get this woman. Likewise, if I buy this speedboat or designer suit, I, too, can attract this romantic partner.

Indeed, these ads went far beyond the standards of acceptability established in the previous decade, when most people considered displaying the backs of the knees a taboo (Goodrum & Dalrymple, 1990).

THE ART OF THE TEASE

Another wave of post World War I advertising gave birth to the materialistic and sexually permissive (at least for men) philosophy embodied in *Esquire*, which included pinups during the 1930s. But the new magazine sensation was *Playboy,* first published in 1953, that was overtly committed to the sensuous pleasures: gourmet food, high fidelity, romantic travel, and of course, sex. With the gradual relaxation of censorship laws, *Playboy's* pinup presentations became progressively bolder reflecting a change in taste. This pattern of presentation was also repeated in advertising, and admakers also used sex to move merchandise more than ever before.

The approach worked. Through the 1940s and 1950s the treatment of sex in advertising shifted from an almost reverent dignity to casual humor. Thus, admakers created a world in which language paid rich dividends and in which sexual images invited the reader's vicarious imaginative participation.

It began with Elliot Springs, owner of Springs Cotton Mills and seven other textile mills, who has been called the "expert on tease." Springs created a new approach by combining the typical sexy image with a humorous sales pitch favoring double entendres and puns. But Springs insisted that the ad sell some Springmaid fabric and that the logo be prominent. For example, one ad (1949, June) showed showed an illustration of a Native American sleeping in a hammock with the headline: "A buck well spent on a Springmaid sheet." And another 1948 ad, "Perfume and Parabolics," used a "girlie" illustration of an attractive skater with her skirt billowing around her legs and her panties exposed to the reader and two elderly gentlemen sitting on a bench (see Fig. 3.4). The copy read:

> During the war, the Springs Cotton Mills was called upon to develop a special fabric for camouflage ... but the Japanese learned to detect it because of its lack of jungle smells.

> To overcome this, when the fabric was dyed, it was also impregnated with a permanent odor of hibiscus, hydrangea, and old rubber boots. This process has been patented, and the fabric is now available to the false bottom and bust bucket business as SPRINGMAID PERKER, made of combed yarns, 37" wide, 152 × 68 approximate count, weight about 3.30, the white with gardenia, the pink with camellia, the blush with jasmine, and the nude dusty. If you want to achieve that careless look and avoid skater's steam, kill two birds with one stone by getting a camouflaged callipygian camisole with the SPRINGMAID label on the bottom of your trademark. (*Tide,* 1948)

Another typical advertisement pictured a pretty young girl having difficulty carrying two bags of groceries, because her panties had slipped to her ankles. The headline read "Watch the Butter Fly," and the copy went on to explain how the Springmaid "Sticker, a special cotton fabric containing rubber," could protect from the "consequences of embarrassing accidents" such as pictured in the ad. The ad lightly closed with this guarantee: "We stick behind our fabric and feel its tenacity so strong that we call it an insurance policy to provide full coverage. Our only competitor comes from a tattoo artist" (*Coronet,* June 1949).

FIG. 3.4. 1948 ad for Springs Cotton Mills.

Still another advertisement sold more than sheets—it promoted sexual intercourse. The illustration depicted an early American military officer with a sword on his hip and a young damsel in his bedroom, while an elderly man could be seen peering through the opened door. The headline "Bundling without Bungling" and copy introduced the advantages of FORT SUMTER sheets. Although sheets no longer stand up to the "knightly slaughter" when men slept with spurs and boots upon their feet, the covers "still stand rips and tears and of laundries, kids, and derrieres." To make the selling point of the quality and durability of the company's sheets, however, the remaining text explained the strenuous test that was applied to each SPRINGMAID sheet, where the fabric was washed 400 times—"that's equal to a generation of wear and tear and vellication" (*Coronet*, 1949). Thus, Springs insisted that the ad sell some Springmaid fabric, the logo be prominent, and the campaigns liven up the textile industry.

Nevertheless, advertising trade journals such as *Tide* considered the copy "ribald" and ineffective, because of phrases like "false bottom and bust bucket, "ham hamper and lung lifter," and "hip harness and bosom bolster" as references to women's undergarments ("Tide Leadership Survey," 1948). Although several magazines refused to run the advertisements because of the copy, prominent newspapers like *The New York Times* and *New York Herald Tribune* accepted the advertisements with no copy changes. Another issue of *Tide* referred to the illustrations as "semi-nudes," then asked whether the advertisements were directed to consumers. "If they are addressed to women, surely they don't speak the same language" (Montgomery, 1948, p. 24). And if they were addressed to the garment industry, these ads were really in the wrong publications, also criticized the publisher of *Printers' Ink* in 1948 (p. 5). Many other readers of the advertisements also complained, calling both the illustrations and copy vulgar. Without doubt, the Springs Mills campaigns pushed the envelope of good taste in advertising.

But what about the Springs Mills campaigns that have page after page of "girlie pictures"? Must the pictures be taken out, pinned up, and considered pinups? After all, many of Springs' artists, particularly Varga and Petty, gained their reputation mainly through magazine pinups. First, the vehicles for the advertisements were "class" magazines such as the *Saturday Evening Post, Holiday, Esquire, Fortune,* and *The New York Times Magazine,* and some of these publications were read by women. In the advertisements, then, the female reader may wish to relate to the model in a variety of ways—not necessarily sexually, amorously, or socially—but perhaps to encourage fuller, glamorous associations or sexual fantasies with the advertised product, that is, to be attractive, well liked, and desirable as a romantic partner. Thus, Springs intuitively recognized that many women readers were susceptible to the same pinup images that had inspired the masses of men.

Ultimately, Springs recognized that sex was phenomenally effective in getting the attention of a jaded reader. However, it worked only if used with certain other principles, explained Goodrum and Dalrymple (1990):

1. The admaker had to treat the reader as an intelligent peer.
2. Once an admaker had the reader's attention with leggy models, the ads had to offer some product benefit to justify getting the reader's involvement, or otherwise the reader would resent the admaker's impudence.
3. The actual sex image should be used with a light touch but with respect, not objectified and taken advantage of. In the case of Springs campaigns, both male and female "sexy" models appeared in the ads.
4. Springs believed the best way of attracting a reader's attention was to show them something that they didn't ordinarily see, since the viewers then had to use their imaginations and become involved in the advertisement. That is, suggestive language and a provocative illustration teasing the reader with an inch-and-half of stocking top were more attractive to the reader than nudes. (pp. 79–80)

To women, the representations may not have been necessarily sexually evocative, but for many, it appears that they elicited a pleasurable response as well as an equal amount of criticism. In fact, the advertising campaign for Springs Cotton Mills proved one of the most successful efforts during the late 1940s and early 1950s, increasing brand awareness and, subsequently, sales. In fact, surveys showed the ads resulted in far greater brand recall than any other campaign from 1947 to 1951. And by the late 1950s, the company had become one of the largest makers of sheets ("The Story," 1963). In the process Springs conditioned the public to accept more explicit advertising. Or did he?

YOU'VE COME A LONG WAY, BABY

Springs' rules and casual humor toward sex in advertising held for many decades, but began to take a series of contradictory modifications under another significant shift in American life. When the postwar baby boom generation came of age, the advertiser's audience had dramatically changed. The Puritan ideal, which stressed the importance of hard work and rewards, had gradually dropped out of favor with youths and had given way to pleasure seeking. The widespread availability of birth control also contributed to this new sense of personal freedom. When Dr. Alfred Kinsey published his 1948 *Sexual Behavior in the Human Male*, the uproar was volcanic. But by 1966, when William Masters and Virginia Johnson published a far more intimate and revealing study, *Human Sexual Response*, the book hardly created a stir.

As advertisers faced increasing pressure to communicate with youth, advertising agencies ever attuned to the tenor of the times began to create new images and craft their messages in provocative new ways.

During the 1960s, the social forces of feminism hit Madison Avenue. Feminists not only addressed the old issues of pay inequities and a lack of opportunity, but also challenged the roles assigned to women in a male-dominated society. Works such as Betty's Friedan's *The Feminine Mystique* (1963) argued that society conditioned women from childhood to think of themselves only as wives and mothers or sex objects. In contrast men were to believe that they could do "men's work" and become leaders in business and politics. Yet women of this era were better educated, more socially and politically aware, and almost half had joined the work force. No longer did women accept that they had to get married, start a family, and dedicate themselves to homemaking. Nor did they accept that they had to be pretty, sweet, and demure. This meant that women were no longer going to be influenced by the same advertising and promotional messages that may have motivated them a few years ago.

Three ad campaigns reflected this change in society's attitude toward women. The prewomen's liberation Maidenform campaign had shown women acting out their supposedly exhibitionist fantasies while displaying their Maidenform bras. One openly erotic advertisement pictured a curvaceous young woman with the headline, "I dreamed I took the bull by the horns in my *Maidenform bra.*" As the years went by, the campaign portrayed women who turned these dreams into reality by penetrating traditionally male-dominated domains, such as financial offices, architects' drawing rooms, and even pool halls. But the ads increasingly infuriated feminists because they pictured the scantily clad women with fully dressed men. And by the late 1960s, some women were burning their bras and not wearing them at all, so Maidenform discarded the campaign.

To reach the new woman, Virginia Slims targeted women buyers and launched one of the longest-running, most successful campaigns in advertising history. With its slogan, "You've come along way, baby," and comparative photographs, the campaign contrasted women of today with those of earlier eras. But the turning point came in 1973, when Revlon's Charlie perfume campaign displayed confident, pant-suited young women pursuing traditionally male-oriented activities. By the end of the decade marketers also realized that growing numbers of women were earning higher salaries. Thus, ads now not only depicted the attractive, professional woman at work but also increasingly pitched her cars, homes, and life insurance. In the 1980s, these values began to reassert themselves in sexually charged advertising from perfume to blue jeans

"The most risqué copy I have seen was for Paco Rabanne's men's cologne," said David Ogilvy (1983, p. 28). One of television's sexiest 30 seconds called "Man in Bed" opened with a French-accented man stirring himself awake as the telephone rang. "Hello," he yawned into the phone. "You snore," a woman's voice informed him. "And you steal the covers," he responded jokingly. As the conversation continues, paintings and discreet camera angles hid his nudity; the viewer never sees the woman. In a gender-role reversal it was now the woman who rose at daybreak to go on a business trip, leaving the lovesick man in bed. A two-page print ad also ran, showing the man in bed, with the commercial script expanded and printed alongside. As a promotional stunt, department stores across the country hired actors to lie on beds placed in store windows and talk with passersby who called from extension phones placed on the sidewalks. Sales for Paco Rabanne went up 25%, and in 1981, the advertisement, created by Ogilvy & Mather, was voted the best to appear in magazines. This foray into sexual adventurism continued with Calvin Klein's promotion of Obsession perfume, whose ads suggested that an erotic fantasy world awaited consumers.

Using sex to sell to teens also became a common image-building tactic. The once humble "dungarees" became big fashion, and big news. For example, in 1980 Sergio Valente, Bon Jour, Calvin Klein, Gloria Vanderbilt, and Jordache spent nearly $40 million in advertising. When Calvin Klein introduced his jeans campaign in 1981, controversy arose over the sexy ads and commercial spots featuring teen star Brooke Shields seducing audiences with her provocative "Know what comes between me and my Calvins? Nothing." Three network-owned stations in New York banned the ads. Nevertheless, sales of the expensive jeans jumped nearly 300% following the first wave of commercials ("The '80s," 1990, p. 19). In another controversy that same year, the Chicago Transit Authority pulled hundreds of bus billboards for the Bon Jour brand due to citizen complaints. The ads showed a model's torso with her jeans unzipped far enough to hint that she was not wearing underwear. And Jordache ran ads of blouseless young women astride similarly clad young men. Many people objected to the sexy jean ads, but before long, people paid extravagant sums for denims that displayed designers' names on their backsides.

These emerging trends also coincided with the marketers' attempt again to redefine the way they advertised to women. Now advertising showed women in two different worlds: the traditional one, a rerun of the 1950s with stay-at-home moms, and a modern one filled with women who hold jobs, have career goals, and derive pleasures from outside the home. Ads creatively addressed such issues as maintaining control without being a superwoman, combating fatigue, balancing work, and so on.

At the same time, a new genre of advertisements emerged that focused on the sensibilities of a new breed of woman, who in turns objectifies men—that is, "reverse sexism." In an upbeat parody one such Diet Coke television commercial featured Lucky Santos as a construction worker, who in a reverse role, is the object of attention of a group of female office workers. Some ads were far more explosive, tapping into some women's "I-don't-need-a-man-attitude." Under the new direction, Bodyslimmers lingerie showed a women from the neck down wearing a one-piece undergarment; the copy read: "While you don't necessarily dress for men, it doesn't hurt on occasion to see one drool like the pathetic dog that he is." Another ad for Hyundai cars featured two women arguing that men buy powerful cars because they are worried about the size of their penis—but the word is never spoken. One says, "He must be overcompensating for a … shortcoming." When a handsome man drives up in an economy Hyundai, the second woman muses, "I wonder what he's got under the hood?" Of course, all women did not share the mindset of the women in this advertisement, so admakers continually faced the challenge of how to reach a new balance, adjusting approaches in favor of women and following the currents of culture.

Expanding sexuality is both prevalent and significant today. The topic is probed, brooded on, and encouraged in adult education, literature, television, films, the Internet, and a myriad of publications—many catering to such specialized interests as homosexuality, sapphism, nudism, and fetishism. Scan recent women's magazines and one will be inundated with innuendo from Bruce Weber's photographs for a Calvin Klein advertising insert in *Vanity Fair* to the Victoria Secret lingerie fashion show on the Internet. Same with Abercrombie & Fitch's racy summer retail catalog, which is displayed in tightly wrapped plastic, intended for buyers 18 or older, and featuring young, unclad male and female models in what the company touts as sexy in a wholesome sort of way. By the standards of *Playboy* or *Penthouse*, the book might seem tame; yet, in fact, today's youth-oriented ads touch on every area of sexual pleasure and perversion.

Even so, the advertising is far less sexually explicit than much of what people can readily find elsewhere in their lives—in films, in magazine features, on cable TV, and in literature. Advertising's explicitness does not provide proof of the depravity of its creators and sponsors, but is evidence that some of the restraints in force are outdated. The irony is that in Europe and South America, where advertising is allowed to deal with sex more openly, the ads don't come across nearly as sexy as American advertising, which is generally less explicit.

If today's young generation of readers are less shocked by open sexuality than their grandparents' coquettish suggestions, can culture be far from a time when any sexual inclination will be freely portrayed in advertising? Can we then see an end to representations of women as sexual objects, which traditionally has been the basis of sex in advertising? And will the next generation be unimpressed with sex as a selling point? This kind of advertising does attract considerable attention and readership.

And it will continue to do so as long as there is sexuality itself. People will be dressing, scenting themselves with perfumes, and beautifying with cosmetics, not only to interest romantic partners, but also to give hidden pleasures to themselves.

REFERENCES

Daniel, C. (Ed.). (1989). *Chronicle of America*. Mount Kisco, NY: Chronicle Publications.
Editorial. (1899, May). *Charles Austin Bates Criticisms*, p. 511.
The 80s: What a decade. (1990, January 1). *Advertising Age*, p. 19.
Fishburn, K. (1982). *Women in popular culture: A reference guide*. Westport, CT: Greenwood.
Fox, S. (1983). *The mirror makers: A history of advertising and its creators*. New York: Vintage.
Friedan, B. (1963). The feminine mystique. New York: Dell Publishing.
Goodrum, C., & Dalrymple, H. (1990). *Advertising in America: The first 200 years*. New York: Harry N. Abrams Inc.
Janello, A., & Jones, B. (1991). *The American magazine*. New York: Harry N. Abrams.
Johnston, P. (1997). *Real fantasies: Edward Steichen's advertising photography*. Berkeley: University of California Press.
Kinsey, A. C. et al. (1948). Sexual behavior in the human male. Philadelphia: W. B. Saunders.
The Ladies' Home Journal. (1929, May). p. 35.
LaTour, M. S., & Henthorne, T. L. (1994). Ethical judgments of sexual appeals in print advertising. *Journal of Advertising, 23*(3), 81–90.
Marchand, R. (1985). *Advertising the American dream: Making way for modernity*. Berkeley: University of California Press.
Masters, W. H., & Johnson, V. E. (1966). Human sexual response. Boston: Little & Brown.
Milestone in the love affair that lasts a lifetime. (1928, May). Palmolive Soap advertisement, *The Ladies' Home Journal*.
Miller, E. G. (1982). *The art of advertising*. New York: St. Martin's Press.
Montgomery, C. (1948, September 10). The women's viewpoint. *Tide*, p. 24.
National markets and national advertising. (1929). New York: Crowell.
Ogilvy, D. (1983). *Ogilvy on advertising*. New York: Vintage Books.
Ostrander, G. M. (1968). The revolution in morals. In J. Braeman, R. Bremner, & E. Walters (Eds.), *Change and continuity in twentieth-century America: The 1920s* (pp. 323–349). Columbus: Ohio State University Press.
Palmolive advertisement. (1928, August). *The Ladies' Home Journal*.
Palmolive advertisement. (1938). Domestic advertisement collection, *J. Walter Thompson*.
Peiss, K. (1999). *Hope in a jar: The making of American's beauty culture*. New York: Owl Books.
Poffenberger, A. T. (1925). *Psychology in advertising* (2nd ed.). New York: McGraw-Hill.

Presbrey, F. S. (1929). *The history and development of advertising.* New York: Doubleday.

Printers' Ink. (1919, May 15). p. 86.

Printers' Ink. (1938). *Fifty years: 1888-1938.* New York: *Printers' Ink.*

Printers' Ink. (1948, December 10). p. 5.

Scanlon, J. (1995). *Inarticulate longings: The Ladies' Home Journal, gender, and promises of consumer culture.* New York: Routledge.

Scott, W. D. (1908). *The psychology of advertising.* Boston: Small, Mayfield & Co.

Springmaid advertisement. (1949, June). *Coronet.*

The story of Springs Cotton Mills, 1888–1963. (1963). Fort Mill, SC: Springs Mills.

"The Story of Woodbury's Facial Soap" (1930, January-February): 5, *J. Walter Thompson Account Files,* box 1, folder: Andrew Jergens Company.

Tide. (August 1948).

Tide leadership survey. (1948, August 27). *Tide,* p. 53.

Vinikas, V. (1992). *Soft soap, hard sell: Personal hygiene in the age of advertisement.* Ames: Iowa State University Press.

Wicklund, R. A., & Gollwitzer, P. M. (1982). *Symbolic completion theory.* Hillsdale, NJ: Lawrence Erlbaum Associates.

Woodbury's Facial Soap National Campaign (1926). 7, Account Files, Andrew Jergens Company, Account Histories 1916–1926, box 1, *J. Walter Thompson collection.*

Woodbury's Facial Soap (n.d.), Account Files, Andrew Jergens Company, Account Histories 1946–1950, box 1, Account Files, *J. Walter Thompson collection.*

Chapter 4

Dark Desires: Fetishism, Ontology, and Representation in Contemporary Advertising

Jonathan E. Schroeder
Royal Institute of Technology, Sweden

Janet L. Borgerson
Stockholm University

Advertising has become a complex societal institution, blending seamlessly into the visual landscape, invoking a range of social, cultural, and ethical issues formerly reserved for the political sphere, and implicating itself in almost all information transfer. Advertising provides a shared common experience for a majority of the world's inhabitants, and a reference point for conversation and interaction. Rippling through visual culture, advertising widely circulates information about the social world, largely through photographic representation. Ads appear everywhere, including art galleries and museums, blurring distinctions between popular culture and fine art. Recently, advertisements have become collected commodities—bought, sold, and traded—prized for their aesthetic and investment value. One particular campaign stands above the rest in this regard—Absolut Vodka.

This chapter takes a look at the fetish, an iconic element of sexuality in visual culture, and introduces a theoretical framework for understanding fetishism in contemporary advertising. Two compelling print advertisements provide a point of departure, highlighting the way photography reifies objects in a fetish-like manner and how advertising capitalizes on cultural stereotypes about fetishism to both communicate certain messages and create novel associations in viewers. Beyond a strict paradigmatic view of the fetish, basic concepts of fetish objects from psychoanalysis and anthropology contribute to our analysis. We begin with a brief introduction to *visual consumption,* a concept developed to cope with the visual aspects of consumption as a critical social and cultural institution (Schroeder, 1998a, 2000). Then we discuss the roles that ontological aspects of visuality and identity perform in marketing communications.

The next section introduces two images from the Absolut print ad campaign. Absolut is a popular, widely heralded, long-running, and iconic ad campaign that demonstrates the triumph of image over product function in marketing discourse. Absolut advertising images are readily available on the Internet, and several books have been written about the brand (i.e., Hamilton 2000, Lewis, 1996). Furthermore, the two "Absolut Au Kurant" ads under consideration feature fetish staples, a black leather corset, and a black garter belt. Fetishism has become an aestheticized signifier, emphasizing the eroticized associations of these ads' photographic images. We include a discussion of liminality as a contributing category in the theoretical framework of fetishism.

How does the fetish function in contemporary visual culture? How do advertisers create powerful and positive images for their products via fetishistic themes? The specimens scrutinized here are meant to be both illustrative and theory building—not merely exemplars of fetishism in visual culture—producing cultural knowledge about visual phenomena. Previous work in this vein includes literary and art historical analyses of a famous Paco Rabanne cologne ad (Stern & Schroeder, 1994), Hawaiian tourism ads (Schroeder & Borgerson, 1999), Victoria's Secret catalog imagery (Schroeder & Borgerson, 1998) and the CK One ad campaign (Schroeder 2000). These papers describe our interdisciplinary interpretive method in considerable detail.

We are not proposing a theory of fetishism per se. Rather, we find fetishism to be a useful conceptual tool for analyzing visual consumption. Visual images constitute a major presence in the modern market—goods are sold via images, and consumers buy products as much for their symbolic qualities as for their utilitarian aspects. Images are imbued with fetish-like attributes in art, advertising, and film. Photography itself has also been called a fetish. In the words of one writer, commenting on the work of Roland Barthes: "Like a fetish, this element—the shoe or dress of the person depicted—expresses and stands for the viewer's desire and, metonymically, for his or her experience of the photograph itself" (Weissberg, 1997, p. 109). We draw on photography theorist Abigail Solomon-Godeau's conception of the fetish as a confluence of factors, including photographic practice and reception (1991; 1993). Fetishism, photography, and advertising combine to produce striking, sexually tinged images designed to promote a basic vision of the good life.

Fetishism, in this case a psychological phenomenon that replaces human relations with commodified object relations, generally revolves around particular items of clothing. Visual representation of fetish clothing often depends on three significant qualities: liminality, blackness, and decontextualization. First, fetishized clothing is liminal, straddling the conceptual and ontological divide between nature and culture. For example, leather derives from natural sources: animals. To convert an animal skin into a wearable garment, however, requires transformative cultural and technological processes. Leather clothing usually exhibits a polished, shiny surface. This shininess visually underscores the liminal quality of fetish apparel; shine or gloss signifies a manufactured characteristic that contrasts with the material's natural essence. Furthermore, fetish clothing is often tight, worn close to the skin, stretched to conform to the body, inscribing the wearer with its liminal qualities. Second, fetish clothing is often colored or dyed black. For example, black is the most common color of leather available. Black, of course, is a racial category; blackness in semiotic terms connotes exoticized identity and a sexualized fascination with the other (Gordon, 1995). Blackness contributes to the fetishization of clothing in part due to black skin's exoticization by the Western world. Third, photographic techniques such as close cropping, lighting, and depth of field visually fetishize objects via isolation and decontextualization. Thus, photography contributes to the fetishization of goods by reifying and eroticizing consumer products.

In this chapter, we present an in-depth analysis of fetish themes in contemporary advertising via an interdisciplinary reading that draws from visual studies, consumer behavior, and critical race theory. This discussion opens up broader considerations of the fetish's role in visual culture. The chapter closes by reflecting on the fetish as a conceptual tool to understand visual rhetoric in contemporary advertising.

VISUAL CONSUMPTION

Identity construction via representation and image management is a central motivating concern in consumer behavior. In one sense, one might say that the consumer produces identity through consumption processes. This apparent paradox—identity production through consumption—characterizes consumer culture. The concept of visual consumption attempts to capture these conceptually complex interactions in a highly visual culture dominated by marketing images (see Schroeder, 2002). Visual consumption refers to engaging with, reading, and responding to signs, symbols, and images (Schroeder, 1998a; 2000; 2002). Articulating perceptual processes around the consumption of representation invokes a complex interaction between producing and consuming images. Visual consumption encompasses critical ways that people experience their world and represent themselves through action, word, and image.

Representation refers to meaning production through language systems (cf. Stern, 1998). Language, then, is central to meaning via its role as a representational system. Recent work utilizing representation as an analytic tool emphasizes how cultural practices—such as laws, rituals, norms, art, and consumption—contribute to meaning production in advertising (Mirzoeff, 1999; O'Barr, 1994; Ramamurthy, 1997; Schroeder & Borgerson, 1998; 2002; Schroeder & Zwick, 1999; Stern, 1998). Conventional views of representation hold that things (objects, people, consumers) exist in the material and natural world, and that their material characteristics define them in perfectly clear terms. Representation, according to this view, is of only secondary importance in meaning making.

Recent thought in the humanities and social sciences that emphasizes how social and cultural forces produce knowledge implies that representation is of primary importance for understanding meaning construction. Representation, in this view, is conceived as entering into the very constitution of things. That is, an object's or idea's meaning is shaped by the very process of representing it via language, picture, or sound (Hall, 1997). Representation, then, is a critical concept for understanding how advertising produces meaning.

Marketing communication works in a broad context to influence the construction of the world through representation and advertising images (cf. Wells, 1997). Advertising operates with a system of visual representation that creates meaning within the circuit of culture, often beyond what may be intended by the photographer, advertising agency, and company whose product is advertised (cf. Ritson & Elliot, 1999). Photography emerged in the 20th century as the most powerful and omnipresent technology of representation, lending its visual power to advertising, the dominant global communication force both in terms of its ubiquity and its support and influence of the vast majority of mass media (Schroeder, 2000). Representation is now inconceivable without photography; the world has taken on what Eduardo Cadava called "a photographic face" (1999). Furthermore, the information technology of photography is central to understanding how advertising produces meaning. This meaning production contributes to advertising's status as representation. However, advertising research often focuses on the internal content of advertisements—what the ad claims, how it links the product to consumer benefits, or the design of the ad—as if visual issues are solely an information processing variable. Moreover, visual issues often are overlooked in advertising research despite their importance in meaning creation (Stern & Schroeder, 1994). Advertising relies on visual imagery to connect the perceptual with the conceptual, the signifier and the signified, the product and the product benefits.

ILLUSTRATIVE EXAMPLE: ABSOLUT VODKA

Absolut Vodka has produced one of the most successful and celebrated ad campaigns since the 1980s. The campaign, which included a new bottle design, transformed an obscure Scandinavian snaps into one of the leading global brands in any product category (see Hamilton, 2000). Absolut Vodka's former name was Absolut brannvin, which meant pure and unflavored vodka in Swedish. The Absolut brand has several line extensions, such as Absolut Citron—a lemon-infused vodka—as well as Absolut Kurant, which is flavored with black currants.

The liquid product has not changed, but Absolut's image has been catapulted into the heights of brand ecstasy by a consistent, long-running marketing strategy that centered around an ongoing ad series that featured the Absolut bottle in a wide variety of characters and guises (Lewis, 1996). Many artists have been commissioned to produce an Absolut ad. Perhaps the most famous example is Absolut Warhol, introduced in 1985 (see Schroeder, 1997). Absolut Kurant also holds an "Absolut Visions" art competition each year, offering cash grants and a group exhibition to winners, selected from art schools such as the Art Institute of Chicago and the Rhode Island School of Design. Absolut has been aggressive in supporting the arts community as well as the gay community in a promotional effort to link its brand with hip trends. For example, an Internet search revealed an Absolut Fetish ad in the form of a black rubber insert imprinted with the Absolut bottle in the British gay magazine *Attitude* (see http://www.absolutad.com/davezzz98.htm). Absolut ads are collected, traded, and displayed by an enthusiastic group of admirers, and ads are offered for sale on many Internet sites devoted to the Absolut ads (e.g., http://www.absolutcollectors.com).

Absolut Au Kurant, a version of the popular and critically acclaimed Absolut campaign, will serve as an in-depth case study. The brand position for Absolut Kurant has evolved into a cutting-edge image, and ads often feature exclusive nightclubs, sexual references, or cool people. Websites featuring Absolut often provide racy recipes for Absolut Kurant flavored drinks, such as the "Peekaboo" and "Absolut Sex."

THE IMAGES

Two Absolut Au Kurant ads constitute the main target of the analysis. One depicts a tight, shiny black leather corset, its lavender-colored laces forming the shape of an Absolut bottle as they crisscross and tightly bind the photographer's model (see Fig. 4.1); the other shows a leg dressed in a black stocking and garter belt, with a tiny purple Absolut bottle-shaped garter

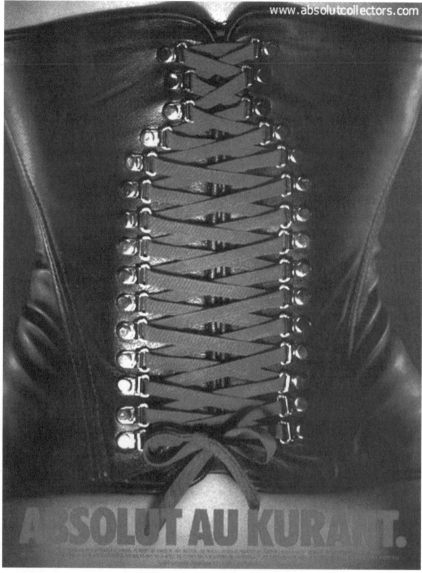

FIG. 4.1   Absolut Au Kurant corset ad.

clip holding up the stocking (see Fig. 4.2). These ads appeared in *The New York Times Magazine* in May and October of 1997, respectively. These provocative, erotically charged images reinforce the Absolut Kurant brand as a cutting-edge sexuality signifier through the use of familiar tropes of bodily representation and photographic techniques of cropping and highlighting.

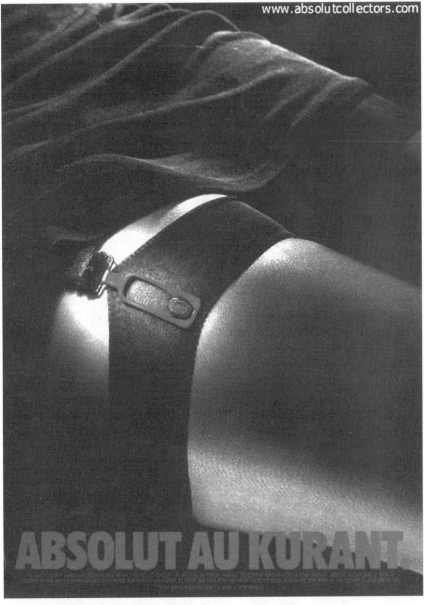

FIG. 4.2. Absolut Au Kurant stocking ad.

Furthermore, an undercurrent of S & M and fetishism is present in the images. An interpretive key to the ad is that opening the Absolut bottle by unlacing or unfastening its representation in the ads leads to sexual activity—or at least an undressed model.

The Corset Ad

The first ad is a bright color photograph of a human torso dressed in a black leather corset with lavender lacing, tightly cropped to show only a small patch of bare white skin, perhaps an inch at the top and two inches at the bottom of the image (see Fig. 4.1). The words "Absolut Au Kurant" run along the bottom of the ad, in lavender capital letters that match the corset's lacing color. A subtle lavender filter gives the corset a purplish cast. The corset's lacing hooks are arranged so that the lavender laces form the shape of a bottle—the Absolut Vodka bottle—with a bow tied at the bottom of the corset. Thus, the laces represent the bottle in the ad.

The laces crisscross the figure, tightly binding the model, pulling in the stomach, and pushing up the chest. These laces signify the effort that goes into being corseted; two people are routinely required to restrict the waist as tightly as shown in the ad. The laces are laced perfectly flat through a series of shiny metal rings, or eyes, which are riveted to the leather. Their bottle-like simulation is familiar from Absolut's ubiquitous and long-running marketing campaign. Thus the laces echo the containing properties of the glass bottle—they hold the "contents" only to release when undone. The message of the ad centers around the resonance between opening an Absolut bottle and consuming the product and opening the black corset and consummating a relationship. The lace-bottle opens up the person within, undressing for potential intimate activity. The Absolut bottle serves as the key prop for sexual readiness. Furthermore, the bottle enables a postmodern transformation of the corset into contemporary erotic signifier, its intertextual sign power fueled by the long-running Absolut campaign. The magic properties of the Absolut bottle are hinted at by these elements, a common theme in liquor advertisements (Williamson, 1978).

The laces also suggest striptease or foreplay. Dressed like this, it will take a while to undo the corset. This sense of slow undressing serves well as a visual signifier of desire and temptation. An invitation is issued: Open the bottle in the ad by undoing the laces; the bow that secures them looks awfully insubstantial. Thus, the viewer participates in sexual ritual. In a fairly simple and straightforward image, Absolut links itself to leather corsets, erotic fetishism, alternative sexuality, and sexual allure.

The Stocking Ad

The basic layout of the Au Kurant ad with stockings (see Fig. 4.2) is similar to the corset ad; both highlight body parts and each tightly crops the image so that no facial identity is revealed. Both have a similar color scheme of black and lavender. Each shows a glimpse of skin, in this case a part of the thigh not covered by black stockings and a short, black skirt. The clip that holds up the black stocking resembles a tiny lavender Absolut bottle. The bottle-clip holds the stocking that covers the model's leg. Opening the garter fastener frees the leg from the confinement of the stocking, a basic move scripted in many music videos, films, and pornography.

These ads say "alcohol provides access." Absolut vodka is the key to undressing. Opening the bottle—in this case the garter clip bottle—paves the way for sexual activity. Both corset and garter exemplify old-fashioned garments—designed in an age before the women's movement, before spandex, and before aerobics. The corset, for example, became a symbol of oppression, molding women to an ideal as confining as the garment. There are other ways to read this ad, however.

Queering the Image

Lavender is the adopted color of the gay rights movement. In the corset ad, we see only the back of the model, and most corsets lace in the rear. Therefore, it is difficult to tell visually whether the model is a man or a woman. True, the upper body reveals a feminine shape, complete with small waist, but this could be from the corset restricting a male body or an effect of the camera angle. Unquestionably, most viewers would see a woman, for corsets are a feminine item, linked to female identity. However, men wear corsets too. Most corset manufacturers feature several models designed for men. Some corset-wearing men are looking to hold in a growing gut or perhaps help a chronically sore back—but many are participating in a bit of gender-bending by donning a fetishistic item, usually out of bounds for male attire.

Corsets change the body when worn tightly laced. They whittle the waist and exaggerate the hips and breast to achieve an "hourglass" figure—an archetype of desirable female form. Likewise, a corset is a convenient way for men to acquire a "female" form—corsets can reduce men's waists, too. A corset will also push a man's breast up and out, a start on obtaining a womanly bosom.

Corsets were originally made from cotton or linen, usually white or off-white. A leather corset is clearly not an old-fashioned type. It is meant for today's sexual libertine. Furthermore, the black corset is an icon of leather influenced sex. By casting a black leather corset in the Absolut Au Kurant ad, the ad director signified transgressive hipness rather than merely waist reduction. The corset depicted is fetishized as an object unto itself, made expressly for sexual display, rather than concealment or restriction.

Hence, the ad's figure can be read as a man in a corset. Is he gay? Not necessarily. One scenario would be a female lover—or perhaps a dominatrix—has laced him into the corset. Perhaps he is wearing it for his pleasure, for the feeling of being firmly held in by tight leather. Absolut ads, of course, can be read as "gay" ads. The corseted figure could be lesbian or bisexual. It is clear that viewers are able to project a range of visions onto this image and, in the absence of clearly identifiable body features, it could easily be seen as a male, opening up a range of possible polysemic interpretations and responses.

In the stocking ad there is also no specific reference to the model's sex, other than the highly feminine clothing. Of course, men once wore hosiery—as any viewer of a film set in the Elizabethan era can plainly see—but now full-length hosiery is mostly reserved for women. Stockings and garter belts or stockings and suspenders are staple props of pinup photography, "R" rated films, music videos, and pornography. A shot of a gartered leg glimpsed through a slit skirt has become an overused trope to titillate (mostly) male desire. However, stockings and garters are also a mainstay of men's efforts to appear female, from drag shows to Halloween costumes. Nothing prevents the viewer from identifying this model as a male masquerading as a female or perhaps experimenting with sexy, feminized—and taboo—clothing. Photographed differently, the ad would not be as open to such interpretations. Like the corset image, the tight cropping produces a malleable picture of interpretive possibilities, including a knowing nod to male cross-dressing or gay fashion. Clearly, Absolut Kurant has created compelling imagery that works differently for different target markets (cf. Lewis, 1997). Given Absolut's presence in the gay market, this is not surprising. These fetishistic images are infused with alternative sexual energy, which is a cornerstone of the Absolut brand strategy.

THE FETISH

A fetish object symbolizes control and release, power and helplessness, sexuality and infantilism. In clinical terms, a fetish may be a dysfunctional response to sexuality; eventually fetish objects replace human contact for arousal and sexual gratification. Fetishism is associated with displacement and disavowal; sexual energy becomes directed toward something other than the genitals, a substitute that is charged with sexual power and attraction (Hall, 1997). Examples abound, but a hallmark of the visual culture of fetish is tight-fitting clothing, particularly those made from materials such as leather and rubber. In popular terms, fetishism often refers to a psychological relationship or an intra-individual practice, but fetishism can fruitfully be considered a kind of cultural discourse (Apter & Pietz, 1993).

The fetish is a useful concept for analyzing marketing communication. It illuminates important aspects of consumers' relationships with products, as well as how marketers create objects of desire (cf. Jhally, 1987). In the magical realm of advertising, goods are readily infused with fetish qualities. Products are worshipped for their ability to complete the self and to help the user gain satisfaction or even ecstasy, and are revered for their capacity to project a desired image. In this way, goods function similarly (in a psychoanalytic sense) to the fetish object, which promises gratification but ultimately is unable to deliver, forever displaced within a fetish relationship. Fetish items are typically linked to sexuality. Furthermore, a fetishized relationship in some cases interferes with the ability to have more "human" relations. Fetishized articles are usually decontextualized and isolated—the shoe that by itself arouses, the black stocking and heel disconnected from any recognizable body.

Two factors underlie the visual power of fetish: associations made through repeated usage of stock items in fashion, photography, and pornography; and what we call the *liminal* element of fetish clothing. The word liminal reflects a gap, a space between, or an edge. Liminal zones are often spaces of uncertainly, creativity, danger, and passion. The space between—a space to be entered or crossed—can be simultaneously exciting and unnerving. Many fetish objects, particularly items of clothing, represent a powerful liminal zone. Absolut's version of the corsets and garter belts, for example, occupy a space between the nostalgic past and the trendy future; they are old-fashioned garments modified for cutting-edge resonance. Corsets contain, yet reveal. Shoes, boots, corsets, stockings are typical fetish items—usually colored black or bright red. In popular discourse, fetish clothing is usually desired by men on women.

Stockings are liminal items. Extremely close fitting, stockings accentuate and conceal the leg, both revealing and covering. Furthermore, the space at the top of the thigh that is left uncovered, save for the taut garter straps that hold up the stocking, represents another in-between zone. This seems to be a key in the fetishization of garters and stockings—the small patch of skin that remains bare, unclothed. Stockings were once made of silk, a natural product transformed by manufacturing into a wide range of textiles and garments. Today most stockings are made of nylon. Furthermore, most hosiery worn is a kind of pantyhose, without the need for a garter belt to keep them up on the wearer's leg. Thus, representations of garter belts nostalgically invoke the past. Although a full discussion of fetishism is beyond the scope of this chapter, we want to spend some time looking at fetish objects and how they are represented in visual culture, using imagery from the world of advertising as illustrative aids. A myriad of things can be fetishized—perhaps anything—but we concentrate on fetish clothing as an iconic implication of the fantasized fetish in advertising photography.

Fetishism in Visual Culture

The visual vocabulary of fetish has become a staple of the culture industries, television, fashion, film, music video, comic books, and advertising. These draw on cultural stereotypes of the fetishist, a male whose sexual identity and gratification is obsessively linked with the fetish object. For fetishism "is not really a *human* perversion at all but a uniquely male one" (Grosz, 1993, p. 39). In classic fetish relationships, sexual desire is projected onto eroticized objects. This projection of lust, of desire, and of want onto a fetish object seems the simplest way to present such imagery, which is usually recruited to lend an edgy sexuality to the advertised product. Ads from cologne to telecommunications networks feature fetish themes of high-heeled shoes, stockings, tight leather, S & M, and bondage (cf. Cortese, 1999). Often these motifs are invoked with a wink to the knowing audience, a hip sign that the viewer understands—and appreciates—what is implied by the image of a handcuff, an extremely high heel, or a leather corset (Goldman & Papson, 1996).

The dominatrix has become a visual fetish icon. The image of a woman—usually dressed in black leather, high-heeled black boots, carrying a whip or riding crop—who desires to inflict both pain and the promise of pleasure on her (usually) male victim seems appropriate to sell most any product. Typical manifestations of this type appear in recent ads ranging from Altoids mints, Johnnie Walker Red whiskey, and Breil watches, to name a few. These ads draw on motifs developed by such mid-century photographers as Horst, Helmut Newton, and Jean-Loup Sieff, who featured women in corsets, leather, and high heels in their photographic work for mainstream fashion magazines. In the 1970s this trend accelerated, pushed by the art world, a growing awareness of "underground" sexual practices, and a market hungry for extreme imagery. By the 1980s, fetish and dominatrix imagery had established a firm place in the visual pantheon of fashion, music video, and film, and was adopted by such mainstream celebrities as Grace Jones, Madonna, and Annie Lennox, and via the photography of Robert Mapplethorpe. Today, fashion designers such as Thierry Mugler, Versace, Jean-Paul Gaultier, and Sisley regularly include fetish-themed clothing in their clothing lines and ad campaigns.

A dominatrix is imbued with a certain power. However, the dominatrix' power revolves around sexual power, a kind of power under oppression; it remains unclear if power in the bedroom translates in a meaningful way to power in the living room, dining room, or boardroom (cf. Borgerson, 2001; Carter, 1978). Furthermore, the dominatrix tends to exist to fulfill male fantasies of passive participation in sexual activity. The fantasy works best if she performs scripted scenarios of seduction and sadomasochism fueled by male desire (Schroeder & Borgerson, 1998; Stern, 1991). In most dominatrix images, the man gets to endure and enjoy. The dominatrix embodies many of the forces of fetishism, for she is a fiercely dressed female who exists to serve sexually. Most popular dominatrix imagery revolves around extreme stereotypes of sexual interaction involving fetish objects, leather, or other accoutrements of "deviant" sexuality (Schroeder, 1998b).

Some may argue that representations of "alternative" sexuality are use-ful to question entrenched norms and push limits of acceptable behavior between consenting adults, but, in general, these images are used to titil-late, tease, and move products off the shelves, not to disrupt notions of cul-tural behavior. Furthermore, the dominant image of the dominatrix hardly expresses the variability inherent in alternative sexuality. Rather, it serves to reinforce stereotypical understandings of the role that power, S & M, and leather play in real relationships. Dominatrix iconography is closely linked to stereotyped notions of fetishism, although there are important distinc-tions between the two concepts. In this analysis, we unpack how fetishism works in contemporary visual culture, and the dominatrix is one icon that deserves further investigation. Others include the henpecked husband, the executive, and the alien.

Visual representation and fetishism work together to create fantasy im-ages of desire and inaccessibility (cf. Borgerson & Schroeder, 1997). Fetish-ism has been discussed from many perspectives, including psychology, anthropology, and Marxism. Advertising images draw on each of these—creating objects of desire through visual techniques and symbols. Psychoanalytic theory holds that a true fetish is based on paradoxical repul-sion and attraction that charges fetish objects with power as it simulta-neously represents titillation and taboo. (Shoes are seemingly an essential fetishistic item, and they probably need a much longer treatment than given here.) Visual representations of fetish objects, made possible by pho-tographic reproduction, mass media, and specialized photographic tech-niques, add another dimension to the fetish concept. Solomon-Godeau (1993) theorized the fetish in 19th-century photography as:

> a confluence of three fetishisms ... the psychic fetishism of patriarchy, grounded in capitalism, shrouded in what Marx calls the "veil of reification" and grounded in the means of production and the social relations they engen-der, and the fetishizing properties of the photograph, a commemorative trace of an absent object, the still picture of a frozen look, a screen for the projective play of the spectator's consciousness. (p. 269)

The fetish emerged as an important marketing tool, via advertising rep-resentations of fetish objects, and the fetish-like worship and power of ma-terial goods inherent in contemporary consumer culture.

Leather, Liminality, and Longing

Fetish clothing—usually of leather, rubber, or other tight-fitting materi-als—stretches over an important cultural and psychological liminal zone of nature versus culture (see Ortner, 1996). Leather and rubber are natural materials, in the sense that they have roots in the natural world—leather as animal skin, and rubber as a botanical extract. When made into clothing, however, each is culturally transformed into a manufactured product (cf. MacKendrick, 1998). Each has a distinct genealogy, yet functions in a similar liminal way. Fur has a history as a fetish material as well, made famous by the Victorian novel *Venus in Furs*, but here we concentrate mostly on leather.

Humans have a long relationship with leather. Part of the contemporary iconography of leather clothing comes from its association with the Nazis and the SS—popularized via film, television shows, and photographs. Only recently has leather been associated with sex, fetishism, or deviance. Leather jackets, once mainly associated with the police, punk rockers, rock and rollers, fighter pilots, and motorcyclists, have undergone a significant transformation in the past 25 years from rebel badge to everyday fashion accessory. Leather pants, formerly reserved mainly for motorcyclists or rock stars, have become a staple of department store clothing lines. Thus, the repertoire of cultural associations for leather accommodate countervailing images of authority and rebellion (see McClintock, 1995).

Many leather-clothed icons are male stereotypes, yet women are most often depicted in eroticized leather. Where do their images come from? Emma Peel, from the British television show *The Avengers*, often wore leather top to toe; Catwoman from the *Batman* movie series sewed her own shiny tight-fitting catsuit; Xena the warrior princess wears stylized leather armor. This is not a huge reservoir of images, and yet the woman in leather plays a powerful role in contemporary visual culture. One recent source for these images is MTV, which provides a playground of fetishized women 24 hours a day. One formula was set by pop group ZZ Top, whose early 1980s videos featured women with "legs," who "know how to use them" often wearing a tight black leather skirt, high heels, and stockings. The video scenario invariably centered around a young man, minding his business, who would ultimately benefit from this "knowledge" and be ushered into the world of sexuality and adulthood by the leather-clad women (cf. Kaplan, 1987). In the absence of compelling icons such as cop or rock star, women are relegated to sexual stereotype. Perhaps leather's sexual significance may diminish somewhat as additional styles of leather clothing become more widely available for both men and women. Of course, leather's connotations vary by culture, too. In Northern Europe, leather pants are commonly worn by women without too much sexual association, but in the United States, leather pants remain "hot."

Leather is also linked to the gay community. Leather often obliquely refers to sexual preference, as in: "Are you into leather?" or "He's a leatherman." Thus, leather in this sense refers to leather as fetish accessory. Although leather clothing has gone mainstream, certain kinds of leather goods—collars, harnesses, leather bras, leather jocks, tight leather shirts for men—remain within the underground domain. Certainly, these are worn and used by people of all sexual preferences, yet many leather items signify homosexual practice, and a "leather lifestyle" more often refers to gay men than to straights. There is a huge market for leather fetish clothing, aimed at both straights and gays, served by catalogs, a growing number of specialty stores and the Internet. Moreover, a "leather community" is often referred to, particularly during public spectacles such as gay pride parades. Leather gains an alternative sexuality image from these associations.

Leather was originally meant for protection outdoors. Wearing these materials inside signals a transgression of a liminal zone between inside and outside, home and away, familiar and exotic. Visual representations of leather draw on these distinctions, because the fetish world is usually indoors. Other fetish icons—shoes, gloves, masks, and so forth—exemplify protection from the elements. These items serve as bestial body extensions. Donning leather may represent gaining animal-like qualities; rubber pushes this transference into an amphibian or almost reptilian world. Leather is a durable material, and this quality signifies tough work or manly outdoor tasks. Visually, wearing leather indoors and particularly in the bedroom appears as a breach of the liminal zone between inside and outside, private and public, perhaps work and pleasure. Leather-infused imagery calls on these associations to build up power and mastery connotations.

Leather is a sensual fabric when processed in certain ways. Variable associations to types of leather are based on their place within the liminal system of nature versus culture. Leather is considered a skin, a natural product of the animal it came from. Most leather sold today is cowhide, but many other animals' hides are made into leather goods: goat, pig, lamb, deer, and so on. The process of turning a hide into a garment is a cultural one; leather is skinned, tanned, dyed, cut, sewn, and finished before it winds up as a jacket or pair of gloves. Thus, leather, especially leather clothing, worn near our own skin, is liminal, between the zones of nature and culture, or what Lévi-Strauss called the raw and the cooked (1983).

Smooth, shiny leather is most often associated with fetishism. Few gloves or corsets shown in contemporary advertising are made of rough suede, or bulky "unfinished" hides. Suede certainly can be sexy, yet it is also "safer" than leather, easier to integrate into a conservative wardrobe, less "suggestive." Suede often appears more like animal skin. Fuzzier and less shiny than leather, suede shows more of the dull nap of the skin. Shininess is an indicator of human handling; leather has to be highly processed to achieve a high sheen. Patent leather, which is perhaps the pinnacle of fetishized leather, undergoes even more finishing to achieve a stiff, almost plastic look that is highly prized by the fetishistic boot licker, at least in stylized representations of the foot fetishist. Patent leather is a hybrid material, originating from a natural source but treated to such an extent that it begins to resemble plastic—that icon of manufactured substance.

A critical factor in fetish clothing is the way it conforms to and transforms the body. The tighter the clothing, the stronger the fetish potential. Tight clothing accentuates the human form, often isolates certain body parts like the pelvis or the breasts, and reveals the body's shape. Tight clingy clothing, for the most part, is a recent development, owing to changes in cultural norms, social mores, and manufacturing technology. Tight leather, of course, is often linked to sexuality and fetishism—particularly in visual representations—due to its capacity to mimic human skin. Skin is natural. A tight fit is often achieved with metal fasteners such as zippers, rivets, hooks or laces, subtle reminders of leather's cultural status as a manufactured good. Tight leather stretching snuggly over the wearer forms a second skin, suggesting a kind of superskin. Leather clothing can be made to fit loosely, but, typically, tight leather populates the cultural imagination. The icon is the *tight* black leather skirt, after all. Of the three adjectives—tight, black, leather—so far we have discussed two. In the next section, we discuss the importance of blackness as a fetishistic signifier.

ONTOLOGICAL IMPLICATIONS OF FETISH IMAGERY

Many things are liminal in the way they fall between nature and culture; it is not this quality alone that accounts for the sensual power of fetishized materials. Visual associations are important and contribute meaning in conjunction with prevailing cultural codes. For example, photography contributes to fetish signification. Kobena Mercer, commenting on Mapplethorpe's photographs of black men, argued that the photographed black skin signifies transgressive fantasy: "the glossy, shining, fetishized sheen of black skin thus serves and services the white man's desire to look and to enjoy the fantasy of mastery precisely through the scopic intensity that the pictures solicit" (Mercer, 1997, p. 293). Thus, the combination of artificial lighting, flash photography, and visualized shininess associated with certain skin (or skin-like garments) animates fetishization processes. Black-and-white photography emphasizes black tones, and implicitly contrasts black with white. Of course, black-and-white pictures do not contain only black and white tones, but millions of varying shades between black and white. The language of photography, however, reinforces a dichotomous conception of black–white, inscribing racial categories with technological markers, in a process of racial fetishism.

Blackness, exoticized via cultural stereotyping processes, is the preferred "color" of fetish iconography. Black, as a Western semiotic category, functions as the antithesis of white—the good. Blackness, in the context of racism, is associated with primitivism, savagery, and the animalistic—the nonhuman, in other words (Gordon, 1995, 1997). Moreover, black is often ontologically linked to nature, white to culture. Blackness, then, has ontological status:

> blackness and whiteness take on certain meanings that apply to certain groups of people in such a way that makes it difficult not to think of those people without certain affectivity charged associations. Their blackness and their whiteness become regarded, by people who take their associations too seriously, as their essential features—as, in fact, material features of their being. (Gordon, 1995, p. 95)

Thus, blackness refers to racial identity in a semiotically charged way.

Tight black clothing such as stockings, tights, evening gloves, or a leather corset represents a second skin. Indeed, skin color has been called "the most visible of the fetishes" (Bhabha, 1983). Tight black leather might be said to resemble what is referred to as black skin. For whites—and most of the models in the images discussed here are white—this representation is another foray into a liminal area, this time of racial categories. The point is not that people in black clothes look black, or somehow experience blackness. Visually, however, their skin is altered toward blackness—it appears "black." This phenomenon led Mercer to conclude "such fashion-fetishism suggests a desire to simulate or imitate black skin" (1997, p. 289). Blackness is associated with fetishism, a deviant sexuality, via representations of white people wearing black skins. That the categories of sexual, animal, and savage characterize semiotic coding of blackness helps explain why most fetish clothing is black. Black fetish clothing is able to signify a sophisticated sexuality via its liminal status and its associations built from elements of visual culture, by means of what Suren Lalvani called "consuming the exotic" (1995).

FETISHISM, FASHION, AND ADVERTISING

Marx introduced the commodity fetish concept in the 19th century and his analysis of the relationship between consumer goods and the market remains important for understanding how fetishism works in consumer culture. Indeed, "fetishism is a term Marx used to characterize the capitalist social process as a whole" (Pietz, 1993, p. 130). Marx did not fully anticipate an economy based on image, one in which the dialectic of the fetish relies less on material things than on symbolic ideas. Advertising's use of photographic technology accelerates this process in a way that seems both readily apparent and unfathomably underscrutinzed. The fetish can function as a tool to understand visual consumption, which is at the heart of present-day life (Schroeder, 2002). Contemporary consumption is highly visual: Web sites crave eyeball capture, advertisers work to break through visual clutter, and the economy is attention focused (Willis, 1991).

Fetish clothing interacts with visual representation in intricate ways. Advertising capitalizes on the visual power of fetish objects through photographic practices that support a reified relationship with things. Ads often represent fetish items devoid of context, visually emphasizing tactile qualities like shininess. Moreover, photography enhances the shine of fetish garments with flash, studio lighting, and image tone. Although nylon hosiery doesn't possess the natural origin of leather the way silk does, its shiny quality is often enhanced via photographic techniques in advertising, and hosiery is employed to sell many products other than itself. The fetish object is also emphasized by the use of composition, cropping, and color. In the Absolut Au Kurant ads, the fetishized bottle is given a contrasting lavender detail color to accentuate and isolate it as a graphic element. Similarly, fetish photographers such as Trevor Watson, John Carey, and Doris Kloster all highlight clothing as the subject of their work, supporting the fetish relationship by visually focusing on decontextualized garments over bodies, isolated things rather than humans (see Borgerson & Schroeder, 2002).

Absolut Kurant continues to promote a cutting-edge image via its advertising campaign, and the two images discussed here have been replaced by many others in the 5 years since they first appeared. The ads can be bought on the Internet, ranging in price from $2 to $16 in September 2001. Many current ad campaigns draw on fetish imagery. A quick look through a stack of recent mass market fashion and lifestyle magazines reveals Gucci loafer worship, Prada fetishism, Gap black leather jeans, Sisley pornography, a Flexform furniture ad usually featuring high-heeled black patent shoes, a Costume National ad featuring more high-heel worship (a man grasping a women's pump-clad leg), and so on. Although most consumers do not exhibit classic fetishism—foot worship, for example—the relationship that many marketing campaigns promote between consumer and goods have many fetish-like qualities.

The fetish relationship—object worship, delusional belief in the power of the fetish, and substitution of human relations with fetish relations—are invoked in the broader dimensions of consumer culture and its aggressive object worship (cf. Giddens, 1993). Fetish themes may attract the eye to products or services in an economy fueled by obtaining consumer attention. Fetishism may also serve to perpetuate sexual stereotypes and gender stereotypes—women are most often the object of the fetishistic attention, or women are portrayed as slaves to fashion (see Schroeder & Borgerson, 1998). Although the advertising images discussed here might embody some transgression of sexual stereotypes, most fetish-themed ads tend to reinforce entrenched visions of human relationships: woman as object, black as exotic, out-of-the-ordinary sex as deviant. Whether or not companies like Absolut benefit from their appropriation of these themes and sell more vodka is another question. The print ads discussed

here are only one component of a sophisticated and spectacularly successful marketing campaign to build the brand identity of Absolut Kurant as
cutting edge, sexy, and hip.

CONCLUSIONS

Advertising routinely appropriates and harnesses the power of fetishism to
sell goods, services, and ideas. In this chapter, we have focused on body images to develop our arguments, but the function of the fetish need not be
confined to bodies, corsets, and stockings—advertising encourages a fetish-like relationship with things in general. In an economy based on images, information, and Internet technology, fetishism—as displacement, as
dysfunction, and as deviance—contributes to a larger project of linking
products with psychological fulfillment, emotional satisfaction, and sexual
gratification. Moreover, advertising is able to create meaning with photographic techniques, injecting new associations into the circuit of culture.
Whereas many campaigns rely on cultural stereotypes (of fetishism, for example), advertising has reached a stage where it produces novel meaning.
The power of advertising to visually fetishize objects continues this trend in
a way that scholars interested in advertising, consumption, and visual communication cannot ignore.

The Absolut Au Kurant ad campaign invokes many issues central to visual culture: advertising and hegemony, representation and ethics, identity
and difference. These two ads invite the viewer to participate in the sexual
realm, a common theme in contemporary ad culture. The Absolut bottle is
graphically represented by corset lacing and a garter belt clip, both closely
linked to erotic fetishism and sexuality. Absolut Vodka may also be positioned as a way to enter the liminal zone—between everyday life and fantasy, between sobriety and inebriation, between mainstream and
alternative. The visual and photographic facets of the ads point to a link between Absolut Kurant and its iconic bottle shape and sexual adventure,
and possibly, gender subversion or at least cross-dressing. The Absolut bottle's graphic presence conjoins retro corset and stocking to contemporary
lifestyles. In addition, the ads capitalize on the semiotic coding of black as
cool, exotic, and sensual.

All of these meanings need not be apparent to any one viewer. Many
campaigns build in diverse target markets in a single ad (see Stern &
Schroeder, 1994). Absolut Au Kurant's leather corset is a fetish sign, an alternative sexuality trope, and an emblem of eroticism. In other contexts,
corsets symbolize the domination of women. Given the logic of the ad,
however, it is unlikely to be read as a statement about women's oppression,
except insofar as women's oppression is fetishized.

Alcohol manufacturers visually reinforce cultural stereotypes that alcohol consumption makes women accessible. Moreover, advertising fetishizes goods by offering them as substitutes for human relationships. By drawing on powerful imagery, Absolut and other advertisers harness the unique properties of visual representation to create a global communication force. In the words of two sociologists, the "power to recontexualize and reframe photographic images has put advertising at the center of contemporary redefinitions of individuality, freedom, and democracy in relation to corporate symbols" (Goldman & Papson, 1996, p. 216). Advertising is not merely a vehicle to move goods. It is a central feature of visual culture, which it supports through its relationship with mass media. Furthermore, advertising imagery functions at several levels simultaneously—unlike the art world, all advertising has a clear, shared purpose to make particular associations between product and image. Absolut desires the viewer to make a positive connection between black leather corsets and black stockings and its Absolut Kurant vodka.

The use of tight black leather and stylized stockings implicates the ads in the liminal zone of the fetish. The ads draw on three fetishism signifiers in visual culture: the hybrid nature of leather and other tight clothing, the exoticization of blackness, and advertising practice of formally reifying objects via photographic technique. Cultural codes such as black leather, garter belts, and the color lavender are bounded by history, place, and identity. In contemporary visual culture, these codes are powerful and striking visual symbols of fetishism and a kind of alternative sexuality. In addition, lavender is the adopted color of the gay and lesbian community. Thus, for many, the association between its appearance in the Absolut Au Kurant ads and gay culture is readily apparent. Paradoxically, some of these readings may conflict with others, reflecting the ad's flexible appeal for different target markets. Further work on identity in advertising is called for, drawing on theoretical frameworks of the "epidermal schema" (Fanon, 1967; Gordon, 1995, 1997), which is how represented skin color semiotically inscribes social, cultural, and racial identity categories and stereotypes.

Advertising no longer merely reflects culture. Nor does advertising only appropriate concepts or images after the art world has produced the original idea. Advertising is intertextual—it often refers to itself—it creates its own heroes and characters. Moreover, the logic of advertising underscores all aspects of modern visual culture. Art historians and literary scholars have been adept at tracing the history of icons, types, and characters in visual representation. The tools of cultural analysis have come in handy here, for advertising borrows heavily from the iconology and teleology of photographic history. However, researchers attempting to understand its meaning-making capabilities miss a great deal by relying solely on rhetorical forms from other cultural arenas—such as fine art, literature, and film—for themes and insights. Researchers in visual studies should strive to show how advertising creates new types and tropes. Further work could delineate how the fetish works in a wide variety of visual contexts and how fetishization has developed as a powerful advertising practice.

Advertising, the face of capitalism, is one of the key engines of visual culture. Understanding advertising requires complex interdisciplinary work, informed by photographic analysis, critical race theory, and communication studies. Of course, advertising is not equivalent to visual culture, nor is its power limited to the visual arena. Advertising, a realm in which photography, fetishism, and cultural values intermingle, stands as the dominant communication force today. The fetish represents a critical concept for understanding visual culture—indeed, the way advertising fetishizes goods and services is basic to contemporary life.

ACKNOWLEDGMENT

An early version of this paper was presented at the Power and Sensuality in Visual Culture conference at Umeå University, Sweden, organized by Raoul Granqvist and Hans Örtegren in November 2000. We thank Karin Becker, Anette Göthlund, Anders Marner, and Irit Rogoff for comments on this project.

REFERENCES

Apter, E., & Pietz, W. (Eds.). (1993). *Fetishism as cultural discourse.* Ithaca, NY: Cornell University Press.

Bhabha, H. (1983). The other question: The stereotype and colonial discourse. *Screen, 24*(4), 18–36.

Borgerson, J. (2001). Feminist ethical ontology: Contesting "the bare givenness of intersubjectivity." *Feminist Theory, 2*(2), 173–187.

Borgerson, J. L., & Schroeder, J. E. (1997). The ethics of representation—packaging paradise: Consuming the 50th state. *Cooley Law Review, 14,* 473–489.

Borgerson, J. & Schroeder, J. E. (2002). Ethical issues of global marketing: Avoiding bad faith in visual representation. *European Journal of Marketing, 36*(5/6), 570–594.

Cadava, E. (1999). *Words of light: Theses on the photography of history.* Princeton, NJ: Princeton University Press.

Carter, A. (1978). *The Sadeian woman and the ideology of pornography.* New York: Pantheon.

Cortese, A. J. (1999). *Provocateur: Images of women and minorities in advertising.* Lanham, MD: Rowman & Littlefield.

Fanon, F. (1967). *Black skin, white masks* (C. L. Markmann, Trans.) New York; Grove Press.

Giddens, A. (1993). *The transformation of intimacy: Sexuality, love and eroticism in modern societies.* Stanford, CA: Stanford University Press.

Goldman, R., & Papson, S. (1996). *Sign wars: The cluttered landscape of advertising.* New York: Guilford.

Gordon, L. (1995). *Bad faith and antiblack racism.* Atlantic Highlands, NJ: Humanities Press.

Gordon, L. (1997). *Her majesty's other children: Sketches of racism from a neocolonial Age.* Lanham, MD: Rowman & Littlefield.

Grosz, E. (1993). Lesbian fetishism? In E. Apter & W. Pietz (Eds.), *Fetishism as cultural discourse* (pp. 101–115). Ithaca, NY: Cornell University Press.

Hall, S. (1997). The spectacle of the "other." In S. Hall (Ed.), *Representation: Cultural representations and signifying practices* (pp. 223–279). London: Sage/Open University Press.

Hamilton, C. (2000). *Absolut: The biography of a bottle.* New York: Texere.

Jhally, S. (1987). *The codes of advertising: Fetishism and the political economy of meaning in the consumer society.* New York: St. Martin's Press.

Kaplan, E. A. (1987). *Rocking around the clock: Music television, postmodernism, and consumer culture.* New York: Routledge.

Lalvani, S. (1995). Consuming the exotic other. *Critical Studies in Mass Communication, 12,* 263–286.

Lévi-Strauss, C. (1983). *The raw and the cooked: Introduction to a science of mythology* (J. Weightman & D. Weightman, Trans.). Chicago, IL: University of Chicago Press. (Original work published 1964)

Lewis, R. (1997). Looking good: The lesbian gaze and fashion imagery. *Feminist Review, 55,* 92–109.

Lewis, R. W. (1996). *Absolut book: The vodka advertising story.* New York: Charles Tuttle.

MacKendrick, K. (1998). Technoflesh, or "didn't that hurt?" *Fashion Theory, The Journal of Dress, Body & Culture, 2*(1), 3–24.

McClintock, A. (1995). *Imperial leather: Race, gender and sexuality in the colonial contest.* London: Routledge.

Mercer, K. (1997). Reading racial fetishism. In S. Hall (Ed.), *Representation: Cultural representations and signifying practices* (pp. 285–290). London: Sage/Open University Press.

Mirzoeff, N. (1999). *An introduction to visual culture.* London: Routledge.

O'Barr, W. M. (1994). *Culture and the ad: Exploring otherness in the world of advertising.* Boulder, CO: Westview.

Ortner, S. B. (1996). *Making gender: The politics and erotics of culture.* Boston: Beacon.

Pietz, W. (1993). Fetishism and materialism: The limits of theory in Marx. In E. Apter & W. Pietz (Eds.), *Fetishism as cultural discourse* (pp. 119–151). Ithaca, NY: Cornell University Press.

Ramamurthy, A. (1997). Constructions of illusion: Photography and commodity culture. In L. Wells (Ed.), *Photography: A critical introduction* (pp. 151–199). London: Routledge.

Ritson, M., & Elliot, R. (1999). The social uses of advertising: An ethnographic study of adolescent advertising audiences. *Journal of Consumer Research, 26*(3), 260–277.

Schroeder, J. E. (1997). Andy Warhol: Consumer researcher. In D. MacInnis & M. Brucks (Eds.), *Advances in Consumer Research* (Vol. 24, pp. 476–482). Provo, UT: Association for Consumer Research.

Schroeder, J. E. (1998a). Consuming representation: A visual approach to consumer research. In B. B. Stern (Ed.), *Representing consumers: Voices, views and visions* (pp. 193–230). London: Routledge.

Schroeder, J. E. (1998b). Consuming sexuality: A case study in identity marketing. In E. Fischer & D. Wardlow (Eds.), *Gender, marketing and consumer behavior* (pp. 27–40). San Francisco: San Francisco State University.

Schroeder, J. E. (2000). Édouard Manet, Calvin Klein and the strategic use of scandal. In S. Brown & A. Patterson (Eds.), *Imagining marketing: Art, aesthetics, and the avant-garde* (pp. 36–51). London: Routledge.

Schroeder, J. E. (2002). *Visual consumption*. London: Routledge.

Schroeder, J. E., & Borgerson, J. L. (1998). Marketing images of gender: A visual analysis. *Consumption Markets and Culture, 2*, 161–201.

Schroeder, J. E., & Borgerson, J. L. (1999). Packaging paradise: Consuming Hawaiian music. In E. Arnould & L. Scott (Eds.), *Advances in Consumer Research* (Vol. 26, pp. 46–50). Provo, UT: Association for Consumer Research.

Schroeder, J. E., & Borgerson, J. L. (2002). Innovations in information technology: Insights from Italian Renaissance art. *Consumption, Markets & Culture, 5*(2), 153–169.

Schroeder, J. E., & Zwick, D. (1999, October). *Consuming masculinity: Advertising, the gaze, and male bodies.* Paper presented at the annual conference of the Association for Consumer Research, Columbus, OH.

Solomon-Godeau, A. (1991). *Photography at the dock: Essays on photographic history, institutions, and practices.* Minneapolis: University of Minnesota Press.

Solomon-Godeau, A. (1993). The legs of the countess. In E. Apter & W. Pietz (Eds.), *Fetishism as cultural discourse* (pp. 266–306). Ithaca, NY: Cornell University Press.

Stern, B. B. (1991). Two pornographies: A feminist view of sex in advertising. *Advances in Consumer Research, 18*, 384–391.

Stern, B. B. (1998). Introduction: The problematics of representation. In B. B. Stern (Ed.), *Representing consumers: Voices, views and visions* (pp. 1–23). London: Routledge.

Stern, B. B., & Schroeder, J. E. (1994). Interpretive methodology from art and literary criticism: A humanistic approach to advertising imagery. *European Journal of Marketing, 28*, 114–132.

Weissberg, L. (1997). Circulating images: Notes on the photographic exchange. In J-M. Rabaté (Ed.), *Writing the image after Roland Barthes* (pp. 109–131). Philadelphia: University of Pennsylvania Press.

Wells, L. (Ed.). (1997). *Photography: A critical introduction.* Routledge, London.

Williamson, J. (1978). *Decoding advertisements.* New York: Marion Boyers.

Willis, S. (1991). *A primer for everyday life.* New York: Routledge.

PART II

Consumer Responses
to Sex in Advertising

Nudity and Sexual Appeals: Understanding the Arousal Process and Advertising Response

Michael S. LaTour
Auburn University

Tony L. Henthorne
University of Southern Mississippi

Serious research about sexual appeals is difficult with so many dirty jokes circulating in the guise of criticism. Consider the following column in *Advertising Age* (Winsky, 1991, p. 22) following the publication of one of our early works:

Does sex sell?

The question has troubled the sages for centuries. I too have pondered the issue, at length, as it were.

My attention has been arrested by the number of moist-lipped, long-stemmed nymphs beckoning from page or tube, as through a gauzy-curtained window.

At long last—Eureka! One shouts—research provides the answer. "Female Nudity, Arousal and Ad Response: An Experimental Investigation" is our veritable Rosetta stone, tucked modestly into the gray pages of the *Journal of Advertising*, Volume 19, Number 4.

Summoning the pantheon of authorities on the subject (Morrison & Sherman, 1972 of course, but also the inestimable Sciglimpaglia, Belch, & Cain, 1978), our intrepid researchers dare nothing less than evaluate "the ability of the arousal construct to explain many of the individual, content and situational differences in response to female nudity in advertising."

A seminal work, my friends.

We begin, of course, with the lucid definition: "Arousal (frequently referred to as activation, energy mobilization, and excitation) is the release of energy into the various internal physiological systems in preparation for overt activity (Duffy, 1972). Arousal has been linked to the formation of affective and cognitive responses."

I opine that the authors report their findings much too shyly, even to an almost unbecoming reticence, as for instance in the use of "purpose" in their linchpin statement, delivered *sans italics*: "We propose a model in which multiple dimensions of arousal intervene between exposure to female nudity in an ad and responses to the ad."

Indeed.

As might be expected, Berlyne's (1960) unidimensional notion of psycho-physiological arousal is rejected in favor of Thayer's (1968) "Activation-Deactivation Adjective Checklist" (AD-ACL) "self-report instrument."

Thayer, you will recall, posited a continuum of physiological activation, ranging from high activation (HA), general activation (GA), general deactivation (GD) and deactivation sleep (DS). The researchers assert: "The two-bipolar-dimensions model combines GA-DS to form dimension A (energy), and combines HA-GD to form dimension B (tension)."

It is wise of our authors so to assert.

To be noted, nonetheless, is their inexplicable silence on Thayer's exclusion of the multiple orgasmic response (for which, see Masters & Johnson, Shere Hite, Bo Diddley, *et al*).

Now then, the results. Needless to say, all of the coefficient alpha scores are in excess of 0.7 and acceptable, exogenous variables notwithstanding, and as Thurber (1935) noted, initiative, referendum, Carborundum.

The authors insightfully note that gender "has a significant effect on arousal." An unexpected conclusion is that under condition of "high nudity, males feel less tension than females (TD1Sex-HA-.205)," as well as "more calmness (TD2Sex-GD.133)," suggesting further research to incorporate subjects' sexual orientation and possible terminal flaccidity, as well as proximity to the rutting season.

One remains troubled, as do the authors, by some nagging ambiguities, particularly those regarding GD, GS and Nerf balls. The contributions of sexual solipsism also need to be addressed, and one certainly must interpret the results with caution in areas where Norwegian bachelors abound.

Those quibbles aside, the authors are to be commended for their breakthrough work: Now we know.[1]

---

[1] Reprinted with permission from the January 28, 1991 issue of *Advertising Age*. Copyright, Crain Communications, Inc. 1991.

This satirical view, although entertaining, further dramatizes the tendency of society to trivialize a very serious issue with profound consequences for advertising practitioners and practices. There is substantial need for addressing the issue of sex in advertising with insightful research and constructive debate. Furthermore, research and constructive debate must transcend both the realms of academic and applied practice so as to promote a mutually healthy interchange on this sensitive, highly consequential topic for all concerned. The effectiveness of the use of sex in advertising is not the only issue here. In fact, we are in general concurrence with the views of Kilbourne (2000) as to the far-reaching sociological implications of the potentially demeaning nature of such portrayals. It is clear that the moral considerations surrounding the perceived portrayal of women as sub-human sex objects should be examined.

Yet, all of this not withstanding, the use of overt sexual appeals in advertising has increased dramatically in recent years (Ford, LaTour, & Middleton, 1999). A reader need only open the pages of a typical general-interest magazine to be exposed to a wide variety of advertisements featuring provocatively posed and (un)attired models in any number of compromising situations promoting a wide variety of consumer products and services. Many long-running and/or classic examples of the genre exist. Who can forget the provocative ads for Obsession perfume and cologne or similarly controversial ads for Calvin Klein Jeans. Among the more memorable recent examples of such advertising are the controversial print ads for Falmer Jeans. These ads typically feature a seminude couple in a highly compromising or suggestive position. Ads of this type are designed to elicit from the target audience what the originators hope is a vicarious experience of sensuality without extreme levels of anxiety or discomfort.

It has long been contended that ad creators must be acutely aware of the reactions (both positive and negative) of their target audience to the use of potentially controversial sexual appeals as ad stimuli (Alexander & Judd, 1986). The effects of an ad may go far beyond that of the target audience, however, and these possible effects should be considered by ad creators and media executives. A magazine or newspaper's entire readership is exposed to the sexually arousing stimuli and many of these readers may formulate an attitude toward the ad (A_{ad})—whether in the market for the product or not. Clearly, this "unanticipated" audience views the rightness of a particular ad, which research has shown carries over to attitude toward the brand (A_b) in question as well as subsequent purchase intention (c.f. LaTour and Rotfeld, 1997). In the 1987 documentary, *Still Killing Us Softly*, Kilbourne provided numerous examples of advertisements targeted to men that in essence reduce women to "dismembered" sexual body parts. No wonder our society seems to be desensitized to brutal crimes and violence against women.

Profound social issues centered on the use of sexual appeals in advertising continue to swirl around us. At the same time, the complex psychophysiological underpinnings of arousal and ad response continue to be studied. As seen in *Advertising Age* column, even psychophysiology can be the object of satire. Yet, now more than ever, a holistic approach that integrates seemingly diverse and unrelated branches of science to the study of the use of sexual appeals in print advertising is needed.

The study of arousal response is a key part of this "greater whole." Specifically, the measurement of arousal as a predictor of attitude toward an ad (A_{ad})—feelings about the ad (e.g., good/bad, positive/negative, favorable/unfavorable)—has been used in fear appeals (e.g., Henthorne, LaTour, & Nataraajan, 1993) as well as sexual appeals (e.g., Henthorne & LaTour, 1995; LaTour & Henthorne, 1994a; LaTour, Pitts, & Snook-Luther, 1990). Typically, arousal has been operationalized along two dimensions: high activation (HA), described as tension; and general activation (GA), described as energy (Thayer, 1989). Generally speaking, these studies found that mildly arousing stimuli (both HA and GA) could have a positive effect on attitude toward the ad (A_{ad}), whereas stimuli that created a high HA (tension) would have a negative effect on attitude toward the ad (A_{ad}). Therefore, excessive tension from sexual appeals is undesirable whereas high energy is desirable (LaTour, 1990).

In fact, the analysis of these arousal dimensions as key underpinnings of response to sexual stimuli has been a fundamental building block of an entire stream of research. For many decades, psychophysiological reactions to environmental stimuli have been looked to as a logical nexus for understanding the complexities of the mind–body interface. A particularly noteworthy finding is that arousal and ad response to a given stimulus differ between men and women (see LaTour, 1990). It is not surprising to see these nuances, especially in light of the modern day "raising of feminist consciousness," which has been shown to impact ad response and intention to boycott the products associated with the offensive ads (cf. Ford & LaTour, 1996).

Given the complex psychophysiology of arousal response to ads, the manifestation of strong feelings about the moral issues at hand becomes part of the "social fabric" that we have studied. Another construct found to influence attitude toward the ad (A_{ad}) is the perception of the lack of ethicality of the erotic appeal (Henthorne & LaTour, 1995). Our previous research established clear causal linkages between ethical dimensions and attitude toward the ad (A_{ad}), as well as subsequent intentions to purchase the featured product. This work and the aforementioned research are undeniably linked, not only in terms of overlapping bodies of theory, but also in terms of issues of consequence for advertising practice and policy.

In the sections of this chapter that follow, we review a series of studies of arousal response to sexual stimuli (cf. LaTour, 1990; LaTour & Henthorne,

1994a; LaTour et al., 1990). Here we establish the differing arousal and ad responses found for males compared to females. A subsequent section explores the ethical issues surrounding nudity in general readership magazines. We then develop implications for future research, and tie this literature to studies we have conducted concerning the development of feminist consciousness and reactions to female role portrayals in advertising.

AROUSAL AND AD RESPONSE
IN THE CONTEXT OF SEXUAL AD STIMULI

The use of sexual stimuli in print advertising has a long and colorful history. The interaction effects of gender and ad treatment on varying dimensions of arousal were originally reported in our early works (LaTour, 1990; LaTour et al., 1990). After seeing a print advertisement showing explicit female nudity (the "nude erotic appeal"), women rated themselves as more tense (high activation or "HA") than men. Similarly, when men viewed the print ad containing the nude erotic appeal, they reported significantly higher levels of energy arousal (general activation or "GA") as compared to tension arousal (LaTour, 1990). This project, along with later work (Henthorne et al., 1993), has made a strong case for the theoretical and empirical robustness of advertising-stimulated tension arousal (HA) and energy arousal (GA) impacting and influencing viewers' impressions of ads.

   In 1994, we undertook a study to extend the original work of LaTour (1990) and LaTour et al. (1990) in two significant ways, first by providing a multiple-group analysis focused on the structural relations within two divergent groups. One group of participants was exposed to a "nude erotic appeal" in which the female model was shown nude sitting on a beach. The second group of participants was shown the "seminude erotic appeal," which was the same ad but showed the model partially obscured by a perfume bottle. Next, we extended the original work by expanding the evaluation of the model to include attitude toward the brand (A_b) as an endogenous variable (see LaTour & Henthorne, 1994b). Attitude toward the brand (A_b) is seen as flowing from attitude toward the ad (A_{ad}), but nevertheless is specific to the brand's image (cf. LaTour & Rotfeld, 1997).

   Figure 5.1 shows the originally hypothesized structural relationships for the ad containing the seminude erotic appeal. This model assumes that a seminude erotic appeal is a moderate stimulus and not sufficiently strong (or out of the ordinary) to produce a negative relationship between high activation (HA) and general activation (GA). Stated another way, a moderate stimulus should result in a positive association between high activation and general activation. Additionally, we expected there to be positive linkages from both arousal dimensions to attitude toward the ad (A_{ad}) and attitude toward the brand (A_b). Using the same rationale as in LaTour (1990), we ex-

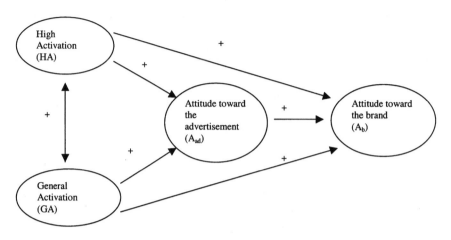

FIG 5.1. Hypothetical model for the seminude treatment group.

pected the linkage between tension and energy to be negative in the ad with the "nude erotic appeal" (see Fig. 5.2). That is, too much tension should deplete energy and result in a negative relationship between HA and GA. Also, we hypothesized there to be a negative link between high activation (HA) and attitude toward the brand (A_b). The outcome of this experiment was highly enlightening. The final models as a result of participant responses are shown in Figs. 5.3 and 5.4. For the sake of parsimony, only the significant paths are included in the diagram.

These results point out that excessive tension arousal can be dysfunctional in this context. That is, HA (tension) is negatively influencing subsequent re-

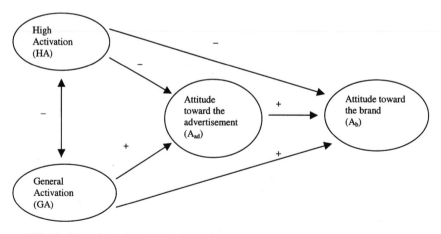

FIG. 5.2. Hypothetical model for the nude treatment group.

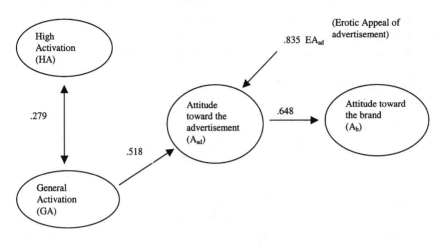

FIG. 5.3. Final model for the seminude treatment group.

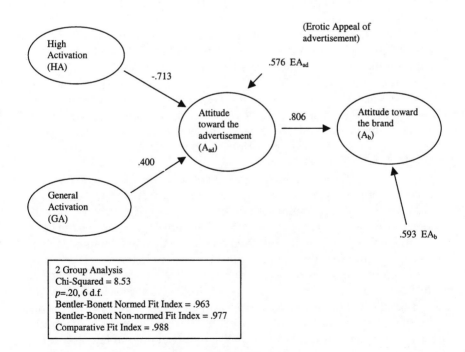

FIG. 5.4. Final model for the nude treatment group.

actions in the nude treatment group. The notion that "sex sells" is strongly undermined by these results—especially among female respondents. As we will demonstrate in a later section, regardless of whether or not the intended target audience of the ad is female, it is of little consequence in terms of social fallout with bottom-line implications. Given all of this, it seems reasonable that the perceived ethics of using such stimuli would have been a heavily researched area—with many issues yet to be addressed.

THE PERCEIVED ETHICALITY
OF THE USE OF SEXUAL APPEALS

To understand consumer reactions (both positive and negative) and some of the ethical dilemmas advertisers face from the use of sexual appeals in print advertising, we have to consider the basic concepts contained in the normative ethical theories of moral philosophy. These fundamental theories can generally be categorized as either teleological or deontological (Murphy & Laczniak, 1981). The primary difference in these two philosophies is their emphasis on the consequence (or lack thereof) of individual action.

The focus of teleological philosophies is on the consequences of individual actions and behaviors in the determination of the outcomes. Teleological philosophies maintain that the individual should examine and determine the likely consequences (e.g., good or bad) of alternative actions/behaviors in a specific situation. A specific action or behavior is considered "ethical" if it produces the greatest balance of good versus evil when compared with all alternative actions (Hunt & Vitell, 1986).

Deontological philosophies, on the other hand, focus on specific actions of the individual without consideration of the consequences of that action. Deontological theory states that the rightness or wrongness of actions and behaviors should be judged by the actions themselves without regard to the outcomes. Thus, deontology opposes the basis tenets of teleology (Fraedrich & Ferrell, 1992).

From a teleological standpoint, the use of sexual appeals in advertising may not be appealing to viewers and may, in fact, produce potentially negative side effects (e.g., gratuitous sex or sexual obsession). Therefore, the consequences of using such sexual appeals in advertising, as well as the basic fundamental rightness of its use, should be of concern to all (Gould, 1994).

Keep in mind that the fundamental component in teleological theory is the amount of good or bad contained *in the consequences* of the act whereas the central component in deontological theory is the amount of good or bad contained *in the act itself*, regardless of its impact on the eventual outcome. But, is it realistic to believe that individuals make ethical decisions or judgments based along the strict lines of teleological or deontological theory? No. Individuals use a blending or mixing of these philosophies when determining ethical judgments (Hunt & Vitell, 1986;

Reidenbach & Robin, 1988). In fact, Tansey, Hyman, and Brown (1992) believed that the use of a controversial ad stimulus could evoke a wide array of related teleological- and deontological-based responses on a single dimension of ethical evaluation.

To examine these theories, we compared responses to two different high-quality black-and-white ad treatments—one containing a strong overt sexual appeal and one containing a mild sexual appeal. Each ad contained the brand name of the jeans at the bottom of the layout (ad treatments are described in Table 5.1). Our findings from this project showed that the use of a highly sexual theme in a print ad was not well received. In fact, its use was viewed as less ethically "correct" than the use of the mild sexual ad. Additionally, and maybe somewhat surprisingly, both men and women expressed serious ethical concerns about the use of the overtly sexual ad (LaTour & Henthorne, 1994a).

A significant gender-by-treatment interaction effect indicated that men in the explicit-treatment group had a more positive attitude toward the ad than woman. This interaction effect, however, was nonexistent for attitude toward the brand, purchase intention, and the perceived ethicality of the use of such ads. This finding indicates that although our society and culture may influence men to be less negative toward such stimuli initially, they do appear to have underlying problems or issues with gratuitous sexual images in advertising, which result in negative feelings about the brand, the ethicality of the use of such stimuli, and intention to purchase the featured product.

TABLE 5.1
Ad Treatment Descriptions

The Mild Sexual Appeal Ad
The male and female models are featured walking together out-of-doors with their arms around each other. The male model's arm is around the shoulder of the female. The female's arm is around the male model's waist, under his shirt. Both models, although fully clothed, are not dressed conservatively. Rather, both models are wearing jeans and tank tops.

The Strong Overt Sexual Appeal Ad
The male and female models are out-of-doors, clearly engaged in a sensual sexual embrace. The female model is leaning against a chain-link fence with her arms raised above her head. The female is completely unclothed, yet her lower abdomen and breasts are covered by the male model. The male model is wearing only jeans with the fly unzipped.

Note. From "*Ethical judgments of sexual appeals in print advertising,*" by M. S. LaTour and T. L. Henthorne, 1994a, *Journal of Advertising, 23*(3), pp. 81–90. Copyright 1994 by *Journal of Advertising*. Adapted with permission.

In a subsequent research project, we explored the structural relations of the variables tested in the previously mentioned study. Using the well-known Reidenbach-Robin (1988) multidimensional ethics scale, we determined to what to extent the reader's judgment of the moral character of the ad (or lack thereof) affected their attitude toward the ad (A_{ad}), their attitude toward the brand (A_b), and their purchase intention (Henthorne & LaTour, 1995). The resulting final model reported that the lack of moral equity/relativism (LACK MOREL; see Fig. 5.5) had a strong, significant negative effect on attitude toward the ad (A_{ad}) and a modest significant negative direct effect on purchase intention. Additionally, both brand attitude (A_b) and purchase intention were impacted negatively through the indirect effects of LACK MOREL. Lack of moral equity/relativism is thought to be a key ethical construct embodying elements of morality of action within a particular social context. Figure 5.5 also features another dimension, lack of contractualism (LACK CONT), which implies the violation of an implicit contract.

The results of this study indicate that the use of high levels of erotic content in print ads may not be perceived as morally right or culturally acceptable to viewers of these ads. While the use of such stimuli may draw additional attention to the ad, the outcome of the continued use of such high levels of erotic stimuli may, in fact, be negative. In other words (as Fig. 5.5 highlights), the perceived lack of moral equity/relativism associated

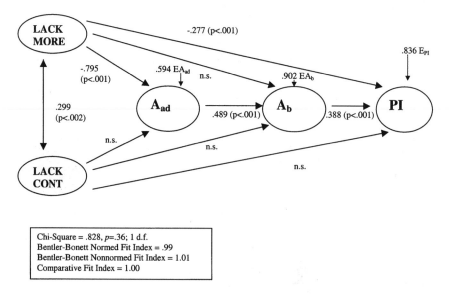

FIG. 5.5. Final two-dimensional model outcome describing moral judgment on advertising outcomes.

with the use of high levels of eroticism in print advertising appears to result in negative feelings toward the advertisement and the brand.

Findings such as those highlighted here should give advertisers considering the use of high levels of erotic content in their ads reason for pause and reflection. Care must be given to determining a priori the likely reaction of their specific target market to proposed ads containing high levels of nudity or erotic content. Additionally, advertisers must consider the possible exposure and negative impact and/or consequences to those individuals not in their target market but who become exposed to the ad inadvertently. These possible negative social consequences to inadvertent exposure may range anywhere from perceived sex objectification (Ford & LaTour, 1993), to perceived degradation of women (Gould, 1994), to negative word of mouth (Miller, 1992).

LINKAGE BETWEEN OUR RESEARCH STREAMS AND FEMINIST CONSCIOUSNESS APPLIED TO THE SEXUAL OBJECTIFICATION OF WOMEN IN ROLE PORTRAYALS

As mentioned previously, the morality of using sexual appeals is a highly charged and complex issue that is related to the psychophysiology of ad response. Indeed, the morality of its use lies in the eyes of the beholder. The relationship between morality and ad response is a dynamic and fluid situation, not static. For example, let us say that an advertising executive ran a successful campaign 5 years ago, using a strong sexual appeal. He or she makes the naïve assumption that the same type of campaign can be repeated today with similarly positive results. However, feminist consciousness-raising is an ongoing process. In fact, a recent article in the *Journal of Current Issues and Research in Marketing* (Ford, LaTour, & Middleton, 1999) indicates that "feminist consciousness" can be raised with mere exposure to a documentary video on the subject.

Specifically, the Ford, LaTour, and Middleton (1999) study manipulated exposure to *Still Killing Us Softly* using a 2 × 2 experimental design (gender by exposure/nonexposure). Kilbourne (1987) made a persuasive case regarding female representation in advertising. She articulated and illustrated how ads often prominently feature women as sex objects. In addition, according to the documentary, it is painfully obvious that there is a "skinny," flawless, and ultimately unrealistic beauty standard promoted in advertising, along with an often callous use of sexual violence toward women.

The most enlightening part of the research findings indicated that women in the "exposure group," compared to women in the "nonexposure group," had a significantly higher score on the Arnott Female Autonomy Inventory (tapping perceived independence from a male-dominated society as a "dimension" of "feminist consciousness"; Ford, LaTour, & Middleton, 1999). Similar results manifested with significantly more negative views of female role portrayals and a significantly more negative image of corporations sponsoring offensive advertising. Additionally, the results showed a significantly greater stated intention to boycott the sponsored product. The negative reactions resulted from viewing a 40-minute video documentary.

Demand artifacts were carefully controlled for and additional testing indicated that sensitivity to women's portrayals endured over time. The bottom line is quite clear. Feminist consciousness-raising is easily facilitated by exposure to the issues. In a sense, women with a raised consciousness see the same things, but see them differently. We believe that psychophysiological response can be a function of this "social exposure." In other words, women who become more sensitized to the issues can, over time, change the outcome of an ad campaign. This clearly has profound and far-reaching consequences.

As can be seen in the modeled results featured in Fig. 5.6, female autonomy leads to negative perceptions of female role portrayals, which in turn increases a negative corporate image and boycott intention. We reported subsequent research that focused on female perceptions of industrial advertising, and confirmed that education appears to be a force for female autonomy and the aforementioned variables (LaTour, Henthorne, & Williams, 1998). Hence, advertisers beware. What was considered "safe" a few years ago (e.g., strong sexual appeals) may result in repercussions in the current environment of raised feminist consciousness.

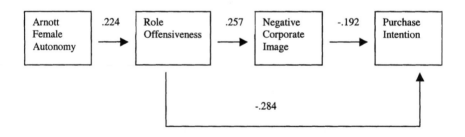

*All paths significant at the $p<.05$ level.
X squared = .855 (2 d.f.). P-value = .652
Bentler Bonett Normed Fit Index = .977
Comparative Fit Index = 1.00

Source: Ford and LaTour, 1996.

FIG. 5.6. A causal model of consequences of raised feminist awareness on corporate image and purchase intention. Reprinted with permission, CtC Press 2002. All rights reserved.

IMPLICATIONS FOR ADVERTISING PRACTICE

There are several critical points that may be inferred from the knowledge accumulated to date.

1. Women with raised feminist consciousness have a propensity to "take action" in response to sexual appeals that are perceived to be inappropriate.

So, let us lay our cards on the table. We are making a case for a chain of events that may result from the continued use of sexual appeals. Women with raised feminist consciousness are not only going to be made tense, but will also be inspired to take action in the form of boycotts against the offending products. Additionally, this negative feeling toward the ad and the offending products can extend to the company and its workplace. This appears to go hand-in-hand with the class action lawsuit filed by female employees of Strohs Brewery concerning the ads featuring the "Swedish Bikini Team" a few years ago. These memorable ads featured the familiar line, "Guys, it doesn't get any better than this," with the voiceover saying "Oh yes it does," as the platinum blondes of the "Swedish Bikini Team" appeared on the scene. Female employees at Strohs filed the lawsuit saying there was a connection between the ads and the way they were treated in the work environment.

This leads to the obvious question, "What should practitioners do about it?" The answer to this is, at least in part:

2. Advertising practitioners should aggressively seek consultation expertise from feminists for the purpose of prescreening possibly "offensive" ads.

As we see it, an enormous problem underlying all of this is the fight by ad executives to break through media clutter by relying on the age-old belief that "sex sells." It is an attempt to get the ad noticed at the expense of other considerations. As a result, the sexy ad that gets noticed may also be sexist. It is clear that there is a difference between what is considered "sexy" and what is considered "sexist" in the present moral and cultural environment. And such is clearly in the eyes of the beholder (see LaTour, Henthorne & Williams, 1998).

As we all know, business and high pressure are common bedfellows. It is no secret that business people often feel the temptation to compromise their ethical standards in order to succeed. We contend, however, that compromising one's basic moral standards extracts a high price, in terms of both personal integrity and integrity in the marketplace. Recognizing this:

3. The perceived ethicality of sexual appeals is of great consequence in the marketplace and, therefore, must be properly assessed.

Our research shows that both men and women have ethical problems with overt sexual appeals. The use of such stimuli evokes highly complex responses. We believe that often this issue is oversimplified or ignored. Given the dynamics of the social fabric surrounding sexual appeals in print advertising, it is no wonder that the psychophysiological underpinnings of people's responses show significant variability. Therefore:

4. Dimensions of arousal response to sexual ad stimuli (tension and energy) should be assessed as a starting point to "diagnose" potential ad response problems.

Our research indicates that women are made significantly more tense than men by overt sexual stimuli. Arousal forms the baseline for feelings as well as subsequent cognition. The resulting manifestation of indignity toward the dehumanizing objectification of women is also a part of this complicated package for advertisers to take into account. Much research remains to be done. The question arises, "Who should do it?"

5. Advertising practitioners need to partner with academic researchers in an effort to facilitate applied research based on the richness of basic research into sexual appeals.

Our recent article on the subject of academic/practitioner partnering (Nataraajan, Henthorne, & LaTour, 1998) makes a strong case for an enhanced "synergistic" partnership between academe and marketing practitioners on critical subjects such as this one. Both parties have much to gain from such a collaborative relationship. Unfortunately, the opportunity for such a relationship is often overlooked.

In summary, our current and future research endeavors seek to explore specific reactions to various manipulations of sexual appeals. In addition to assessing various attitudinal and ethical issues, we will also examine arousal response and a variety of "feminist consciousness" dimensions as covariates. Specifically, both the Arnott Female Autonomy inventory as well as dimensions of the Liberal Feminist Attitude and Ideology Scale (LFAIS) will be incorporated (cf. Levonian-Morgan, 1996). As emphasized earlier, it makes sense to meld these aforementioned research streams in this way. In so doing we hope empirically to elucidate the linkages between psychophysiological response, feminist consciousness, and perceived ethicality of sex in advertising. We are, in essence, still seeking answers to the basic fundamental questions at issue: "Does sex sell, and if so, how much sex is too much?"

REFERENCES

Alexander, M. W., & Judd, B., Jr. (1986). Differences in attitudes toward nudity in advertising. *Psychology: A Quarterly Journal of Human Behavior, 23*(1), 27–29.

Ford, J. B., & LaTour, M. S. (1993). Differing reactions to female role portrayals in advertising. *Journal of Advertising Research, 33*(5), 43–52.

Ford, J. B., & LaTour, M. S. (1996). Contemporary female perspectives of female role portrayals in advertising. *Journal of Current Issues and Research in Advertising, 18*(1), 81–95.

Ford, J. B., LaTour, M. S., & Middleton, C. (1999). Women's studies and advertising role portrayal sensitivity: How easy is it to raise "feminist consciousness?" *Journal of Current Issues and Research in Advertising, 21*(2), 77–87.

Fraedrich, J., & Ferrell, O. C. (1992). Cognitive consistency of marketing managers in ethical situations. *Journal of the Academy of Marketing Science, 20*(3), 245–252.

Gould, S. J. (1994). Sexuality and ethics in advertising: A research agenda and policy guideline perspective. *Journal of Advertising, 23*(3), 73–80.

Henthorne, T., & LaTour, M. S. (1995). A model to explore the ethics of erotic stimuli in print advertising. *Journal of Business Ethics, 14*, 561–569.

Henthorne, T. L., LaTour, M. S., & Nataraajan, R. (1993). Fear appeals in print advertising: An analysis of arousal and ad response. *Journal of Advertising, 22*(2), 59–69.

Hunt, S. D., & Vitell, S. (1986). A general theory of marketing ethics. *Journal of Macromarketing, 6*, 5–16.

Kilbourne, J. (1987). *Still killing us softly*. Cambridge, MA: Cambridge Documentary Films.

Kilbourne, J. (2000). *Can't buy my love: How advertising changes the way we think and feel*. New York: Touchstone.

LaTour, M. S. (1990). Female nudity in print advertising: An analysis of gender differences in arousal and ad response. *Psychology & Marketing, 7*(1), 65–81.

LaTour, M. S., & Henthorne, T. L. (1994a). Ethical judgments of sexual appeals in print advertising. *Journal of Advertising, 23*(3), 81–90.

LaTour, M. S., & Henthorne, T. L. (1994b). Female nudity in advertisements, arousal and response: A parsimonious extension. *Psychological Reports, 75*, 1683–1690.

LaTour, M. S., Henthorne, T. L., & Williams, A. J. (1998). Is industrial advertising still sexist? It's in the eye of the beholder. *Industrial Marketing Management, 27*(3), 247–255.

LaTour, M. S., Pitts, R. E., & Snook-Luther, D. (1990). Female nudity, arousal and ad response: An experimental investigation. *Journal of Advertising, 19*(4), 51–62.

LaTour, M. S., & Rotfeld, H. (1997). There are threats and (maybe) fear-caused arousal: theory and confusions of appeals to fear and fear arousal itself. *Journal of Advertising, 26*(3), 45–59.

Levonian-Morgan, B. (1996). Putting the feminism into feminism scales: Introduction of a liberal feminist attitude and ideology scale (LFAIS). *Sex Roles, 34*(5/6), 359–391.

Miller, C. (1992, November 23). Publisher says sexy ads are OK, but sexist ones will sink sales. *Marketing News, 26*, 8–9.

Murphy, P., & Laczniak, G. R. (1981). Marketing ethics: A review with implications for managers, educators and researchers. *Review of Marketing 1981* (pp. 251–266). Chicago, IL: American Marketing Association.

Nataraajan, R., Henthorne, T. L., & LaTour, M. S. (1998). Reinforcing the importance of the marketing practitioner–marketing academic interface. *American Business Review, 16*(2), 109–112.

Reidenbach, R. E., & Robin, D. P. (1988). Some initial steps toward improving the measurement of ethical evaluations of marketing activities. *Journal of Business Ethics, 7*, 871–879.

Tansey, R., Hyman, M. R., & Brown, G. (1992). Ethical judgments about wartime ads depicting combat. *Journal of Advertising, 21*(3), 57–74.

Thayer, R. E. (1989). *The biopsychology and mood and arousal.* New York: Oxford University Press.

Winsky, J. (1991). Science as sex partner. *Advertising Age, 62*(4) 22.

Chapter 6

The Effects of Sexual Appeals on Physiological, Cognitive, Emotional, and Attitudinal Responses for Product and Alcohol Billboard Advertising[1]

Annie Lang
Indiana University

Kevin Wise
Stanford University

Seungwhan Lee
Indiana University

Xiaomei Cai
University of Delaware

Although outdoor advertising, more commonly referred to as billboard advertising, ranks behind all major media forms in terms of total advertising revenue (Coen, 2001), it is an important part of the media mix for many products. Billboard advertising is unique because it can reach a large number of viewers, and these viewers have only a few seconds to process the message. Sexual themes have been shown to generate attention to advertising, and they are often used to promote alcohol products. The emotional nature of sexual appeals may help predict how billboard messages are processed by viewers. As such, this chapter reports the results of three related studies that assess similar variables to determine if the effects of sex-

[1]This research was conducted under a sub-contract on a grant to Michigan State University from the Robert Wood Johnson Foundation. The authors wish to thank Chuck Atkin, Michigan State University, and Esther Thorson, University of Missouri, for their support of this research.

ual appeals differ when the billboard is advertising alcoholic beverages compared to nonalcohol products, as well as other related processes. The limited-capacity processing model is used as a framework to understand how sex appeals affect processing, attitudes, and memory (Lang, 2000).

LITERATURE REVIEW

Information Processing of Mediated Messages

The limited-capacity model of media processing (Lang, 2000) is a data-driven theoretical approach that has proven useful for investigating the processes and mechanisms underlying media effects. In this model, message recipients are defined as information processors, the media as some mix of audio or visual information, and the message content as the topic, genre, and information contained in a message. Message processing is the allocation of a limited pool of processing resources to the cognitive processes required for recipients to make sense of a message. Processing a message includes (but is not limited to) the parallel cognitive subprocesses (or tasks) of encoding, storage, and retrieval.

Comprehension of a message involves the continuous and simultaneous operation of these subprocesses. New information from the message is continuously attended to, encoded into short-term or working memory, processed, and stored. Previously held information (required to understand the message) is concurrently retrieved, associated with the new information, and stored again. Information encoded earlier in the message is being stored as later information is being encoded.

In general, because it is not possible for a message recipient to encode and store all the information in a message, the recipient continuously selects which information in the message to encode, process, and store. The amount of information that can be attended to, encoded, and stored has an upper bound created by the availability of the recipient's processing resources, which are limited. Viewed in this way, message processing, although it "feels" simple, is in fact a complex and difficult cognitive task. How large a portion of a message is successfully encoded, stored, and eventually retrieved is determined by the level of resources required by and allocated to the various subprocesses involved in viewing. The message recipient, the medium, and the content all affect how resources are allocated to processing the message.

The message recipient controls some aspects of the allocation of processing resources by making decisions about whether to watch, how carefully to watch, and how hard to try, based on how interesting the subject is, how relevant the information is, or simply whether the message recipient wants to remember it (Gantz, 1978). This voluntary or controlled allocation of processing resources is a relatively long-term process occurring over minutes or hours. Similarly, characteristics of the recipient (like familiarity with the topic, emotional response to a topic, etc.) partly determine the level of resources required to make sense of and store the message.

The medium itself may also control the automatic allocation of processing resources through the elicitation of orienting responses (ORs) in recipients. These ORs are automatic, reflexive attentional responses to changes in the environment or to stimuli that people have learned signal important information. In television, for example, ORs are elicited by structural features like cuts, edits, movement, flashes of light, and sound (Lang, 1990; Lang, Geiger, Strickwerda, & Sumner, 1993; Reeves et al., 1985; Thorson & Lang, 1992). This automatic allocation of resources is a relatively short-term response, occurring over seconds. In other media, ORs can be elicited by the appearance of a message or by graphic aspects of a message (Borse & Lang, 2000; Lang, Lee, Chung, & Zhao, 2001; Wise & Lang, 2001).

The content of the message can also invoke both automatic and controlled allocation of processing resources. Aspects of content, such as relevance and difficulty, can elicit controlled allocation of processing resources (Basil, 1994a, 1994b; Thorson & Lang, 1992). Other aspects of content, such as emotion, elicit automatic allocation of resources (Lang, Dhillon, & Dong, 1995; Lang, Newhagen, & Reeves, 1996; Newhagen & Reeves, 1992). Recent studies also suggest that the presence of "risky" products, such as condoms, alcohol, and cigarettes, may also elicit orienting responses and arousal (Lang, Lee, Chung, & Zhao, 2001).

In summary, the limited-capacity model makes the following general predictions: (a) The message recipient allocates an overall level of processing resources to the message processing task based on goals and interests; (b) the recipient's goals influence the proportion of resources allocated to the various subprocesses (such as storage and retrieval); (c) structural and content features of the message elicit orienting behavior and the automatic allocation of resources to encoding; (d) both content and structural attributes can elicit arousal that increases the allocation of resources to encoding and storing the message; (e) when there are insufficient resources available to carry out all the subprocesses, some aspect(s) of processing will be performed less well.

Applying this perspective to studying the effects of sexual appeals in alcohol- and product-billboard advertising requires answering the following questions:

1. What aspects of the structure of alcohol and product billboards will engage the automatic resource allocation system?
2. What aspects of the content of the billboards will engage the automatic resource allocation system?

3. What demands does the billboard medium place on cognitive load?
4. What aspects of the medium will engage the controlled allocation processes?

The answers to these questions should allow us to predict variations in orienting behavior, resource allocation, recognition, cued recall, and free recall for messages being presented.

First to be addressed are the aspects of the structure of billboards that might engage automatic processing. Structural features that elicit automatic-attention responses generally are features of a message that introduce change into the environment. To some extent, the answer to this question will vary depending on context. In experiments 1 and 2, participants will view the billboards one at a time on either a projection screen or a computer monitor. In these situations the viewer's task is to look at the billboards and rate their response. Thus, the appearance of the billboards is predictable and expected. Initially, the appearance of a billboard might elicit an orienting response, but this is likely to habituate quickly (Lang et al., 2001). In experiment 3, participants are instructed to focus on a driving video. The billboards appear on a computer monitor in their peripheral vision. In this case, as may be the case in the real world, the appearance of the billboards probably does elicit orienting (Borse & Lang, 2000).

The second question asks which aspects of the content of these billboards might elicit automatic processing. It seems likely that both sexual appeals and the presence of alcohol may elicit automatic attention responses. Research suggests that sexual content in still pictures elicits automatic attention in viewers (Lang, Bradley, & Cuthbert, 1997; Lang, Gilmore, Cuthbert, & Bradley, 1996; Lang, Greenwald, Bradley, & Hamm, 1993). Similarly, recent research has shown that the presence of "risky" products (e.g., alcohol, cigarettes, condoms) changes the nature of the orienting response to images presented on a computer screen (Lang et al., 2001). This would suggest that both ads containing alcohol and ads containing sexual appeals would elicit more automatic attention than billboards that do not contain them.

The third question asks about the cognitive load imposed on the message recipient by the medium. Billboards are designed to be read quickly. In experiment 2, the rate of presentation of the billboards is a constant 7 seconds per billboard. In experiment 1, rate of presentation is under the viewer's control, so cognitive load is fairly low. In experiment 3, viewers are instructed to focus on the driving video, with the billboard as the secondary stimulus. In this instance, cognitive load is higher, but not overwhelming.

The fourth question asks which content feature of these billboards might elicit controlled processing. In experiments 1 and 2, an attempt has been made to control the allocation of controlled processing resources by asking the respondents to pay close attention to the billboards and informing them that they will be tested on their memory for the billboards after viewing. However, in experiment 3, an attempt was made to allocate controlled processing to the driving task. In this case, allocation of controlled processing resources to the billboards is likely to reflect the interests and idiosyncrasies of the individual recipient. It seems likely, for example, that drinkers might allocate more resources to alcohol billboards than nondrinkers.

Based on the answers to these questions, it seems likely that the presence of both sexual appeals and alcohol will increase automatic allocation of resources to the processing of the billboards. In addition to eliciting attention, it seems likely that sexual appeals will also elicit emotion in billboard viewers. The following section reviews, briefly, some of the interactions of emotion and information processing of media messages.

Emotion and the Processing of Media Messages

The use of emotion to attract, persuade, and entertain is common. A great deal of research has attempted to determine if emotional messages are more persuasive (Tan, 1986), more attention-getting (Gunter, 1987; Lang, Newhagen, & Reeves, 1996; Newhagen & Reeves, 1992), or more memorable than messages without emotion (Basil, Schooler, & Reeves, 1991; Lang, 1991; Lang & Friestad, 1993; Newhagen & Reeves, 1992). Much of this research has explored the effects of emotional valence (i.e., whether a message is positive or negative) on various processing and effects variables (Lang, 1991; Lang & Friestad, 1993; Reeves, Lang, Thorson, & Rothschild, 1985; Basil et al., 1991; Thorson, Christ & Caywood, 1991).

Although the results of this research are not completely consistent, three conclusions can be drawn. First, message valence significantly effects memory for television messages. Second, most studies show that negative messages are remembered better than positive ones. Third, virtually all of the studies show emotional messages are remembered better than nonemotional ones. Critics of this research (Lang et al., 1995) have suggested that this literature's inconsistencies result from focusing exclusively on valence and ignoring the impact of arousal.

Dimensional theories of emotion (P.J. Lang, 1984; P.J. Lang, Bradley, & Cuthbert, 1997; Osgood, Succi, & Tannenbaum, 1957) conceptualize emotion as having two primary dimensions: valence and arousal. The valence dimension is conceptualized as a continuous affective response ranging from pleasant (or positive) to unpleasant (or negative). The arousal dimension is defined as a continuous response ranging from "energized, excited, and alert" to "calm, drowsy, or peaceful." Within this framework, research on the effects of emotional valence on the processing of media messages becomes an investigation of only one dimension of emotion. Yet research by P. J. Lang and colleagues on memory for emotional media (slides, sounds, and text) suggests that arousal plays a much more important role in memory for mediated messages than does valence. For example, Lang and colleagues have measured viewers' cognitive, affective, and physiological responses to emotional pictures chosen to vary on the arousal and valence dimensions. This work (Bradley et al., 1992) shows that arousing slides are remembered much better than nonarousing slides and that when the arousal dimension of emotion is controlled, there is little effect of valence on memory. Rather, both positive and negative slides are remembered better than neutral (or nonemotional) slides. When an effect of valence is found, positive pictures are remembered better than negative ones when arousal is controlled. Lang et al., (1995) replicated this research using televised messages. They found that arousing messages were remembered much better than calm messages and positive messages were remembered slightly better than negative messages when arousal was controlled.

Not only are arousing messages remembered better, but many studies suggest that the presence of arousing content in various types of messages (print, slides, audio, television) compels attention and automatically increases the resources allocated to process a message (Bradley, 1994; Bradley, Greenwald, Petry, & Lang, 1992; Lang, 1991, 2000; Lang, Bolls, & Kawahara, 1996; Lang, Bolls, Potter, & Kawahara, 1999; Lang et al., 1995; Lang et al., 1996; Lang, Zhou, Schwartz, Bolls, & Potter, 2000; Lang, Fitzsimmons, Bradley, Cuthbert, & Scott, 1996; P. J. Lang, Gilmore et al., 1996). Research done by the first author of this chapter and colleagues has examined whether arousing television content increases resources allocated to message processing (Lang et al., 1995; Lang et al., 1996; Potter & Lang, 1996). Results consistently show that when content is rated as more arousing, viewers have slower reaction times and slower tonic heart rate levels indicative of greater resource allocation. From a limited-capacity point of view, this means that arousing messages require more resources to process and therefore may overload processing sooner than less arousing messages.

In addition, Lang (2000) has suggested that the presence of arousing content in the media message not only allocates resources to attention and its associated subprocess of encoding, but also automatically allocates resources to memory—specifically to the subprocess of storage. Lang and colleagues (Lang, 2000; Lang, et al., 2000) demonstrated that messages containing arousing content consistently show higher cued and free-recall scores (indicative of better storage) compared to messages that do not contain arousing content, even when there is no difference in recognition levels (indicative of encoding).

Based on this research, it seems likely that sexual appeals will elicit an emotional response. That response is likely to be positive and arousing. Positive arousing emotional responses should increase both encoding and storage of message contents. Thus, billboards containing alcohol and/or sexual appeals should be recalled and recognized better than those that do not contain alcohol or sexual appeals. Furthermore, this effect will be more pronounced in experiment 3 where cognitive load is higher.

Alcohol, Sexual Appeals, and Attitudes

In addition to looking at processing variables, the present research also examines the effects of sexual appeals and the presence of alcohol on attitude toward the ad and intent to purchase. In general, sexual appeals are frequently used in consumer advertising (Percy & Rossiter, 1992). Results generally suggest that sexual appeals increase attention to advertisements but not necessarily to the product or brand information (Belch, Belch, & Villarreal, 1987; Reichert, Heckler, & Jackson, 2001). Thus, although sexual appeals may increase processing of elements of the advertisement, they may not direct this extra processing to relevant aspects of the ad such as product information or brand name. On the other hand, Yoon and his colleagues (Yoon, Bolls, & Lang, 1998), in a study looking at presence or absence of arousing content in television advertising, found that ads containing arousing content generated more positive attitudes toward the ads and brands and elicited somewhat better brand recall than ads that did not contain arousing content. However, although some of the arousing content in that experiment was sexual, some was not. In the experiments presented here, it seems likely that the presence of arousing content will increase both attitude toward and memory for the brand because cognitive load is low. As a result, increasing the resources allocated to attention and storage has a greater chance of resulting in the brand being stored.

Little information exists about how the presence of alcohol in billboards will affect attitudes toward the ad or purchase intent. One possibility is that the increase in arousal (and possibly attention) associated with alcohol will result in more positive attitudes toward the billboards. In general, the presence of arousing content has been shown to increase liking for media messages (Lang et al., 1999; Lang, Schneider, & Deitz, 1999; Lang et al., 2000; Yoon et al., 1998). If so, this increase in liking might also increase purchase intentions. Similarly, the increase in arousal associated with alcohol should increase storage, and therefore, recall for the alcohol billboards.

Thus, the general hypotheses for these experiments are that: (a) the presence of either alcohol or a sexual appeal will increase attention; (b) the presence of either alcohol or a sexual appeal will increase arousal; (c) increases in attention should increase encoding, which should lead to greater recognition memory for billboards with alcohol and sexual appeals; (d) the presence of arousal should increase resources allocated to storage, which should increase recall for billboards containing sexual appeals and alcohol;

(e) both the presence of alcohol and the presence of sexual appeals will increase attitude toward the ad and intent to purchase.

EXPERIMENT 1

Experiment 1 was designed to measure behavioral and physiological responses to the billboards. This experiment has four dependent variables: (a) time spent looking; (b) heart rate to measure attention; (c) skin conductance to assess the arousal dimension of emotion; and (d) facial electromyography (EMG) to measure the valence dimension of emotion. The specific hypotheses for this experiment are:

H1:   The presence of a sexual appeal in a billboard will increase attention, and this will result in a decrease in heart rate and an increase in time spent looking.

H2:   The presence of alcohol in a billboard will increase attention, and this will result in a decrease in heart rate and an increase in time spent looking.

H3:   The presence of a sexual appeal in a billboard will result in more positive and less negative valence, and this will result in an increase in zygomatic muscle activation and a decrease in corrugator muscle activation.

H4:   The presence of a sexual appeal in a billboard will result in an increase in arousal, and this will result in increased skin conductance.

H5:   The presence of alcohol in a billboard will result in an increase in arousal, and this will result in increased skin conductance.

RQ 1: This research question asks if there are any interactions between any of the primary factors and drinking behavior or gender?

METHOD

This experiment is a mixed 4 (Order of Presentation) × 2 (Sexual Appeal) × 2 (Product Type) × 3-5 (Message) factorial design.[2] Sexual Appeal, Product

---

[2]The number of messages in each Sexual Appeal × Product Type category varied from 3-5. There were two cells with four messages, one with three, and one with five. The original design called for four messages per cell. However, an error in setting up the stimulus programs resulted in five ads in one category and three in another. This error was not observed until after data had been collected. Because repeated measures analysis of variance requires a balanced design, all analyses were done in two ways to rectify this problem. First, the design was run with three messages per cell (eliminating the requisite number of messages by random selection in the three cells with more than three messages). Second, repeated measures analyses were run on the means for each cell (eliminating the repetitions factor). The results were virtually the same for both approaches. The results of the means analysis are reported here because it includes all data collected.

Type, and Message were all within-subject factors. Billboards with sexual appeals generally contained suggestive images of people (some were men and some were women). Order of presentation was the only between-subjects factor. Participants were randomly assigned to view one of the four orders of presentation. There were no significant Order effects and this factor will not be discussed further.

Participants. Sixty-one participants were recruited from an introductory telecommunications class and a campus-wide, interdisciplinary participant pool. All participants were given monetary compensation and some received extra credit.

Procedure. All participants were greeted on arrival at the research site and asked to sign an informed consent statement. Prior to beginning the billboard phase of the experiment, participants viewed about 30 minutes of television. Participants were seated in a comfortable chair, approximately 2 feet away from an 18-inch color monitor. A standard computer keyboard mounted on a wooden board was placed across the participant's lap. Participants were instructed to view each billboard for as long as they desired, and then to press any key on the keyboard to bring up the next billboard. This pattern was repeated until the participant had viewed all 16 billboards.

The billboards used in the study were scanned from actual photographs taken by the researchers or pictures of billboards taken from advertising textbooks and trade books. Each billboard was put into one of four categories: sex/alcohol, no sex/alcohol, sex/not alcohol, and no sex/not alcohol. There were four orders of presentation, each one systematically constructed to ensure that each billboard category appeared in every possible location.

The presentation of billboards and measurement of time spent looking at each billboard was controlled by the program Superlab. When the participant hit any key to continue to the next billboard, she or he saw a blank screen for 5 seconds (to allow collection of baseline physiological data), followed by presentation of the new billboard. Physiological data collection was time-locked to stimulus presentation.

Dependent Variables

Attention. Attention was measured in two ways. First, time spent looking at each billboard was interpreted as an indicator of interest or attention to the message. Second, deceleration in heart rate was used to index allocation of resources to the message (Lang, 1990).

Valence.   Facial EMG was used as a covert measure of valence. Activation in the smiling (zygomatic) and frowning (corrugator) muscles was measured during viewing. Research suggests that zygomatic activation is associated with liking and positive emotion whereas corrugator activation is associated with dislike or negative emotion (Bolls, Potter, & Lang, 2001).

Arousal.   Arousal was measured using skin conductance. Skin conductance is an accurate measure of activation in the sympathetic nervous system, which is one possible definition of arousal. It has also been shown to be highly correlated with self-reports of arousal (Bolls et al., in press; Lang et al., 1995; P. J. Lang et al., 1993).

Physiological Recording Techniques

Heart-rate data were collected using three standard Beckman electrodes; one electrode was placed on each forearm, with a third ground electrode placed just above the wrist. Skin conductance was gathered using a pair of standard Beckman AG/AGCL electrodes placed on the palmar surface of the participant's nondominant hand. Corrugator and zygomatic EMG were measured with identical pairs of Beckman mini AG/AGCL electrodes, placed slightly above the participant's right eyebrow and cheekbone, respectively.

The signals measured for physiological data passed from the electrodes to Coulbourne couplers. The heart rate signal was passed through a bioamplifier to a Coulbourne bipolar comparator connected to a Coulbourne one-shot, and finally, into a computer that measured the milliseconds between heart beats. Heart rate data was initially collected as milliseconds between beats, then converted to beats per minute. The EMG signal was sampled at 50 Hz and passed from the electrodes to a bioamplifier through a contour following integrator and into the A/D board of the computer. Skin conductance was collected using a Coulbourne skin conductance module and was also sampled at 50 Hz.

RESULTS

Hypothesis 1 predicted that sexual appeals would increase attention. The prediction is for a main effect of Sexual Appeal on time spent looking and heart rate. The main effect of Sexual Appeal on the time spent looking data was significant [$F(1, 53) = 8.12, p < .006$]. Participants looked longer at billboards containing sexual appeals ($M = 13,585.53$ milliseconds) compared to those that did not contain sexual appeals ($M = 12,066.76$ milliseconds). There were no interactions of Sexual Appeal with either drinking behavior or gender.

The main effect of Sexual Appeal on the heart-rate data was not significant [$F(1,34) = 1.65, p < .21$]. However, there was a significant Gender × Sexual Appeal interaction [$F(1,34) = 3.87, p < .05$] shown in Fig. 6.1. As can be
seen, sexual appeals had little effect on heart rate for women; they paid
equal amounts of attention to billboards with and without sexual appeals.
For men, however, sexual appeals had a large effect; men paid more attention to billboards with sexual appeals. There were no interactions with
drinking behavior.

Hypothesis 2 predicted that attention (time spent looking, heart rate)
would be greater for billboards containing alcohol products compared to
billboards that did not contain alcohol products. The main effect of Product
on time spent looking was not significant ($F < 1$). There were no interactions
with drinking behavior or gender.

The main effect of Product Type on the heart rate data also was not significant ($F < 1$). The Drinking Behavior × Product Type approached significance [$F(1, 32) = 3.55, p < .069$]. This interaction suggested that heavier
drinkers (8.47 average drinks per week) paid more attention to nonalcohol
billboards than did lighter drinkers (.82 average drinks per week).

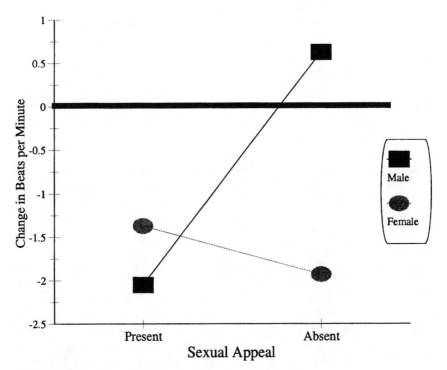

FIG. 6.1. Sexual Appeal by gender interaction on heart rate.

Hypothesis 3 predicted that Sexual Appeals would lead to more positive and less negative emotional responses. The prediction is for a main effect of Sexual Appeal on the facial EMG data. The main effect of Sexual Appeal on the change in zygomatic muscle activity approached significance [$F(1, 40)$ = 1.65, $p < .206$]. There was no change in activation in smiling muscles from baseline to viewing for the billboards that contained sexual appeals (M = .00) whereas there was a decrease in activation, indicative of less smiling, for billboards that did not contain sexual appeals ($M = -.02$).

The main effect of Sexual Appeal on the frowning (corrugator) muscle activity was significant [$F(1, 40) = 6.13, p < .018$] but in the opposite direction from the prediction. There was, however, greater corrugator activity during viewing of billboards that contained a sexual appeal (M = .125) compared to billboards that did not contain a sexual appeal (M = .025). This suggests that either there was more frowning while viewing billboards containing sexual appeals or, it may indicate, an increase in attention. The corrugator muscle, in addition to being strongly related to valence, is also moderately related to attention. There were no interactions with gender or drinking behavior.

Hypothesis 4 predicted greater smiling and less frowning while viewing billboards containing alcohol. The main effect of Product Type on the change in zygomatic muscle activity approached significance [$F(1, 40)$ = 1.50, $p < .22$]. There was a small increase in zygomatic muscle activity during viewing of alcohol billboards (M = .005) and a decrease in zygomatic muscle activity while viewing not alcohol billboards ($M = -.025$) suggesting slightly more positive valence during alcohol billboards compared to product billboards. In addition, there was also a significant Sexual Appeal × Product Type interaction [$F(1, 40) = 5.52, p < .02$]. This interaction is shown in Fig. 6.2. As can be seen in the figure, there is the greatest activation in the zygomatic muscle, signifying greater positive emotion, when viewing billboards with both alcohol and sexual appeals. The main effect of Product Type on the change in corrugator muscle activity also approaches significance [$F(1, 40) = 3.56, p < .07$]. Mean change in corrugator activity is .035 micro volts for the alcohol billboards compared to .115 for the product billboards, signifying less negative valence for alcohol billboards.

Hypothesis 5 predicted that the presence of sexual appeals and alcohol in billboards would increase arousal. Thus, the prediction is for a main effect of Sexual Appeal and Product Type on the skin conductance data. Neither main effect was significant. Instead, there is a three-way Gender × Product Type × Sexual Appeal interaction. Perusal of this interaction showed that there was no effect of Product Type when Sexual Appeals were absent. However, in the presence of a Sexual Appeal, the effect of Product Type was large and had opposite effects for men compared to women. Spe-

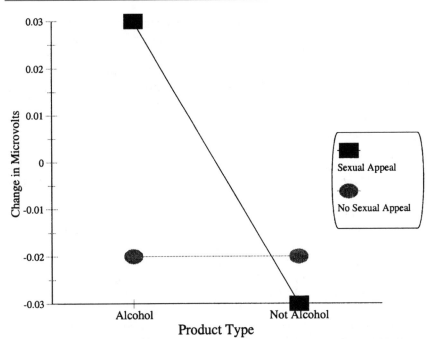

FIG. 6.2. Product Type by Sexual Appeal interaction on the zygomatic EMG data.

cifically, for men Sexual Appeals decreased skin conductance (arousal) for alcohol billboards and increased skin conductance for product billboards. For women, Sexual Appeals increase skin conductance for alcohol bill-boards and decrease skin conductance for product billboards.

Finally, there is a significant Drinking Behavior x Sexual Appeal inter-action on the skin conductance data. Light drinkers show greater skin conductance responses when there are no sexual appeals whereas heavy drinkers show greater skin conductance responses when sexual appeals are present.

DISCUSSION

Experiment 1 tested the general theoretical propositions that the presence of sexual appeals and alcohol would increase attention, arousal, and posi-tive valence. Although the results are somewhat mixed, there is general support for these propositions. For example, this study clearly showed that the presence of a sexual appeal increased attention to the billboards. First, billboards with sexual appeals were looked at for a longer period of time than those without sexual appeals. Furthermore, although there was no main effect in the heart-rate data, there was a significant interaction with gender. This interaction showed that the presence of a sexual appeal in the billboards significantly increased resource allocation for male participants but had little or no effect on resource allocation for women.

Second, when both sexual appeals and alcohol were present there was significantly more activation in the smiling muscles, indicating greater positive valence compared to all other conditions. In addition, there was some evidence that both sexual appeals and alcohol, alone, increased positive emotional responses and decreased negative emotional response.

Last, there was some support for the premise that the presence of sexual appeals in billboards would elicit arousal. Rather than the expected main effects of Sexual Appeal and Product Type, interactive effects were present. Specifically, sexual appeal in a billboard increased arousal only for heavier drinkers, women viewing alcohol billboards, and men viewing product billboards.

Thus, it seems reasonable to conclude that the presence of sexual appeals in product and alcohol billboards clearly increases attention, seems to increase positive valence, and, at least for some groups, increases arousal. The presence of alcohol in billboards also altered participant responses to the billboards. In particular, the presence of alcohol seemed to increase positive valence and decrease negative valence, with the effect being particularly pronounced when sexual appeals were present. In addition, the presence or absence of alcohol significantly alters the effects of gender and sexual appeal on arousal. The presence of alcohol did not significantly affect any of the attention variables.

Taken together, these results suggest that sexual appeals increase attention, positive valence, and arousal (at least for some groups). The presence of alcohol has no apparent effect on attention, but does increase positive valence, and mediates the effects of sexual appeal on arousal.

EXPERIMENT 2

Experiment 2 uses the same stimuli used in experiment 1 to investigate the effects of Sexual Appeal and Product Type on encoding (e.g., recognition), attitudes, and self-reported emotional response. Whereas the billboards were presented on an 18-inch computer monitor in the first experiment, billboards were projected onto a wall-sized screen for this experiment. In experiment 1, respondents viewed the billboards alone, did not rate the billboards, and viewed each billboard as long as they liked. In experiment 2 respondents viewed in groups, saw each billboard for 7 seconds, and rated their emotional and attitudinal responses to each billboard. Finally, following a distractor task, respondents' memory for the billboards was tested. Specific hypotheses for this experiment are:

H1:   The presence of sexual appeals and alcohol will increase recognition for billboards.

H2:   The presence of sexual appeals and alcohol will increase self-reported arousal and positive valence ratings.

H3:   In general participants will have more positive attitudes toward billboards that contain alcohol and sexual appeals.

METHODS

Design.   The design of this experiment is the same as that used in experiment 1: Sexual Appeal (2) × Product Type (2) × Messages (3-5) × Order of Presentation (4). The same stimuli used in experiment 1 were used in experiment 2.

Participants.   Forty-two participants were recruited from both an introductory telecommunications class and a campus-wide interdisciplinary participant pool. All participants were given monetary compensation and some received extra credit for participation.

Procedure.   All participants were greeted and signed an informed-consent form. Participants viewed the stimuli in groups of 5. The billboard stimuli were projected onto a wall-sized screen. Participants, seated about 10 feet from the screen in comfortable chairs, viewed 16 commercials and 16 billboards projected on the screen. Participants were randomly assigned to view either the commercials first or the billboards first. Following presentation of each message, respondents rated their emotional responses to the message. Following viewing of all 32 messages, participants took a speeded recognition test. Following the recognition test, participants completed a demographic and substance use questionnaire, and were dismissed.

Dependent Variables

Recognition.   Encoding was assessed as recognition. Respondents were seated at a computer monitor. Thirty-two billboards were presented on the screen for 3 seconds each. Sixteen of the billboards were foils and 16 were billboards they had actually seen. Accuracy of response was recorded by the computer running the Superlab program.

Emotional Response.   Participants were instructed to rate their emotional response to each billboard immediately following viewing. Participants rated their emotional response using the SAM scale. SAM (the Self Assessment Manikin) is a three-dimensional pictorial emotional rating scale (P. J. Lang et al., 1993). Participants rate their emotional response in terms of arousal, valence, and dominance. Only the arousal and valence ratings are discussed here.

Attitudinal Ratings. Participants rated how much they liked each billboard and how likely they would be to buy the product in each billboard on a 10-point scale.

RESULTS

Hypothesis 1 predicted that there would be main effects of Sexual Appeal and Product Type on the forced choice recognition data. The main effect of Sexual Appeal on the recognition data was not significant. The main effect of Product Type on the recognition data was significant [$F(1, 29) = 24.95, p < .000$]. Participants recognized 83% of the alcohol billboards compared to 64% of the product billboards. There were no interactions with drinking behavior. However, there was a Gender × Product Type interaction. Men recognized 83% of the alcohol ads and only 53% of the product ads, whereas women recognized 84% of the alcohol ads and 72% of the product ads. Thus, the effect of Product Type was greater for men than for women.

The Sexual Appeal × Product Type interaction approached significance [$F(1, 29) = 2.82, p < .100$]. This interaction showed that when no sexual appeal was present participants recognized 83% of alcohol billboards compared to 70% of product billboards. When a sexual appeal was present, participants recognized 83% of alcohol billboards compared to only 59% of product billboards. Thus, the effect of Product Type is larger when sexual appeals are present.

Hypothesis 2 predicted that both the presence of alcohol and the presence of sexual appeals would increase arousal and positive valence in viewer's self-reported emotional responses. The main effect of Sexual Appeal on arousal was not significant although the means are in the right direction. The main effect of Sexual Appeal on valence was significant [$F(1, 40) = 36.06, p < .000$]. Billboards with sexual appeals were rated more positively ($M = 6.11$) than billboards without sexual appeals ($M = 5.34$). In addition, there was a Product Type × Sexual Appeal interaction [$F(1, 40) = 29.67, p < .000$], shown in Fig. 6.3. As can be seen in this figure, Sexual Appeals increased positive valence for billboards that did not contain alcohol but had no effect on positive valence for billboards that did contain alcohol products.

The main effect of Product Type on the SAM arousal ratings was significant [$F(1, 40) = 17.28, p < .000$]. Billboards containing alcohol were rated as more arousing ($M = 3.51$) than billboards that did not contain alcohol products ($M = 2.78$). There was no main effect of Product Type on the valence ratings.

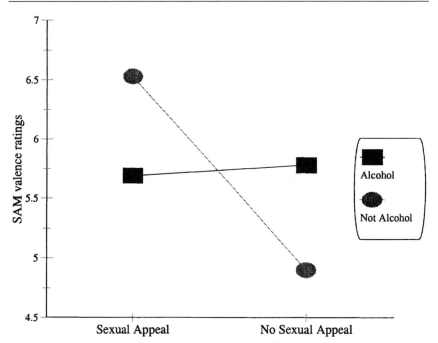

FIG. 6.3. Product Type by Sexual Appeal interaction on the SAM valence ratings.

In addition, there were no significant interactions of drinking behavior or gender on the arousal and valence ratings data.

Hypothesis 3 predicted that participants would like and be more likely to buy products in billboards containing sexual appeals and alcohol compared to those that contained no sexual appeals and no alcohol. The main effects of Sexual Appeal on liking and intent to purchase were not significant, but there was a significant Sexual Appeal × Product Type interaction for liking. The presence of a sexual appeal increased liking for nonalcohol billboards but decreased liking for alcohol billboards. The main effect of Product Type was significant for both liking [$F(1,37) = 23.71, p < .00$] and intent to purchase ($F(1,37) = 12.31, p < .00$). Participants liked alcohol billboards better (alcohol = 5.48, nonalcohol = 4.89) and were more likely to say they would buy the products (alcohol = 5.42, nonalcohol = 4.14).

DISCUSSION

In general, the results of this experiment suggest that the effect of Sexual Appeals in billboards differs depending on whether alcohol or nonalcohol products are being advertised. Sexual Appeal had no main effect on recognition but did increase the effect of Product Type on recognition. Alcohol billboards were recognized much better than product billboards, especially when a sexual appeal was present.

Both Sexual Appeal and Product Type had significant effects on emotional response. Both variables increased ratings of positive valence. The effect of sexual appeals on valence was particularly strong for alcohol billboards. Product Type had a significant effect on arousal ratings, and alcohol billboards were rated as more arousing than product billboards. Interestingly, as in experiment 1, there was no significant main effect for Sexual Appeal on arousal. On the other hand, unlike experiment 1, there is a main effect of Product Type on arousal.

Finally, both Sexual Appeal and Product Type significantly increased intent to buy the products in the billboards, and the presence of alcohol resulted in greater liking for the billboards. Sexual Appeals, on the other hand, increased liking only for nonalcohol products.

EXPERIMENT 3

Experiment 3 looks at the effects of Sexual Appeals and Product Type on recognition, free recall, free brand recall, and intent to buy and use the products. In this experiment, unlike the first two experiments, viewing the billboards is the secondary task, whereas viewing a driving video is the primary task. This represents an attempt to increase psychological external validity to further investigate the effects of sexual appeals and product type on the processing of billboard advertising. The hypotheses tested in this experiment are:

H1: Billboards with sexual appeals and alcohol will be recognized better than those without sexual appeals and alcohol.

H2: Billboards with sexual appeals and alcohol will be free-recalled (billboard and brand) better than billboards without sexual appeals and alcohol.

H3: Billboards with sexual appeals and alcohol will receive more positive attitudinal evaluations and purchase intention than those without sexual appeals and alcohol.

METHOD

Design. The same design and billboard stimulus materials were used in this experiment. In addition to the billboard stimuli, participants in this experiment viewed an 18-minute 13-second driving simulation video projected onto a large screen. Thirty-two images were simultaneously presented on an 18-inch computer monitor located to the right of screen. The driving video simulated normal, nontaxing driving through a me-dium-size city, out onto the highway, and down the highway. The 32 im-ages shown on the computer monitor were shown in one of two presentation orders. Sixteen of the 32 images were snapshots of scenes and objects normally seen on the side of the road. The other 16 were the bill-board stimuli used in experiments 1 and 2.

Respondents.   Forty-seven students from a freshmen-level telecom-munication class participated in the experiment for extra credit and com-pensation. Respondents participated in groups of five.

Procedure.   Participants viewed the driving simulation video pro-jected onto a large screen. To the right of the projected screen, there was a computer monitor. On that monitor an image appeared at a randomly se-lected point once within every 34-second period. Each image was shown for 7 seconds and disappeared. Participants were instructed to imagine that they themselves were driving on the highway and that the images appear-ing on the monitor were natural things they would see along the highway. Participants were told that when images appeared on the screen they were not to pay special attention to those images but should behave as they would if they were really driving down the road.

After viewing the driving simulation video, respondents were taken to another room to complete the free-recall test. They were instructed to write down a description of all the billboards they could remember seeing. After the free-recall test, participants, one at a time, completed a speeded recogni-tion test on the computer. Following the memory tests, participants were given an attitude test. This test listed 32 products, half of which they had seen in billboards and half they had not. For each product, participants rated how positively they felt about the product and how likely they would be to use the product in the future. Finally, participants completed a ques-tionnaire about their drinking behavior and their expectations about alco-hol consumption. No limit was placed on the length of time subjects had to complete the free-recall, attitude, and expectancy tests. Respondents were thanked and dismissed.

RESULTS

Hypothesis 1 predicted that participants would have better recognition for billboards that contained sexual appeals and alcohol. The main effect of Sexual Appeal on the recognition data was significant [$F(1, 45) = 7.43, p < .01$]. Participants recognized 91% of the billboards containing sexual ap-peals compared to 83% of the billboards not containing sexual appeals. The main effect of Product Type on the recognition data was not significant.

There was no interaction with gender, drinking behavior, or between Sexual Appeal and Product Type.

In addition to the main effect of Sexual Appeal on the recognition data there was also a main effect of Sexual Appeal on the latency to response data [$F(1, 45) = 9.99, p < .01$)]. Participants were slightly slower recognizing billboards containing sexual appeals ($M = 1328.53$ milliseconds) than they were recognizing billboards that did not contain sexual appeals ($M = 1235.85$ milliseconds). This finding suggests that although respondents were more accurate for sexual appeals, they took longer to make the decision.

Hypothesis 2 predicted that free recall and free brand recall would be better for billboards containing alcohol and sexual appeals. The main effect of Sexual Appeal on the free recall data was significant [$F(1, 45) = 13.27, p < .00$]. Participants were able to recall more of the billboards containing sexual appeals ($M = .50$) than billboards that did not contain sexual appeals ($M = .26$). The main effect of Sexual Appeal on brand free recall was also significant [$F(1, 44) = 3.78, p < .058$]. Participants free-recalled the brand name for billboards containing sexual appeals ($M = .32$) slightly better than they did for billboards without sexual appeals ($M = .25$).

There were also main effects of Product Type on both the free recall [$F(1, 45) = 4.77, p < .034$] and brand free recall data [$F(1, 44) 8.07, p < .01$]. Participants free-recalled more billboards containing alcohol ($M = .47$) than billboards that did not contain alcohol ($M = .39$). In addition they free recalled more of the brands from billboards containing alcohol ($M = .26$) than for billboards that did not contain alcohol ($M = .20$).

Finally, for the brand free-recall data there was also an interaction of Product Type with Drinking Behavior. Heavy drinkers free-recalled more alcohol brands ($M = .27$) than did lighter drinkers ($M = .31$). On the other hand, light drinkers free-recalled more nonalcohol brands ($M = .26$) than did heavier drinkers ($M = .20$).

Hypothesis 3 predicted that both Sexual Appeal and Product Type would have significant main effects on liking for the billboards and intent to use the products. There were no significant main effects of either Sexual Appeal or Product Type on either liking or intent to use the product. Instead there were significant interactions of the Sexual Appeal and Product Type factors with Drinking Behavior. For ratings of how much they liked the billboards, the interaction of Drinking Behavior was significant with both Sexual Appeal [$F(1, 38) = 5.94, p < .02$] and Product Type [$F(1, 38) = 7.99, p < .01$]. For the Product Type interaction, light drinkers preferred nonalcohol billboards ($M = 5.18$) to alcohol billboards ($M = 4.26$). Heavier drinkers, on the other hand, preferred alcohol billboards ($M = 5.96$) to nonalcohol billboards ($M = 5.05$). For the interaction of Sexual Appeal with the drinking behavior, the presence of a sexual appeal increases liking for light drinkers and decreases liking for heavy drinkers.

The only significant effect on the intent to use rating was a significant Drinking Behavior × Product Type interaction [$F(1, 39) = 7.11, p < .01$]. This interaction showed that lighter drinkers were less likely to intend to use alcohol products ($M = 2.90$) than heavier drinkers ($M = 5.23$) and more likely to use nonalcohol products ($M = 4.75$) than heavier drinkers ($M = 4.45$).

DISCUSSION

In this experiment, when viewing the billboards is a secondary task rather than a primary task, the effects of Sexual Appeals on processing of billboards were much more pronounced. The presence of a sexual appeal in a billboard increased recognition, free recall, brand recall, and liking for billboards. As in previous experiments, Product Type also had significant effects but they were diminished in this experiment. There was no effect of Product Type on recognition although there were significant effects of Product Type on brand and free recall. Finally, in this experiment the evaluative components—liking and use—showed significant interactions with drinking behavior (which were absent in experiment 2). Not surprisingly, heavier drinkers evaluated alcohol billboards more positively than light drinkers. Interestingly, how much participants liked billboards with sexual appeals was also mediated by Drinking Behavior. Specifically, light drinkers preferred billboards with sexual appeals whereas heavier drinkers preferred billboards without sexual appeals.

CONCLUSION

Perhaps the most interesting finding in these studies is that the effect of sexual appeals in billboard advertising varies as a result of the type of product being advertised. In these three studies, the effects of sexual appeals were consistently being altered by the presence or absence of alcohol in the billboards. Generally, sexual appeals are predicted to have their effects by increasing attention and arousal in message viewers. In these studies, clear evidence that sexual appeals increased attention was found. The data did not, however, clearly support the hypothesis that sexual appeals increased arousal in viewers. Instead, Product Type consistently interacted with sexual appeals when arousal was the dependent variable.

   Limited-capacity theory predicted that sex and alcohol would increase attention. In experiment 1 two measures of attention were used—time spent looking and heart rate. Results partially supported this theoretical prediction. The presence of a sexual appeal increased time spent looking for everyone but there was no effect of alcohol. On the other hand, heart rate decreased (indicating greater attention) for alcohol ads for heavy drinkers and sexual appeals for men. Taken together this suggests that sexual appeal has a slightly greater ability to increase attention, but, if the viewer drinks alcohol, product type will also result in an increase in attention.

Arousal was measured using both self-report and physiological measures. In experiment 1, skin conductance was used to measure arousal. The major effect was a three-way Gender × Sexual Appeal × Product Interaction. Sexual Appeals increased arousal for nonalcohol ads for men and alcohol ads for women. Sexual appeals decreased arousal for alcohol ads for men and nonalcohol ads for women. In experiment 2, on the other hand, a self-report measure of arousal was used. Here, the presence of alcohol increased self-reported arousal for all viewers and there was no effect of sexual appeal on arousal.

Thus, there is evidence that both sexual appeals and alcohol increase attention and arousal, but the pattern of results across measures and experiments is not entirely consistent. The physiological measures suggest that sexual appeals are both more arousing and more attention-getting for men, but that this is mediated by product. The only physiological effect found for women was that sexual appeals increased arousal for alcohol ads and decreased arousal for product ads.

Another prediction was that both alcohol and sex would increase positive attitudes toward the messages. In experiment 1 this was tested using physiological measures. Both alcohol and sex resulted in more smiling when they were present compared to when they were absent. Alcohol also resulted in less frowning when it was present compared to when it was absent. Sexual appeals, on the other hand, resulted in slightly more frowning when they were present. Thus, the physiology generally supports the hypothesis that there will be more positive valence during alcohol and sexual messages. Mixed results are available on the question of whether the amount of negative valence is decreased. In experiment 2, valence was measured by having viewers self-report their emotional valence and their liking for the billboards. In experiment 3 viewers self-reported their liking. Viewers reported feeling more positive affect during sexual appeal billboards in experiment 2 as predicted. In addition, both liking and valence had significant Sexual Appeal × Product Interactions, thus viewers reported more positive affect during sexual appeals in nonalcohol ads compared to alcohol ads in both experiment 2 and experiment 3. Viewers also reported liking alcohol ads better than nonalcohol ads in experiment 2 but not in experiment 3. In experiment 3, only the heavy drinkers liked the alcohol ads better. Overall, it appears that sexual appeals and alcohol clearly increase positive valence—but that valence can vary.

Limited-capacity theory goes on to predict that if a variable increases attention it should also increase recognition for the message. If it increases arousal, then recognition and recall should improve as well. And, if arousal is equal—positive messages may be remembered slightly better than negative messages. Overall, the results taken together suggest that both alcohol and sexual-appeal billboards should be remembered better than nonalcohol and nonsexual billboards. These hypotheses were tested in experiment 2 and 3 and were basically supported. In experiment 2 alcohol ads were recognized better than nonalcohol ads and there was an interaction with sex appeal. In experiment 3 sexual billboards were recognized better than nonsexual billboards, but product type was not significant. For recall both sexual appeals and product type had significant positive effects.

Given this pattern of findings, the theoretical predictions made by the limited-capacity approach are largely supported. Differences in results across measures and experiments, however, deserve further study. Are the differences in arousal between experiment 1 and experiment 2 due to screen size? We know that screen size affects arousal, so this is a distinct possibility. Are the differences in recognition between experiments 2 and 3 due to the fact that processing the billboard is a secondary task in experiment 3 and a primary task in experiment 2? Again, this seems likely and suggests that the impact of both product type and sexual appeal is mediated by context and task requirements.

Having said that, it is still clear that sexual appeals have effects on both cognitive processing and emotional and evaluative response. Experiment 1 produced strong evidence that the presence of a sexual appeal increased attention to the billboards. Experiments 1 and 2 demonstrated that the presence of a sexual appeal can increase arousal, particularly for nonalcohol billboards and for men. Experiments 2 and 3 showed that sexual appeals increase recognition and free recall for billboards. Finally, experiment 3 showed that when ad viewing is the secondary task (which is the more externally valid condition) sexual appeals had strong effects on recognition, free recall, and brand recall for the products advertised in billboards.

Interestingly, the effects of sexual appeals were not demonstrable for intent to purchase the product. Instead, a sexual appeal increased ratings related to liking for the billboards. This may suggest that although sexual appeals are a useful tool for increasing attention to, arousal, and memory for an advertisement, they may not serve to motivate intent to buy or intent to use the product.

Further research should investigate the effects of Sexual Appeals for a variety of products that differ in terms of their ability to elicit arousal. It would be interesting to determine if sexual appeals lose their functionality when used to promote products that are inherently arousing. If this were the case, that might suggest that sexual appeals should be used primarily to promote products that lack the ability to elicit arousal on their own. This deserves further study because some of the interactions reported here suggest that the presence of a sexual appeal actually decreases the effectiveness of the advertisement when the product is arousing (or at least when the product is alcohol).

REFERENCES

Basil, M. (1994a). Multiple resource theory I: Application to television viewing. *Communication Research, 21*, 177–207.

Basil, M. (1994b). Secondary reaction-time measures. In A. Lang (Ed.), *Measuring psychological responses to media.* Hillsdale, NJ: Lawrence Erlbaum Associates.

Basil, M., Schooler, C., & Reeves, B. (1991). *Positive and negative political advertising: Effectiveness of ads and perceptions of candidates* (pp. 245–262). Hillsdale, NJ: Lawrence Erlbaum Associates.

Belch, G. E., Belch, M. A., & Villarreal, A. (1987). Effects of advertising communications: Review of research. In J. Sheth (Ed.), *Research in marketing* (Vol. 9, pp. 59–117). New York: JAI Press.

Bolls, P., Potter, R. F., & Lang, A. (2001). The use of facial EMG to measure emotional responses to radio. *Communication Research, 28*(5), 627–651.

Borse, J., & Lang, A. (2000, May). *The effects of web banner advertisements: A study of the impact of animation and interactivity on memory, click-through, attention, arousal, and affect.* Paper presented at the annual meeting of the International Communication Association, Acapulco, Mexico.

Bradley, M. M. (1994). Emotional memory: A dimensional analysis. In S. H. M. V. Goozen, N. E. Van de Poll, & J. A. Sergeant (Eds.), *Emotions: Essays on emotion theory.* Hillsdale, NJ: Lawrence Erlbaum Associates.

Bradley, M. M., Greenwald, M. K., Petry, M. C., & Lang, P. J. (1992). Remembering Pictures: Pleasure and arousal in memory. *Journal of Experimental Psychology, 18*(2), 379–390.

Coen, B. (2001). *Bob Coen's insider's report.* Retrieved http://www.mccann.com/insight/bobcoen.html.

Gantz, W. (1978). How uses and gratifications affect recall of television news. *Journalism Quarterly, 55*, 664–672.

Gunter, B. (1987). *Poor reception: Misunderstanding and forgetting broadcast news.* Hillsdale, NJ: Lawrence Erlbaum Associates.

Lang, A. (1990). Involuntary attention and physiological arousal evoked by structural features and emotional content in TV commercials. *Communication Research, 17*(3), 275–299.

Lang, A. (1991). Emotion, formal features, and memory for televised political advertisements. In F. Biocca (Ed.), *Television and political advertising, Vol. 1: Psychological processes; Vol. 2: Signs, codes, and images* (pp. 221–243). Hillsdale, NJ: Lawrence Erlbaum Associates.

Lang, A. (2000). The limited capacity model of mediated message processing. *Journal of Communication, 50*(1), 46–70.

Lang, A., Bolls, P., & Kawahara, K. (1996, May). *The effects of arousing content and production pacing on television viewers' arousal and allocation of processing resources.* Paper presented at the Midwest Artificial Intelligence and Cognitive Science Conference. Available: http:www.cs.indiana.edu/event/maics96/proceedings.html.

Lang, A., Bolls, P., Potter, R. F., & Kawahara, K. (1999). The effects of production pacing and arousing content on the information processing of television messages. *Journal of Broadcasting and Electronic Media, 43*(4), 451–475.

Lang, A., Dhillon, K., & Dong, Q. (1995). The effects of emotional arousal and valence on television viewers' cognitive capacity and memory. *Journal of Broadcasting and Electronic Media, 39*(3), 313–327.

Lang, A., & Friestad, M. (1993). Emotion, hemispheric specialization, and visual and verbal memory for television messages. *Communication Research, 20*(5), 647–670.

Lang, A., Geiger, S., Strickwerda, M., & Sumner, J. (1993). The effects of related and unrelated cuts on television viewers' attention, processing capacity, and memory. *Communication Research, 20*(1), 4–29.

Lang, A., Lee, S., Chung, Y., & Borse, J. (2001). *Task not medium: Orienting to web banner advertisements.* Unpublished manuscript, Institute for Communication Research. Indiana University, Department of Telecommunications.

Lang, A., Lee, S., Chung, Y., & Zhao, X. (2001, May). *It's the product stupid: Do risky products compel attention and elicit arousal in media viewers?* Paper presented at the International Communication Association, Washington, DC.

Lang, A., Newhagen, J., & Reeves, B. (1996). Negative video as structure: Emotion, attention, capacity, and memory. *Journal of Broadcasting and Electronic Media, 40*(4), 460–477.

Lang, A., Schneider, E. F., & Deitz, R. (1999, August). *Emotional experience and physiological arousal during violent video game playing: Gender, experience, and presence matter.* Paper presented at the Association for Education in Journalism and Mass Communication, New Orleans.

Lang, A., Zhou, S., Schwartz, N., Bolls, P., & Potter, R. F. (2000). The effects of edits on arousal, attention, and memory for television messages: When an edit is an edit can an edit be too much? *Journal of Broadcasting and Electronic Media, 44*(1), 94–109.

Lang, P. (1984). *Cognition in emotion: Concept and action.* New York: Cambridge University Press.

Lang, P. J., Bradley, M. M., & Cuthbert, B. N. (1997). Motivated attention: Affect, activation, and action. In P. J. Lang, R. F. Simons, & M. T. Balaban (Eds.), *Attention and orienting: Sensory and motivational processes.* Hillsdale, NJ: Lawrence Erlbaum Associates.

Lang, P. J., Fitzsimmons, J. R., Bradley, M. M., Cuthbert, B. N., & Scott, J. (1996). *Processing emotional pictures: Differential activation in primary visual cortex.* Poster session presented at the 2nd annual Functional Mapping of the Human Brain conference, Boston, MA.

Lang, P. J., Gilmore, R., Cuthbert, B. N., & Bradley, M. M. (1996, October). *Inside picture processing: Emotional modulation of ERPs from the cortical surface.* Paper presented at the Society for Psychophysiological Research, Toronto, Canada.

Lang, P. J., Greenwald, M. K., Bradley, M. M., & Hamm, A. O. (1993). Looking at pictures: Evaluative, facial, visceral, and behavioral responses. *Psychophysiology, 16,* 495–512.

Newhagen, J. E., & Reeves, B. (1992). The evening's bad news: Effects of compelling negative television news images on memory. *Journal of Communication, 42*(2), 25–41.

Osgood, C., Succi, G., & Tannenbaum, P. (1957). *The measurement of meaning.* Urbana, IL: University of Illinois.

Percy, L., & Rossiter, J. R. (1992). Advertising stimulus effects: A review. *Journal of Current Issues and Research and Advertising, 14,* 75–90.

Potter, R. F., & Lang, A. (1996). *Arousing messages: Reaction time, capacity, encoding.* Paper presented at the annual meeting of the Association for Education in Journalism and Mass Communication, Anaheim, CA.

Reeves, B., Lang, A., Thorson, E., & Rothschild, M. (1985). Emotional television scenes and hemispheric specialization. *Human Communication Research, 15*(4), 493–508.

Reeves, B., Thorson, E., Rothschild, M., McDonald, D., Hirsch, J., & Goldstein, R. (1985). Attention to television: Intrastimulus effects of movement and scene changes on alpha variation over time. *International Journal of Neuroscience, 25,* 241–255.

Reichert, T., Heckler, S. E., & Jackson, S. (2001). The effects of sexual social marketing appeals on cognitive processing and persuasion. *Journal of Advertising, 30*(1), 13–27.

Tan, A. (1986). *Mass communication theories and research.* New York: Macmillan.

Thorson, E., Christ, W. G., & Caywood, C. (1991). Effects of issue-image strategies, attack and support appeals, music and visual content in political commercials. *Journal of Broadcasting and Electronic Media, 35*(4), 465–486.

Thorson, E., & Lang, A. (1992). The effects of television videographics and lecture familiarity on adult cardiac orienting responses and memory. *Communication Research, 19*(3), 346–369.

Wise, K., & Lang, A. (2001, May). *Cardiac orienting and recognition for text appearing on a computer screen.* Paper presented at the annual meeting of the International Communication Association, Washington, DC.

Yoon, K., Bolls, P., & Lang, A. (1998). The effects of arousal on liking and believability of commercials. *Journal of Marketing Communication, 4,* 101–114.

Chapter 7

Sex(haustion) Sells: Marketing in a Saturated Mediascape

Collin Gifford Brooke

Syracuse University

Much like comedy or dress styles, advertisements age rapidly. A successful marketing campaign may indeed earn its company an initial competitive advantage, but that advantage fades quickly unless it is translated into brand loyalty. Advertising is based on fashion in the broadest sense, and as such, is subject to a combination of competitors' imitation and entropy. In the absence of a monopoly, the fundamental marketing challenge facing any company is to distinguish itself from its competitors, however momentarily. Faced with literally dozens of choices in some cases, advertising must provide consumers with some rationale for choosing one product rather than another, particularly when so little distinction exists among the products being advertised.

If this weren't enough, consumers are more sophisticated in their approach to visual texts than ever before. According to Rushkoff (2000), the relationship between marketers and their consumers is best understood as a "race," and this is in sharp contrast to the unidirectional manipulation and deception traditionally attributed to advertisers. The more spectacle that we are exposed to, the less spectacle itself affects us. The more technologically sophisticated the images become, the less impressed we are with images that don't push that envelope. Our mediascape fills with advertising at an unprecedented rate, and we are increasingly desensitized to the messages marketed at us.

Certainly advertisers have not stood still. In our credit-dominated economy, we provide companies with overwhelming amounts of data simply by virtue of spending money. The information available from our credit companies and vendors themselves can be compiled on a scope and at a rate that was inconceivable not so long ago. The broadcast model of marketing is quickly giving way to an era of pinpoint psychographics (see Rushkoff, 2000), a surprisingly accurate account of our income levels, attitudes toward spending, and market preferences. Relationship marketing is an advertiser's dream come true, translating the habits of our daily lives into an increasingly precise, individually targeted marketing plan that very nearly executes itself.

Despite the level of sophistication at both ends of the marketing equation, or perhaps because of it, analyses of advertising often cling to antiquated notions of how marketing functions. We are quick to dismiss advertisers as crass manipulators, and advertising itself as base deception. Nowhere is this lack of critical sophistication more apparent than in the truism, repeated in countless student essays and routinely appearing in local television news features, that "sex sells." A cliché that benefits from the fact that it would be impossible to verify or disprove, the idea that "sex sells," that sexual imagery somehow makes advertising more effective, is very nearly a given, not unlike the popular perception of subliminal advertising (see Twitchell, 1996). However, this cliché glosses over the use of sexual imagery, use that has changed considerably throughout the history of advertising, in a way that retards our understanding of advertising as a whole.

In this chapter, I borrow from Benjamin (1968) the notion of *aura* in an attempt to describe both the process by which "sex sells" and also a more nuanced account of how sexual imagery functions (or fails to function) in our contemporary mediascape. For Benjamin, the idea of aura is intimately tied to technology (specifically in terms of its ability to reproduce a given work), and I argue that recent developments in information technology are shaping our responses to spectacle-based advertising, including the use of sexually charged material. There is some reason to believe that these changes are not simply fashionable, that they are instead part of a larger change in our relationship to consumption.

ADVERTISING IN A POST-DESIRE ECONOMY

This strategy for exorcizing [sic] the body by means of the signs of sex, for conjuring away desire through the overkill of its staging, is a good deal more efficient than good old repression founded on taboo.(Baudrillard, 1992, p. 23)

As Twitchell (1996) noted in *Adcult USA*, "the idea that advertising creates artificial desires rests on a profound ignorance of human nature, on the hazy feeling that there existed some halcyon era of noble savages with purely natural needs" (p. 12). The platitude that "sex sells" operates as a variation on this theme: Sex in advertising creates false desires by linking the product to the seemingly irresistible image of sexuality. Critics such as Taflinger (1996) based this hypothesis on a distinction between intellectual and/or cultural appeals and those appeals that target our baser, physical instincts, such as self-preservation and sexual desire. In such cases, the "false desire" for the product is metonymically linked to an instinctive desire. As a model of the way sex functions within advertising, this explanation has many problems, not the least of which is its tendency to treat the relationship between nature and culture as uncomplicated. Setting those problems aside for the time being, however, we must consider this model in the context of our contemporary mediascape.

To say that advertisements age rapidly is to anthropomorphize a particular quality of these texts, one that, following Benjamin, I want to describe as the *aura* of advertisements. Although I continue my focus on sexually charged advertising, it is important to recognize that the idea that "sex sells" might more properly be understood as "spectacle sells." That is, sex is certainly an obvious example of the spectacle found in advertising, but it is not the only one, and I would argue that the aura I describe here is just as relevant to the Taco Bell chihuahua as it is to supermodels. Sex is simply the most familiar subset of what I would call *"spectacle advertising."*

Benjamin's (1968) discussion of aura takes place in the essay "The Work of Art in the Age of Mechanical Reproduction," where he discussed the effects of rapidly developing reproductive technologies (photography, cinema) on art. According to Benjamin, the aura of a work of art is connected to its "unique existence," a quality threatened by reproduction:

> [T]hat which withers in the age of mechanical reproduction is the aura of the work of art. [...] One might generalize by saying: the technique of reproduction detaches the reproduced object from the domains of tradition. By making many reproductions it substitutes a plurality of copies for a unique existence. (p. 221)

Authenticity and reproducibility are inversely related for Benjamin; those forms of cultural expression that rely on reproducibility do not partake of aura in the same way that the work of art does. For Benjamin, this "emancipates" the work of art from its dependence on ritual; "instead of being based on ritual, [the total function of art] begins to be based on another practice—politics" (p. 224).

To a certain degree, however, Benjamin jumped the gun. It may seem odd to consider applying Benjamin's traditional aesthetic to advertising, expression that is "designed for reproducibility," but I would contend that Benjamin errs in establishing a stark contrast between authenticity and reproducibility. His assumption here suffers from the same mistake that is glossed over in the platitude that sex sells; it abstracts the text/work from its reception. The first time that a potential consumer is faced with spectacle in advertising, it does not matter that millions of other copies of that spectacle appear in other magazines or on other televisions. That first encounter carries with it some measure of aura; it attracts and holds the attention of the viewer. However, it also fades with time, as each individual viewer sees it subsequently. As the image is reproduced *for the individual*, it loses its aura for that person. She or he becomes desensitized.

The epigraph for this portion, from Baudrillard's (1992) *Transparency of Evil*, suggests another angle from which to consider the life cycle of the aura. The cultural category of taboo is another source of aura, one that gains its power both from reinforcement and attempted transgression. When Jenny McCarthy posed for a series of Candies shoe advertisements sitting on a toilet with her underwear around her ankles, the taboo nature of the advertisements attracted its fair share of attention, but it also weakened the taboo being violated, both in terms of the ads themselves and any subsequent use of that motif. To put it another way, advertisements that accrue aura from violating taboos both desensitize the viewer to the violation and weaken the taboo that they violate.

To say that advertisements age, then, is to acknowledge the diachronic character of their reception by an audience, and to include the notion of aura as a quality of those texts, understanding it as a variable rather than an absolute. There is another dimension to aura, one that I attempt to detail in the next section, but for the moment, I want to lay some groundwork for that discussion. The idea of aura puts the notion that "sex sells" to the question; in short, it reveals the cliché for the unsupportable generalization that is. These sorts of generalizations run the risk of what Morris (1990), following Hall (1981), called *cultural dopism*, the tendency to perceive audiences as "distracted, absent-minded, insouciant, vague, flighty, skimming from image to image" (p. 24). Cultural dopism, a position roughly analogous to what Davison (1983) called the *third person effect* in mass media theory, assumes certain qualities (or their lack) on the parts of nonacademic audiences, regardless of context. Such audiences, in this view, are incapable of the "contemplation" practiced by academic cultural theorists, and are therefore susceptible to the machinations and manipulations of advertisers.

Morris suggested that taking the opposite tack, arguing that "consumers are not 'cultural dopes' but active, critical users of mass culture" (p. 21), has been enabling for cultural studies, but it nevertheless reproduces the logic of cultural dopism. In its efforts to generalize about the audience, cultural dopism overgeneralizes. The most "distracted" viewer is capable of disarming sophisticated advertising, and the most "contemplative" academic is equally capable of being seduced by that same advertising (see, e.g., chap. 8 of Twitchell, 1999). The problem with this complexity is that it saps analysis of its critical force; any argument that acknowledges the full range of capabilities possessed by consumers will not be able to make definitive claims. Morris offered one account of the problems we face, however, when we ignore consumers' reality:

> If a cultural dopism is being enunciatively performed and (valorized) in a discourse that tries to contest it, then the argument in fact *cannot* move on, but can only retrieve its point of departure as "banality" (a word pop theorists don't normally use) in the negative sense. (p. 24)

Cultural dopism effectively becomes a tautology; regardless of which side of this attitude a critic starts with, and the assumption is inevitably recycled by the conclusion.

Deprived of arguments that assert either a morally suspect, complicit audience or one that is composed of Twitchell's "noble savages" being victimized by evil advertising, where can we turn? The alternative that I pursue here understands the activity of advertising as competition in an attention economy, which is to say that advertisements compete for our attention in an analogous way to products and services competing for our money. Approaching advertising as one element among many in an economy of attention implies a number of things. First among them is the fact that we should bracket off any concerns with the motives and intentions of advertisers themselves. Even were their motives not as straightforward and explicit as they are, advertisements are like any text—their reception cannot be predicted with any accuracy. A second implication is one that audience can play only a subordinate role in our analysis. There is no "everyman" by which we can accurately gauge the effect of a given advertisement, much less its effect when it enters the mediascape. Just as there is a vast range of sophistication when it comes to audience, an equally broad range of possibilities makes relying on audience response impossible.

Ultimately, I am asking the same question that every marketer asks: How is it that an advertisement can get an audience to pay attention? Faced with two advertisements—one that employs sexual imagery and one that does not—there is little question as to which will attract the first glance of a viewer. But what happens when Pepsi hires Britney Spears and CocaCola responds by signing Christina Aguilera? What happens when a marketing campaign, whether it employs sex as a strategy or not, enters the larger economy where it must compete for attention that, advertisers hope, involves more than a casual glance? These questions cannot be answered through the analysis of individual advertisements, or even the analysis of advertising as a genre, because they are not the only texts to compete for our attention. In a culture increasingly defined by the remote control, advertisements compete not only with each other, but also with the whole range of choices available to consumers, with other channels, not to mention other media.

It is certainly possible to become discouraged at the thought of making any substantive claims with respect to advertising, given the overwhelming amount of competition that it faces. This, in fact, is the same dilemma facing advertisers themselves:

> Uncertainty is understood to be a part of the entire system. [...] Marketers know that consumers may be able to faithfully redescribe an advertisement, but neither name or [sic] use the product. This is the reason for the creation of more and more elaborate systems of "monitoring, measurement and modelling [sic]" which connect television, to store, to user, to product. (Sawchuck, 1984, p. 95)

Just as advertisers redouble their efforts to chart and demonstrate the effectiveness of their marketing, it is possible for us to ask what it is that advertising does that obliges us to pay attention. This is inevitably an interpretive enterprise, one that can only surmise why consumers *have paid* attention, why particular campaigns appear to have succeeded and other have failed.

In the next section of this chapter, I offer an analysis of a particular strategy, one that signals a change in the way that certain advertisements ask us to pay attention. But first, I want to prepare for that analysis with some related claims about what I am calling both our contemporary mediascape and the economy of attention within which advertisements operate. It is no accident that the work of advertisers is more difficult now than it has ever been. It has become commonplace for cultural critics to note that we now live in an age characterized by information overload. As Shenk (1997) noted in *Data Smog*,

> With information production not only increasing, but *accelerating*, there is no sign that processing will ever catch up. [...] And as we enjoy the many fruits of this burgeoning information civilization, we also have to learn to compensate for the new and permanent side effects of what sociologists, in an academic understatement, call a "message dense" society. (p. 30)

But information overload is in some ways a nonissue; those who have experienced the explosion of information must adapt, certainly, but for many, it is simply a fait accompli.

Other than making it more difficult for marketers to distinguish their products, how has this information explosion affected us? I would suggest that we now operate in a mediascape characterized by a shift in the fundamental nature of desire, that we are living in a postdesire economy. I do not mean by this that as postmodern subjects, we have ceased to desire. Nor am I suggesting that our economy of production has altered substantially. Rather, I am claiming that information overload, and the significant portion of this phenomenon fueled by advertising, creates in our attention economy what Zizek (1991) described as a *deadlock of desire*. In *For They Know Not What They Do*, Zizek articulated this deadlock:

> Desire is never aimed at some object but is always desire "squared"—the subject finds in himself a multitude of heterogeneous, even mutually exclusive, desires ... the question with which he is thus faced is: Which desire should I choose? Which desire should I desire? (p. 131)

In its incessant attempt to attract our attention, marketing no longer operates at a level of restriction sufficient to guarantee success. Cross-medium and market advertising, sponsorships, and product placements have all contributed to an attention economy that is saturated with appeals to our desires. To return to Twitchell briefly, it can no longer be a question of real and false desires, if indeed it ever was. As Rickert (2001) observed, "when the symbolic order no longer provides the coordinates for desire, our consititution as subjects of desire is properly transformed." The deadlock of desire (and the desire I reference in the phrase *post-desire*) is a deadlock of what we might call *first-order desire*, where the choice is between possessing a particular object or not. The diffusion of advertising throughout the mediascape makes this first-order desire impossible, as Rickert explained:

> The existential crisis of the subject is no longer which object to choose (from the multitude of other competing objects) that will provide its meaningful, magical comforts, but rather how can I choose now, or feel secure in my choice? The objects for which we so brazenly create narratives of desire have achieved their revenge—alive with magical meaning, their commodity sacredness has suffused the entire realm of objects. Every choice is partial, provisional, potentially the wrong choice—a better object always lurks around the corner, or we have ourselves become unable to make a choice that identifies us as the proper desiring/desired subject. (p. 2)

This deadlock is the flip side of Rushkoff's "arms race" (2000) that marketers and consumers unknowingly engage in. The pervasiveness of Adcult raises the stakes for advertisers who must combat both their competitors and the growing sophistication and indifference of their targeted audience. But it also affects consumers, for whom choices become increasingly complex and difficult.

The current interest in what is called *branding* is one response to this escalation (see Gad, 2000; Gobé, 2001; Thomson, 1998; Todreas, 1999). Alluding both to product brands and to the permanent scarification of cattle, the process by which producers create and reinforce brand positioning and familiarity is the subject of many recent books and studies. From our perspective, however, brand loyalty may best be described as a euphemism for "consumer fatigue"; what corporations perceive as a positive attraction and attachment to their brands may in fact be a sign of consumer indifference. The ability to identify oneself as a "Coke drinker" or "Toyota driver" may be less a matter of loyalty than a matter of releasing oneself from the burden of choosing from among the myriad other products clamoring for our attention and money. We might see the ill-fated 1985 release (and subsequent withdrawal) of "New Coke," as a cautionary tale about what happens when choice is reintroduced into a brand.

And this, ultimately, is what I mean by describing our economy as post-desire. It is not that we have ceased to desire—such a cessation would be nearly impossible—but rather that our contemporary mediascape has effected an inversion of desire. We desire more, but what we desire more of is *less*, less noise, less choices, less burden. Almost every articulation of information overload carries with it a concurrent call for what would initially be *more* information, but in the form of filtering, a means for us to prioritize the information we already have, to free us from the Sisyphean task of filtering it ourselves. In this sense, these analyses parallel (and often overlap) with our status as consumers. We want information that will free us from information; analogously, our desire for less is no less commodified than what I am calling our *first-order desire*. We still attempt to achieve and satisfy our desire through commodities, but we want those commodities to free us from the work of desire.

I hope to demonstrate in the next section that we have not drifted as far from our topic as it may seem. That "sex sells" is a truism for the era of first-order desire; sexual desire is only ever satisfied temporarily, and when advertisements appeal to sex, the desire evoked cannot be satisfied. Is it possible for the sexual appeal in advertising to survive the transition to a postdesire economy? Yes and no. In the next section, I offer one model of sexual appeal that has enjoyed recent success in television advertising, but in the section that follows, I argue that recent developments in information technology have begun to suggest limitations for this particular strategy.

YOU GOTTA GET THIS LOOK: SEX(HAUSTION) SELLS

> What is sought today is not so much health, which is an organic equilibrium, as an ephemeral, hygienic and promotional radiance from the body—much more a performance than an ideal state. In terms of fashion and appearances, what we seek is less beauty or attractiveness than the right *look*. (Baudrillard, 1992, p. 23)

In 2001, in anticipation of its 15th anniversary of advertising during the Super Bowl, Pepsi announced a cross-platform promotional campaign. Users of the Yahoo! web site would be offered the chance to choose their favorite Pepsi commercial from the past 15 years, and the commercial that received the most votes would be broadcast during the Super Bowl. As it turns out, the commercial garnering the most support was one titled "Two Kids" from 1991, featuring supermodel Cindy Crawford. At first glance, this choice might seem to contradict the trajectory of my argument thus far—who better than one of the archetypal supermodels to defend the currency and potency of sexual appeal in advertising? While "Two Kids" was

indeed a "break" for Cindy Crawford in that it made her a household name
for a national audience, the commercial itself actually inaugurates the trend
that I'm discussing in this essay.

"Two Kids" opens out in the country, in an unnamed heartland state. In
the middle of this farmland, two preteen boys are leaning against a fence
watching the day pass. Up drives a red sports car, and out steps Crawford,
clad in a bikini top and cut-off shorts. She approaches a nearby vending machine, selects a Pepsi, and the two boys are struck almost wordless. The
camera begins a slow pan up the length of Crawford's body, and the boys
express their admiration, not for the supermodel herself, but for the "new
can" design that Pepsi is debuting in the commercial.

This commercial operates on many levels, most of which are readily apparent to even the casual viewer. The viewer is interpolated as male, and he
is encouraged to make the connection between Crawford and Pepsi, and in
this sense, the commercial is simply one more in a long line of ads that take
advantage of sexualized imagery. However, "Two Kids" is also an example
of what Rushkoff described as *wink* marketing, where the audience is invited to be "in on the joke." In this case, the unsophisticated boys notice a
can of soda rather than an obviously rich supermodel, and we are encouraged to share a chuckle at their oversight (or undersight, as it were). These
two interpretations combine to form a third, implicit level of interpretation.
We pay more attention to Crawford, but the advertisement implies that perhaps it is our urban cynicism, an attitude that these country boys do not
share, that affects our reception of the scene. Rather than asking us to identify with the boys, this commercial consciously introduces a gap between
our perception and theirs. Perhaps there is some homespun wisdom in the
boys' observation, and there is something so special about Pepsi that it is
worth our attention despite Crawford's presence.

Whether or not the product itself is special, this particular strategy certainly has been. It has produced a number of imitators, including several
commercials still active at the time of this chapter; Taco Bell, Burger King,
and Raisin Bran are all currently running ads that feature male consumers
choosing their products over attractive women. Nor should we overlook
the "classic" ad featuring female office workers who gather during to stare
at a male construction worker during his break drinking Diet Coke. There
is, of course, a sense in which these commercials simply represent an escalation on the part of the marketers, an attempt to appeal to an audience that is
increasingly jaded and more likely to appreciate irony than a straightforward appeal to sex. But as I indicated in the last section, I think that this
strategy is symptomatic of a larger shift in the sensibility of consumers;
these commercials are more than attempts to catch up with the audience.

One of the issues postponed in the previous section was the question
of aura, and how it can be achieved in a medium that, with VCRs, is al-

most infinitely reproducible. In other words, how can any image affect us or induce our desires when we are constantly bombarded by visual stimulation? The key is what Benjamin described as the work of art's *unapproachability*, the very quality that appears to be frustrated by widespread replication. In the case of a painting, for example, it was at one time simply the fact that the painting existed in a private collection, was displayed at a museum on a limited basis, and/or could only be viewed at a specific juncture in space and time. With the development of sophisticated reproductive methods, artworks' unapproachability must be achieved in different ways. Much of the world's "great art" is available in poster form, and so their aura is recuperated in different ways, such as the prices that such art fetches in international auctions. The aura of a Monet comes not from the beauty of the art itself, but rather the possession of the material object, the image itself having been reproduced and made accessible to anyone willing to visit a museum gift shop or to perform a rudimentary web search.

In the case of digital media, however, the difference between the original footage of "Two Kids" and video of the 2001 Super Bowl is negligible at best. There is no "original commercial," no restricted economy within which an alleged original might recuperate some sort of aura. Typically, this is true of any mass cultural artifact, or rather any artifact, if Baudrillard's analysis of the vacated categories of the aesthetic, political, and social is to be believed. From the perspective of the marketers, however, this is old news; the very process of creating a buzz for a product is not based on the notion of restricting access but rather the saturation both of the market and the minds of consumers. Pepsi wants us to think of its products when we think about getting a soda. In this way, marketing aspires to category dominance (Twitchell, 1996), the position of companies like Kleenex and Xerox, whose brand names are quite literally synonymous with the products they sell, despite their lack of monopolies.

I would contend that this is also a species of aura, albeit not the same type that Benjamin described. It is an aura that relies on a product's availability, rather than its unapproachability. We might find evidence for this brand of aura in the explosion both of talk shows in the last 10 years and more recently of "reality television." In many ways, celebrity once followed the model of aura proposed by Benjamin, where access to celebrity (and celebrities) was strictly controlled. Now, celebrity is less a matter of a particular talent than it is the time to respond to open casting calls for reality shows or the willingness to air dirty laundry in front of a syndicated audience. Despite the occasional backlash, what once was vilified as tabloid journalism now has multiple cable networks devoted to the practice and even occasionally garners critical acclaim (in the case of shows such as VH1's *Behind the Music*). As an audience, we have made the transition from celebrities whose aura came precisely because of their distance from us to celebrity (in general) whose aura comes instead from the perception that we might experience it ourselves.

In the case of "Two Kids," Pepsi dramatizes this transition, contrasting the unapproachability of the wealthy supermodel and the constant availability of Pepsi. But this is true of any commercial that relies on sexual imagery; the unapproachability of sex evokes desire in an audience that marketers hope consumers fulfill by turning to the product whose availability the advertisement also communicates. In this sense, consumption provides the missing step in the enthymeme advanced by the commercial. We see a supermodel and desire him or her, the model is drinking Pepsi, and we know that the model is unavailable to us, so we complete the circuit of desire by settling for the product as an approximation of our frustrated desire. The difference in "Two Kids," and in advertisements based on a similar strategy, is that we are presented with a closed circuit, an enthymeme whose missing step has already been filled in by the characters in the commercial. The protagonists of this advertisement do our desiring for us; these advertisements present us with a complete marketing–consumption cycle, which raises the question of where we as an audience fit into that cycle.

Or, to put it another way, what is the point of an advertisement that simulates the very evocation and consummation of desire rather than including us directly within that process? When the mediascape bombards us with choices, a strategy like this is almost a relief. These advertisements offer us the position of *having desired* without actually expending the energy that desire requires in an age of media saturation. In such advertisements, it is not the sex that is selling us, but rather the opportunity to avoid the inevitable compromise that decades of sexually charged advertisements have led us to expect. By closing the circuit, these commercials vacate sex as a category or an object of desire; how else can we explain ads where the position of the (sexual) object is occupied by celebrities like Bob Dole (Viagra and Pepsi), Ruth Westheimer (Clairol), and green M&Ms ("What is it about the green ones?"). We are so accustomed to the narrative of desire suggested by sexually provocative advertisements that these advertisements need no longer provoke. In fact, as the strategy behind "Two Kids" suggests, it clarifies matters considerably if they don't even bother. It is enough (and perhaps even advantageous) that someone else desires the object.

Baudrillard (1992) argued that our age of simulation encourages us to forgo the pursuit of beauty in favor of what he termed the *look*, the performance of attractiveness rather than its achievement. In an analogous fashion, these advertisements offer us the performance of desire rather than the actuality. For consumers who are exhausted by the endless choices available to them, desire and choice itself results in the deadlock discussed in the last section. The answer to this deadlock, the way that (as

Rickert noted) we can "feel secure in [our] choice," is to embrace those products that other people have already chosen. It is a matter of appearing fashionable without going to the trouble of determining what is in fashion. When recent Old Navy commercials, for example, tell us that "You gotta get this look," they are marketing their clothes only indirectly. They are actually selling us relief from having to figure out what the "look" is; they are selling us less. In this way, the notion of less has acquired its own aura. But I would argue that the traditional media that we think of when we think of advertising (television, magazines, billboards) are not the native habitat for this marketing strategy. In the final section of this chapter, I suggest that this is a strategy whose effectiveness is most evident when we turn to more recent information technologies.

CUSTOMERS WHO HAVE BOUGHT THIS BOOK
HAVE ALSO BOUGHT …

> I hate this supermarket/ But I have to say it makes me think/ A hundred mineral waters/ It's fun to guess which ones are safe to drink/ Two hundred brands of cookies/ 87 kinds of chocolate chip/ They say that choice is freedom/ I'm so free it drives me to the brink.
>   (Joe Jackson, "It's All Too Much" from *Laughter and Lust* album)

The strategy embodied by "Two Kids" is significant enough on its own, but its most recent occasion, Pepsi's cross-platform marketing campaign, introduces another layer of interest for our purposes in this essay. While thousands of people visited Yahoo! to cast their votes for this and other Pepsi commercials, pundits and commentators found that this campaign didn't exactly represent the cutting edge of what is called fusion advertising. Green (2001) of Dataquest dismissed the campaign as "fake inclusion and weirdly offensive," regarding the "choice" of commercials as an insult to the intelligence of consumers. The idea that consumers would be interested in viewing QuickTime videos of the commercials, and then choosing one to see during the Super Bowl, does seem to overestimate the amount of fascination that these commercials have for the audience. The idea that we would want to choose the method of our manipulation seems counterintuitive, but as I hope to demonstrate, there is a sense to this strategy.

That sense has little to do, however, with the original and initial attempts to market on the Internet. When the World Wide Web first entered the mediascape as a fully fledged medium in its own right, it represented a new frontier in countless ways. The response from advertisers was comfortingly predictable. First-generation marketing web sites were built, and URLs included in print and television advertisements, according to the same "gee-whiz" sense of novelty that fueled the expansion of the web in the first place. In addition to URL placement (and spam advertising over email and Usenet groups), the first wave of marketing took the form of banner advertising.

Banner advertising operates according to the structure established for more traditional media. In magazines and on television, content is interrupted by advertisement according to fairly standardized percentages (a 30-minute situation comedy, for example, typically contains 7 minutes worth of commercials). Banner advertising follows this model, allowing advertisers to purchase a minor percentage of the screen real estate on a given page. Unlike advertising in traditional media, web-based advertising can be verified according to "click-throughs," or the number of people who click on the banner, and subsequently visit the site being advertised. To click on a banner, users must first notice them, and thus this first-wave of Internet advertising relied on the same visual logic as other media.

However, this type of advertising suffers from the same problems with aura as its analogues in other media; viewers become desensitized to banners quickly. And again, unlike commercials in more traditional media, just as the success of banner can be charted, so too can its failures. According to studies by Nielsen (Nielsen, 1997; Nielsen, 2000), click-through rates have steadily decreased from 2% (1995) to 0.5% (1998) to 0.2% in May 2000. Although the failures of banner advertising have been complicated—Pagendarm and Schaumburg (2001) suggesed that navigation style has been insufficiently considered as a factor in these studies—the fact remains that this sort of advertising, while it may not be any less successful than another, can be precisely quantified in its failure. Faced with exact numbers of how many users *don't* click through a banner, it may be more comforting for advertisers to simply return to traditional media where they are blissfully ignorant of their failure.

Why don't banner advertisements work? There are a number of reasons, many of which rely on the differences between the Internet and traditional media. Television viewers and magazine readers are conditioned to expect advertisements, and content producers in those media have responded to those expectations, pacing the content to allow for commercial interruptions. Moreover, viewers can surf channels and readers can turn the page; a certain amount of our exposure is involuntary, but we do exert a measure of control over that exposure. When the majority of web users access pages via Internet connections that are less than instantaneous, banner advertisements (particularly those that are animated or that come from banner ad services and reside on another server) are perceived not only as interruptions, but as obstacles as well. Another advantage of the web, the relatively low costs of publication, proves to be a disadvantage to banner advertising; it is more difficult for a user, even when that person acknowledges the "necessity" of television commercials, to accept the download delays associated with banners. It is no accident that the formula for online success has changed for particular genres; a search engine like Google, although it does advertise the scope of its indexing, appeals to users specifically through the lack of advertising on its search page. If anything, the desire for less is more protracted on the Internet, and banner advertising, which flies in the face of that desire, seems doomed to long-term failure.

There are online models of marketing that have enjoyed success, however. Amazon Books, arguably the most successful e-commerce site in the brief history of the Internet, provides a major example, and it is from this site that the title for this section comes. When a user looks up a book on Amazon, the description of that book comes with purchase options, industry reviews, and all of the elements that the average consumer would expect. But another feature also appears, one that may represent Amazon's most significant contribution to the growing field of e-commerce. Users are informed that people who have purchased this book have also purchased other books, and the site lists several. From the perspective of a consumer, this is a notable feature, particularly if one is interested a field of knowledge or authorial style or genre. Just as one would see and scan the titles of books that surround your choice in a store, this feature gives prospective buyers a chance to browse the shelf, as it were. Additionally, this browsing is not conditioned by alphabetical order or the whim of stockpeople; the connections between your book and these others are motivated by other consumers. Amazon records purchases, and each time we look up a book, we are treated to a glimpse of the portion of that database that pertains most immediately to our particular interests.

Many of the other features of the Amazon site are variations on this theme. Those consumers willing to identify their professional affiliations are tracked as well; it is possible to see what members of a given academic department at MIT, for example, are reading right now. Frequent visitors are encouraged to submit their own evaluations of books, reviews that themselves can be evaluated by future visitors and whose authors are ranked (and marketed). Users are encouraged to compile reading lists for their interests, which are then broadcast to users who purchase books from those lists. They can also set up wish lists and email them to potential gift-givers. The purchase cycle now includes a page where you can email friends a 10% discount on the books that you've just bought; if your friends avail themselves of the discount, the value of the discount is also credited to your next purchase. While interactivity was the buzzword for Internet development for some time, Amazon has put its own spin on the idea. The interactivity at Amazon is built around the community of consumers, and in many ways, it's achieved a life of its own. As Moulthrop (2000) observed, Amazon is perhaps the one store that gains credibility by permitting (and even encouraging) negative evaluations of its merchandise; they "can afford to unsell the books that line its virtual shelves" (p. 273). There are countless reviews of books that attempt to dissuade potential customers.

The success of Amazon, therefore, is not about books; nor is it the fact that the choice they offer exceeds the capacities of a physical bookstore. The value added by Amazon is grounded in the community that these features both serve and reinforce. Every time that a user follows one of these links, and every time that the site "unsells" a book, Amazon is building consumer capital. And they are doing this in a way that seems to invert the traditional composition of advertisement. If the first advertisements provided information cast in the language and appearance of promotion, Amazon's site features do the opposite, promoting their site in the guise of providing consumers with information. Amazon sets up what is called a *feed-forward* loop, the value of which comes from being able to follow (and reinforce) tendencies established by previous consumers. This strategy is entirely appropriate for an era of second-order desire; Amazon is offering customers the option of choosing books according to statistical patterns of consumption, generated from the customers who have chosen before them. Why browse for a book of a particular genre, style, or subject when you can get the book right away and enjoy the position of *having browsed* without expending the energy?

I hope that the parallel I am drawing between Amazon's "service" and the strategy behind commercials like "Two Kids" is becoming apparent. Designed for a medium that encourages spectacle, "Two Kids" can only hint at the method that Amazon achieves to perfection; in essence, "Two Kids" is a clumsy attempt to start the kind of feed-forward loop that Amazon provides. More recent examples have grown more sophisticated. Raisin Bran's slogan ("Breakfast is Back") asserts a trend that doesn't exist outside of the advertisement; Old Navy's "look" that we "gotta get" is an implicit claim that others before us have already confirmed the style's status. To buy into these commercials has little to do with spectacle. Instead, they are asking to buy into the trends they advocate, the possibility that consumers before us have already done our choosing for us. But this is a method of promotion that can only be achieved in a medium that combines the point-of-sale access of the World Wide Web with the information gathering and organizing abilities of a database; our vague grasp of the site mechanics at Amazon, the way it tracks our purchases and records them, is what lends the site and therefore its recommendations some validity. In this sense, "Two Kids" is an example of what Johnson (1997) identified as a "message waiting for [its] medium to come" (p. 36), a strategy that could only be implemented imperfectly in a broadcast medium like television. In short, what "Two Kids" and other commercials like it hint at is the possibility of "information agents."

Without delving too specifically into the field of artificial intelligence, information agents represent one of the most recent ideals of that field. According to Perry (1996), "The agent technology is being researched to 'engage and help all types of end users' with such tasks as 'information filtering, information retrieval, mail management, meeting scheduling, selection of books, movies, music, and so forth'" (par. 2). Information agents are programs that, ideally, would anticipate our wants and needs in a given area, based on pattern analysis of our previous behavior. Hendler (1999) explained the conditions for information agents in the following way:

> A good Internet agent needs these same capabilities. It must be *communicative*: able to understand your goals, preferences and constraints. It must be *capable*: able to take options rather than simply provide advice. It must be *autonomous*: able to act without the user being in control the whole time. And it should be *adaptive*: able to learn from experience about both its tasks and about its users preferences. (par. 11)

Information agents, in other words, represent a prosthesis of individual choice. If agents that can anticipate our desires automate the process by which we make our choices as consumers, we will have fully entered the era of second-order desire. We will have achieved the security in our choices that Rickert (2001) questioned, by occupying the position of *having chosen* without ever having to choose.

CONCLUSION(S)

If we are not the ones actually doing the choosing as consumers, then spectacle advertising is pointless, like marketing to people with no influence or control over disposable income. Marketing may attract my attention all it wishes, but if I have software agents making my decisions, that attention will never be translated into purchases. However, this is not an overnight change, despite the success of sites like Amazon. It could be argued that the book market is one that has been quite resistant (although not completely) to spectacle advertising. Furthermore, much of our culture is based on spectacle, and this is not likely to change soon; it would be the equivalent of abandoning the genre of the movie trailer in favor of more extensive movie reviews and ignoring the pleasure that spectacle brings. Finally, the impossibility of verifying the success of a print or television advertisement is a strength, for its lack of success cannot be verified either. It is likely that spectacle advertising carries with it enough inertia to guarantee its continued health.

And yet, the unparalleled explosion of the Internet, a medium designed (initially) for the storage and dissemination of information, suggests the model that this chapter elaborates. Consumers are not cultural dopes for the most part; in markets where all of our options are promoted through spectacle, promotional success depends less on spectacle than it does on the absence of alternatives. And the success of sites like Amazon and Google suggests that consumers are more than happy to pursue alternatives to spectacle when they exist. These alternatives rely on a different sort of aura from that produced by spectacle, an aura that depends on the availability of the information sought. In the case of Google, information is immediately available, rather than mediated through banner advertisements and complicated layout or design.

Such immediacy has its price, and often that price is mediation, but mediation that is invisible to the consumer. This is why we miss the point if we disparage Pepsi for the strategy of encouraging consumers to "pick their poison," to decide how they will be manipulated. In a very concrete sense, information agents will do just that. In many cases, however, the decision process is one that we will not have access to, as consumers or marketers. While we will benefit from the perception that our choices are immediate (and unmediated), the fact of mediation will remain. At least part of the future of marketing must include an understanding of this brand of promotion, an understanding of how to intervene in the processes by which information agents make consumers' choices for them. Advertising in some spheres of the market will have to incorporate the knowledge of how to appeal to information agents, knowledge that is much more complex than the cliché of trotting out a scantily clad supermodel or pop singer and handing him or her a can of Pepsi. Advertisements age rapidly, but advertising must age more quickly, if it is to keep up with technology and engage future generations of consumers.

REFERENCES

Baudrillard, J. (1992). *The transparency of evil: Essays on extreme phenomena*. London: Verso.

Benjamin, W. (1968). The work of art in the age of mechanical reproduction. In Hannah Arendt (Trans.), *Illuminations: Essays and reflections*. New York: Shocken.

Davison, W. P. (1983). The third-person effect in communication. *Public Opinion Quarterly, 50*, 1–15.

Gad, T. (2000). *4-D branding: Cracking the corporate code of the network economy*. Upper Saddle River, NJ: Prentice Hall.

Gobé, M. (2001). *Emotional branding: The new paradigm for connecting brands to people*. New York: Allworth.

Green, H. (2001, January). There's no fizz in Pepsi's E-promotion. *Business Week Online*. Retrieved October 15, 2001 from http://www.businessweek.com/technology/content/0101/ ep0122.htm

Hall, S. (1981). Notes on deconstructing "the popular." In R. Samuel (Ed.), *People's history and socialist theory* (pp. 227–239). London: Routledge.

Hendler, J. (1999, March). Is there an intelligent agent in your future? *Nature web matters*. Retrieved October 15, 2001 from http://www.nature.com/nature/webmatters/agents/agents.html

Johnson, S. (1997). *Interface Culture: How new technology transforms the way we create and communicate*. New York: HarperCollins.

Morris, M. (1990). Banality in Cultural Studies. In P. Mellencamp (Ed.), *Logics of television: Essays in cultural criticism* (pp. 14–43). Bloomington: Indiana University Press.

Moulthrop, S. (2000). Error 404: Doubting the web. In A. Herman & T. Swiss (Eds.), *The World Wide Web and contemporary cultural theory* (pp. 259–275). London: Routledge.

Nielsen, J. (1997, September). Why advertising doesn't work on the Web. *Alertbox*. Retrieved October 15, 2001 from http://www.useit.com/alertbox/9709a.html.

Nielsen, J. (2000, May). Methodology weaknesses in Poynter Eyetrack Study. *Alertbox*. Retrieved October 15, 2001 from http://www.useit.com/alertbox/2000514_weaknesses.html

Pagendarm, M., & Schaumburg, H. (2001). Why are users banner-blind? The impact of navigation style on the perception of web banners. *Journal of Digital Information, 2.1*. Retrieved October 15, 2001 from http://jodi.ecs.soton.ac.uk/Articles/v02/i01/Pagendarm/

Perry, L. (1996). Emotionware. *ACM Crossroads, 3.1*. Retrieved October 15, 2001 from http://www.acm.org/crossroads/ xrds3-1/emotware.html

Rickert, T. (2001). *Notes on an economy of undesire*. Unpublished manuscript.

Rushkoff, D. (2000). *Coercion: Why we listen to what they say*. New York: Putnam.

Sawchuck, K. (1984). Semiotics, cybernetics, and the ecstasy of marketing communications. In D. Kellner (Ed.), *Baudrillard: A critical reader* (pp. 89–116). Cambridge, MA and Oxford: Blackwell.

Shenk, D. (1997). *Data smog: Surviving the information glut*. New York: HarperCollins.

Taflinger, R. (1996). *You and me, babe: Sex and advertising*. Retrieved October 15, 2001 from http://www.wsu.edu:8080/ ~taflinge/sex.html

Thomson, K. (1998). *Emotional capital: Capturing hearts and minds to create lasting business success*. Lanham, MD: Business Book Network.

Todreas, T. (1999). *Value creation and branding in television's digital age*. Westport, CT: Quorum Books.

Twitchell, J. (1996). *Adcult USA: The triumph of advertising in American culture*. New York: Columbia University Press.

Twitchell, J. (1999). *Lead us into temptation: The triumph of American materialism*. New York: Columbia University Press.

Zizek, S. (1991). *For they know not what they do: Enjoyment as a political factor*. London: Verso.

Chapter 8

Toward a Theory of Advertising Lovemaps in Marketing Communications: Overdetermination, Postmodern Thought and the Advertising Hermeneutic Circle

Stephen J. Gould

The City University of New York

A *lovemap* is a concept that researchers may use to represent the approach consumers take to their own sexuality. Advertisers may be guided by this concept when creating advertising with sexual themes. I describe it in terms of prior concepts, namely the general and consumer lovemaps, and then go on to develop an extension of these for an advertising lovemap. The *general lovemap* concept comes from the work of John Money (1984, 1986), a renown sexual researcher who has studied the complex and interacting biological, psychological, and social roots of sexual behavior. According to Money (1984, p. 165), this lovemap "carries the program of a person's erotic fantasies and their corresponding practices." Money also determined that individuals at some point in life, usually an early one, develop a basic orientation to sexuality that they carry forward, even as they evolve in response to the environment. Sometimes this lovemap may even be traceable to a single event that made a strong impression.

I carried this concept into the consumer behavior and advertising areas by suggesting that consumers embody and ornament their lovemaps with products, services, and consuming practices, routines, rituals, and symbols (Gould, 1991a, 1992, 1995a). These phenomena comprise what I called a *consumer lovemap*, which may be defined as "including those aspects of the more general lovemap which involve consumption, i.e., the purchase and use of products in attracting a mate, engaging in sexual activity, and developing and maintaining sexual-love relationships" (Gould, 1991a, p. 381). This consumer lovemap is also very much reflective of consumers' general sexual identities and may be related to other aspects of identity, including gender, age, and ethnicity. However, the lovemap should also be viewed more dynamically than the term *identity* connotes because it is not merely static, but also involves change processes of personal development, social interaction, and energy and mood self-regulation (Gould, 1991b, 1997).

From the point of view of developing marketing communications, an extension of the consumer lovemap needs to be considered, namely the advertising lovemap. The advertising lovemap is the cultural embodiment of all aspects of sexuality that are relevant to, and are contained in, advertising. Of course, it is also appropriate that this construct implies what is not explicit as well (e.g., sexual nuance as opposed to explicit sexuality). With regard to that, the advertising lovemap can be applied to provide a guide as to what is perceived as sexual, what the boundaries are, and what is appropriate and effective in advertising. It also may be applied to both consumers and advertisers. Thus, consumers would map advertising from their own point-of-view (e.g., "those ads are very sexy") and advertisers would generally map advertising with an emphasis on those consumer lovemaps (e.g., "consumers find those ads are very sexy and respond to them accordingly").

There are many examples to illustrate these two lovemaps. Fetishism, for example, is an excellent illustration of lovemap-driven behavior in that it maps the trajectory of how physical objects can become a source of sexual arousal as opposed to a person (e.g., collecting shoes and being sexually aroused by them). What is more relevant to advertisers is that consumers generally map products in sexual contexts in relation to their own sexual experiences with other people. Thus informed by their own experiences, as well as advertising and opinion leaders, consumers develop various fantasies, dream worlds, projections, schema, and scripts that guide them in their sexual behavior with others and that they often repeat over and over again (Gould, 1991a, 1992). For example, they may dress in clothing they believe makes them sexually attractive to potential sexual partners or they may set up their dream-world living spaces with such consumer goods as appropriate fragrances or lava lamps to make the sexual act more pleasurable. Reflecting their lovemaps, consumers also vary in their attitudes toward nudity in advertising. For example, different gender, age, or lifestyle segments may like different sexual themes or models.

Another way, and perhaps for some the best way, to comprehend these lovemaps is introspectively to imagine your own, a powerful method or exercise for informing your research (Gould, 1991b; 1995b). The idea of such an exercise is not so much to generalize or project your own experience onto others, but rather to uncover the relevant elements and processes involved in sexual advertising and consumer perceptions. You may apply this method to any or all of the elements discussed in this chapter. It is also useful to repeat the exercises over time to increase your familiarity with them and generate continuing experiences and evolving insights.

What products, services, or advertising do you associate with sexuality? What ads enhance your sexual experience? Can you trace these ads in your own mind to earlier experiences that *sexualized* these consumer goods or messages—some experience that caused you to associate them with attracting a sexual partner or engaging in sex? For example, you may have carried over something you used with a former partner into your present sex life. The use of other goods may be harder or impossible to trace, but thinking about them in this way should give you an idea of the consumer lovemap as something that associates at least some consumption and advertising response with sexuality. As another related exercise, reflective of postmodern change processes, consider how perceptions of sexuality have been modified over your lifetime in the use and design of products and in their advertising. For example, think of how the Sexual Revolution, the Women's Movement, and the sexuality expressed by young people of different eras have influenced society. To paraphrase an Oldsmobile ad, this is not your Father's (or Mother's) sexuality anymore. Or is it? You decide.

CHARACTERISTICS AND FUNCTION OF THE ADVERTISING LOVEMAP

The *advertising lovemap* can be understood in terms of three broad characteristics: (a) holism, (b) synergy, and (c) flexibility. The advertising lovemap is holistic in terms of representing consumers' sexuality with respect to advertising as a whole, and it consists of a number of interacting components (i.e., sexual perceptions, attitudes, and behavior). It is this whole that needs to be studied and addressed by the advertiser, even if only one component or dimension is the focus. Second, these components must be seen as having a synergistic relationship with one another so that the lovemap is something that should be viewed as more than the sum of its parts (e.g., response to sexual ad appeals is tied to myriad personal experiences). Third, lovemaps are flexible so that their components are not set in stone, but evolve over time. Moreover, advertisers may study and apply their understanding of these components/dimensions and their holism/synergies in ways that suit their own agendas and aims without being confined to prior thought or constraints. In this sense, ads are the semiotic signs that convey meanings, albeit not necessarily fixed ones. Instead, as reflected in postmodern thought that postulates continual flux, the signs themselves are constantly evolving and play off each other to construct meaning. For example, sexual explicitness in advertising as a sign of sexuality in general is constantly changing with respect to such things as degree (e.g., degrees of nudity or of simulating the sex act), accoutrement worn (e.g., types of clothing or jewelry worn), and type of model who may be shown in sexually explicit ways (e.g., variations in gender, age, sexual orientation, or ethnicity).

The function of advertising lovemaps is to help comprehend the following:

- consumer behavior and response to marketing communications programs by describing product use behavior related to stages in the sexual encounter process (i.e., attracting a mate and engaging in sexual behavior);
- consumer segmentation based on individual-difference aspects of the lovemap;
- degrees of positive or negative erotic responses to advertising appeals;
- differences in various attitudinal and behavioral responses to erotic ads (e.g., recall and recognition, attitudes toward the brand and ads, purchase behavior);
- differences in attitudes regarding the ethics of erotic appeals, among others.

In an important sense, lovemaps can be viewed as directing scripted behavior in which products and services are included as erotic, stimulating props (Gould, 1992). Within these lovemaps, relatively unconditioned sexuality is joined with sexually conditioned (sexualized) products to drive both direct (e.g., having sex and using sex toys) and indirect sexual behavior (e.g., dressing in a erotic fashion). Such sexualization is used in advertising to render even what seems to be the most inert consumption activity as a highly sexually charged one. For example, an advertisement for the Fireman's Fund in *The New York Times Magazine* utilizes a sexy model showing a lot of skin, albeit from the back, to sexualize loss insurance (see Fig. 8.1). Using the back to show skin is actually visually ambiguous (a characteristic of much postmodern sexual advertising) because at first it deceptively appears as if the model is nude since we usually see her necklace from the front. The image seductively tricks us into involvement with the ad.

THE OVERDETERMINATION
OF THE ADVERTISING LOVEMAP

The advertising lovemap is an overdetermined phenomenon that simply means it has multiple roots, including psychological, psychoanalytic, social, and cultural ones (Devereaux, 1980). Thus, it is multidimensional, as

FIG. 8.1.   Advertisement for the Fireman's Fund illustrating the sexualization of insurance.

well as developmental, evolving, and coterminous with the life of any consumer. It is also coevolving with the environment. For example, technological innovation has added new forms of sexual relating (e.g., virtual sex,
phone sex). In a postmodern sense, values and mores are ever changing as
well, so that what is acceptable or not, tasteful or not, is in constant flux.
Here, we can examine this overdetermined lovemap, and as shown in Fig.
8.2. Consider it in terms of four major dimensions: (a) individual consumer
differences, (b) product differences, (c) cultural differences, and (d) advertising differences.

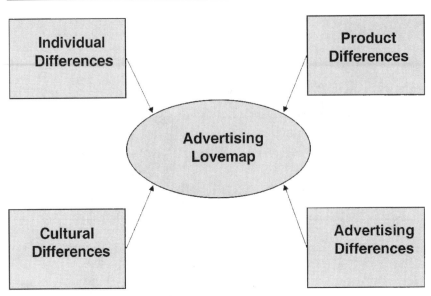

FIG. 8.2. The elements of the Advertising Lovemap.

Individual Differences

Most studies of sexuality in the general areas of marketing and advertising have focused on individual differences in response to sexual appeals. Here, we briefly review gender and two less-studied variables: erotophobia–erotophilia and sexual energy.

Gender. Regarding gender and research on sex, it has been stated that "the inclusion of gender in terms of one's own sex seems to be *sine qua non* of any sexual research, especially as many sex-based, gender differences have been found in sex research" (Gould, 1995a, p. 399). Moreover, the gendered elements of sexuality—both in relation to advertising and marketing communications—are very much contested and caught up in the constant enactment and shifting of gender roles and relationships. Even what gender "is" in terms of a broad conceptualization beyond mere male and female designations (e.g., examining masculinity and femininity as psychosocial constructs) remains an issue. With regard to advertising responses, gender has been found to influence attitudes toward sexuality in advertising, with men generally being more favorable in their attitudes than women (e.g., Fetto, 2001), and with women often being portrayed in ads in more explicit ways than men (Reichert, Lambiase, Morgan, Carstarphen, & Zavoina, 1999). Such gender differences have persisted when considered in terms of the lovemap and attitudes toward products when they are viewed and/or used in sexual contexts (Gould, 1995a).

Erotophobia–Erotophilia.   Individuals appear to have varying degrees of attraction or avoidance of sexual matters. Those said to be more open or attracted to sexual matters are said to be erotophilic, whereas those who are less open are or who actively seek to avoid sexual matters or behavior are said to be erotophobic (Fisher, Byrne, White, & Kelley, 1988). Thus, some consumers will perceive images or products in a more sexual way than other consumers will perceive these same objects. For the first group, these images or products are more sexually salient. For example, in one study, erotophilic consumers tended to rate products as having more sexual applications than did more erotophobic consumers (Gould, 1995a). This variable has also been theorized as being related to advertising, because erotophilic consumers will be more responsive to sexual themes than will erotophobic consumers (Gould, 1994).

Sexual Energy.   Sexuality and vital energy have a longstanding historical and worldwide relationship. Sexuality is very often viewed in energy terms, because the desire and ability to engage in sexual behavior are expressions of energy. Vital energy is a phenomenon connected to consumers' physiological functions but is also psychophysiological in nature with regard to sensations and consciousness of it (Gould, 1991b). It may also be construed phenomenologically as an experiential and subjective aspect of existence. The use of energy in advertising is widespread and many products are concerned with expression or revitalization of that energy.

There are several ways that sexual energy as a manifestation of vital energy may be viewed. First, consumers make choices about projecting energy into behavior. Advertising's tendency to sexualize many aspects of life may influence choices, but may also cause consumers to perceive things in sexual terms. This leads to the second point: Eexual energy is projected into many other aspects of life and is often reflected in advertising in the use of attractive models who embody sexual energy and transfer it to products. Third, sexuality as energy may be created or spent. Many products and ads address this aspect of energy and sexuality (Gould, 1991b). Finally, sexual energy will also reflect individual differences in terms of consumers' perspectives.

Product Differences

Products (and services), when seen from a sexual point of view, are or become an inherent part of consumer lovemaps. Consumers, in constructing their lovemaps, seek a fit between themselves, their scripts and schemas, and the products they include in the lovemap (cf. Mosher, 1988). Some products are clearly more sexually charged than others (associated with sexuality; Gould, 1995a). However, there are also situational aspects because some products may appear at once to be tied directly to sexuality, and yet have other applications depending on the circumstances of their use. For example, makeup may be used to convey both sexy and nonsexy looks (Fabricant & Gould, 1993). The same woman, for example, may wear different types of makeup, one for night where the signals are much more sexual and one for day where they may be less sexual. Products may also be transformed or sexualized through advertising. For example, relatively nonsexual products can be associated with sexuality and/or sexual innuendo and connotation (Gould, 1995a).

This product-difference effect is part of what has been called the *economy of desire*, a construct that looks at the totality of desire, including sexual and nonsexual desires (Gould, 1995a). For example, consider the Adbusters website ad spoof that displays a beautiful female model and presents her desires, including consuming, acquiring, eating, drinking, and dressing, as well as sexual desire, as somehow correlative and integrated (Adbusters, 2001). There is also a sense of play between sexual and nonsexual matters as evidenced by the "Molson Export—Promised Her Sex" commercial in which a male out with a group of buddies in a bar is seen calling another friend to join them and declaring: There's a time for sex and a there's a time to take it easy with the guys. It's all about balance ("Molson Export," 2001).

Some products also may be more associated with different stages of the sexual experience, such as attraction of a mate or involvement in the sex act itself. In my study of these stages in which consumers rated various products in relation to their sexual application, a product by stage interaction was found that indicated that cars, for example, were more associated with the attraction stage as opposed to the sex-act stage, whereas lighting in the bedroom was just the opposite (Gould, 1995a).

Cultural Differences

Although it is well known that different cultures may have widely varying sexual mores, this idea has been little explored in the marketing, consumer research, or advertising fields. Boddewyn (1991) documented the fact that advertising standards and regulations regarding it are quite variable across the world. Moreover, Boddewyn indicated that regulations are in ever-present flux. Here, we want to add to this standards approach a cultural layer that reflects current theoretical thought about the impact of culture and cultural construction on individuals and marketing communications. Indeed, standards may be viewed as a cultural artifact that reflects the attempt to codify and control sexuality (Foucault, 1990). With respect to marketing communications, cultural values and other factors of culture focusing on standardized versus adaptive aspects of advertising across the world have also been explored and documented (de Mooij, 1998). This cultural layer is also one that needs to be added to the individual and product layers considered earlier. In one respect, we might see this process as examining the relationship between cultural and individual fantasies, myths, and discourses.

In this regard through ongoing research, Barbara Olsen and I are investigating a new concept, the *cultural consumer lovemap*, which complements the individual consumer lovemap (see Olsen & Gould, 1999). It reflects how a culture perceives sexuality and behaves sexually. Much as an individual tends to react sexually in certain specific ways, cultures may do much the same thing, albeit on a more collective level. For example, there are certain culturally prescribed ways potential sexual partners are to meet, become involved, and approach sexual issues. This internalized cultural consumer lovemap also serves as the standard against which individuals perceive, form, and judge their own lovemaps (Olsen & Gould, 1999). However, although consumers can never be separate from their own omnipresent cultures, they can also draw on these resources to shape it in their own fashion. Thus, in our study of Jamaican consumers with a focus on their music, we find that music at once embodies established cultural values and addresses them in new ways. Much the same can be said for advertising, which in general embodies these ever-shifting phenomena.

As another component of the cultural consumer lovemap, consider how cross-cultural differences may be expressed, hybridized (cross-culturally mixed), or embodied in advertising. For example, ponder the idea of vital energy and imagine how cross-culturally it may transform the way sexuality is understood and practiced in a paradigmatic way. Vital energy is viewed in different ways throughout various cultures. Asian cultures in particular are very much concerned with vital energy and maintain various sets of practices concerned with sustaining it (Gould, 1991b). Moreover, some cultures, again especially some Asian cultures, focus on practices that utilize this energy in its sexual form to transform themselves (Gould, 1991c). For example, Gould and Minowa (1994) reported on the packaging theme of a Japanese revitalization product that concerns restoring vital energy. Thus, this sexual energy perspective illustrates how the cultural consumer lovemap functions in channeling consumer sexuality into products and advertising in specific, culturally determined ways.

Advertising Differences

Advertising, as a mirror of everyday life, will reflect various lovemap differences (i.e., individual, product, and cultural differences). In any case, advertising captures these other determinants of the lovemap, and its construction of sexuality in its own terms reflects the advertising lovemap.

Moreover, although it may be useful in some contexts to think of an overall advertising lovemap, it is perhaps more germane in others to consider multiple advertising lovemaps. Thus, advertising with different target audiences or dealing with different products will contain differences in the way sexuality is expressed. Varying degrees of nudity or bodily exposure, for example, are common signs indicating sexuality in advertising. For example, Dudley (1998) found that nudity was very persuasive in a suntan lotion ad in contrast to a product-only ad, in spite of the nudity simultaneously being perceived as somewhat offensive.

Other signs of sexuality that generate differences among ads include various sounds and music, the presence of sexy models, their poses and looks, interaction with the intended gaze (e.g., who is expected to see this ad?), sexual terms or talk, and various degrees of explicit or implied sexual behavior. These characteristics may interact with individual or cultural differences in terms of degrees of comprehension, deemed appropriateness, and acceptance. They also interact with product differences in terms of appropriateness to the product. Altogether, there may be complex interactions that can be seen as reflected in consumer lovemaps in terms of the dimensions of the fit of the ads with consumers' notions of sexuality and their responsiveness to such advertising.

THE ADVERTISING HERMENEUTIC CIRCLE

Thus far, we have considered several aspects of a consumer's existence that can influence his or her sexual behavior, especially in relation to the advertising lovemap. These are individual difference, product difference, cultural, and advertising factors. At this point, it is important to establish the process of how these dimensions relate and function together. The central process is embodied in what may be called the *advertising hermeneutic circle*. The circle borrows from the concept of the hermeneutic circle in which an interpreter of a text goes back and forth between the text and the interpretation. A text may be almost anything involving thought, but here it refers to any form of marketing communications, including written, spoken, musical, and visual elements. All these elements and the messages they convey are interpreted by the consumer and applied in various acts of interpretation, development of brand attitudes, and purchase behavior. The communications attempt to respond to consumer lovemaps while simultaneously helping to inform or change them. Thus, the actions of the consumer also serve as feedback to the advertiser. In this regard, the hermeneutic circle might be viewed as a dynamic feedback loop that continually cycles. For example, consumers use advertising to keep up with the latest trends in what is "cool" in terms of attractive dress, while advertisers simultaneously strive to keep up with what consumers think is cool.

This hermeneutic approach is also rooted in or informed by a phenomenological perspective in which consumers experience and locate their own views of those experiences (Thompson, Locander, & Pollio, 1990). Moreover, although *a priori* theories or themes may be considered, the market researcher is encouraged to look to the consumer's view in the form of interview texts and observations for emergent themes. The hermeneutic circle encourages this process by providing a vehicle for such emergence to take place. Here, we are not so interested in the investigator as much as the circle applied by the consumer or advertiser. Thus, consumers will construct interpretations of their own sexual behavior reflexively moving back and forth among various acts, perceptions, personal thoughts, and social messages. These processes include iteratively going back and forth among experiences of advertisements, perceptions of ads, and imitation of ads. In this regard, consumers make further decodings of marketing communications and engage in a constant comparison process between external and internal perspectives. Advertisers apply a similar interpretive-process circling among ads, agency and advertiser communications, internal communications, market research, and consumer responses.

A generalized description of the hermeneutic circle is important for our present purpose because it helps us to capture, map, and position the role of marketing communications with relation to sexuality. The elements of the circle involve movements between the individual and culture, a good portion of which is mediated by advertising and other marketing communications. In this regard, the theoretical approach is agnostic about the significance and meaning of directions followed because there is not a presupposition that the consumer is merely reacting in a one-way passive manner to cultural constructions. Thus, cultural aspects of lovemaps may be seen as percolating up from the actions and perceptions of consumers as it is informing them and their behavior. As an exercise, think about how your own perceptions of sexuality reflect the culture around you and advertising in particular. Can you detect any direction or flow between yourself and your culture?

In pursuing the hermeneutic understanding of the advertising lovemap, there are some ancillary transfer processes that abet this perspective. An important part of the transfer process is analogical, in which consumers attempt to understand something unfamiliar by relating it to something familiar in the form of analogy, metaphor, or metonym (Lakoff & Johnson, 1999; Morgan & Reichert, 1999). With respect to sexuality, some communications, for example, may stimulate direct sexual arousal with relatively explicit sexual portrayals whereas others may take on sexual connotation, double entendre, or innuendo. Recent work with respect to metaphors has suggested that much of our thought is embodied (i.e., concepts are developed from and grow from our experience of living in our bodies; Lakoff & Johnson, 1999).

In this regard, one particular metaphor that is especially apt for considering the relationship of consumers' sexuality and their response to advertising is the metaphor of "seeing is touching" (Lakoff & Johnson, 1999). In this sense, Lakoff and Johnson concluded that there is a primary human experience in which the visual and tactile exploration of objects is correlated. Indeed, a recent study applying discourse analysis of consumer texts suggested that some consumers likened sexual advertising to art and found its expressive qualities to be very positive in investing tangible products with symbolic meaning (Elliott, Jones, Benfield, & Barlow, 1995). Thus, if we view most advertising as largely visual, we can further surmise that it is correlated with consumers' tactile experiences and/or with their visualizations of such experiences in their mind's eye when seeing a commercial. We would also suggest that auditory cues in ads operate through a similar correlative conflating, or even synesthetic mechanism. Moreover, we can theorize a conflative or correlative structuring of all the senses that allows advertising to represent and stimulate consumer sexuality so that its effect becomes correlated with or transferred to products. We should note that this conflationary process results in both verbal and sensory consumer phenomena. For example, on seeing a certain commercial, the consumer may say, "That's a *hot* commercial." She feels aroused by the commercial in a physical-sensory way and correlates that with the metaphor of hotness.

In another sense, advertising may be said to fetishize products or create a fetish in its own right. Advertising itself is not sexual attraction or the sexual act, but it does convey something about sex through the hermeneutic circle between it and consumers. The sexual-transfer role of advertising is an important one for marketers when attempting to influence purchase behavior. In this role, it involves transferring both meaning and affect to products. Based on such transfers, consumers may choose to *tangibilize* the experience of ads by applying the product in their own lives (cf. Belk & Wallendorf, 1990). Advertising thus facilitates transfers of meaning in an ongoing hermeneutic circle between consumers and advertisers. Affect transfer is not unrelated to meaning transfer but is defined in terms of the emotional facets of an ad that are transferred to a product. In this sense, sexual arousal may be viewed as a form of affect, and affect transfer is the means by which products are sexualized. Many advertising cues may act to facilitate this sexualizing transfer process, including such things as arousing models, sexual themes, the depiction of sexual scenes, sexually associated music, and double entendre. For example, a commercial for the FX Network acts to transfer sexuality to its network and its X Show by rewording the National Anthem to include sexual references throughout (FX Network, 2001). The anthem begins with the words, "Oh, sex, sports, beer, breasts" and continues from there through "centerfold," "Miss November," "ménage á trois," "lingerie," and "crazy, steamy, jungle sex."

Reflecting on this hermeneutic-sexualization process from the lovemap perspective, we find that consumers generally have a set of cues embedded in their consciousness that may have arisen from childhood, but may also have evolved over their lifetimes. Advertising is one of the instruments of sexual socialization that informs consumer lovemaps. In this role, advertising also hermeneutically facilitates the omnipresent segmentation of lovemaps. For example, Valdivia (1997) illustrated how different lingerie catalogs with quite different styles are created for different women. Sexual segmentation in general may be as simple as male–female, straight–gay, or it may involve complex tastes relating to specific sexual practices (e.g., S&M). Tastes in particular are complex because some consumers may respond vicariously to the tastes of others but not engage in particular sexual practices themselves. For example, although S&M themes have played out in advertising, many consumers may respond to such themes but not engage in S&M themselves. As such, we identify a key part of the consumer lovemap, namely that some consumers construct their lovemaps based on their being a part of a specific sexual taste group or community, whereas others borrow vicariously from that group.

THE ADVERTISING LOVEMAP IN THE POSTMODERN AGE

Having explored the advertising lovemap and its various dimensions, we now turn to the vexing perspective of the postmodern and how it might problematize our conceptualizations. In postmodern terms, the hermeneutic circle of lovemap construction may be understood in terms of a never-ending cycle of (re)signification and constantly shifting tastes (Baudrillard, 1983). Postmodern and related poststructuralist thought privileges the transience of existence as opposed to the universals that seem to serve as the foundation of prior thought. Although this might at first appear inconsistent with the scientific point of view that seems to seek out such universals, it is less so when the scientific research method is considered because it continually strives to overthrow established theories. Thus although we should not airbrush out the differences, we should nonetheless recognize the major element of flux common to both approaches.

In the present context, postmodernism suggests a lack of rigidity in the construction of the advertising lovemap. For example, in the marketplace, there may be a variety of versions of the lovemap that are encountered by different versions of the self (cf. Simon, 1989). At the same time, there are aspects of life that appear to be more enduring. In fact, there is a paradoxical negotiation between the relatively longstanding and the relatively novel, transitory or postmodern (Gould & Lerman, 1998; Thompson & Hirschman, 1995). The longstanding reflects themes that appear to be virtually continuous whereas postmodern themes are reflective of a culture in which social structures and values appear to be under siege by forces of hyper-change and fragmentation.

Reflective of the advertising lovemap's overdetermination, postmodernist advertising also juxtaposes themes and playfully tweaks consumers' imagination. For example, a recent series of ads for various clothing manufacturers and stores in *The New York Times Magazine* contained models in sexy poses and with sexy gazes. Each ad also had a different theme, including: "On the Edge," "Russian Revolution," "Baby-doll Punk," "Black Power," "Second Skins" with a sub-theme "Zoology is Destiny," "Hippie Chic," "New Chicks on the Block," "Wide, They Said," "Leather and Lace," and "The Showmen" (actually two women). These themes intermingle sexuality with other themes in mockingly playful ways, at once tempering sexuality and then exaggerating it. For example, as shown in Fig. 8.3, the "Second Skins" ad plays on clothing as skin, ala Marshall McLuhan, and zoology (biology) as destiny, ala Darwin. With all its seeming complexity, the excitement of shedding superfluous skin to reach the flesh is not lost on the audience.

The postmodern hermeneutic circle may also involve some cross-culture-based transformations that reconstrue sexuality altogether. For example, I have been an observer of a previously obscure practice from India and Tibet known as Tantric sex (Gould, 1991c). Suddenly, it has become *an item* as it has surfaced on HBO and in other popular outlets. The Tantric perspective shifts consumers' sexual focus to a practice of elaboration and spiritual or yogic dimensions, much different from conventional Western perspectives. Yet, Tantric sex is making its presence felt in Western circles. Such a shift as this suggests that there is not "one sexuality," but instead a multiplicity as expressed by the cultural consumer lovemap. I include this Tantric form of sexuality here, because although advertising concerning it is mainly restricted to goods directly related to it, at least at present, I predict that such a perspective will be coopted and utilized by mainstream advertising at some point as the advertising lovemap evolves.

Technology is also a major factor in the fluidity of postmodernity. New forms of communication alter the cultural landscape by transforming how consumers view themselves. For example, consider the Internet, which reflects the play between culture and individuals very well. The Internet has afforded individuals the capacity to reach one another by disintermediating the process of utilizing hierarchical media, in which they never did reach others (e.g., broadcast television). Moreover, through such transformative phenomena, there has emerged what might be called *peer-to-peer advertising* or *peer-to-peer direct marketing* in which consumers commercialize and attempt to reach other consumers with their products and services. Web-based auctions would be another example of peer-to-peer marketing,

FIG. 8.3   Advertisement titled "Second Skins," illustrating postmodern sexual playfulness.

although auctions are generally less sexually charged than are some webcam sites.

In this context, advertising serves not only to reflect identities and roles but also to problematize them through play and through challenge. Things are unsettled and fluid, if not altogether confusing. In this respect, longstanding elements are utilized in combinatorial construction so that the constant new of postmodernity is produced. The old never quite dies and the new never quite takes hold. With respect to sexuality, enduring themes about men and women continue but they are constantly being transformed in the play of hyper-evolving cultural forces. Sexual roles are in constant negotiation and advertising becomes an instrument in the hands of these forces.

IMPLICATIONS FOR THE FUTURE
OF THE ADVERTISING LOVEMAP

What is the future of the advertising lovemap? Two overall trends for re-searchers, managers, and policymakers may be discerned: (a) the ongoing dynamic hermeneutic of the lovemap, and (b) the evolution of related tech-nology-media effects.

Dynamic Hermeneutic of the Advertising Lovemap

There is a constant hermeneutic cycling between the longstanding and postmodern in producing advertising lovemaps. Sexuality is never a set-tled matter and new manifestations and phenomena will arise, even as they appear to reenact more established phenomena. For example, the cultural war over explicitness and restraint in sexual advertising will con-tinue although new players and new forms shape the battle. Likewise, themes such as S&M crop up as if new, and are in fact new in context, but they are also historical with roots as far back as we care to look. In this re-gard, sexuality will be constantly problematized. Thus, readings of even a single ad may vary widely, as evidenced by the three quite different sexual and gendered readings of a Moet & Chandon champagne ad provided by Brown, Stevens, and Maclaran (1999) that reflect varying perspectives constructed in part by the male gaze versus the female voice. Such a multi-ple readings approach suggests not only that consumers may differ, but also that they may produce various unintended readings that are not fore-seen by advertisers (Gould, 1994). Moreover, as consumers' sexual per-ceptions and roles evolve, their sexuality, or at least the meanings they apply to it, will be transformed.

One major feature of this hermeneutic concerns the sexualization or even pornographication of advertising communications. Such sexualization is especially notable on the web, but also is present in television and print magazine advertising (Kuczynski, 2001). This sexualizing hermeneutic is characteristic of postmodernism, with shifts that transform sexual meanings on an ongoing experimental basis, often led or guided by pornography as a sexual opinion leader. For example, a recent fashion layout in the French magazine, *Vogue Hommes*, deconstructed masculine sexuality by displayed a male model in poses akin to females, mimicking in its art direction an Italian porn magazine, *Bel Ami* (Trebay, 2001, p. B8). The model was "... posed supine, his legs elevated, wearing little more than a studded crop top." The ad was viewed as controversial and deconstructive of masculine sexual psychology because it put men in a "woman's pose" when straight men, at least, do not want to see other men portrayed in this way (Trebay, 2001). We should expect such deconstructive play and sexualization of advertising to be a continuing, if not dominant trend.

Evolution of Technology and Media Effects

The evolution of technology and the media is greatly shaping expression of the advertising lovemap in the contemporary environment. For example, the popularization of Tantric sex is tied in with the continuing evolution of cable television. Beyond that, we have seen the emergence of such phenomena as phone sex, virtual sex, and the like. These practices have opened up the boundaries of sexual behavior and marketing communications toward an even more ubiquitous, if contentious presence, in which sexuality seems to squirm into areas that were either not seen as sexual media before or help to shape new media from the outset (e.g., the Internet). For example, search through a number of categories on the web (e.g., "mature women") and it's likely that you will turn up several pornographic sites. Thus, a major feature of the web as a lovemap construct is how much it is sexualized. Furthermore, new developments such as broadband will likely play even larger roles in this sexualization process because so much more can be done with it. For example, one can easily envision marketers testing the limits of sexual explicitness in advertising over such media.

Technology is also facilitating the peer-to-peer marketing phenomenon, both in relation to sexuality and other areas. Advertising has always had a tension between using "real people" and actors. In the sexual arena, this plays out as another hermeneutic dynamic in which consumers variously seek out both real people and attractive celebrities on whom they project their desires (digital characters as they evolve may be still another element in this dynamic). Thus, there are the coevolving phenomena of amateur sexual videos and web sites on the one hand, and the continuing seeking out of beautiful models and celebrities in sexual roles on the other. We can model this process in a way that is similar to the Wheel of Retailing model in which discount retailers come in and supplant higher-priced retailing institutions until they also come to raise their prices only to be undercut themselves. Here, we would suggest in similar fashion that new sexual types, such as amateurs, arise to undercut commercialized forms of sexuality. Peer-to-peer activity also takes time and energy from the use of mass media and thus will be a major factor in the use of media. Media strategists will have to deal with this potential paradigm shift in media usage, driven in large part by sexual activity. Moreover, one of the characteristics of sexuality, especially for males, appears to be the desire for novelty and diversity. Amateur sexuality seems to be a rich source for those taste factors as does the constant shifting of celebrity types in the sexual arena. New technology and the constant thrill and presence of the "new" make fulfilling those desires easier. Thus, marketers are forced to constantly embrace new forms and find new stars, as individuals seek out novelty in sexuality to keep their sexual energy stimulated.

CONCLUSION

One thing is certain: Sexuality is such a rich but contested area of consumer culture and life that it has never been fully addressed in advertising (not to mention any site of communication), and perhaps never will be. But advertising's very richness and the diversity of advertising lovemaps leaves room for a great deal of creativity, not only to develop marketing communications but also simultaneously to design products and services to meet the needs of sexually motivated consumers. Your own comprehension of these lovemap processes can be informed by experientially relating to the lovemap through exercises, as well as through more conventional research. For the moment, I have just indicated some trends that seem visible, and I have also examined the advertising lovemap as an embodiment and mapping of these trends. The rest I leave to the ongoing magic of life and your own ability to apply imagination to your understanding of them.

REFERENCES

Adbusters (2001). *Manufacturing desire*. Retrieved July 20, 2001, from http://adbusters.org/magazine/28/desire/4.html.
Baudrillard, J. (1983). *Simulations*. New York: Semiotext(e).
Belk, R. W., & Wallendorf, M. (1990). The sacred meaning of money. *Journal of Economic Psychology, 11,* 35–67.
Boddewyn, J. J. (1991). Controlling sex and decency in advertising around the world. *Journal of Advertising, 20,* 25–35.
Brown, S., Stevens, L., & Maclaran, P. (1999). I can't believe it's not Bakhtin!: Literary theory, postmodern advertising, and the gender agenda. *Journal of Advertising, 28,* 11–24.

De Mooij, M. (1998). *Global marketing and advertising: Understanding cultural paradoxes*. Thousand Oaks, CA: Sage.

Devereaux, G. (1980), *Basic problems of ethnopsychiatry*. Chicago: University of Chicago Press.

Dudley, S. C. (1998), Consumer attitudes toward nudity in advertising. *Journal of Marketing Theory and Practice, 7*, 89–96

Elliott, R., Jones, A., Benfield, A., & Barlow, M. (1995). Overt sexuality in advertising: A discourse analysis of gender responses. *Journal of Consumer Policy, 18*, 187–218.

Fabricant, S. M., & Gould S. J. (1993). Women's makeup careers: An interpretive study of color cosmetic use and "face value." *Psychology and Marketing, 10*, 531–548.

Fetto, J. (2001). Where's the lovin'? *American Demographics, 23*, 10–11.

Fisher, W. A., Byrne, D., White, L. A., & Kelley, K. (1988). Erotophobia-erotophilia as a dimension of personality. *The Journal of Sex Research, 25*, 123–151.

Foucault, M. (1990). *The use of pleasure: The history of sexuality, Volume 2*. New York: Vintage Books.

FX Network (2001). *National Anthem*. Retrieved July 19, 2001, from www.adcritic.com/content/fx-network-the-x-show-national-anthem.html.

Gould, S. J. (1991a). Toward a theory of sexuality and consumption: Consumer lovemaps. In R. H. Holman & M. R. Solomon (Eds.), *Advances in consumer research, 18* (pp. 381–383). Provo UT: Association for Consumer Research.

Gould, S. J. (1991b). The self-manipulation of my pervasive, perceived vital energy through product use: An introspective-praxis perspective. *Journal of Consumer Research, 18*, 194–207.

Gould, S. J. (1991c). The import of Asian sexual psychotechnologies into the United States: The 'new woman' and the 'new man' go 'tantric'. *Journal of American Culture, 14*, 19–23.

Gould, S. J. (1992). A model of the scripting of consumer lovemaps: The consumer sexual behavior sequence. In J. Sherry & B. Sternthal (Eds.), *Advances in consumer research, 19* (pp. 304–310). Provo, UT: Association for Consumer Research.

Gould, S. J. (1994). Sexuality and ethics in Advertising: A research agenda and policy guideline perspective. *Journal of Advertising, 23*, 73–80.

Gould, S. J. (1995a). Sexualized aspects of consumer behavior: An empirical investigation of consumer lovemaps. *Psychology & Marketing, 12*, 305–413.

Gould, S. J. (1995b). Researcher introspection as a method in consumer research: Applications, issues and implications. *Journal of Consumer Research, 21*, 719–722.

Gould, S. J. (1997). An interpretive study of purposeful, mood self-regulating consumption: The consumption and mood framework. *Psychology & Marketing, 14*, 395–426.

Gould, S. J., & Lerman, D. B. (1998). "Postmodern" versus "long-standing" cultural narratives in consumer behavior: An empirical study of NetGirl Online. *European Journal of Marketing, 32*, 644–654.

Gould, S. J., & Minowa, Y. (1994). "Are they saying the same thing?" An exploratory study of Japanese and American automobile advertising. In B. G. Englis (Ed.), *Global and multinational advertising* (pp. 193–204). Hillsdale, NJ: Lawrence Erlbaum Associates.

Kuczynski, A. (2001, March 12). Racy magazine ads expose inconsistency in publishers' stance. *New York Times, 150*, pp. C1, C11.

Lakoff, G., & Johnson, M. (1999). *Philosophy in the flesh: The embodied mind and its challenge to Western thought*. New York: Basic Books.

Molson Export (2001). *Promised her sex*. Retrieved July 19 2001, from www.adcritic.com/content/molson-export-promised-her-sex.html.

Money, J. (1984). Paraphilias: Phenomenology and classification. *American Journal of Psychotherapy, 38*, 164–179.

Money, J. (1986). *Lovemaps*. New York: Irvington.

Morgan, S. E., & Reichert, T. (1999). The message is in the metaphor: Assessing the comprehension of metaphors in advertisements. *Journal of Advertising, 28*, 1–12.

Mosher, D. L. (1988). Pornography defined: Sexual involvement theory, narrative context, and goodness-of-fit. *Journal of Psychology and Human Sexuality, 1*, 67–85.

Olsen, B., & Gould, S. J. (1999). Jamaican DJ music lyrics and postmodern consumption: Liberatory for whom? In E. Arnould & L. Scott (Eds.), *Advances in Consumer Research, 26* (pp. 43–45). Provo, UT: Association for Consumer Research.

Reichert, T., Lambiase, J., Morgan, S., Carstarphen, M., & Zavoina, S. (1999). Cheesecake and beefcake: No matter how you slice it, sexual explicitness in advertising continues to increase. *Journalism and Mass Communication Quarterly, 76*, 7–20.

Simon, W. (1989). Commentary on the status of sex research: The postmodernization of sex. *Journal of Psychology and Human Sexuality, 2*, 9–37.

Thompson, C. J., Locander, W. R., & Pollio, H. R. (1990). The lived meaning of free choice: An existential-phenomenological description of everyday consumer experiences of contemporary married women. *Journal of Consumer Research, 17*, 346–361.

Thompson, C. J., & Hirschman, E. C. (1995). Understanding the socialized body: A poststructuralist analysis of consumers' self–conceptions, body images, and self–care practices. *Journal of Consumer Research, 22*, 139–154.

Trebay, G. (2001, March 20), Men's fashion does without clothes. *New York Times, 150*, B8.

Valdivia, A. N. (1997). The secret of my desire: Gender, class, and sexuality in lingerie catalogs. In K. T. Firth (Ed.), *Undressing the ad: Reading culture in advertising* (pp. 225–250). New York: Peter Lang.

PART III

Cultural Impact and Interpretation

Chapter 9

Advertising and Disconnection[1]

Jean Kilbourne

It is almost impossible to imagine what our popular culture would look like if women's bodies weren't objectified and dismembered. We are so used to this that it is hard to believe that it has not always been so. In fact, the eroticized imagery of women has been part of the general cultural landscape, not relegated to the world of pornography and sex clubs, for only the past 50 years or so. It is true that there have been erotic images of women in art for centuries, but mass technology has made it possible for these images to constantly surround us. Unlike art, advertising always yokes these images to products. The point is not to arouse desire for the woman, but to arouse desire for the product. Robert Schultz describes these images as "scattered like parks or resorts, little retreats for the male imagination, strokes to the ego and hooks for commerce."

I've been talking about the exploitation of women in advertising since the late 1960s and it was the subject of my 1979 film *Killing Us Softly: Advertising's Image of Women*. It is certainly no longer news. However, it is more extreme and pervasive than ever before. Women's bodies are not only used to attract attention to the product in increasingly absurd ways, as when a nude woman is used to sell a watch or breasts are used to sell fishing line, but increasingly the woman's body morphs into the product, as in the ad for "the Sak." And this objectification is related to addiction and substance abuse in ways that are complex and that have not been explored.

It is becoming clearer that this objectification has consequences, one of which is the effect that it has on sexuality and desire. Sex in advertising and the media is often criticized from a puritanical perspective—there's too

---

[1]Reprinted with the permission of The Free Press, a Division of Simon & Schuster, Inc., from CAN'T BUY MY LOVE: How Advertising Changes the Way We Think and Feel (originally published in hardcover entitled DEADLY PERSUASION) by Jean Kilbourne. Copyright © 1999 by Jean Kilbourne.

much of it, it's too blatant, it will encourage kids to be promiscuous, and so forth. But sex in advertising has far more to do with trivializing sex than promoting it, with narcissism than with promiscuity, with consuming than with connecting. The problem is not that it is sinful, but that it is synthetic and cynical.

Sexual images in advertising and throughout the media define what is sexy and, more important, who is sexy. To begin with, sex in advertising in the mass media is almost entirely heterosexist—lesbian, gay, or bisexual sex is rarely even implied in the mainstream media (aside from the occasional male fantasy of lesbianism as two beautiful women waiting for Dick to arrive). We are surrounded by images of young, beautiful heterosexual couples with perfect hard bodies having sex. Women are portrayed as sexually desirable only if they are young, thin, carefully polished and groomed, made up, depilated, sprayed, and scented—rendered quite unerotic, in fact—and men are conditioned to seek such partners and to feel disappointed if they fail.

We never see eroticized images of older people, imperfect people, people with disabilities. The gods have sex, the rest of us watch—and judge our own imperfect sex lives against the fantasy of constant desire and sexual fulfillment portrayed in the media. To a great extent, the images define desirability—our own as well as others'. We can never measure up. Inevitably, this affects our self-images and radically distorts reality. "You have the right to remain sexy," says an ad featuring a beautiful young woman, her legs spread wide, but the subtext is "only if you look like this." And she is an object—available, exposed, essentially passive. She has the right to remain sexy, but not the right to be actively sexual.

Just as women and girls are offered a kind of ersatz defiance through drinking and smoking that interferes with true rebellion, so are we offered a pseudo-sexuality, a sexual mystique, that makes it far more difficult to discover our own unique and authentic sexuality. How sexy can a woman be who hates her body? She can act sexy, but can she feel sexy? How fully can she surrender to passion if she is worried that her thighs are too heavy or her stomach too round, if she can't bear to be seen in the light, or if she doesn't like the fragrance of her own genitals?

In the world of advertising, only young people have sex. Not only are young women valued only for their sexuality, but the rest of us end up in a culture arrested in adolescence, surrounded by teenage fantasies of sex and romance, a culture that idealizes the very things that make real intimacy impossible—impulsive gratification, narcissism, distance and disconnection, romanticism, and eternal youth. Sex in advertising is about a constant state of desire and arousal—never about intimacy or fidelity or commitment. This not only makes intimacy impossible—it erodes real desire. The endless pursuit of passion is fueled by a sense of inner deadness, emptiness—and it is doomed to failure, like any addiction. Passion inevitably wanes and one is alone again, empty.

When we think about it, the people in ads aren't sexy because of anything unique to them. They have no personal histories. They mostly look alike and are interchangeable. They very rarely look at each other. "The only downside to female guests that stay over for breakfast is they leave with your nicest shirts," says an ad featuring a man getting dressed. His back is to the young woman in his bed, who is covering herself up as if embarrassed. People in ads like this aren't lovers—they are sexy because of the products they use. The jeans, the perfume, the car are sexy in and of themselves. The answer to the question posed by one ad, "What attracts?" is the perfume being advertised, which means these particular partners are irrelevant. They could easily be with anyone else who happened to be wearing Jovan musk. Advertising even tells us that "Shi Cashmere is sexier than skin!" Often the people in the ads are grim—there is no humor, no quirkiness, none of the individuality that defines the truly erotic.

Although the sexual sell, overt and subliminal, is at a fever pitch in most advertising, depictions of sex as an important and profound human activity are notably absent. It is a cold and oddly passionless sex that surrounds us. A sense of joy is also absent; the models generally look either hostile or bored. Passionate sex is one way that we can experience the oceanic, the transcendence of our own boundaries. But this can only occur between subjects, not objects. Sex certainly cannot and does not always have to be sacred and transcendent, but it is tragic for a culture when that possibility is diminished or lost. As psychologist Linda Pollock says, sexual pleasure is significantly more important and, at the same time, significantly less important than our culture holds it to be.

This notion that sexiness and sex appeal come from without rather than within is one of advertising's most damaging messages. Real sexiness has to do with a passion for life, individuality, uniqueness, vitality. It has nothing to do with products or with all the bored, perfect-looking models embracing that we see all around us. If Jeremy Iggers's definition of the erotic as "a heightened sense of aliveness" is true, then surely, in a world in which beautiful people so often look more dead than alive, it is the car ads that most promise an erotic experience. We live in a culture that is sex-crazed and sex-saturated, but strangely *unerotic*.

Advertising constantly confuses real sexuality with narcissism. Identical models parade alone through the commercials, caressing their own soft skin, stroking and hugging their bodies, shaking their long silky manes, sensually bathing and applying powders and lotions, and then admiring themselves at length in the mirror. We're subjected to a steady barrage of messages telling us that all that matters is the immediate fulfillment of our needs and desires. "We are hedonists and we want what feels good," de-

clares a Nike ad. We are the heroes of every ad. "You deserve a break today." "Go for it." As an ad for a bath product says, "Entering Willow Lake.
Population: One. You."

"A celebration of laughter ... love ... and intense happiness," says the ad
for Amarige perfume. But all we see is a woman who seems to be in the
throes of orgasm caressing her own throat. We don't need partners any
more. This is perfect disconnection.

This has been taken even further in some recent ads where the models
are literally kissing themselves. Supermodel Linda Evangelista appears in
one such ad as a woman and a man. Transvestite RuPaul is featured in another, in which RuPaul the guy nuzzles RuPaul the babe. She is no doubt
wearing "Narcisse" perfume and he "Égoïste."

This adolescent attitude toward sex is further reflected and reinforced by
all the ads (and situation comedies and films) that turn sex into a dirty joke.
Countless ads use sophomoric double entendres, such as "We keep it up
longer" (for a radio station), "Your ability to score has just improved" (for a
video game), and "You never forget your first time" (for alcohol and for a
discount store). An ad for shoes in a British magazine aimed at young people features a photo of a blonde in the throes of passion (or dead—it's hard
to tell) and the copy "Half way up Mount Caroline. Realised I'd forgotten
my safety gear. Made a speedy descent." An American ad for cruises asks
the question, "What's your idea of fun?" A beautiful woman slyly replies,
"Licking the salt off my husband's margarita." When sexual jokes are used
to sell everything from rice to roach-killer, from cars to carpets, it's hard to
remember that sex can unite two souls, can inspire awe. Individually these
ads are harmless enough, sometimes even funny, but the cumulative effect
is to degrade and devalue sex.

I do not mean to imply for a minute that sex has to be romantic, soft, nice,
domesticated. We inevitably objectify ourselves and each other sexually,
which is fine as long as there is reciprocity, as long as we all can be subjects
as well, and never merely objects. As Ann Snitow says, "The danger of
objectification and fragmentation depend on context.... The antipornography campaign introduces misleading goals into our struggle which in-
timates that in a feminist world we will never objectify anyone, never take
the part for the whole, never abandon ourselves to the mindlessness or the
intensities of feeling that link sex with childhood, death, the terrors and
pleasures of the oceanic." Far from abandoning the erotic, we need to take it
back from the commercial culture that monopolizes it.

Perhaps most important, advertising and the popular culture define human connection almost entirely in terms of sex, thus overemphasizing the
relative importance of sex in our lives (and marriages) and under-
emphasizing other important things (friendship, loyalty, fun, the love of
children, community). According to poet Robert Hass, the art of the por-

nographer "consists in the absence of scale." There is no sense of scale in advertising, no sense of what is of greater or lesser importance. Life is rich and varied, with so many aspects that are important and meaningful—political, occupational, educational, creative, artistic, religious, and spiritual aspects. Sex is certainly one of these important aspects but, as Sut Jhally says, "Never in history has the *iconography* of a culture been so obsessed or possessed by questions of sexuality and gender." Men's magazines are filled with erotic images of perfect women (which also litter our highways and fill our TV screens). And women's magazines are filled with desperate articles about how to keep our men sexually happy—explicit instructions for fellatio, recommendations to try new things like anal sex.

The magazines for single women, like *Cosmopolitan*, are breathless, risqué ("Drive Him Wild in Bed: The Surprising Places He Wants You to Touch," "Be the Best Sex of His Life," and "Rated X: Sex Lessons of a Paris Madam" are typical cover stories). The ones for wives and mothers are more instructive (how to have romantic quickies, revive your sex life with a weekend in the Caribbean). When I read these magazines, I can almost feel the fatigue between the lines—oh, my God, in addition to working full-time and spending "quality time" with the children and remembering everyone's birthday and being responsible for all the planning of our lives and all the emotional work of the marriage, I also have to schedule passionate interludes and put on a garter belt and stockings and learn the latest sexual positions. No wonder I need a drink or a cigarette or a pint of ice cream.

Perhaps not surprisingly, at the same time that we are surrounded by these images and exhortations, many therapists and marriage counselors say that a chief complaint of many people, both single and married, these days is lack of desire. According to one sex therapist, "Sexual boredom is the most pandemic dysfunction in this country."

A 1999 study published in the *Journal of the American Medical Association* found that sexual dysfunction (such as lacking interest in or enjoyment of sex, performance anxiety, or inability to achieve or hold off orgasm) is an important public health concern, affecting 43 percent of women and 31 percent of men. The study, considered the most comprehensive look at American's sex lives since the Kinsey Report of the late 1940s, surprisingly found that the rate of sexual problems, aside from impotence, is not closely correlated with age. More than 1 in 4 women aged 18 to 29 said they do not find sex pleasurable and young women (aged 18 to 31) were more likely than older women (in their 40s and 50s) to report a lack of interest in sex, anxiety about performance, pain during intercourse, or an inability to achieve orgasm.

Not surprisingly, victims of childhood sexual abuse reported much higher rates of sexual dysfunction, with male victims 3 times more likely to experience erectile dysfunction and female victims twice as likely to have arousal disorders. "Traumatic sexual acts continue to exert profound effects

on sexual functioning, some effects lasting many years beyond the occur-
rence of the original event," the study authors wrote.

But even those who have not experienced trauma are often unhappy
and dissatisfied with their sex lives. Another major survey found that a
third of women respondents and a sixth of men were uninterested in sex.
One-fifth of the women but only one-tenth of the men went so far as to say
that sex gave them no pleasure. Although one advertiser joked about all
this in an ad claiming that "37% of women prefer shoe shopping to sex," it
is decidedly unfunny to those who are afflicted. Sexual dysfunction is associated with unhappiness and poor quality of life, especially for women.
In a sea of sultry images, many people are dying of thirst, drying up. Now
it may be that these people are perfectly "normal," but in an overheated
culture have no idea of what normal desire is. We're not morons. We know
that slipcovers won't lead to great sex and that a cruise won't bring a dying marriage back to life. However it is hard not to believe that other people are having more fun and that there is something wrong with us.

Syndicated columnist Dan Savage thinks that the way we talk about
sex contributes to this unhappiness and destroys a lot of perfectly de-
cent relationships. "When we talk about trying to bring the divorce rate
down," he says, "maybe we should do it by creating a society where we
don't insist a relationship is over when the sexual passion in gone."
Raymond C. Rosen, one of the authors of the JAMA study, said that too
often people's perceptions of what their sex lives should be like are
shaped by articles in magazines that suggest everyone else is having
great sex all the time. "As a scientist, it makes my hair stand on end," he
said. "It's terrible."

Perhaps these sexy images have the same effect as violent images: They
lead more to desensitization than to imitation. As Norman Cousins said:

> The trouble with this wide-open pornography is not that it corrupts, but that
> it desensitizes; not that it unleashes the passions, but that it cripples the emo-
> tions; not that it encourages a mature attitude, but that it is a reversion to in-
> fantile obsessions; not that it removes the blinders, but that it distorts the
> view. Prowess is proclaimed but love is denied. What we have is not libera-
> tion, but dehumanization.

A recent issue of Sky, a magazine targeting young people, contained the
following letter in the advice column: "My problem is that I don't enjoy
sex any more. I am a virile 22-year-old. I regularly have sex with my girl-
friend, but I have no pleasure any more…. Is there something that I'm doing wrong?" The advisor replied, "Shootin' air, eh, babe? You've caught
the sex problem of the '90s: pelvic apathy…. Actually all that's happening
to you and your bald best mate of 22 years is that you've both managed to
forget there's another human being slaving away at the far end of your

plank. Remember that person with the high voice and the lipstick?" This exchange was an unwittingly ironic counterpart to all the "sexy" ads throughout the issue. And how dehumanizing to refer to a woman, someone's lover, as "that person with the high voice and the lipstick."

Meanwhile, *Mademoiselle* offered this advice to young women whose arms start to ache while pleasuring their partners: "Your best bet—short of looking meaningfully at the bedside clock or developing the forearms of Martina Navratilova—is to get him to give you a hand."

In 1997, NBC featured a story about some college students—men and women—who regularly make a practice of getting drunk together and then having sex with whomever happens to be nearest at hand. According to one student, it is a great way to get his sexual needs met quickly without the "time-consuming" hassle of actually dating and getting to know somebody.

In a world filled with fast-food chains and junk-food advertising, many people are deliberately starving themselves or gorging themselves into oblivion. Consuming food for which we have no real appetite, we are never satisfied and lose our ability to gauge our own hunger. In a similar way, the barrage of constant sexual images and perfect bodies being offered up to us like delectable pastries (or perhaps popsicles) leaves us sexually numb and out of touch with our own desire. We can get almost any kind of ethnic food in our hometowns these days, and we also have more sexual choices than ever before in terms of partners and techniques. But when eating is divorced from hunger and appetite, and sex is divorced from desire and relationships, both experiences become onanistic, solitary, unfulfilling.

Of course, all these sexual images aren't intended to sell us on sex—they are intended to sell us on shopping. The desire they want to inculcate is not for orgasm but for more gismos. This is the intent of the advertisers—but an unintended consequence is the effect these images have on real sexual desire and real lives. When sex is a commodity, there is always a better deal. The wreckage that ensues when people try to emulate the kind of sexuality glorified in the ads and the popular culture is everywhere, from my house to the White House. And many who choose not to act on these impulsive sexual mandates nonetheless end up worrying that something is wrong with them, with their flawed and ordinary and all-too-human relationships.

So, all these blatant sexual images that surround us actually are more likely to lead to disconnection rather than to connection. And substance abuse and addiction, especially for women, is often a response to disconnection. Advertising doesn't cause this disconnection, of course, just as it doesn't cause addiction. But it does objectify women's bodies, making it more difficult for women to feel safely "embodied" and thus furthering a sense of dissociation. And it creates a climate in which disconnection and dissociation are normalized, even glorified and eroticized. And finally it deliberately offers addictive products—alcohol, cigarettes, food—as a way to cope with the pain this causes.

Far from improving, the situation continues to get worse. We are so used to blatant sexual images these days that advertisers have to constantly push the envelope in order to attract our attention, to break through the clutter. Increasingly, in order to shock us into paying attention, they borrow images from the world of pornography—which is a world of violence, a world of utter disconnection.

REFERENCES

Apostolides, M. (1998). *Inner hunger: A young woman's struggle through anorexia and bulimia.* New York: W. W. Norton.

Cousins, N. (1975, September 20). *Dehumanization.* Saturday Review.

Dear Karen (1996, December). *Sky* magazine, 226.

Greggis, A. (1997, August 16). Mainstream soft-core porn at the checkout. *Boston Globe*, C1, C6.

Howe, P. J. (1999, February 10). Study finds many in U.S. experience sex problems. *Boston Globe*, A1, A18.

Iggers, J. (1996). *The garden of eating: Food, sex, and the hunger for meaning.* New York: Basic Books.

Jhally, S. (1989). Advertising, gender and sex: What's wrong with a little objectification? In R. Parmentier & G. Urban (Eds.), *Working papers and the proceedings of the Center for Psychosocial Studies*, No. 29.

Johnson, R. (1998). Advice for the Clinton age. *New York Times Magazine*, 59–61.

Kilbourne, J. (1977). Images of women in TV commercials. In J. Fireman (Ed.), *TV book*. New York: Workman.

Kolata, G. (1998, June 21). Women and sex: On this topic, science blushes. *New York Times*, 3.

Laumann, E. O., Paik, A., & Rosen, R. C. (1999). Sexual dysfunction in the United States. *Journal of the American Medical Association, 281*, 537–544.

Moog, C. (1991, Spring/Summer). The selling of addiction to women. *Media and Values*, 20–22.

Pollack, L. (1998, April). *Lusty women.* Paper presented at a symposium at the spring meeting of the Division of Psychoanalysis, Boston, MA.

Schultz, R. (1995, Autumn). When men look at women: Sex in an age of theory. *The Hudson Review*, 365–387.

Snitow, A. (1985). Retrenchment versus transformation: The politics of the antipornography movement. In V. Burstyn (Ed.), *Women against censorship*. Vancouver: Douglas and Mcintrye, 116.

Wylie, M. S. (1997). Our trip to bountiful. *Family Therapy Networker*, 29.

Chapter 10

Adcult and Gender[1]

James B. Twitchell

University of Florida

IS IT TRUE BLONDS HAVE MORE FUN?

To find any battle against Adcult's intrusion into popular culture, we must go to the women's movement. During the last generation a steady parade of Cassandras, from Betty Friedan to Naomi Wolf, has contended that the commodification of gender is not just a nuisance but a handicap. I must say that I do not find the feminist critique of advertising entirely fair-minded, but I give it because it is the only coherent indictment of Adcult that has ever had a political following, and it has produced real changes in the industry.

The feminist criticism starts with the relatively simple proposition from 18th-century empiricism: esse est percepti, to be is to be perceived. What we take ourselves to be is how we perceive ourselves to be perceived. And we see ourselves in the media. Before the argument cleaves into gender-based concerns, let's have a look at something both sexes share that is literally at the edge of self and other—our epidermis. For our skin is literally what we show to the world of our selves. And what we put on our skin is what we see on the skins of others and how we want ourselves to be seen.

Having clean skin is a modern concern—instilled, aided, and abetted by companies in the 19th century that were producing surpluses of an everyday product, namely, soap. At the beginning of this century most people cleaned the skin of their entire body only once a week. On Saturday night, both in anticipation of the sabbath and as a result of the organization necessary to supply sufficient hot water, the family bathed. The soap people used was made from animal fats leached through ashes. Such soap was labor in-

---

[1]From *Adcult USA* (1996). New York: Columbia University Press; pp. 142–160. Reprinted with the permission of the publisher, Columbia University Press, and James B. Twitchell, Department of English, University of Florida, P.O. Box 117310, Gainesville, FL 32611-7310.

tensive to produce, unwieldy to use, and smelly. Hair was washed once a month as the soap tended to add oil, not remove it. The toothbrush was unknown. The mouth, like the armpit, certainly produced odors, but they had not yet been labeled offensive. In face, because they were the norm, they may well have not been "smelly" at all.

The mass production of soap made from vegetable oils rather than from organic materials, and the serendipitous discovery by James Gamble that overbeating the mixture would aerate it sufficiently so that it would float, and that this floating could be associated in consumers' minds with purity ("Ninety-nine and forty-four one hundredths percent pure"), allowed Ivory to separate itself from other soaps like Pears' and Sapolio and advertise its "ownership" of purity. The importance of Palmolive as a soap name is lost to us, but it announced to early users that no animal fats were used.

The other matter that should not be forgotten, and which was known to the upper classes, is that the human skin feels better when clean. The most important reason factory-made soap succeeded was that it was useful. By 1938, when the Scripps-Howard newspaper chain polled a cross-section of its readers in 16 cities, soap ranked second only to bread as an essential. At the same time, soap was becoming second to food in advertising volume (Vinikas, 1992, p. 93). The cultural ramifications were considerable. A new term, hygiene, was coined, the cosmetics industry began, and the concept of gender was profoundly changed.

Skin was not alone. Soon those other uncharted territories of the body became colonized. No crevasse, cave, or gully would go uncharted. Consider Listerine, which started as a hospital disinfectant. You would have been considered vile had you swirled it around in your mouth at the turn of the century. It should be used on the walls of operating rooms. Looking for a way to extend product application, Gerard Lambert, the mildly dissolute heir of the family business (at Princeton in the 1920s he had been chauffeured from building to building), came across the term halitosis in a medical journal. Lambert never cared much for the chemical business, but he loved to write ads and now he did. In his reminiscential essay "How I Sold Listerine," he tells of how in the early ads he told the story of how "a young lassie lost the lad of her dreams" for reasons that we learn only by checking an asterisk. There, separated from the copy, is the offending condition that has caused so much modern love to go sour—halitosis. With a dedication worthy of an obsessive-compulsive, young Lambert steadily increased his advertising until he had saturated magazine and newspaper culture. By 1928 he was the third-largest advertiser in magazines. By the 1930s, although he had to give up the claim of Listerine as aftershave lotion, the mouth was his.

In Adcult all the senses are up for grabs. Sight, of course, is self-evident. But take touch. From "the skin you love to touch" (thought by Albert

Lasker to be the introduction of sex into advertising) to "reach out and touch someone" (to sell telephone use), the exploitation of "being in touch" is omnipresent. Shaving the underarms and legs to make them touchable is recent. Kissing on the lips is far more popular in a culture that sells special lip colors than in those with natural skin. Although no one has applied a kissometer, we probably kiss more in the 1990s than in the 1890s, in large part because of the concept of "kissable lips." To some Freudians the painting of lips in shades of red, the act of French kissing with plunging tongues, and even the injecting of silicone to make them appear chubbier, is a far more sophisticated translation of nether labia than advertisers may ever have intended. But if you look at lipstick ads in women's magazines, you may not be so sure.

But the really powerful sense in Adcult is smell. How else to explain the underarm deodorant Odorono? And what of the long-dormant but still linguistically resonant campaign of Lifebuoy soap, based on just the initials of what we all know so well as B.O. The business of deodorization could not have been successful without the germ theory of illness. The concept of bad germs hiding on the body ready to charge out and ambush the forces of good health was more than a powerful trope. It was the selling tool of an entire industry. Being able to link the smell of rot with the appearance of such bad germs was the trigger of ersatz hygiene.

The programming of the senses, the social bells and whistles of bad odor, was not created in Adcult but exploited by it. The Cleanliness Institute, founded by the Association of American Soap and Glycerine Producers, inundated not just the media but the school system with expert advice on hygiene. It lobbied for special classes in hygiene and got them. That the rise of modern scientific medicine, directed by principles of observation and experimentation, should have been hijacked by the descendants of the patent medicine industry is no surprise. That it remains so powerful is a surprise, however. Much of the revenue flow of the major pharmaceutical companies in modern America, companies like Warner-Lambert, Bristol-Myers Squibb, Schering-Plough, American Home Products, Merck, and Upjohn, is not from proprietary drugs but from the over-the-counter concoctions to correct some natural deficiency or defend some body part from the attack of germs.

To some degree the germ theory is the basis of gender differentiation in the West. For once you remove dirt from the skin, pyorrhea from the mouth, and sweat from the armpit, the next step is clear: replenish, restore, replace, recreate. Cascading forth from the cosmetological cornucopia come all manner of deodorant sprays, antiperspirants, mouth washes, breath fresheners, foot powders, depilatories, scented shampoos, douches, clothes fresheners, and especially facial paint. To market many of these products, gender needs to be separated from sex. Sex is biological. Gender is cultural.

Arguably the most lasting contribution of Adcult is the ongoing creation and maintenance of gender. Until the 1920s men and women generally shared the same ideas and tools of cleanliness. Get rid of grime. The Gillette safety razor allowed men to more easily remove the natural growth of facial hair in a daily morning ritual. Women's ritual also centered on the face. Face painting, once reserved for prostitutes ("painted ladies") became an accepted routine in presenting the self for the day. It became required display for evening. Once the natural oils and dirt had been removed, the concept of cover-up became essential. Put on a face. Change the self. Look female. And be prepared to do this repeatedly during the day. Lacquering the soma with lipstick, eyestick, eyelash stick, fingernail stick became commonplace. Cosmetology became a science. Ideals like Miss America were spun out as examples of the perfectibility of this science when properly applied. Dressing and undressing became fetishized, because taking off and putting on was fundamental to femalehood. Gender was being branded.

Were women in the early 20th century duped by the onslaught of cosmetics? Were they cajoled against their better judgment to wash off their natural selves and paint themselves anew? And for whom did they do this? Recall Helen Resor's line for Woodbury soap, which revolutionized Adcult: "For the skin you love to touch." Who is the "you" who touches your skin? You or he? Just who was your face for? Recall Shirley Perkoff's line, "The closer he gets, the better you look." Why wasn't it "The closer you get the better he looks?" Did the faceless corporations of "the beauty industry" use the various new media of women's magazines to promulgate a culture of the subjection of the female self to the male other? (It need not be mentioned that most cosmetic advertising is written by women to appear in magazines edited by women—admittedly in parts of corporations run by men, the majority of stock in which is owned by women. Big deal.)

In one of the few dispassionate treatments of modern cosmetology Vincent Vinikas writes in *Soft Soap, Hard Sell: American Hygiene in an Age of Advertisement*:

> Advertising certainly stimulated demand of lipsticks, powders, rouge, eye makeup and the rest. But the phenomenal surge in the sale of cosmetics cannot be credited to the new vehicles of mass persuasion that appeared in the early 20th century. Instead, we must look at structural realignments in gender relations, as women assumed a more public identity than had been accorded them in the past. This reinterpretation of the meaning of female in America was signaled by Suffrage, the birth control movement, new conception of motherhood, and the development of new frameworks of opportunity for women beyond the confines of the home. It is only within the context of this fundamental change in the apperception of the woman's place—the conditional acceptance of the "New Woman"—that the cult of feminine beauty becomes comprehensible. (1992, p. xv)

Certainly, we can see this transformation to New Womanhood if we leave the powder room for a moment and look sideways into the workplace. As the demand for clerical workers increased with industrialization, it was met with the increasing supply of well-educated women. The job of secretary, which until modern times had been the role of confidant or deputy to an important personage (secretary = someone who could keep a secret), became not just gender but machine linked. The telephone and the typewriter became the tools of the receptionist-secretary. In 1890 women did 60 percent of the typing jobs in the United States, in 1900 it was 77 percent, and by 1920 it was 90 percent. To be sure these jobs now carry a sense of belittlement, as in the term *Girl Friday*. Today's feminist wouldn't be caught dead operating in such a job. In Adcult the working woman is now pictured as jauntily swinging her Louis Vuitton briefcase as she enters the boardroom. Or she pats a male rump en route to Somewhere Important as in the infamous Charlie perfume ad of the 1970s. But the next generation of women may well find this Enjoli woman ("Bring home the bacon, fry it up in a pan") just as ridiculous as we find the image of the secretary in the 1950s, mooning over her new IBM Selectric. However, at the time women were moving into the workforce, they remarked upon no such degradation. Quite the opposite. The "new woman" was the woman at last independent of the stultifying confines of the family and at last earning an independent wage.

How we look back in the brief history of Adcult is always determined by what we see today. In a museum show as revealing of current sensitivities as knowledge of the past, the Cooper-Hewitt recently displayed the tools of the mid-century American secretary. The informing premise of "Mechanical Brides: Women and Machines from Home to Office" was that somehow "they" were "gendering" the workspace for "us," and vice versa. The manufacturers of typewriters, telephones, and ironing boards were concocting and advertising a life for women devoid of real promise and excitement, to keep women if not servile then at least uncomfortable. You could not enter that marketplace as you were. You had to be re*fashioned*.

This view of woman-as-victim was especially true in the descriptive catalog. There is, however, a world of difference between shaping wants and needs and getting in the way of them. Herbert Muschamp, culture critic for the *New York Times*, made a central point about Adcult in his review of the show:

> So why has Cooper-Hewitt tried to tell its story as a narrative of deception? Because deception requires that someone is fooled, and someone else is doing the fooling. It sets up a plot of victims and oppressors. And what "Mechanical Brides" wants to illustrate is not simply that appliances are designed for women, but that they are also designed to keep women in their place. The secretary smiling at her desk has been duped into accepting a better typewriter instead of a better life. The curves and colors of her new Royal remind her that she is valued chiefly for being pretty.

The case is not airtight. The advertisements do show women in subservient positions: washing their husbands' pants or taking their bosses' dictation. But it is far from clear that the sexy new typewriter is what dragged the woman into the typing pool or discourages her from climbing out of it. In fact, since consumers mostly are women, the warped case could also be made that they're the ones responsible for trapping men into roles of insufferably rigid masculinity. How do we know that some husbands in the 1950s didn't secretly long to drop their lawn mowers, pull on satin gloves and flash their wives the "Sheer Look?"

The point is that the objects presented in this show invite more complex reading than the show itself allows. For instance, the secretary's smile may simply register that her new typewriter is a better piece of equipment. (When I worked as a secretary, I may not have grinned from 9 to 5, but the I.B.M. Selectric III was a joy to use.) Then, too, the transformation of industrial appliances into highly styled objects reflected something more than the entrance of women into lower echelons of the work force. It also reflected the broader shift in the nation's economy from manufacturing to service industries that set a higher store on image. (1993, p. C1)

I pause on Muschamp's point because the same consciousness that informs "Mechanical Brides" (even the show's title distorts McLuhan's thesis in his book of the same title) is at the heart of the feminist indictment of Adcult. To a degree this view comes from the academy's love affair with Marxism. In its macrocosmic form everything is cultural politics. In its microcosmic form individuals are invariably victims. The so-called Frankfurt theorists of the 1950s and 1960s essentially argued that what we see in popular culture is the result of manipulation of the many for the profit of the few. The manipulators, a.k.a. "the culture industry," attempt to enlarge their "hegemony" by establishing their "ideological base" in the hearts and pocketbooks of the mindless. The masters of the media strive to "infantilize" the audience, to make it both docile and anxious and consumptive with "reified desire." The lords of Adcult are predators, and what they do in no way reflects or resolves genuine audience concerns.

We may think advertising is "just selling a product," but this is not so. It is selling the oppression of consumption. The weak and marginalized, especially the female and the black, are trapped into a commodifying system, a "false consciousness" and a "fetishism" that only the enlightened can correct. Not to worry, however. It just happens that the fully tenured, university-based critic who is making this argument is one of the enlightened.

Indeed, much of modern feminism indicates that many young women were paying too much attention in college. Certainly one of the most articulate recovered victims of Adcult's suffocating oppression is Naomi Wolf. The subtitle of her best-selling 1991 book—*The Beauty Myth: How Images of Beauty Are Used Against Women*—begs the question and gives the lie too much hope of objectivity. Had she spent less time in Women's Studies and more time reading history, she might have been less willing to contend that quite suddenly, just when she was entering her teenage years, the world completely changed. Essentially her thesis is that just when feminism was finally liberating women from "the men who hold them back" by providing economic independence, sexual freedom, career opportunities, and reproductive control, male-dominated culture fought back through its manipulation of the cosmetic, medical, media, and especially advertising worlds to enforce the draconian "beauty myth."

"We are in the midst of a violent backlash against feminism that uses images of female beauty as a political weapon against women's advancement: the beauty myth," is Wolf's point. This oppressive beauty myth is inflicted on millions of innocent women thousands of seconds each day by the incessant unreeling of unreal images of beauty. Advertising has become sexual harassment. Want to know why there are so many anorexics, so much cosmetic surgery, so many ad-fat womens' magazines touting fat-free diets? Ask Madison Avenue; it knows. Want to know why those string-bean images are omnipresent? Ask the men in the $300 billion cosmetic surgery industry, in the $33 billion diet industry, and in the $20 billion cosmetics industry; they know.

It is not the male bashing that I find upsetting (well, okay, a little), it is her ahistorical economy of mind. Please don't misunderstand. Why some women purge themselves, have breast implants, apply acid to their faces to peel off the wrinkles, go on innumerable, often dangerous, diets (according to one study, 90 percent of women say they have been on a diet and 20 percent of "normal" women binge once a month), and why fashion magazines have come to favor photo spreads of women wearing dog collars and chains and penciled-on bruises in order to advertise some colored grease to cover the lips, are parts of important cultural matters. It is self-evident that advertising plays a reflecting (and shaping) role in this process.

But the concept of doing something to your body to make it "beautiful" is no more new to girls than that adolescent boys are often sent out in a rite of passage to do some kind of group violence. If you stand in the right place and adjust your blinders just so, it will seem that the antisocial and often frightful behavior of young men in college fraternities is unique to our "troubled times." But it's not. It is our current expression of something far more deeply infused with culture *and* biology. Like all other myths, these bracketing events are up for grabs. They are never imposed on an unwilling culture. Advertising is the folklore of a commodity culture. As such it articulates and redirects, but it does not invent behavior. If it did we would all be wearing Corfam shoes, drinking Tab, New Coke, and Schlitz, lathering with Sapolio, brushing with Pepsodent, painkilling with Lydia Pinkham elixirs, listening to music on our eight-track stereos, watching video on our Beta machines, and tooling around in Edsels.

What happens to adolescent girls in Adcult is different from what happened two generations ago, in part because the products are so different. But the cult of feminine beauty is as old as the cult of the male warrior. (And, who knows, maybe just as obsolete.) Look at the ugly bags and sexy wenches in Chaucer or Shakespeare. Look at fairy tales, for goodness' sake. What is Cinderella all about? Revlon did not make this nonsense up, although it merchandises it. And it merchandises it because the myth still has resonance. The face of a woman has been a commodity for some time. How else to explain the mythopoetic powers of Cleopatra and Helen of Troy? A FACE THAT LAUNCHES SHIPS—a copywriter's dream headline. Her idealized shape expands and contracts. Breasts in particular come and go: relatively big in the 1950s when housewifery was central; small in the 1920s and the 1960s when suffrage and liberation were central. No one said that Twiggy made women anorexic. But flat-as-a-pancake Kate Moss is now offered as a sign of the manipulations of a male-dominated culture out to render the female helpless.

Far from being victims of a new deception, female anorexics stand in a long tradition of women who have internalized cultural imperatives to obliterate their sexuality for any number of reasons. It may be as appropriate to blame the inchoate ideals of feminism for the youthful confusions about power and control as it is to blame the hopelessly perfect images in the media.

In a howler of massive proportions Wolf claims some 150,000 deaths each year from anorexia, and she blames this "holocaust" (her word, please) on the industries of oppression. "How," she asks, "would America react to the mass self-immolation by hunger of its favorite sons?" A good question made all the more provocative by the fact that the statistic is utter nonsense. The National Center for Health Statistics reports that the annual toll from anorexia is fewer than 100—usually around 50, although in 1983 it spiked up to 101. To her credit Wolf has promised to correct the error in future editions. However, the distortion is as purposeful as it is powerful, for it allows her to invoke the most powerful analogy of the 20th century. The image has already been picked up by textbooks used in Women's Studies. Modern life for young women in Adcult is like living next to a death camp.

To be sure, men have always been involved in matters of feminine beauty. This didn't start yesterday or even the day before. Remember the Judgment of Paris? As long ago as the third century A.D. Tertullian devoted a whole treatise to the subject of female dress, forbidding women to wear certain clothes or decorate their hair. All women, he wrote, should dress "as Eve mourning and repentant." Who can deny that his purpose was to control female sexuality and consolidate male power? And what of Thomas Aquinas, who implicitly acknowledged the bargain offered to compliant women when he wrote that nuns by renouncing sexuality "are promoted to the dignity of men whereby they are liberated from the subjection of men." Rascals have been around for a while. And what of cultures different from ours, like present day Iran, where the chador is used to protect otherwise oh-so-powerful men from the temptations of female flesh? And, for that matter, what was the Holy Roman Catholic Church doing with the cult of the virgin Mary?

Dark forces ("male institutions," "the economy," "Madison Avenue," "the power structure," "the cosmetics industry"), alarmed by the onward march of women, are not on the offensive, all due respect to the conspiracy and victim crowd: Catherine MacKinnon (feminist law), Andrea Dworkin (rape theory), Susan Faludi (backlash conspiracy), and Naomi Wolf (beauty myth). Women are not being systematically enervated by men just as the sisterhood struggles to be powerful. The idea that women are so utterly victimized by the way they are portrayed in their magazines that they starve themselves and become sick has a certain alluring simplicity. If only human nature were so simple. But anorexia and bulimia are multifactoral disorders more attributable to biology, environment, and personality than to the appearance of scrawny models in Diet Coke ads. This is not to deny the sexist nature of much of the media, or the reflective *and* aspirational nature of images cast in that media, but only to deny that conspiracy is the explanation.

Wolf tells an interesting story that she herself might ponder. Once, just before she was to deliver a lecture at a university, she was summoned to meet a group of women's studies majors to be sure she was right thinking. "Isn't the act of writing a book," asked a young woman accusingly, "in itself exclusionary to women who cannot read?" There are many answers to this transcendentally dumb question, short of howling in disbelief. One is that while it may be comforting to feel like a victim, it is usually counterproductive to act like one. This is not a gender-based problem. Listen to the bleats of full-grown white men in Detroit contending that the Japanese and Germans have stolen the American car market. By building better cars perhaps?

Having said that, it is of more than passing interest to see how much ads have changed, not so much because of feminist observations but from market pressure, a market that has changed because of feminism. If you watch early afternoon television, which used to be the entertainment ghetto for women, you will see few of the "two consumers in a kitchen"—type of advertising made standard by Procter & Gamble. If women today are house prisoners, their concerns are for personal injury lawyers, schooling programs like Hooked on Phonics, mortgage companies, Conway Twitty records, relief from vaginal itch, and a lot of kids' paraphernalia like diapers and toys. If you watch television ads for kitchen products, you are likely to see not frustrated housewives pleading for Mr. Clean or The Man from Glad, but Elayne Boozler controlling kitchen odor with Fantastik and wisecracks.

Television is filled with ads portraying women as being in control. What of the Maidenform ads (made at Ogilvy & Mather entirely by women) symbolically depicting the diversity of women with a rapid succession of 30 women's clothed torsos, each sporting different pins, with slogans ranging from "Right to Life" and "My Body, My Choice" to "No Pain, No Gain" and "Support Recycling." What of the Blockbuster ad in which the working heroine forgoes a date with a handsome man in order to watch a movie alone. Or the feisty woman at a gas pump telling us how she bought this Subaru, and how the '69 Mets choked. As I write this, two prime-time ads are poking fun at gender roles in advertising. In a Diet Coke commercial women office workers leer at a construction worker who takes off his shirt and opens the soft drink. The spot closes with their agreement to meet again tomorrow. And in a Hyundai ad women make suggestive comments about men who confuse flashy automobiles with virility. A hunk drives by in the economical Hyundai. Voyeurism? Certainly. Reverse sexism? Hardly. How come? Women are the target audience of both products.

In magazine ads Bamboo lingerie ridicules men for using words like *headlights*, *door knockers*, and *melons* and ends with the tag line, "Bamboo Lingerie, a company owned by two women. Put that in your pipe and smoke it." Liz Claiborne shoes flaunts the line, "Aren't there enough heels in your life?" while her fragrance ads use the theme "Reality is the best fantasy of all" and depict real-looking women in everyday situations. A new Maidenform "still-life" magazine ad shows a lacy bra lying on a table next to a stack of best-selling books by women. How about Nike's "You are not a goddess and you are never going to be a goddess" and its "You'll never be perfect" print ads? And Nike's three new black-and-white TV spots—its first TV campaign aimed at women—include one that says a woman's life should be as much of an announcement as her "selfish and shattering" scream at birth. Another advises, "Don't rush. The world rushes enough as it is."

In no way do I mean to overlook the "You've come a long way, baby" or the "I dreamed I was ... in my Maidenform Bra" genre, or the use of pubescent eroticism in selling jeans, or the uniformly over-the-top cosmetic ads of women's magazines. Whether she is the Breck Girl, the Cover Girl, or the Cosmo Girl, the one girl she is *not* is the girl next door. Nor do I want to pretend that the Johnnie Walker, Calvin Klein, Virginia Slims et al. campaigns don't exist. But I do want to argue that this aspect of advertising is neither new nor oppressive. Would that it were so, many an advertiser might hope. Sex doesn't sell, but it certainly captures attention. The Springmaid Sheet ads of the 1930s, the busty women on the Coke calendars, the endless use of sex to focus concentration on cigarettes, automobiles, beer, and what-have-you were the steady diet of the generation of women who produced the generation of women who now find themselves helpless before the onslaught of Adcult.

Ann Simonton, onetime beauty contestant and now director of Media-Watch—a nonprofit feminist group that "monitors sexism," makes the case:

> The ad industry has managed to mainstream pornographic images and desensitize the populace into accepting the humiliation of women in advertising. By porno I mean the use of a woman's sexuality as if it were some kind of commodity for sale. (Strnad, 1993, p. S6)

If women were so thoroughly desensitized for so long, how could they perceive their plight? And what of men who can't buy the right kind of toilet paper, leave watermarks on the glassware, and are invariably too stupid to know what to do when they have a cold? How desensitized are they? In Adcult men spend a lot of time lying abed moaning about how awful they feel. Only occasionally do they even know what to do for a headache. Let men become the primary buyers of such goods and you'll see the roles change. Women will be lying around moaning about what to do when they feel punk.

This shift is evident in slow motion in beer ads. Men used to be the primary consumers and *buyers* of beer. What did we have for ads? Endless bimbos in steamy pickup bars with voiceovers assuring us the "The night belongs to Michelob," which any fool knew really meant the "chick" is yours if you buy this beer. Now women are buying more beer and the advertising is shifting direction.

Sometimes the shift in mythography gets stuck and we can see it up close. A few years ago Hal Riney & Partners did a send-up of the "get a beer, get a chick, celebrate the beer" tradition with its now infamous Swedish Bikini Team campaign for Stroh's Old Milwaukee brand. To understand the parody you needed to know that for years the Old Milwaukee commercials had featured young males out fishing, hiking, and generally bonding and, come sun-down, drinking that beer and sighing in unison, "It doesn't get any better than this." In the send-up the fellows are all set to deliver the tag line when the Swedish Bikini Team arrives by raft or parachute or whatever. The joke is that the buxom beer bimbos (who are all wearing outrageous blond wigs) are clearly aware of the ridiculousness of the situation. The boys were quite wrong to think that "it doesn't get any better than this." It does. The punch line was missed in an avalanche of complaints, including some from women who worked in the brewery and thought they were being ridiculed, even harassed. As often happens in Adcult, the bikini team went on the cover of *Playboy*. The campaign was pulled, but it did show, if only for a second, the same shifting mythology of beer that has forever changed beer ads and literally shrunken the bosom of the St. Pauli Girl.

Gender differences are often confused with purchasing differences. When was the last time you saw a woman used in an automobile ad as an ornament? Forget it. In fact, some cars, like the Ford Probe, have so cornered the female market that no men even appear in the advertising. About half of all car-buying decisions are now made by women, compared with less than a third before the 1980s. Men buy most of the shaving cream, which is why the Gunilla Knutson "Take it off, men, take it all off" ad for Noxzema was such a success. And still is. Men also buy most of the small office products (fax machines, copiers), which is why Sharp Office Products runs the campaign with the sharply angular and steely technodominatrix who makes a point of repeating, "When I say Sharp, I mean business."

However, women buy most of the fragrances for men, which is why so many brands are keyed to perfume. Eternity for Men, Giorgio for Men, Passion for Men are all sold at the women's counter. So when Chanel does a television ad for Égoïste cologne for men (to be bought by women), it is an arty spot of 32 women screaming in French from their apartment windows. Dressed in ball gowns and long gloves, they yell such insults as "Miserable one" and "How could I have lived so long and been so disgraced?" all in French. Then they slam their shutters in unison against this cad. In focus groups the men had trouble understanding the message. They thought the French was important to translate. But women understood: this is how she wants her man to be. In such cases males are a "nice to" have, not a "have to" have audience. However, men still buy Old Spice. So the ad for them is the sailor home from the sea with the chick on his arm, tossing his Old Spice to young dweebs who so desperately need it.

Another example: young men buy their own pants. Their ads resemble the Bugle Boy campaign in which lots of sexy women are shown trying on men's jeans. But 60 percent of jeans for men older than 25 are bought by women. Hence the Dockers casual pants ads, in which the camera pans the butts and crotches as a bunch of guys have a chucklefest, are for women. So too is the send-up of the traditional male-bonding scene in which we see three golf buddies pitying a fourth for not being able to escape the clutches of his wife for a little weekend play. The scene shifts to the bedroom of the fourth as he is in the arms of his wife, having a far better time than he ever could have had on the links.

What we hear when we listen to the racket of Adcult is often deafening. It often seems as though a New Year's noisemaker is wailing the pitches of Calvin Klein, Benetton, or any of the in-your-ear campaigns designed to be fingernails on the chalkboard. But in truth, advertising is one of the most conservative forces in culture. It is more metronome than trumpet. Although individual ads do indeed claim the outer edge of acceptability, and their memorability often depends on this outrageousness, the accumulated force of commercial selling is more like a slow and continuous drumbeat of social norms. Again what commercial language does here with gender is exactly what all organizing systems do: it externalizes deep, cul-ture-specific, occasionally even biologic, concerns and ties them to specific physical goods. In so doing Adcult behaves far more like a religion, gaining power as it colonizes distant aspects of life, making them part of a coherent pattern, than like an oppressive dictatorship forcing innocent and helpless consumers to give up their better judgment in order to aggrandize some evil mercantile power.

REFERENCES

Lambert, G. B. (1957). How I sold Listerine. *Fortune* (Eds.) *The Amazing Advertising Business*. New York: Simon & Schuster. 49–59.

Muschamp, H. (1993, August 20). Women, machines and the sexual revolution. *New York Times*, C1.

Strnad, P. (1993, October 4). Nothing tops the woman's touch. *Advertising Age*, S6.

Vinikas, V. (1992). *Soft soap, hard sell: American hygiene in an age of advertisement*. Aimes, IA: Iowa State University Press.

Wolf, N. (1991). *The beauty myth: How images of beauty are used against women*. New York: William Morrow.

Chapter 11

Subliminal Sexuality: The Fountainhead for America's Obsession[1]

Wilson Bryan Key

*"The great majority of mankind is satisfied with appearances,
as though they were realities, and are often more influenced
by things that seem than by those that are."*
—Niccoló Machiavelli, 1520

HOW SUBLIMINALS REMAIN SUBLIMINAL

My experiences with subliminal perception over the past 25 years, since publication of *Subliminal Seduction* and my subsequent four books on the subject, were often bizarre though frequently quite humorous. A refined sense of humor is a basic necessity in dealing with the subliminal dimension. This is a subject area few readers know about, but more significantly most simply do not wish to know about. Subliminal manipulation abounds in the media world around us. Even presidential candidate George W. Bush used subliminal techniques in his campaign commercials ("rats"), then lied profusely in his refusal to admit it. His ad director, Alex Castellanos, is considered an expert in subliminal techniques. When a tachistoscopic display was discovered spliced into a Bush ad, it made news for several days, and then disappeared into the limbo of scandals that abound in many U.S. elections.

Media will generally avoid the subliminal issue, if possible, to protect their advertisers whose art and copy are saturated with the hidden persuaders. In media, one never bites the hand that feeds. The average citizen lives usually in denial (a perceptual defense) about the subject. Few appear capable of consciously accepting their vulnerability to media manipulation. Even fewer can admit to themselves having been gullible or perceptu-

---

[1]Printed with the permission of Dr. Wilson Bryan Key. Copyright © 2002 by Mediaprobe, Inc.

ally illiterate as they stumble through life blindly believing they think for themselves. Almost everyone believes they can easily discriminate between fantasies and realities, and are untouched by billions of dollars of media pumped into their brains annually. Americans desperately wish to believe they think for themselves—the fundamental assumption necessary to optimize a return on media investments. Simply put, consumers must believe ads do not work in order for them to work successfully.

Subliminal communication has been a commercial reality for a very long time. Well over 500 serious research studies, published mostly in academic journals over the past century, validate the effects of subliminal stimuli upon 10 measurable areas of human behavior—pretty much the entire behavioral package. Subliminal stimuli have been scientifically shown to affect conscious perception, emotional responses, drive-related behaviors, adaptation levels (AL), verbal formulations, memory, perceptual defenses, dreams, psychopathologies, and most of all driven by proprietary commercial research—purchasing and consumption behaviors. The vast amount of secret proprietary research produced by ad and marketing organizations on the subliminal issue is difficult to obtain. Should the issue ever surface in court, however, any competent attorney would have a field day doing discovery.

Norman Dixon, in his two books *Subliminal Perception: The Nature of a Controversy* and *Preconscious Processing* ponderously documents an exhaustive quantity of published academic experimental research supporting the effects of subliminal stimulation upon behavior. Like so many simplistic experimental psychologists, however, separating himself from the real world, he never once suspected commercial applications of his scientific evidence—which would have been readily apparent on billboards outside his London office. Anton Ehrenzweig's *The Hidden Order of Art: A Study in the Psychology of Artistic Imagination* superbly hypothesizes subliminal perception as the basis for creativity in music, art, poetry, and literature. There is much nourishment here for deep, multi-dimensional, and serious thought.

Further research on whether subliminals effectively change behavior still occasionally appears in academic journals—tantamount to re-examining the wheel as a useful technological device. The more serious question persistently avoided is what socio-cultural effects developed after half a century or more of an environment saturated with commercially directed subliminal influences—which the population is incapable of detecting, understanding, or even acknowledging—forces which control their destiny. There are few psychological, social, and medical pathologies in the United States, which do not have roots in advertising.

A recent estimate held that 10–20% of mainstream U.S. advertising contained sexual information. The estimate considered only cognitive, consciously available depictions of behavior, nudity, models, or promises of sexual fulfillment and intimacy. As long as one considers only the obvious, the estimate—though quite conservative—appears reasonable. Include the subliminal dimension of communication, however, and the input of information into the brain (without conscious awareness) of sexual material easily approaches 80–90% of commercial media. In this all-pervasive ocean of sexualized people, products, ideas, and information, few consumers even suspect an enormous, bizarre, invisible environment has been created to milk them out of their money, allegiances, and power. Curiously, the exploited and manipulated become the staunchest defenders of the forces that victimize them.

Media industries have been outspoken about what ads have done *for us*. As consumers, we should be more curious about what they are doing *to us*. But, magicians can never reveal to audiences how illusions are created. Sophisticated use of both cognitive and subliminal (the two are inseparable) communication techniques provide power to make of the world virtually anything desirable. Driven by unconscionable greed, today's media environment appears to have resulted in something closer to a garbage can. A dangerous paradox allows media to camouflage what has happened. It is impossible to separate observers from what they are observing.

Objectivity, or the fantasy of it, is a basic myth in most social systems. Individuals take their media for granted, trust it most if not all of the time, and stumble through life oblivious to what may really be going on around them. Few writers have seriously considered what occurs when media fantasies become far more desirable than realities. The fantasies become the dominant forces in our lives, ranging from our preferences toward an underarm deodorant to our selection of a presidential candidate.

Some years ago, I worked on a fictional movie script, which depicted a foreign conspiracy to control a major U.S. ad agency. The movie, *Agency*, starred Lee Majors and Robert Mitchum. The United States was to be corrupted via subliminal media manipulation. Sexual and social restraints were to be abolished. During a story conference, one of the more thoughtful producers questioned, "What would happen in the real world if someone actually did what our story line proposes? Would it be possible to corrupt an entire nation?"

Having written five books on subliminal media manipulation, I paused and thought carefully before answering. I finally replied, "Walk over to the window and look out into the street. It has already happened. But we did it to ourselves."

The motion picture industry has been deeply into subliminal perception for decades. Subliminals have been discovered in a broad range of Disney productions. For example, in *The Lion King*, "SEX"es float gracefully in cloud formations throughout the film. In *Who Killed Roger Rabbit*, the animated sexualized female character exposes her genitalia subliminally. In

The Little Prince erect penises decorate backgrounds as playful towers. Animation provides directors with complete control of every square centimeter of a frame.

Tachistoscopic high-speed flashing displays are frequently inserted in animated children's programs such as *Alf*. William Friedkin used subliminal audio and video extensively in *The Exorcist*—an early subliminal tour de force. Later in *Cruising*—a film about the gay leather bars in New York—Friedkin loaded the film with subliminal sexual pornography in both audio and visuals. He bragged that in his movie *Jade*, a strongly sexualized epic at the cognitive level, he utilized heavier subliminal content than he had ever before put into a film. *Jade* was itself pornographic dealing with prostitution, sexual promiscuity, and a rich variety of sexual deviations at cognitive levels, enhanced for the unconscious with subliminal pornographic stimuli. Nonetheless, *Jade* was not formally considered a pornographic production.

Since becoming involved with subliminal communication roughly 25 years ago, I have been astonished—and often amused—at the delicate dances performed by so-called scholars in their avoidance and denials of the subject. It is easy to rationalize why ad hustlers and their academic sychophants ignore the subject in their relentless pursuit of the fast buck. But, many presumably solid citizens approach the subliminal issue with awe, even fear, and an awkward hesitation, emotions usually reserved for an IRS audit or the threat of a herpes infection.

THE SKEPTICAL INQUIRER

I was interviewed roughly 25 years ago by a distinguished editor of a prestigious academic communication journal. The interview preceded publication of my first book *Subliminal Seduction*, which over the years reached 2.5 million copies in print, including translations. Similar interviews were frequently repeated over the next quarter century. I was overwhelmed when this distinguished editor called me personally. I had submitted an article on subliminal advertising. I was, at the time, an unknown author, rarely published in academic journals, serving as an assistant professor at a state university—not very impressive credentials.

"We found your piece on subliminals unusual and quite interesting," he said. I held my breath. Maybe this was my chance to enter the halls of academic scholarship. This might even get me tenure. He continued, "We wondered, however, why you avoided footnotes and validations for your conclusions."

"I don't understand your question," I replied in surprise. "I thought my facts and conclusions were simple, obvious, direct, and sustainable to anyone looking at the illustrations. I merely described what I perceived. Can you explain what you mean?" I chose my words carefully, straining to project a warm, congenial tone in my voice. But, the opportunity for social criticism was irresistible. "I assumed your readers would be visually literate," I added.

"You used a Kanon Cologne ad (see Fig. 11.1) to support your thesis. You alleged the hand and bottle were painted, not a simple photograph of the

FIG. 11.1. Ad featuring Kanon cologne.

objects. How do you know this allegation is true?" I detected a subtle tightening in his pronunciation as he articulated the verb "alleged."

"Did you call the editor of *Playboy* magazine to confirm your hypothesis," he asked. "Yes, of course," I replied. "I also called the ad agency that designed the ad."

"Did they confirm your analysis," he demanded.

"Not exactly," I answered. "They simply shouted obscenities at me."

"Sir," I tried to reply calmly, to the point, and with what I hoped would be perceived as humility and restraint, "Please compare your left hand with the hand portrayed in the ad. There are major discrepancies between the knuckle's distance from the end of the thumbnail to the distance from the knuckle to the wrist. They are totally disproportionate to what appears in an actual hand."

"Yes, that is curious, I must admit," he replied. "But," he continued, "How can you be certain some individuals might not have a left hand comparable to that in the ad?"

"Sorry," I replied apologetically. "I looked all over our campus and did not find a man's left hand that came close. By the way," I could not help but add, "the hand in the ad has no fingers. You may have missed this small detail."

His response was immediate. "The fingers could have been hidden in the dark shadows behind the bottle," he said with a victorious note in his voice. I wondered for a moment whether to compliment his critical perceptual skills, but decided to avoid an argument and look at other details in the hand.

"If you study the palm and the wrist and compare them with your left hand, they are complete distortions of the real thing," I said. "You might even conclude the wrist and palm look far more like male testicles. The thumb has been painted to appear far more like an erect penis of somewhat prodigious proportions."

He inhaled sharply, "Do you have any empirical evidence that the hand in the ad is not an actual hand? Who can validate your questionable conclusions? You have made a serious allegation toward a respected product and the publication in which they advertise. You must provide some sort of proof," he said adamantly. His hostility was now on the surface.

I considered asking simply that he compare his own left hand with a penis, but felt it might appear an insult. I still half-hoped I might talk him into publishing my article.

"Did you notice the knife blade on the cork about to slip," I inquired. "Such a slip would result in a disaster for the man trying to open the Kanon bottle."

"My God! You have an incredible imagination," he replied. "In your piece you wrote some psychological nonsense about castration fear. What is your evidence?" he demanded.

I thought at first I might suggest he talk to students. Most young men will discuss to a friendly questioner their castration fears. Editors of the so-called men's magazines utilize castration fear as a major theme in copy and art. I thought I had better keep my mouth shut if I was ever to see my article in print.

The editor continued, "Your allegations about the dead beagle with a chisel through its head in the lower right portion of the ad we found sustainable. Until you pointed it out, none of us had noticed the dog. But, how could a dead beagle ever sell Kanon Cologne? If you can come up with real proof about the hand, knife, and dog, we might consider publishing your piece. Once again," his voice was now commanding, "how do you know your conclusions are true?"

"One more item," he concluded. "As these magazines have mainly young male readers, your conclusion that the ad would sell Kanon Cologne through an appeal to latent homosexuality and castration fear is absurd. Those paragraphs must go!"

I ended our conversation abruptly. I hung up.

The above conversation was not exaggerated. I have participated in dozens of such conversations over the past quarter century, often with men or women who somehow achieved the title of communication scholars. Subliminal communication is frightening to a great many scholars. Some are simply in denial, not an unusual perceptual defense among scholars, but others know clearly that subliminals are a taboo subject in the United States. Universities serve individuals and institutions that control and manage society and the ad media they own and operate.

I recall sound advice from a dear friend and colleague, Marshall McLuhan, who wrote the preface for *Subliminal Seduction* while I fought to survive attacks upon my work at the University of Western Ontario. "Never waste time arguing with fools, especially experts, bureaucrats, and academics. Most merely mimic and follow their leaders, threatened by innovation and creative insights." McLuhan was a very wise man.

"Mmmmmmmm MOISTER!"

"There have been moist layer cakes before. But now there's SuperMoist!" This is a lovely thought for those obsessed with chocolate. The Betty Crocker ad (see Fig. 11.2) was published in a score of women's magazines over several years. The best way I have found to study art is to first relax. Five deep breaths, slowly inhaled and exhaled, are a good start. As the body and mind relax, fine details in art and music slowly surface. As you view the ad, let your eyes wander, find their own direction and focus, as your *foveas* (the central cluster of cells in your eyes' retinas) saccade (move from point to point) across the ad. Relaxation, however, is the most important step in unlocking

FIG. 11.2. "MMMMMoister." Ad featuring Betty Crocker Super Moist Cake Mix.

your perceptual restraints. This process may be compared to audio perception. When you go to bed at night with music on the radio, the sound appears
to grow louder and louder. Your perception of volume becomes more sensitive as you relax. The radio only appears to grow louder.

There appears a perceptual quality in the chocolate cake picture that has
been called *synesthesia,* simply a sensory crossover effect where through visual stimuli, you can taste and smell the rich chocolate in the cake. These are
projective perceptions. Possibly the most important synesthesia effect, however, is tactile—the perceptual projection of touch. Tactile is our most vital
sensory capacity. "Moister" is of course tactile. A fundamental ingredient in
any meaningful art experience is the synesthesia effect, a subliminal perception. Merely glancing at certain textures—latex, satin, silk—can be sexually
arousing for many individuals. In good music, synesthesia effects are important. Ravel's *Bolero* depicts a slow, sensuous orgasmic buildup. Beethoven
composed the *Ninth Symphony,* considered by many the single most magnifi-
cent musical composition ever, without ever hearing the music. He was totally deaf when he composed the masterpiece. He experienced the complex
harmonics visually through the written notes on paper. Many composers develop this ability as they progress through their careers.

Concentrating on the chocolate cake-mix ad, on the surface the most blatant type of banality, might even appear absurd until you realize produc-

tion costs on this single ad could have ranged from $70,000 to $100,000. The cake ad was painted, of course. It is not real cake. It actually appears far tastier and more desirable than real cake. And, the publication budget for this two-page masterpiece approached $10 million in *Reader's Digest* and scores of women's magazines. Art, especially in this case, must be highly functional. To justify its investment, the ad must sell at least $50 million in Betty Crocker's cake mix—a major transaction in our economic system. When a reader perceives the ad, he or she rarely devotes more than an instant to the perception. It most likely would not surface cognitively. Fewer than 5% of readers who perceived the ad actually read the copy.

If the Betty Crocker ad is to change the lives of the millions of readers who perceived it for a few seconds by inducing their purchase of the cake mix, it must work inside the brain instantaneously. The ad would unlikely elicit a cognitive response and, as one of the 1,200 sales inducements perceived daily by average Americans, would not be consciously recalled. Individuals do not perceive an ad, then rush down to the nearest Safeway and scoop up every available box of the product. It may be days, weeks, or even months before they are in a situation where they could purchase the mix. The ad is worthless unless it can evoke a delayed response.

In conventional cognitive wisdoms, advertising—irrespective of how brilliant the art-work—appears a waste of money, time, and effort. But, if you know that perception is *instantaneous*—at both conscious and unconscious levels—a few seconds of exposure is really a very long time. Less than 10% of such a perception is cognitive, the remainder subliminal unless you have been specifically trained. And, if you knew that perception is also *total*, that meanings and every detail are retained in unconscious memory indefinitely, perhaps for a lifetime. Finally, if you knew that around 1918 a Viennese physician, Otto Poetzle, discovered that unconscious memories can be hypnotically programmed to stimulate delayed action responses days, weeks, or even months after their initial perception. If you knew all of this, you might begin to understand the cake ad could constitute a major life event after a momentary perception.

As your relaxed eye and mind wander across the picture, you may not notice several discrepancies in the design. The fork is a salad fork, usually small, much too small to support a large, moist slice of chocolate cake. Artists often insert dissonance, things illogical or unreasonable, in their work. Dissonance appears to stimulate unconscious perception—a primary effect—and rarely draws cognitive attention. Under hypnosis, individuals easily perceive dissonant detail. As your eyes lazily wander the design, you might notice the crumbs in the slice. Painted under a magnifying lens, small letters appear among the crumbs—such as S, E, and X, not necessarily in that order.

"Icing on the cake" is a traditional American metaphor that describes not only the sweetest, richest portion of a pastry, but also a special reward added to a promise of indulgence. When your eye wanders along the top of the cake, the rich succulent flavor and odor assaults your subliminal senses. True, you can tell the icing is sticky as well as moist (tactile responses), but no chocolate enthusiast could ignore the lush pile of chocolate icing above the heel of the slice. Remember, virtually every individual in the Western world has eaten Betty Crocker. The mixes are internationally renown.

At first glance, the pile of icing on the heel of the cake appears dissonant. Logically, it should appear as thin as the top icing. The baker, or artist, may have had icing left over and dropped a large glob on the heel. Considering that this artwork cost more than $50,000 and will involve an investment in media of several million dollars, such dissonant detail is unforgivable by conventional wisdoms. At this point, inspect the detail in Fig. 11.3. The chocolate icing has been sculpted to appear as a tumescent female genital. The painted details are anatomically correct—major and minor labia and clitoris. The artist had certainly researched the subject exhaustively. Chocolate, of course, provides the genital with black ethnic characteristic. As the headline perhaps redundantly announces—"Mmmmmm Moister!"

The Betty Crocker ad demonstrates the incredible power of human repression to hide important information from our cognitive processes. Millions of consumers, both men and women, perceived the ad. None consciously dealt with the subject matter that they concealed (repressed) from themselves. It was not the artist who concealed the exposed genital, but the individual viewers of the ad. Yet, no one—as the artist and executives who produced the ad accurately predicted—consciously recognized the genital. Unconsciously, of course, such powerful information could remain in their unconscious memory indefinitely.

I included Betty Crocker's Moister in my book *The Age of Manipulation*. The ad was directed at female consumers, as the Kanon ad was directed at young males. Illogical? You might think the gender of the genitalia should have been reversed. But, subliminal manipulation appears most successful when the content is taboo. Most social taboos in all cultures involve either sex or death—the two universal polarities of human life. Homosexuality in America, as the Clinton administration discovered when they confronted a homophobic U.S. culture, evokes fierce phobic reactions, quite unlike those in other world cultures.

My files contain hundreds of subliminal genital ads. If your sexual fantasies appear strange from time to time, there could be good reasons. It appears quite possible U.S. sexual phobias have been nourished by media's taboo subliminal content. Unfortunately, at the moment, it appears impossible to penetrate the complex cause-and-effect relationships between media and socio-psychological phenomena. Someone should be looking into this. Unfortunately they are not.

FIG. 11.3. Close up of sexualized Betty Crocker icing.

In the United States, news—not unlike toilet paper and underarm deodorants—is relentlessly merchandised and exploited for profit. Very rarely is a news photograph published without retouch work. Retouching can heighten contrasts between figure and ground, emphasize content detail obscured by poor lighting, and actually add new material not in the original photograph. Retouch artists can easily work the word "SEX" into a picture either in mosaic patterns or individual letters. "SEX" embeds can either be painted in with an airbrush, etched into engravings, or electronically embedded with digital photography. A digital camera provides complete control over every square centimeter of the picture.

Most individuals can, if they learn relaxed perception, consciously perceive the "SEX"es. They are embedded just above the threshold of visible cognition. For example, on a scale from 0 to 10, the embeds would be apparent at full contrast at 10, while at 0 nothing appears. Subliminals must be embedded as close to 0 on this scale, or as faintly as possible, without the embed disappearing. Conventional wisdoms hold that the stronger the image, the more powerful. With subliminals, however, the weaker or more faint they are the more powerful is the effect. As with the Betty Crocker ad, subliminals must never intrude cognitively to be effective.

The easiest way to find embedded "SEX"es in art is to first take several deep breaths, relax, and allow your eyes lazily to scan the picture. Once again, do not strain to perceive what you are searching for. Strain and tension will keep the subliminal hidden from cognitive perception. These embedded "SEX"es allow media to sexualize everything in the society, especially those subjects where sex would be considered taboo. I collected numerous printed cards with portraits of Jesus Christ where "SEX"es were exhaustively embedded in hair, face and clothing. "SEX"es appear to sell Christ extremely well, as many Christians are obsessed with the subject.

A consensus among artists I have spoken with is that if artwork is well done and skillfully crafted, embedded subliminals will enhance the work emotionally. Subliminals will not make good art out of poor craftsmanship. Audio engineers who record popular music have testified that audio subliminals are the final creative polish to a good tape to embellish the emotional impact of the composition. Audio subliminals are often added to sound tracks after the initial recording where punch-ins (inserted obscenities, etc.) are integrated into the composition with millisecond precision. Punch-ins can be reversed, slowed down or speeded up to be stored indefinitely in the unconscious, probably appearing later for use in sexual fantasies, purchases, or other behaviors.

"SEX" thoroughly saturates U.S. media, sexualizing virtually everything in the society. The word "SEX," symbolizing the strongest human drive system, is so familiar only two of the letters are necessary. The consumer fills in the missing letter in a Gestalt closure. Even look-alike or missing letters will work to establish the SEX identification. The letters on automobile trunks, for example, include Honda SE 1, Mazda ZX 7, Dodge 600 ES, Datsun ZX, Datsun 200 SX, Mercury ZX 7, Mercedes SE 4, and Toyota SE 5.

YOUTH AND VIRILITY THROUGH "SEX"ES

The omnipresent "SEX"es in media lay the groundwork for our society's major obsession. The *Time* magazine portrait of George W. Bush is a well executed, though typical example of subliminal retouching (see Fig. 11.4). *Newsweek's* comparable Bush cover portrait used essentially the same technique. Most magazines covers (an ad for the magazine) are similarly retouched and restructured. Bush, of course, was heavily cosmetized for the portrait. His eyelashes were painted darker to make him appear younger. A portion of the left side of his face was darkened. Shadowing a face usually suggests subliminally that the person portrayed is hiding something. Shadowing either makes the portrait more sinister, more dramatic, or both.

The pupils, the dark central opening of the iris, have been slightly enlarged, suggesting subliminally that the subject is tense, alert, or sexually stimulated. Bush is portrayed in the cover as very young, boyish. His grin might lead you to believe he had just made Eagle Scout. Remember, every square centimeter of the portrait has been expertly retouched. The portrait has very little to do with the subject's reality. It actually conceals reality.

The "SEX" embeds, often in very small mosaics, cover his face. Many are very small, but can be viewed comfortably with magnification. More obvious, larger "SEX"es were marked on an overlay and photographed for the illustration. Discovering SEXes can be difficult for some individuals. Once again, it is helpful to relax. Try half a dozen slow deep breaths, then permit the eyes to roam effortlessly and unguided across the portrait. When the eye finds one of the three letters, you can usually connect the remaining two lightly embedded on the surface (see Fig. 11.5).

Virtually all celebrity photographs, and certainly those on magazine covers, are embedded with "SEX"es. Photographer-artists usually retouch them with an airbrush, but they can be embedded in numerous ways—photo superimpositions, engraving, or electronically via a digital camera. Such professional portraits can cost thousands of dollars.

Once an individual becomes relaxed, the discovery of the "SEX"es can become quite engrossing, if you have nothing more exciting to do at the moment. The "SEX" letters combine all basic design elements—curves, horizontal and vertical lines, and diagonals. It is most unlikely such design elements could be random projections. Arguments have been made that the "SEX"es could be projections—the mind is making them up. I used to take my classes outside the building to lie on the lawn for an hour to study cloud formations. You would be astonished at the filthy language and

FIG. 11.4. Unmarked cover of *Time* magazine featuring President George W. Bush.

scenes reportedly going on in the clouds. These are projections, not unlike responses to the famed Rorschach inkblots. All humans project, all of the time. To separate the "SEX"es from projections, I use several rules. The letters must be in the same typeface, equidistant letters, and other individuals must readily identify them. Fantasy projections are usually recognizable

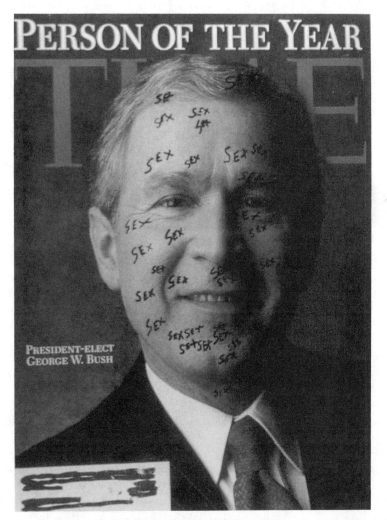

FIG. 11.5 "SEXes" revealed on George W. Bush's face.

because they will be perceived differently by other individuals, or not at all. The question, of course, is highly sophisticated. How does one discriminate between fantasies and realities? Are "SEX"es really there, purposefully designed by someone? Or, is the observer making them up, merely fantasizing. In a technologically advanced society such as ours, media can make fantasies far more appealing, sexually desirable, and of course, more expensive than reality could ever become.

The airing of subliminals is prohibited in the United States and outlawed in several other nations. The Federal Communications Commission and Federal Trade Commission have ruled subliminals are contrary to the public interest because they are clearly intended to be deceptive and are therefore restricted. Courts have ruled subliminals are subject to First Amendment protection. The techniques are also prohibited in voluntary professional advertising and broadcasting codes. Most recently, the Bureau of Alcohol, Tobacco, and Firearms (ATF) ruled to prohibit subliminals in alcohol beverages advertising—spirits, beer, and wine. I wrote a large portion of the ATF ruling. So much for opposing sin and favoring motherhood. Like so many laws in the United States, they are selectively enforced. Clever people spend their lives and energies working to circumvent the law. Seemingly inexhaustible commercial artists continue to design new, creative, subliminal techniques and strategies. Few in the general pubic are even aware they are the victims in an immoral game. U.S. politicians would never critically oppose an ad media's major income source.

Over the years, I have testified before U.S. Senate and Canadian House of Commons committees. They were always polite, amused, appeared fascinated, and even sometimes shocked. But, nothing changed and the various legal prohibitions continued to be ignored. ATF used subliminal techniques in their attack upon the Branch Davidian compound in Waco, Texas. The subliminals were actually engineered by Green Beret Delta Force officers, working under ATF supervision, who embedded hidden voices in Gregorian Chants and in the death screams of animals being sacrificed which they amplified into the compound with powerful outdoor speakers. These officers referred to the audio techniques as a weapons system.

And finally, George W. Bush used subliminal embeds in his election campaign commercials. In the famed "RATS" commercial for Bush, the word "RATS" was spliced into the commercial. The tachistoscoped display appeared for roughly 1/50th of a second superimposed over the word "bureaucrats" which appeared cognitively on screen. The embed was discovered by Fox TV News which ran the story, but no one picked up on it. The ad ran 4,000 times during a two-week period at a cost of $4 million. The subliminal was aimed at discrediting Democratic bureaucrats and their medical proposals.

A retired Boeing technical writer, Gary Greenup in Seattle, again discovered the flashing insert. He called the Seattle TV media, which brushed him off. Generally, media will run a subliminal story if they must, but ignore the issue on behalf of their advertisers—most of whom use subliminal tricks. Greenup then called the Democratic National Committee who sent staff members to interview him. By afternoon, the "RATS" campaign commercial was in the hands of *The New York Times*.

George. W. Bush and his ad director, Alex Castellanos, had their cover story ready. Castellanos is widely known as an expert on subliminal advertising. Bush called the notion of subliminals "bizarre and weird," making light of the commercial. Bush explained, trying to lie his way out of the problem, "One frame out of 900 hardly in my judgment makes a conspiracy. I am convinced this is not intentional. You don't need to play, you know, cute politics," he piously added.

Alex Castellanos, the Republican ad director, said he flashed the letters "RATS"—the tail end of bureaucrats—so the ad appeared more visually interesting, and it was just a coincidence it came out "RATS". "It's a visual drumbeat," he said. "People get bored watching TV. You are trying to get them interested and involved."

Castellanos insisted the use of the word was "purely accidental. We don't play that way. I am not that clever." The embeds were directed to denounce Gore's prescription drug plan where "Bureaucrats decide." Castellanos earlier had used subliminal racist themes during a campaign for Jesse Helms in North Carolina against a black opponent.

To anyone interested in studying subliminal techniques, my suggestion is usually to study good art and music. Artists have been using subliminals for centuries, as have the great composers. The Bigallo Crucifix, as cited in my book *Age of Manipulation*, dates to 1240-70. I also cited works using subliminals by Dürer, Hieronymus Bosch, Michelangelo, Holbein the Younger, DaVinci, Titian, Rembrandt, and Picasso in *The Clam-Plate Orgy*.

So, finally, one might reasonably wonder why—with so many people studying communication in the United States—the subject of subliminals is denied, ignored, circumvented, discouraged, and even forbidden? I collected a file of letters over the years from high school and college teachers who had been threatened with sanctions or chastised for using my books in their courses and including them in their reading lists. The study of subliminal communication has become the new subversive threat to media control of U.S. culture.

Marshall McLuhan once commented that "George Orwell's *1984* actually happened around 1930. We just did not notice anything had changed, much as Orwell had predicted." Big Brother had convinced intellectuals to study only the cognitive (what is consciously perceived): psychology, sociology, anthropology, art, and linguistics. Behaviorism, the psychological theory that disavows the unconscious, studies only obvious cognitive behaviors. What you see, hear, smell, taste, or feel is what you get. Behaviorism remains a monumental anti-intellectual, farcical triviality, but the major perspective prevalent in academic America.

REFERENCES

Dixon, N. F. (1971). *Subliminal perception: The nature of a controversy*. London: McGraw-Hill.

Dixon, N. F. (1981). *Preconscious processing*. New York: John Wiley & Sons.

Ehrenzweig, A. (1970). *The hidden order of art: A study in the psychology of artistic imagination*. London: Paladin.

Key, W. B. (1973). *Subliminal seduction: Ad media's manipulation of a not so innocent America*. New York: Signet.

Key, W. B. (1977). *Media sexploitation*. New York: Signet.

Key, W. B. (1986). *The clam-plate orgy and other subliminal techniques for manipulating your behavior*. New York: Signet.

Key, W. B. (1989). *The age of manipulation: The con in confidence, the sin in sincere*. New York: Henry Holt.

Key, W. B. (1992). *Subliminal ad-ventures in erotic art*. Boston: Branden.

PART IV

Contexts and Audiences

Chapter 12

Masculinism(s) and the Male Image: What Does It Mean To Be a Man?

Barbara B. Stern

Rutgers, The State University of New Jersey

FEMINISM AND MASCULINISM

Before the advent of feminism and the rise of women's studies, everything male was assumed to be the "norm" and everything female the "other" (de Beauvoir, 1949 [1952]). Predetermined sex roles based on biological sex were viewed as static containers for men and women, with appropriate gender traits and behaviors assigned to each sex. However, the rise of men's studies problematized the construct of gender such that the question "What does it mean to be a man?" could no longer be answered simply as "the social norm."

The justification for men's studies is that if the "sex-role paradigm" assumes masculinity as the normative standard of reference, changes as a result of the women's movement are ignored. Men's studies problematize gender categories and challenge the sex-role model in which each sex fits (or does not fit) pre-existing roles. It is characterized by a new model of relational and multidimensional gender roles, in which the meaning of masculinity is that it changes. This model posits the social construction of gender, with definitions of masculinity "historically reactive to changing definitions of femininity" (Kimmel, 1995, p. 14). That is, changes in the definition of either term act as prompts for the reevaluation of definition of the other one.

These reevaluations have led to a crisis of contemporary masculinity (Seidler, 1997), characterized by the breakup of the formerly monolithic concepts of *masculinity* and *femininity*. There is no longer a simplistic single masculinism, but, rather, many and changing masculinisms. Successive waves of social construction have broadened the construct to include biological sex as well as class, race, age, ethnicity, and sexual orientation.

The source of masculinist scholarship is the field of men's studies, which has become an accepted discipline that has its own organization (Men's Studies Association of the National Organization for Men Against Sexism), scholarly journals (*masculinities*, formerly the *Men's Studies Review*, and *The Journal of Men's Studies*), and print and online bibliographies (August, 1994, Kibby, 2001). However, it is a discipline that can only be understood in light of feminism, for the feminist movement set in motion a masculinist movement, and a basic premise (Kimmel, 1987) is that men's studies arose as a response to the challenge of women's studies. Definitions of masculinity evolved in the course of dialectical masculinist–feminist discourse and theory development, and changes are likely to be ongoing. Just as the study of femininity dealt with the oppression of women by male objectification, so too does the study of masculinity deal with the oppression of men by objectification.

Feminists often categorize advertisements as a locus of oppression, the carrier of images denigrating women by representing them as passive objects of the male "gaze" (Stern, 1993). Here, women are shown as passive objects of desire, gazed on by men actively engaged in evaluating and controlling whatever they look at. Quite recently, however, the concept of the "female gaze" (Schroeder & Zwick, 1999) has been introduced into the advertising literature, and the feminist technique of role reversal (Fetterley, 1977; Stern, 1993) has been used to support the claim that men too are often depicted as eroticized, fetishized, and vulnerable objects of desire.

Nonetheless, sociocultural factors more complex than the substitution of one sex for the other are responsible for changing interpretations of male body imagery (Sandikci & Ringberg, 1999). It seems likely that men and women will continue to be both subjects and objects of the gaze, for not only have men as well as women been influenced by feminism, but also by masculinism. To address the shifts in male imagery brought about by the dialectic, let me begin with a brief summary of the evolution of masculinism.

A GENERATION OF MASCULINISMS

Although the definition of masculinity is recognized as fluid, evolving, and dialectically progressive, there has been little research on the impact of changing definitions on advertising. Nonetheless, advertising serves as the primary lexicon of gender images, responsible for the wide dissemination of currently relevant masculine and feminine imagery (Bordo, 1999). Although advertisements are considered the repository of "beefcake and cheesecake" images (Jones, Stanaland, & Gelb, 1998), more research attention is paid to the present than to the past, albeit a recent and relatively short span of time. Thus, it seems fair to say that the history of masculinism, rooted in the concept of male oppression, is not nearly as well-known as that of feminism. Thus, the following brief summary of a generation of masculinisms provides background necessary to understand the catalog of today's male body images.

The iconic book that launched the masculinist movement in the United States was Warren Farrell's *The Liberated Man*, published in 1975, over a decade after Betty Friedan's *The Feminine Mystique* (1963), the book that launched contemporary feminism. Friedan's book inspired the women's movement, which quickly became organized via the New York National Organization of Women (NOW), started in 1967. Throughout the late 1960s, women's consciousness-raising groups grew in popularity and influence. Farrell was closely associated with New York NOW, and was on its first board of directors. He attended numerous women's liberation meetings, and in 1970 founded the first men's liberation group. In 1971, he founded the NOW National Task Force on the masculine mystique, which became the organizational base of the men's movement. He had been working on his book since 1969, and as the chronology indicates, his focus on masculinism is intertwined with his experience of early feminism.

The men's movement led by Farrell and others set out to liberate men from stereotypes, often viewed as emblems of male oppression. Herb Goldberg's, *The Hazards of Being Male: Surviving the Myth of Masculine Privilege* (1976) focuses on the cultural disempowerment of men just as Friedan's earlier book did on women (1963). Current masculinist study parallels new feminist interest in social construction, aiming at discovering multiple representations of maleness (Cohan, 1997; Rotundo, 1993). Just as feminism disrupted the idea of femininity as a monolithic construct, so too does masculinism challenge masculinity, implying that feminist theories of resistant reading can now be generalized to men and women.

Pluralistic masculinisms (Clatterbaugh, 1996) have been described in terms of eight men's "movements," with different perspectives flowing from responses to feminist viewpoints. That is, the perspectives begin as reactions to one or another aspect of feminism, for the history of masculinism cannot be written without that of feminism. A short summary follows.

1. *Conservative.* An early 1970s response to feminism was spurred by anger and a desire to resume the status quo. This was the "first wave of resistance," in which rage against "liberated" women (Lyndon, 1992) spurred the growth of antifeminism, which called for a return to the moral and biological imperatives viewed as "natural." From this perspective, the traditional "place" for each sex was what it had been before the disruptive feminist upheaval.

2. *Profeminist.* At the same time, a liberal profeminist movement also arose, led by Farrell and others. In opposition to the conservative privileging of masculinity and maintenance of the patriarchy, this more radi-

cal perspective focused on the need for both men and women to break out of restrictive roles so that both could achieve self-realization. Traditional views of masculinity were viewed as outmoded, in need of being replaced by new behaviors informed by feminist values.

3. *Men's Rights*. By the mid-1970s, antifeminism centered on the status of men as the oppressed group, a concept popularized by Goldberg (1976). He argued that far from men being privileged in relation to women, the feminist privileging of women works in tandem with the degradation of men. He and others claimed that the new sexism of male-bashing, as well as the older sexism of woman-bashing, was detrimental to both sexes.

4. *Socialist*. Evidence of sexism in the liberal movements of the 1960s and early 1970s (Civil Rights, Workers' Rights, and so forth) spawned a reaction by the late 1970s on the part of left-leaning men. From the socialist perspective, masculinities were seen as grounded in the capitalist society, inevitably patriarchal. Economics and class structure determine masculinity, based on the kind of work one does, the control one has over others' labor, and the responsibility one has for the products of labor. In this society, men are the producers who control labor and money, and women are the consumers of the fruits of male resources.

5. *Spiritual (mythic) "Iron Men."* In the late 1980s and early 1990s, interest in things spiritual arose, and Robert Bly's *Iron Man* (1990) explored masculinity from the perspective of its roots in Jungian myths and archetypes. Bly claimed that men are unsettled by the challenges of feminism and have become overly feminized in response to women's demands for changes. He proposed that masculine myths can help men recover a sense of spiritual values, and thereby escape the trap of rationalism in an authentically male way. Despite the argument that his call for spiritual regeneration is not antifeminist, a focus on "warriors" and "wildmen" carries a great deal of historical antifemale baggage.

6. *Gay Rights*. In the early 1980s, the spread of AIDS unified gay men, for starting in 1982, AIDS was recognized as an epidemic that at the time was thought to afflict gay men primarily. By the end of the decade, gays had begun to self-identify as an oppressed group and, in response, turned to publicizing their new perspective on masculinity (Mosse, 1996). They argued that the legacy of homophobia suppressed the important part that prejudice played in the development of "modern manliness." Gays claimed that the concept of masculinity was derived from homophobia, and they challenged accepted sociocultural distinctions between what is masculine and what is feminine. The roots of homophobia in this century were traced to the end of the last one, in which the ho-

mosexual was viewed as an outsider, a countertype to the dominant male stereotype. Outsider status forced gays either to attempt to imitate the ideal of manhood or to define themselves in opposition to the ideal, for they were not able to come out openly at this time.

7. *African-American Rights.* Also in the late 1980s and early 1990s, Black men defined themselves as an oppressed group facing unique difficulties because of the legacy of racism. They attacked antiblack racism as a formative feature of dominant masculinity, arguing that Black men were historically emasculated by the institution of slavery and that they continue to be disempowered by White dominance.

8. *Evangelical Christian Movement—The Promise Keepers.* In a recent return to conservativism, the religious movement founded in 1990 reaffirms the traditional prefeminist sex roles. It claims that men should be the providers—the heads of families—although men have not necessarily done so in the past, as feminists pointed out. The platform is that society is in moral crisis now for two intertwined reasons: Men have abdicated their responsibilities, and women have been so influenced by feminism that they have usurped men's roles.

In summary, contemporary masculinity (Seidler, 1997) is a collection of different masculinities engaged in a dialectical discourse with different femininities. Men's backlash against women has been—and probably will continue to be—triggered by feelings of powerlessness summoned up by a failure to recognize themselves in the powerful male images exposed by feminists. Although men collectively may still recognize a sense of superiority to women, individual men are becoming increasingly doubtful.

THE "MANLY IDEAL": DEFINITION BY COUNTERTYPES

Once masculinity became an object of study, closer attention to the origins and contemporary definitions of ideal-male images began taking place. The origins of ideal images lie in the traditional differentiation of male and female bodies in accordance with biological functions and physical appearance. Historical research (Mosse, 1996) on the concept of modern masculinity focuses on its evolution from the mid-18th century, when Wincklemann's "manly ideal" of physical beauty (Irwin, 1972) became the normative model. Male beauty—the ideal of masculinity—was the foundation of middle-class society and reflected traditional values and normative standards of appearance, behavior, and social values. Modernism reified the ideal of the Greek god, whose physical beauty was made manifest in the White Anglo-Saxon male (Wincklemann's "ideal beauty"). The manly ideal based on differing ideals of male versus female beauty remains current, with *male beauty* viewed as emblematic of the enduring division between the sexes.

In the 19th century, the physical, intellectual, and moral components of the manly ideal were augmented by a socioculturally codified differentiation between men's and women's proper "place" (Bordo, 1999). Different spheres were set forth as appropriate to each sex—the world for men, and the home for women. The 20th century inherited the physical and sociocultural image of the true man as one who has overcome the female components of his nature (Weininger, 1906/ 1975).

Nonetheless, the definition of manliness is not restricted to that which is "against" womanliness, for it also includes that which is "against" male countertypes. Insofar as mankind was presumed to seek perfection through beauty, physical appearance was taken as a sign of intellectual and moral worth. The male ideal's facial and bodily beauty signified superiority, harmony, measured movement, and moderation in contrast to countertypes whose physical ugliness was equated with inner deformity, perpetual movement, and excess. In the 18th century, philosophers and early anthropologists developed aesthetic criteria to differentiate the ideal manly man from the marginalized outsider whose physical disorder was viewed as the outward expression of moral defectiveness. Among these countertypes were vagrants, Jews, homosexuals, madmen, and criminals, all of whom were considered diseased in some way. Disease was viewed as a visible sign of vice, and the straight nose of the Greek classical man was contrasted with the hook nose of the Jew, the squashed nose of Blacks, and the malformed or diseased noses of social outcasts. Homosexuals were especially denigrated as countertypes, considered ugly in body and facial features, and the late 19th century's fear of homosexuality (Bordo, 1999) reaffirmed the "manly man" ideal.

But in the 1950s, the Beat Generation rebelled against this ideal, which embodied modern society's worship of respectability, order, and progress. Beat authors such as Jack Kerouac, William Burroughs, and Alan Ginsburg encouraged wild and passionate joy in bodily expression as opposed to respectability, and disharmony of the body as opposed to orderliness and symmetry. Androgyny was expressed by men with long hair, thin bodies, and lack of muscular definition, taken as a statement against normative masculinity and femininity. The untraditional look conveyed the image of androgynous men as a "third sex," a countertype to the manly man automatically ranked as the first sex.

Thus, the manly ideal has been defined by looking and behaving differently not only from women, but also from countertypical men, with heterosexual men constructing masculinity in terms of perceived differences from both femininity and homosexuality. This makes the stereotypical manly man multifaceted, for he must be differentiated from both the opposite sex and the same-sex homosexual (Mishkin, Rodin, Silberstein, & Striegel-Moore, 1987). Given that the manly ideal is the basis of stereotyping, the number and variety of male countertypes suggests that a closer look at masculine stereotyping is necessary.

MALE STEREOTYPING

The generic male stereotype is active, in accordance with Berger's dictum (1972) that "men act and women appear." Popular culture is a repository of men in action, immersed in what they are doing, and media images reinforce action no matter the type. One of the most popular male stereotypes is the superhero—a god, demon, or destroyer—who derives from Greek tragedy and comprises the most active and aggressive category of men who invade and dominate. In this group are athletes, soldiers, superheroes, and even killers (e.g., Superman, the Terminator, and Freddy Kreuger). A recent manifestation is the literally robotic man, whose appearance resembles that of an action-hero toy.

At the opposite extreme is the stereotype of the male-bonder, derived from "genre" works such as westerns, police procedurals, and science fiction (Cawelti, 1976). The stereotype reveals a macho man (think John Wayne), ordinarily expected to ignore emotional sensitivity and view the body merely as an arena of exercise and sexual performance, who bonds with other men in a way that cannot be labeled effeminate (Bordo, 1999). What makes this possible is the juxtaposition of a raw, active, and primitive lifestyle in which love and death are intermingled. Danger and death legitimize male bonding, for manly men are permitted to show deep feelings toward other men in these situations.

Still, despite the popularity of manly men, masculinist researchers following Goldberg (1976), continued to point out that men have grown fed up with and angry at stereotypical constraints (Horrocks, 1994). Whereas feminists complain about male dominance, masculinists argue that the situation is the reverse, for men die earlier, endure anxiety and depression without seeking treatment, and feel lonely and abused. Arguing against the feminist claim that men enjoy power, Horrocks considered men despairing, for they are forbidden to show any feelings other than aggression. Not surprisingly, new stereotypes that rewrite or subvert older ones have sprung up, among which are men as androgynous, gays, and minorities, such as Blacks, Hispanics, and Asians.

The androgynous man subverts the macho hero by presenting a man who is more passive, neurotic, narcissistic, and haunted by uncertainty. James Dean, Montgomery Clift, and Leslie Howard are representative of this type, along with Woody Allen—the modern anti-macho man. The Charles Atlas body-builder stereotype—in current parlance, a man on steroids—is the antithesis of the androgyne, more characterized by sensitivity than by brute strength. The traditional body builder existed as a stark contrast to the weak, passive female, and his extreme upper-body muscle development was set off by narrow hips to emphasize the difference from females, whose wide hips were viewed as necessary for childbearing.

Whereas the androgyne is feminized in appearance and demeanor, the new gay stereotype is defined by overt phallicism, for the homosexual is often associated with promiscuity and uncurbed lust. This image reflects rebellion against the conservative heterosexuals who gave us the patriarchy, and is thought to be both exciting and subversive (Horrocks, 1994). Black male images are also subversive, different from and counter to images of White men. Black-audience magazines such as *Stylin* present the African aesthetic as a subversive challenge to the fashion practices of European American Whites, emphasizing visual liveliness versus restraint and decorum. The "in your face" attitude characteristic of street culture is expressed via images of defiance of the prevailing code of dress and behavior. Thus, many stereotypes now coexist, change, merge, and coalesce, giving rise to a reconsideration of what the ideal male body might be.

THE IDEAL BODY: "MUSCULAR MESOMORPH"

Body image plays a significant role in a man's feelings of body satisfaction and self-esteem. The concept of an ideal male body still reflects the equation of beauty and goodness (Mosse, 1996), for societal benefits accrue to attractive men, generally considered to be happier, more successful, and more in control of their lives than those who are unattractive. The manly male is associated with the prevailing cultural view of masculinity, centered on the "shoulds." Men "should" be powerful, strong, effective, and even domineering or destructive when necessary. Male musculature is the symbolic embodiment of these traits, and men view their body image and potency as related.

The ideal body type is the "muscular mesomorph," a man with an average but well-proportioned build, in contrast to the ectomorph, who is thin and weak-looking, or the endomorph who is fat. Upper-body strength is one physical dimension of body-image satisfaction, for the current ideal muscle-man conforms to the triangular aesthetic—he has a well-developed chest, defined arm muscles, and wide shoulders tapering to a narrow waist. A related dimension is physical conditioning, with the ideal man in "good shape," displaying a high energy level, flat stomach, stamina, and the "right" weight in proportion to height. Facial attractiveness also counts. The aesthetic of handsomeness requires clear tanned skin, abundant healthy hair, a sculptured nose, and nonprominent ears. All told, the manly man can be satisfied with his body when it conforms to the ideal, signifying power, grace, and potency.

Bordo viewed male dissatisfaction with body image as a "gold mine for consumerism" (1999, p. 220). Men are concerned about their appearance, and the role of the body image in men's lives has led to significant marketing activity. Men have been found to be very aware of images of their own body and of the ideal body, and have expressed the greatest dissatisfaction about weight, chest size and musculature, and waist size. Men are conscious of having to stave off fat, flab, and the signs of old age. Not surprisingly, marketers develop and advertise products to fill the gap between the actual and the ideal. Increased emphasis on dieting, body-sculpting, and exercise regimens characterized the 1980s, which saw the rise in popularity of gyms, low-calorie products, and personal trainers. Commercials such as the "Diet Coke®" spot featuring a hunky construction worker drinking the diet drink legitimized male attention to weight. By the 1990s, facial and body surgery for men became accepted as ways of transforming their actual self-image into the ideal one. The emphasis—or overemphasis—on outer beauty has also been linked to dysfunctional body-image behaviors such as "bigorexia" (reverse anorexia) and an excessive number of cosmetic surgeries.

SEXUALIZATION OF THE BODY IMAGE

In a 1994 survey (Horrocks), men were asked about how they would like to see themselves—that is, what their ideal self-image is. They answered that they would like to be sexy, good-looking, and attractive to women. Action qualities such as assertiveness and decisiveness were ranked lower than appearance. One explanation is that the manly-man ideal has been influenced by responses to diminished differences from women on dimensions such as occupation, lifestyle, and cognitive traits (Kimmel, 1987). The current "muscular backlash" represents a wish to preserve the ineradicable, biologically driven physical differences. According to "polarization" theory, male and female ideals are physical and symbolic opposing extremes. Alhough depiction of the extremes may vary from culture to culture, the dualistic opposition remains a constant.

The Penis: The Last Taboo

Ads both reflect and affect culture, often celebrating the young, lean, and muscular male body (Horrocks, 1994), and male bodies are frequently depicted as sexual fetishes. Whereas fetishism was formerly expressed in ads by the face and upper body, ads in the 1980s emphasized the thigh, belly, buttocks—and penis. In so doing, ads challenged the taboo against depiction of the penis characteristic of modern patriarchal culture. Cultural historians offer a variety of reasons for the taboo, among which are the following: overly exciting for other men to view; too daunting for men to live up to; too vividly stimulating a fear of castration; very embarrassing in directing attention at a body part that is visibly out of control; and, above all, too tempting to women voyeurs bent on evaluation.

The driving force for the overturn of this taboo was the cultural change brought about by gay men's aesthetics and marketing clout. *The Advocate* (a gay periodical) pointed out in the early 1980s that gay men had considerable buying power, and male clothing designers—notably Calvin Klein—capitalized on this target market (Bordo, 1999). The first ad to violate the taboo against depicting buttocks and penises in main-stream ads was Calvin Klein's 1983 ad for underwear, in which the model's penis outline was visible. The ad aimed at maximum exposure, for it was placed on a billboard in Times Square as well as on bus shelters throughout Manhattan.

The Bruce Weber photo used in the ad exemplifies patriarchal fears. The model's muscular and athletic build is the aesthetic norm not only for straight men but also for gays (Bordo, 1999), serving both as an exciting and anxiety-provoking image. Furthermore, the model's facial demeanor is "feminine," for his gaze is averted, allowing no eye contact, and his posture is one of sexual supplication. He projects passive receptivity and vulnera-bility, for he is looking downward. Most tellingly, the ad challenges the tra-ditional phallic symbolism that establishes generic male superiority to all women by giving cultural permission to women to be voyeurs of men.

What is new here is the role reversal in the gaze, in which a near-naked man is the object of the sexual gaze, and men *and* women are presumed to be gazers. This is far from the traditionally male display of the stare or "eye fuck," a signal of in-your-face masculinity. In contrast, the ad presents a man who is stared at, a passive body dependent on another's gaze, which overturns male cultural conditioning to avoid being put in a vulnerable po-sition where one can be sized up. As Hamilton pointed out, "today's tight-fitting men's pants expose your every shortcoming," adding that "getting stared at was a revealing experience" (2000, p. x).

The image of male passivity, vulnerability, and dependence as objects to be gazed at raises the question of whether or not men experience the same resistance to objectification as do women. Resistance theory posits women's experience in reading male texts as a process whereby women are forced to identify against themselves. Fetterley (1977) argued that women can only possess a more authentic view of their own experience when they resist the text and take a stand against male empowerment. This process in-volves "taking control of one's reactions and inclinations" and reinterpret-ing text via "therapeutic analysis" (Schweickart, 1986, p. 50). Exposure to feminist ideas stimulated women's perception of interpretive strategies as male-dominant, which enabled them to become resisting readers. Post-feminist women have learned to resist identification with inauthentic images in male texts to gain an authentic view of the female self.

Authenticity of images was explored in a recent Future Foundation survey (1999), "Sexing the Media," designed to probe the way that changing social trends impact media consumption. Among the most interesting findings about the treatment of gender in advertising is that both women (48%) and men (26%) are dissatisfied with the way that they are represented. Furthermore, women (39%) and men (27%) claim that there is too much sex in advertising, and both state that advertising does not depict their lives realistically. Yet women's resistance exceeds men's, for even now many people still answer "What does it mean to be a man?" by stating that "being a man means having a penis" (Lewittes, 2000, p. 73). However, advertisements that show a penis as an object to be stared at, measured, compared to others, and fantasized about seem likely to generate resistance. Just as women rebelled against the reduction of the body to a series of sexual parts, so too may men and women object to the similar treatment of men.

MASCULINISM RESISTANCE AND RESEARCH

Research identification of varied and shifting masculine images grounds the call for male resistance, and resisting readers are urged to take a stand against inauthentic representations of male experience—for example, objectification by a "female gaze." Men are becoming more aware of and resistant to inauthentic views of masculinity as a result of exposure, not only to feminist perspectives, but also to masculinist reevaluations. In this way, research in men's studies parallels feminist research not only by identifying male body imagery, but also by examining resistance to it. Both sexes are now positioned on a reactive continuum ranging from acceptance of body images to resistance, and the theory originally presented in feminist research has entered masculinist research as well.

In applying Fetterley's theory of role reversal (1977) to male readers, masculinists aim at raising the consciousness of men readers by showing them that they are forced to identify with male representation running counter to personal experience. However, resistance is a slow-growing phenomenon, one that has not yet become widespread, and much of the research is change-oriented. For example, the Men's Studies Press specifically aims at stimulating resistance, for it is "committed to publishing the best in *activist* men's studies material," with *activist* a term that "connotes a change-oriented value system that encourages men to live lives that reflect respect for all" ("Mission Statement," 2001). Furthermore, books such as Dotson's *Behold the Man: The Hype and Selling of Male Beauty in Media and Culture* (1999), investigate the lack of public resistance to culturally constructed ideals of male beauty made manifest in advertising. Masculinist research on different interpretations of male body imagery (Sandikci & Ringberg, 1999) appears to precede political change, just as feminist research on demeaning female images did.

But it is important to emphasize that men's studies is still in its infancy, as the "Fact Sheet" of *The Journal of Men's Studies* (2001) pointed out: The journal's mission is to publish "original scholarship in the *emerging* men's studies field." The robustness of the discipline is evidenced by the sheer number of works listed in bibliographies, many of which are kept up-to-date online (see Kibby, 2001). For example, the American Men's Studies Association's online bibliography is described as "only the beginning of a growing online Men's Studies bibliography" (Avery, 2001). As the field grows, so too does its specialization, for evolutionary progress has broken the monolith of masculinity. Numerous sub-categories reveal diverse research agendas, with the AMSA's bibliography listing 20 categories, among which are "Men's Bodies," "Men's Health," "Masculinity," "Media," and "Homosexuality" / "Heterosexuality," with advertising the conduit between representation and perception.

This specialization follows the pattern of an ongoing dialectical dialogue with feminism, which progressed from a singular perspective to many different ones such as "Liberal," "Women's Voice," and "Poststructuralist" (Bristor & Fischer, 1993). The masculinist research corpus reflects the evolutionary stages of the men's movement, in which different focal points of multiple masculinisms emerged over time. The points often connect in current research, for historical stages tend to run concurrently in the first generation of a movement. For example, at a 2001 Promise Keepers conference, Steve Farrar, head of a Texas ministry, declared that "We need a release of the Holy Spirit to set guys free from bondage," quoting Thoreau's comment that "a lot of men are living lives of quiet desperation" (Niebuhr, 2001, p. A-12). The topic of "misandryny," now standing beside its counterpart "misogyny," echoes Goldberg's description of the harnessed male (1976, p.1).

As Jourard pointed out in 1971, the constraints on men lead to physical and mental problems, for an oppressive lifestyle generates illness, allowing "disease and death to gnaw into [a man's] substance without his clear knowledge" (1971, p. 40). However, a generation later, masculinist research aims at disseminating knowledge about health issues, and a new journal, *The Journal of Men's Health*, is slated to appear in 2002, published by the Men's Studies Press. Several topics of interest are related to advertising imagery, including "men's bodies and body image" and "marketing to and engagement of men in health care" (*MSP Newsletter*, 2001). Objects of interest include images of men in women-dominant careers such as nursing and elementary school teaching, as well as the influence of class, race, and sexual orientation on what is perceived to be masculine. The broad focus incorporates postmodern anti-capitalist perspectives drawn from Afrocentrism, Marxism, and Queer Theory to particularize the generic "masculinism" by examining differences among men, just as feminist researchers did earlier. In summary, research in men's studies follows the same general pattern set by women's studies, one that is characteristic of emerging disciplines. The pattern is one of ongoing discourse, for research is conducted in a cultural environment that of necessity includes changes and reactions to them. In many situations, "women's studies" has been relabeled "gender studies," and although men's studies have not yet come under this rubric, it seems only a matter of time before cultural studies of masculinity and femininity connect under the same banner.

REFERENCES

Avery, A. P. (n.d.), *Annotated American men's studies association bibliography*. Retrieved November 29, 2001, from http://mensstudies.org/bibliography/manbib.htm.

Berger, J. (1972). *Ways of seeing*. New York: Penguin Books.

Bly, R. (1990). *Iron John: A book about men*. Reading, MA: Addison-Wesley.

Bordo, S. (1999). *The male body: A new look at men in public and in private*. New York: Farrar, Straus and Giroux.

Bristor, J. M., & Fischer, E. (1993). Feminist thought: Implications for consumer research. *Journal of Consumer Research, 19*, 518–536.

Cawelti, J. G. (1976). *Adventure, mystery, and romance*. Chicago: University of Chicago Press.

Clatterbaugh, K. (1996). *Contemporary perspectives on masculinity: Men, women, and politics in modern society*, New York: Westview Press.

Cohan, S. (1997). *Masked men: Masculinity and the movies in the 1950s*. Bloomington: University of Indiana Press.

de Beauvoir, S. (1949 [1952]). *The second sex*. New York: Vintage Books.

Dotson, E.W. (1999). *Behold the man: The hype and selling of male beauty in media and culture*. New York: Haworth Press.

Fact Sheet (2001). *The Journal of Men's Studies*. Retrieved November 29, 2001, from http:// www.mensstudies.com/mission.html.

Farrell, W. (1975). *The liberated man: Beyond masculinity: Freeing men and their relationships with women*. New York: Bantam Books.

Fetterley, J. (1977). *The resisting reader: A feminist approach to American fiction*. Bloomington IN: University of Indiana Press.

Friedan, B. (1963). *The feminine mystique*. New York: Dell Publishing.

Future Foundation (1999). Sexing the media. Retrieved April 14, 2000, from http://www.thefuturefoundation.com/sexingthemedia.htm.

Goldberg, H. (1976). *The hazards of being male: Surviving the myth of masculine privilege*. New York: The New American Library.

Hamilton, B. (2000, November 5). Front and center: Today's tight-fitting men's pants expose your every shortcoming. *New York Post*, p. 39.

Horrocks, R. (1994), *Masculinity in crisis: Myths, fantasies, and realities*. New York: St. Martin's Press.

Irwin, D. G. (1972). *Wincklemann: Writings on art*. New York: Praeger Publishers.

Jones, M.Y., Stanaland, A. J. S., & Gelb, B. D. (1998). Beefcake and cheesecake: Insights for advertisers. *Journal of Advertising, 27*, 33–52.

Jourard, S. (1971). *The transparent self* (Rev. ed.). Princeton: Van Nostrand Press.

Kibby, M. (2001). Bibliographies. *Masculinity and representation.* Retrieved, November 29, 2001, from http://www.newcastle.edu.au/department/so/kibby.htm.

Kimmel, M. S. (1995). *Manhood in America: A cultural history.* New York: The Free Press.

Kimmel, M. S. (1987). Rethinking masculinity: New directions in research. In M. S. Kimmel (Ed.), *Changing men: New directions in research on men and masculinity* (pp. 9–24). Newbury Park CA: Sage.

Lewittes, M. (2000, October 31). It's a man's, man's, man's, man's world. *New York Post,* 73.

Lyndon, N. (1992). *No more sex war: The failures of feminism.* New York: Bantam Books.

Men's Studies Association Newsletter. 2001. Retrieved November 30, 2001, from http://www.mensstudies.com

Mishkin, M. E., Rodin, J., Silberstein, L. R., & Striegel-Moore, R. H. (1987). The embodiment of masculinity: Cultural, psychological, and behavioral dimensions. In M. S. Kimmel (Ed.), *Changing men: New directions in research on men and masculinity* (pp. 37–52). Newbury Park, CA: Sage.

Mission Statement (2001). *Men's studies press.* Retrieved November 29, 2001, from http://www.mensstudies.com.

Mosse, G. L. (1996). *The image of man: The creation of modern masculinity.* New York: Oxford University Press

Niebuhr, G. (2001, May 21). Promise keepers still draws crowds. *The New York Times,* A–12.

Rotundo, A. E. (1993). *American manhood: Transformations in masculinity from the revolution to the modern era.* New York: Basic Books.

Sandikci, O., & Ringberg, T. (1999, October). *Advertising and sexual imagery: A post-structuralist approach.* Paper presented at the meeting of the Association for Consumer Research, Columbus, OH.

Schroeder, J. E., & Zwick, D. (1999, October). *The gaze, the male body, and advertising: A visual analysis.* Paper presented at the meeting of the Association for Consumer Research, Columbus, OH.

Schweickart, P. P. (1986). Reading ourselves: Toward a feminist theory of reading. In E. A. Flynn & P. P. Schweickart (Eds.), *Gender and reading: Essays on readers, texts, and contexts* (pp. 31–62). Baltimore, MD: The Johns Hopkins University Press.

Seidler, V. J. (1997). *Man enough: Embodying masculinities.* London: Sage.

Stern, B. B. (1993). Feminist literary criticism and the deconstruction of advertisements: A postmodern view of advertising and consumer responses. *Journal of Consumer Research, 19,* 556–566.

Weininger, O. (1975). *Sex and character.* New York: Putnam. (Original work published 1906)

Chapter 13

Media at the Margins: Homoerotic Appeals to the Gay and Lesbian Community

Gary R. Hicks

Southern Illinois University, Edwardsville

Contemporary advertising abounds with sexually ambiguous images. Who's to say that the perfume ad that features a near-naked woman is designed to appeal only to men? And whereas a straight audience can see the image of handsome young men playing touch football in a Tommy Hilfiger ad as an symbol of American manhood and, on a quite different level, the joys of consumerism, gay readers might see a lightly veiled homoerotic scene. For years, mainstream advertisers have utilized what Lukenbill (1999) called social, sexual, and image *codes* to sell products to mainstream markets while making gays and lesbians feel connected. This form of "doublespeak" uses innuendo and images that can be decoded by people "in the know."

The subtlety with which advertisers insert homoerotic images into ads targeted at mainstream audiences can be viewed as nothing short of an art form. Ads that employ these dual messaging images—attractive to both heterosexuals and gays—have been used successfully for years to sell products such as clothing, alcohol, and tobacco. When these same advertisers began using more overt sexual imagery to reach out to a lesbian and gay market, the codes took on a different role. In recent years, mainstream advertisers have begun placing their ads with more blatantly homoerotic images in the gay press to attract the gay and lesbian community, and, more specifically, its money. This attention to the gay consumer is not unwarranted. Although common myths about large disposable incomes among gays have mostly been debunked, the lesbian and gay community does represent a potential market of millions. A 1997 ad by the National Gay Newspaper Guild noted that gays and lesbians make up a $35 billion market and that they are 11.7 times more likely to be in a professional work position and 8 times more likely to own a computer notebook than heterosexuals.

This chapter examines the "mainstream" sexual advertising that now frequently appears in such gay and lesbian publications as *The Advocate*, *Out*, and *Instinct*. By means of textual analysis, these ads may be studied not only to see both their blatant and hidden sexual images and innuendo, but also to consider their images and messages within the larger issue of gay and lesbian politics and its place within society.

MASS MEDIA AND THE CONSTRUCTION OF SEXUALITY

Postmodern scholars have argued that sexuality is socially constructed, created through the continuous interplay among individuals, society, and those institutions that make up culture (Foucault, 1978). Among these institutions, media have been cited as the most important contemporary factor in the socialization of gay men and lesbians. The media influence not only how nongay society views gays, but also how lesbians and gay men see themselves. The frequent lack of positive gay images within other institutions of society—family, church, school—make media an even more important source of information about gay and lesbian issues and identities. A 1984 study indicated that self-identification by gays is not even possible until an identity is acknowledged by the media (O'Neil, 1984). Gay people, like all people, define themselves in relation to their environment. In a mediated world, this environment is in turn shaped by media images. As Kellner (1994) wrote, the power of the mass media cannot be underestimated when it comes to helping us define where we as individuals fit within the grand scheme of things. This scheme, it can be argued, has been historically heterosexist and injuriously homophobic.

The mass media provide, as Gross (1994) suggested, a "common ground" from which members of a diverse culture can derive shared meanings and basic understandings of how the world works, of how things are. Power in its truest sense comes not only from the ability to facilitate a shared awareness of the gay experience, but also from actually *creating* this common understanding of what it means to be gay or lesbian in society. Some who hold this immense power include those who run television networks, publish magazines, direct advertising agencies, and manage Fortune 500 companies. Much of what constitutes gay identity today has been created, or at the least modified, by corporate and media organizations—institutions that are generally conservative and mostly white, male, middle-aged and heterosexual.

A MARGINAL COMMUNITY

The emergence of the homosexual as a minority figure occurred at mid-20th century through the convergence of politics and science. World War II provided social and sexual contacts never before available to millions of gays and lesbians. The release in 1948 of Alfred Kinsey's *Sexual Behavior in the Human Male* (followed in 1953 by a book focusing on women's sexuality) acknowledged that upwards of 10% of the population is at any time homosexual. Armed with scientific validation and the presence of large numbers of gay people who transplanted themselves to major American cities after the war, early gay-rights leaders such as Harry Hay made the first tentative steps toward formulating the idea of being gay into an identity. During this time in American history, "… every move a homosexual made was fraught with the danger of self-disclosure and subsequent persecution" (Hay, 1996). Although the liberating forces unleashed by these political and social phenomena would be kept covert during much of the 1950s (including a complete absence of homosexual images in advertising), they provided the springbed from which the consciousness movement of the 1960s and 1970s would arise (Miller, 1995).

Heterosexual America of the 1950s was settling into the post-war economic expansion with little regard for homosexuals. While advertisers zeroed in on the emerging middle class with pitches for products that would help make the American dream a reality, homosexual America remained invisible. Worse than invisibility, homosexuals maintained their own cover for threat of prosecution. "Every evening spent in a gay setting, every contact with another homosexual or lesbian, every sexual intimacy carried a reminder of the criminal penalties that could be exacted at any moment" (D'Emilio, 1983).

If the 1950s represented "a period of wintry despair for homosexuals in the United States" (Gross, 1993), the 1960s were not much better. Although Americans were consumed with new societal and sexual freedoms, concerns over the needs of gay America did not register on most people's radars. At a time when basic civil rights were still being sought and the anti-Vietnam war movement was overshadowing many other concerns, homosexual rights "were the last priority on an already overburdened national agenda" (Herdt & Boxer, 1993). When the media did pay attention to gays and lesbians, their portrayals were anything but flattering.

In a 1964 *Life* magazine article titled "Homosexuality in America: The 'Gay' World Takes to the City Streets," the writers concluded that homosexuals had been "rejected by the 'straight' world," and made reference to "fluffy-sweatered young men," who wear the "attention-calling clothes that the 'gay' world likes." The article continued to reference issues of male prostitution and cross dressing (Mardi, Sanders, & Mormor, 1994). This is one example of how the media saw gay life in the 1960s.

Throughout the 1970s, as women, people of color, and other marginalized members of society became more vocal in their demands for equality and societal benefits, gays and lesbians also took a more visible, more political stance. "Out of the Closets and Into the Streets!" became the slogan for a new, more open way of "being" gay. Sizable numbers of lesbians and gay men were finding their way out of the closet, and insisting that others find the courage to do the same. In 1973 the American Psychiatric Association finally deleted homosexuality as a category of mental illness. Being "out" was the new imperative of the gay liberation movement, an imperative that not only "transformed the meaning of 'coming out'" (D'Emilio, 1983), but was responsible for changing the very nature of the movement itself. Although not as militant and in-your-face as the 1980s rallying cry used by Queer Nation—"We're Here, We're Queer, Get Used to It"—the demand by gays for gays to be open about their identities represented a monumental shift from earlier ideas about gay life, gay community, and gay responsibility. American television, particularly situation comedies, discovered gays in the 1970s but typified them as sources of comic relief, further marginalizing the community. The advertising industry, long credited with staying on top of—if not initiating—cultural shifts, was nowhere to be seen as the gay community took its first tenuous steps toward visibility.

By 1980, the work of the past decade seemed about to pay off. More than 100 of the nation's largest companies had adopted personnel policies that prohibited discrimination on the basis of sexual orientation, and 40 cities across the country had passed similar laws (Kaiser, 1997). The political power of the gay community was at an all-time high. The time to safely come out of the closet, it seemed, had come. By the end of 1981, fear of another kind of enemy pushed many gay men back in. It was in the media that most people first heard of AIDS, an illness that at first seemed to be affecting only gay men. As the 1980s progressed, media coverage helped to merge the gay identity with an AIDS identity. Television dramas about AIDS either made gays appear as promiscuous deviants or portrayed them as objects to be pitied.

By the 1990s, a generation of young gay males had come of age with no memory of sex before AIDS. For them, "… sex, love, queerness, and AIDS have all been inextricably linked from the very beginning" (Kaiser, 1997). The impact of the illness on gay society actually served to lead many community-minded people out of the closet and led to the reappropriation of words and symbols that were once used to denigrate gays and lesbians. An example can be seen in activists' use of the word *queer* as almost a mantra of empowerment.

MEDIA AND GAY VISIBILITY

It is undeniable that gay men and lesbians have become more visible in society than at any time in the past, and that much of that visibility can be seen as positive. More openly lesbian women and gay men hold political office than at any time in the nation's history, television programs that revolve around the multi-dimensional lives of gay characters have topped the ratings charts, and queer theory courses have multiplied within university curricula. But what is the gay *identity* here at the beginning of the 21st century? What role have media played in forming it? To what end are advertisers using that identity to market their products, and in what ways are these advertisements themselves further defining what it means to be gay or lesbian? Are gays and lesbians portrayed as normal, law-abiding citizens who happen to be attracted to the same sex, or as outcasts who participate in risky, deviant sex acts? What do sexually suggestive advertisements teach gay people about themselves? Much of what emerges depends on a mediated definition. When it comes to media images, few are as powerful as advertisements, and few have been so off-limits to the representation of gay and lesbian people and issues. In a media environment where one mainstream newsmagazine, *Time*, can run a cover story on an openly lesbian comedian ("Roll Over," 1997) and a year later question how tolerant Americans are of gay people ("For Better or Worse," 1998), the world of advertising to lesbians and gay men has, until recently, remained a bastion of conservative messages and no-risk images.

The earliest gay publications can be traced to the 1960s. They contained little advertising overall, and none that could be considered mainstream. Some advertisers pointed to the presence in the early gay magazines of ads for pornography, gay bars, and escort services as the reason they kept their distance. As some national gay and lesbian publications, such as the *Advocate*, matured into respectability, and new magazines were launched, mainstream advertisers rethought their position in the 1990s. Major corporations such as IBM, United Airlines, R. J. Reynolds, and Absolut Vodka became regular advertisers in the gay press. Most of their ads, however, were the same ones that were placed in mainstream publications. When the advertising became more obviously targeted to the gay market, the images remained the same as in the "straight" advertisements, only the gender of the models changed. An ad for Safeco Insurance that ran in a 2001 *Advocate* features two men sitting on a floor surrounded by boxes and drinking coffee. Having just purchased a home, as the ad implies, this couple can rest easy because they are covered by Safeco insurance.

FROM "SAFE" SEXUALITY TO HOMOEROTIC EXPLICITNESS

Selling with sex or the suggested promise of sex is nothing new in advertising. Although it has become a truism that sex sells, a review of the past century of advertising shows that the kind of sex that sells is of the "red-blooded, all-American, heterosexual variety." The sight of Brooke Shields contorting in tight jeans while declaring, "Nothing comes between me and my Calvins," might have raised some eyebrows for pushing the envelope of advertising standards a few decades back, but it was still well within the socially sanctioned boy-meets-girl brand of sexual image. Of course, no one in the 1970s seriously viewed the Calvin Klein ads as an example of lesbian eroticism. But when Anheuser-Busch in 1999 ran an ad in gay media showing two male arms with hands intertwined (see Fig. 13.1) and the slogan, "Be Yourself and Make It a Bud Light," right-wing religious groups mounted a boycott of Anheuser-Busch products. Before ultimately deciding to stand by its campaign, the company set up phone numbers that people could call to voice their support or opposition to the ad.

Although the image of two people of either gender simply holding hands can hardly constitute blatant sexual imagery, the beer ad was among the first for a mainstream product to use same-sex models with flesh touching flesh. Subsequent ads from both Anheuser-Busch and other companies have continued to push the boundaries of advertising proprieties.

Among the first, and most surprising, ads to feature a same-sex image was a Coors beer ad that appeared in gay magazines in 2000. What makes it surprising is that the Adolph Coors Company was the target of a boycott by gay consumers in the 1970s. At the time, gay rights groups had accused the company, controlled by a family deeply involved in right-wing politics, of discriminating against its gay and lesbian employees. Anti-Coors sentiment was so strong among gay beer drinkers that a research analyst for Coors wrote about how company employees were encouraged not to mention for whom they worked during business trips to San Francisco (Burgess, 1993).

The Coors ad campaign shows how much society has progressed in 20 years. In 2000, an advertisement for Coors Light beer appeared in an issue of *Instinct*, a gay male lifestyle magazine, that featured two hunky male models in an idyllic country scene, posed beside a bicycle built for two with food and a six-pack of Coors Light in a picnic basket (see Fig. 13.2). One model has his hand around the other's shoulder as they both gaze outward from the page. Except for both models being of the same gender, this image has been used countless times by advertisers to sell products like clothing and perfume. In the same issue an Anheuser-Busch ad occupies the back cover. The image is of an empty beer glass sitting on a counter in what appears to be a gay bar. Above the glass is the slogan, "You're Out!" It is im-

FIG. 13.1. "Be yourself and make it a Bud Light." Ads like this contributed to a boycott of Anheuser-Busch product.

FIG. 13.2. This ad for Coors Light appeared in *Instinct*, a gay male lifestyle magazine.

portant to note that *Instinct*, like all of the magazines mentioned in this chapter, is not pornographic. However, this issue, which attracted advertisements from two of the world's largest brewers, contained articles with titles such as, "Loosen Up! Get Your Man to Sexperiment," and "Slut or Stud? Another Night, Another Notch." Although major mainstream corporations such as Coors and Anheuser-Busch definitely do not advertise in pornographic magazines, it is important to note that the editorial content of these magazines is not necessarily bland, either.

Although many of the mainstream advertisers limit the sexual nature of their ads to romance, such as in the Coors Light ad, more are becoming bolder in both sexual innuendo and image. In a 2000 issue of the *Advocate* a Miller Lite ad asks for reader participation in bringing two handsome gay men together (see Fig. 13.3). In a bar scene, one model is posed on the far left of the ad while the other is on the far right. The model of the left has a line marked "A" next to him, while the model on the right has one marked "B" next to him. The ad's copy reads, "Connect A to B and Celebrate with Miller Lite." The reader who actually goes so far as to follow these directions ends up making the models touch bodies, one model's hand rubbing against the other's.

PHALLOCENTRIC APPEALS

Almost an entire genre of ads has emerged around the tilted or exploding image of a bottle. A 1995 Bud Light ad showed a beer bottle jutting from the page at an angle so reminiscent of an erect penis that mere coincidence is hardly believable. While the use of sexual images in ads targeted to heterosexual male audiences has long been a staple for the beer industry, the provocative nature of those ads seem somehow diminished by the ordinariness attached by society to heterosexual imagery. To a general audience, the image of a bottle positioned to resemble an erect penis appears more threatening when it is known that the intended target is another male. A Slates Clothing ad takes the image one step further with an ad in a 1999 *Advocate* featuring a bottle at the same exact angle as the bottle in the beer advertisement (see Fig. 13.4). In the Slates ad, the cap has been removed and the contents of the bottle are spewing out and filling the page. Although the similarity of this image to male ejaculation is striking, a more interesting question is just what this has to do with selling clothing.

Another clothing company, Diesel, appropriated homoerotic fantasies of uniformed sailors in an ad featuring a naval ship full of young attractive men coming home to port. In the foreground are two hunky men in their sailor whites, lips locked in a passionate kiss. Like the Slates ad, there is no presence in the ad of any Diesel clothing. A 2001 Bud Light ad shows a black-and-white photograph of a muscular man's body wearing only a pair

FIG. 13.3.   "Connect A to B and celebrate with Miller Lite."

FIG. 13.4. This ad for Slates clothing appeared in the *Advocate*.

of cut-off blue-jean shorts and combat boots (see Fig. 13.5). His hand holds a beer bottle, but his head has been completely cropped out of the picture. The cut-offs, the boots, and the anonymity provided by the headless, faceless torso is reminiscent of much gay male erotica.

An advertisement by Interflora that promotes sending flowers for Valentine's Day has appeared in both the British gay lifestyle magazine *AXM* and U.S. publications. The romantic image is of three red rose blooms connected by a single long stem. One of the blooms is at the top of the stem while the other two are snuggled together at the bottom. The image by itself appears to be a portrayal of male genitalia, but once the caption "Floral Sex" is read, the intent of the advertiser become unmistakable.

One of the most sexually bold ads appeared in a 2000 issue of the *Advocate*. Again from Anheuser-Busch, this Bud Light ad is photographed from beneath a glass-top table (see Fig. 13.6). Visible through the glass are the bottoms of Bud Light bottles, along with the removed metal caps. At the top of the ad are the words, "Tops and Bottles." There is no overt message nor any hint of nudity in this ad, but for the gay reader, the innuendo is clear. Men who are the penetrators in anal sex are called tops; those who are penetrated are called bottoms. Can this ad be viewed as simply a clever play on words, or is there a more profound message? Does it reinforce or create an identity for a gay reader? If so, what identity? Another Bud Light ad features the simple picture of a six-pack of Bud Light bottles. The caption reads "Nice Package." Again, the sexual innuendo is clear to the gay reader. When Anheuser-Busch advertises to heterosexual audiences, it uses proudly stepping Clydesdale horses, wise-cracking frogs, and the ubiquitous sports figure. For the gay market, the image is one-dimensional, focusing on sexuality, and in the case of this ad, notions of blatant sexual activity.

LESBIAN IMAGES

If sexual images are the way mainstream advertisers reach out to gay men, what about appeals to lesbians? Most advertising targeting lesbians in the gay press contains images of attractive women, mostly fully clothed, and rarely doing anything more erotic than embracing. A very romantic ad specifically targeting lesbians—although it might indeed appeal to heterosexual males—is for Disaronno Originale Amaretto (see Fig 13.7). Against the backdrop of Florence, two young women are shown on the cover of a matchbox. While they are embracing, one woman's head is on the other's shoulder and they are fully clothed. At the bottom of the ad is the image of a lit match and the words "Light A Fire." In what may be the most provocative of lesbian-themed ads, the Prada clothing company ran an ad featuring two women facing each other lying together in a hammock with their legs

FIG. 13.5. "Be yourself. Make it a Bud Light." Eye candy for the gay male audience.

FIG.13.6. "Tops & Bottles." A double-entendre for gay male sex positions (tops and bottoms).

FIG. 13.7. "Light A Fire." This ad appeared in the gay press, but has appeared in mainstream magazines as well.

spread wide in a 2001 issue of *The New York Times'* monthly magazine *The Fashion of the Times*.

Despite these ads, those featuring women present more subtle representations of sexuality than in ads focused on gay men, leaving how the ad is construed up to reader's imagination and sexual orientation. A study of advertising directed to heterosexual audiences found a significant increase in the explicitness of images of both female and male models from the early 1980s to the early 1990s. However, whereas 11% of male models were found to be dressed provocatively in 1993 advertisements, 40% of women were (Reichert, Lambiase, Morgan, Carstarphen, & Zavoina, 1999). Is society simply more accustomed to seeing women in sexual roles? Is it that these images, popular in their extreme form in men's pornography, are really not much different from those that regularly appear in magazines such as *Cosmopolitan* and *Glamour*? In her book, *The Beauty Myth*, Naomi Wolf compared the advertising content of ordinary women's magazines with pornographic images and found very little difference outside of the degree of explicitness (Wolf, 1991).

Of course, another reason why suggestive ads with women are viewed differently from those with men could be reflective of women's perceived place in society's power hierarchy. The notion of women portrayed sexually with other women is not as threatening to a male-centered culture in which male homosexuality is often viewed as an affront to male privilege. "One of the most effective ways to demean a man in many societies continues to be to question his masculinity, and allude to the possibility that he may be homosexual" (Dubin, 1992, p. 435).

BUYING IN OR SELLING OUT?

In a society where the government imposes a "Don't Ask, Don't Tell" policy on gays in the military, in which AIDS activists chant "Silence Equals Death," and where state legislatures are tripping over themselves to enact laws to deny lesbian and gay couples many of the privileges that heterosexuals take for granted, it would seem that visibility at any cost would be the mantra of the gay movement. But does visibility in mass media serve gay and lesbian causes? The mainstream media often present gay life as one-dimensional, usually revolving around sex. This is the same image painted in many of these "gay" advertisements. Are these advertisements, and the corporate lust for gay dollars that make them possible, proof that lesbians and gay men have further entered mainstream life, or are they just another example of how popular culture and commerce work together to keep minority groups marginalized and powerless? Is the advertising industry, long given credit for both reflecting American culture and moving it forward, serving as a harbinger of changes to come in society as a whole? Is the willingness of advertisers to use sexually suggestive gay-themed images an indication of progressive thinking, or simply an effective means to tap into a lucrative market? If so, will these ads actually produce the brand loyalty that the advertisers expect? A recent study showed that the majority of gays and lesbians feels that companies are reaching out to them through advertising for financial gain, and not as a way to enhance the community's stature in society (Gardyn & Fetto, 2001). And so, these questions are not easily answered. Certainly it is unwise to give powerful advertisers too much credit for progressive thinking or to underestimate their propensity for confusing people for markets and for manipulating communities for monetary gain.

REFERENCES

Burgess, R. J. (1993) *Silver bullets: A soldier's story of how Coors bombed in the beer wars.* New York: St. Martin's Press.

D'Emilio, J. (1983). *Sexual politics, sexual communities: The making of a homosexual minority in the United States, 1940–1970.* Chicago: University of Chicago Press.

Dubin, S. C. (1992). Gay images and the social construction of acceptability. In P. Nardi & B. Schneider (Eds.), *Social perspectives in lesbian and gay studies: A reader* (pp. 434–466). London: Routledge.

For better or worse: In Hawaii, a showdown over marriage tests the limits of gay activism (1998, October 26). *Time, 152*(17), 43–44.

Foucault, M. (1978). *The history of sexuality.* New York: Random House.

Gardyn, R., & Fetto, J. (2001). In broad daylight: Marketers who want to target homosexuals may have better luck using mass media than gay-specific venues. *American Demographics, 23*(2), 16.

Gross, L. (1993). *Contested closets: The politics and ethics of outing.* Minneapolis: University of Minnesota Press.

Gross, L. (1994). What is wrong with this picture? Lesbian women and gay men on television. In J. Ringer (Ed.), *Queer words, queer images: Communication and the construction of homosexuality* (pp. 143–156). New York: New York University Press.

Hay, H. (1996). *Radically gay: Gay liberation in the words of its founder.* Boston: Beacon Press.

Herdt, G., & Boxer, A. (1993). *Children of horizons: How gay and lesbian teens are leading a new way out of the closet.* Boston: Beacon Press.

Kaiser, C. (1997). *The gay metropolis: 1940–1996.* Boston: Houghton Mifflin.

Kellner, D. (1994). *Media culture: Cultural studies, identity, and politics between the modern and the postmodern.* London: Routledge.

Kinsey, A. (1948). *Sexual behavior in the human male.* Philadelphia: Saunders.

Kinsey, A. (1953). *Sexual behavior in the human female.* Philadelphia: Saunders.

Lukenbill, G. (1999). *Untold millions: Secret truths about marketing to gay and lesbian consumers.* New York: Harrington Park Press.

Mardi, P. M., Sanders, D., & Mormor, J. (1994). *Growing up before stonewall: Life stories of some gay men.* London: Routledge.

Miller, N. (1995). *Out of the past: Gay and lesbian history from 1869 to the present.* New York: Vintage Books.

O'Neil, S. (1984). The role of the mass media and other socialization agents in the identity formation of gay males. In S. Thomas (Ed.), *Studies in Communication,*

   Vol. 1: Studies in Mass Communication and Technology (p. 201). Norwood, NJ: Ablex.

Reichert, T., Lambiase, J., Morgan, S., Carstarphen, M., & Zavoina, S. (1999). Cheesecake and beefcake: No matter how you slice it, sexual explicitness in advertising continues to increase. *Journalism & Mass Communication Quarterly, 76*(1), 7–20.

Roll over, Ward Cleaver and tell Ozzie Nelson the news: Ellen Degeneres is poised to become TV's first openly gay star. Is America ready or not? (1997, April 14). *Time, 149*(15), 78–85.

Wolf, N. (1991). *The beauty myth: How images of beauty are used against women.* New York: Doubleday.

Chapter 14

Sex—Online and in Internet Advertising

Jacqueline J. Lambiase

University of North Texas

Cyberspace appeals to human imagination, and its infinite creative spaces have provided fertile sites for display of ideas, products, entertainment, competition, and the human form itself. By some, it is imagined to be a global village, connecting people and supporting their digitally composed relationships through bits instead of atoms. Other popular media representations, however, construct the Internet as an economic pyramid in which *dot-coms* fight for viability and eyeballs. Hierarchy in this narrative becomes paramount because a few large companies continue to consolidate Web properties in order to maintain profitability. It is the idea of connectedness versus the idea of capitalism, and some Web sites try to have it both ways. Particularly in the economic survival scenario, advertising and its formulas have been tested and reimagined to serve profitability in a medium that, until the mid-1990s, had little to do with the desire for large-scale, mainstream capitalistic enterprise (Lambiase, 1999).

Into cyberspace, then, the "sex sells" advertising mantra has migrated from other media forms. Whether the mantra actually works is beside the point. It, like many traditional media tools and strategies, is being exported into new media and tested in the new environment. As a medium, the Internet has been a friendly place for display of sexual content, mostly in the forms of soft and hard pornography. In this sense, "sex" itself does sell and it is profitable. Yet popularity of sex-related content on the Web is seldom mentioned in mainstream media, where news reports about Web-based pornography are few (except in coverage of illegal traffickers) and where rankings by Internet audience-tracking services ignore the popularity of such sites. Although Internet pornography has been scrupulously sanitized or removed from most broader discussions about the medium, it thrives nonetheless as a kind of mixture of those two Internet narratives, that of openness for communication and of dot-com profitability. And its presence affects everything else within the medium. One high-profile example of this phenomenon is Yahoo's attempt to revamp and expand its *e-tailing* services into more sex-oriented products, an action that was received in April 2001 by a flood of mainstream media criticism and 100,000 e-mail messages from Yahoo users in 36 hours (Goldman, 2001; Hansell, 2001, Perry 2001). In this environment, then, content filters are not the only obstacles for the same kind of mainstream sexual content that advertising uses for an increasing number of products.

Because no published research exists on the topic of sexual appeals in Internet advertising, this chapter outlines two areas that will be of interest to those who study sexual appeals, as these researchers begin to scrutinize this new media domain. The chapter proceeds from the general to the specific, first from a broad overview of the medium itself to specific examples of sexual appeals and strategies found in cyberspace. The first section traces the environment of the Internet itself and addresses these questions, among others: Is sex-tinged advertising suitable for the Internet, considering the medium's history and its current use? Does the abundance of sexual content on the Web affect advertising efforts tinged with sex? Does a generalized audience for much of the Web's most popular mainstream content hinder efforts by advertisers to use gendered and sexualized content in ads?

The second area to be outlined focuses on current Web advertising techniques and email-based marketing efforts and their relationship to sexual appeals. Among questions to be addressed are these: Does the Web's environment fundamentally change the ways that sexually oriented appeals are used by advertisers and their targets? Are gendered spaces on the Web able to use sex-tinged ads much like their off-line counterparts of gendered magazines? Are ads more "capable" because users can experience a kind of immediacy not available off-line, by clicking through to streaming video, product web sites, and other experiences and functions? Could attitudes about privacy and *spamming* limit advertisers' ability to reach audiences by email due to fear of backlash? Last, this section addresses technology culture and particularly the development and use of cyber models, as these impinge on advertising.

SEX IN THE GLOBAL VILLAGE

McLuhan's global village narrative (1964) has attached itself to the Internet, being seen by some as possible in principle if not in practice (Poster, 1990). Many others have used McLuhan's narrative to legitimize their own agendas for either connectedness or capitalism. Negroponte (1995) asserted "the true value of a network is less about information and more about community" (p. 183). In the days before dot-coms became preeminent, other scholars (Bolter, 1991; Landow, 1993; Lanham, 1993) endowed the Internet with democratizing attributes, whereas others raised questions about this quality (Carstarphen & Lambiase, 1998; Cherny & Weise, 1996; Herring, 1993, 1996). With the advent of banner advertising and the emergence of sites such as Amazon.com in 1995, the most popular narrative of the Internet changed from an electronic socio-political marketplace to simply an electronic marketplace where goods may be bought and sold conveniently; Amazon's own trademarked slogan, after all, is "earth's biggest selection" of consumer goods. Lurking near the edges of this developing dot-com narrative has been the vitality of sex-related sites, first touted in electronic bulletin board and Usenet groups in the 1980s and early 1990s (Needham, 2001; Salik, 1995). These sites at first either directed people to distributors of erotic and pornographic content or provided primitively coded files that could be reconstructed on a user's computer, but many evolved into e-commerce sites distributing their own sexual content (Needham, 2001; Salik, 1995). Although much about the Internet economy appears in fuzzy outline, there is at least one indisputable fact: The Web offers an exhaustive amount of sex-related content. Sites with sex-related content are money-makers. And if Internet users seek sex-related content, then they're in luck because these sites—as well as advertisements for these sites—may be found easily through search engines and at portal sites for sexual content.

Traces of these sites' popularity may be found in places not concerned about the sensibilities of mainstream audiences. Internet users easily find sex of all sorts on the Web, and sexual content has been one of the main engines driving development of the medium. Particularly during the 1990s, development of Internet technologies can be closely tied to the medium's ability to distribute sexual content at a new level of privacy (Bedell, 2001; Needham, 2001). In fact, sexual content often drives people's desires to obtain access to new media technologies, even at initially high costs (Bedell, 2001; Klein, 1999; "Adult Sites," 1999). One other contemporary example would be the quick popularity of the videocassette recorder in the late 1970s and 1980s. Yet even the VCR, with its reliance on tapes and their distribution in the physical world, could not cloak users' identities as well as the Internet, which allows an exchange of unseen bits of information to flow into someone's private domain, with only a credit card charge as evidence of the exchange. (Of course, hard-drive memory and browser caches can provide traces of content accessed, too.)

Internet users' behavior also confirms the importance of this medium's sexual content. Alexa Research found *sex* to be the most popular search term between March 1999 and January 2001, based on more than 42 million search pages viewed in aggregate by users at 10 portal or search engine Web sites: altavista.com., aol.com, excite.com, go.com, google.com, goto.com, lycos.com, msn.com, netscape.com, and yahoo.com (Pastore, 2001). Among the other top 20 search terms in this study were *porn/porno/pornography* (4th), *nude/nudes* (13th), *xxx* (15th), and *playboy* (19th). An Associated Press article quotes an estimate that "10,000 adult sites may be bringing in as much as $1 billion a year" (1999). Another estimate from Google.com puts the number of unique Web pages at 1.4 billion, with 12% of these devoted to sexual content and pornography (Goldman, 2001).

Statistics about traffic at top mainstream sites have yet to gain credibility (Stempel & Stewart, 2000), and tracking at top sex-related sites is hard to come by. Definitions used for tracking visitors have not been standardized, and mainstream tracking companies like Nielsen and Jupiter Media Metrix do not include sex-related sites in their rankings. For October 2001, Nielsen NetRatings ranks AOL Time Warner properties at the top of its "Top 25 Web Properties," with 66 million unique audience members at home; number 10 on that list, eBay, has 16.3 million unique audience members for that month (NetRatings.com, 2001). Media Metrix ranked AOL Time Warner at 83.9 million unique audience members at home and at work for that month (MediaMetrix, 2001). SexTracker ranks only soft and hard pornography sites that subscribe to the service and allow public distribution of their ratings, using real-time data gathered from traffic patterns at the sites themselves. Its top-ranked subscriber, Smutserver.com, recorded 195.6 million unique audience members for the first 30 days of October 2001 (SexTracker.com, 2001). Yet comparing mainstream and sex-site rankings remains impossible because of differences in how these companies define *users, unique audience,* and other terms. SexTracker defined its unique audience as

> people who have either never before visited your site, or people who have not visited in at least 24 hours. If you have a large percentage of unique visitors you may conclude that once surfers see your site once on any given day, they do not return for at least 24 hours. For free sites, you want unique visitors; they are much more likely to click on advertising banners and make you money. (SexTracker, 2001)

Based on this definition, SexTracker's top site, Smutserver.com, had a minimum of 6.5 million unique audience members for October if every unique visitor returned to visit the site every day. A more likely scenario is that most unique users did not return every day of that month, so the total number of visitors would be much higher and place the site among the top 10 sites overall, if such rankings for both mainstream and sex-related sites were available. Nielsen and Media Metrix defined *unique audience* differently; even if a user visits a site 10 times in one month, that person is counted as one unique audience member for that month (Kopytoff, 2000). Because "web site traffic measurements diverge widely, depending on who is counting and how," these rankings are questioned by advertisers and Web site owners who maintain their own gauges of traffic to their own sites (Kopytoff, 2000; Stempel & Stewart, 2000). The broader audience debate aside, there is evidence that sites serving up sex-related content attract huge audiences.

The Mainstream and Pornographic Dichotomy

Sexual appeals in Web advertising, then, appear in a different sort of media environment than sexual appeals in mainstream media. Although mainstream broadcast media may tolerate depictions of sexual intimacy in shows such as *Friends* and *NYPD Blue* and in commercials for Victoria's Secret, access to even mild pornography is available only to subscribers of special cable or satellite programming. The *New York Times Magazine* often covers sexual topics in its feature stories and runs Jewelry.com ads depicting scantily dressed female and male models wearing little but jewelry, but pornography is not available inside its covers. The Web, of course, provides both mainstream and pornographic content with the click of a mouse. This reality seems to have driven many Internet companies to make obvious hard-line distinctions between mainstream and pornographic content, distinctions that are taken for granted in off-line media. Conversely, some Web sites imitate formats while toning down content to attract the large numbers of Internet users who seek such content. Most all statistics from Internet companies that track the medium's top Web sites usually exclude sites with pornographic content, as discussed earlier. In this way, sex is often purged from discussion about the medium's character, purpose and user habits, just as Yahoo.com was forced by its mainstream audience to purge advertisements for sex sites and to reorganize its directory service for such sites in early 2001.

So, although this global village, at first glance, seemed to be a democratizing place that leveled hierarchies, it currently is a place where the same old gender hierarchies have been reestablished by objectification of sexualized bodies, usually women's, through marketing Web sites, advertising, photo galleries sponsored by Dallascowboys.com and Maximonline.com, and soft and hard-core pornography (see Fig. 14.1). Content on the medium is also placed in hierarchy, with the mainstream dot-com world officially ignoring the presence of a thriving pornography business, while recognizing it as a path to profitability especially in hard times, as the Yahoo case illustrates. The Web is now a venue in which women worldwide are both making profits (mostly Westernized countries; see Needham, 2001) and being exploited in greater numbers than ever (Bartlett & Mitchell, 2000), to feed the appetite of a newly gathered worldwide audience for images of all sorts. Into this environment, advertising's use of sex to sell will continue

FIG. 14.1. Ad from Maximonline.com.

some of the patterns of desire established in off-line media, as the next section discusses. But the self-conscious distinctions made by Internet companies concerning pornographic and nonpornographic Web content,
especially as illustrated by the Yahoo.com case, should signal caution to
those who would use sex to sell on the Internet.

     Web designers revamping Baywatch.com in 2000 were aware of the chal-
lenges of the mainstream–pornography dichotomy, when trying to shift the
Web site toward 18- to 35-year-old men and away from the 24- to
54-year-old women who watch the show. One of the goals of the redesign
meant not "caving into the lucrative temptations of Internet porn," but still
focusing on the beautiful women in the show who would appeal to men
while not offending female fans (Gruenwedel, 2000). After the redesign,
photo galleries at the site featured women and a few men, mirroring a format found on soft-core pornography web sites. Although the medium may
support old-media sensibilities within its digital environment, its easily accessible and often hard-core sexual content may be more likely to repulse

users looking for mainstream content and Web sites looking for profitability from these mainstream users.

IN CYBERSPACE, SEXY (AND SEXIST) ADS FIND YOU

It really comes down to two of the basics of persuasion: Audience and context matter when sexually oriented advertising is created. One study (Reichert, Lambiase, Morgan, Carstarphen, & Zavoina, 1999) shows a marked difference between the amount of sexually oriented advertising in mainstream magazines such as *Time* and *Newsweek*, compared to gendered magazines such as *Cosmopolitan*, *Redbook*, *Esquire*, and *Playboy*, with the latter group featuring more. On the Web, these conditions may proscribe where or whether sexually oriented advertising is used. Mainstream Web sites such as Amazon.com and CNN.com, which attract visitors from across demographic groups and from cultures around the world, may be more cautious about accepting certain kinds of advertising, and advertisers themselves may work to produce banners or pop-up ads deemed appropriate for a worldwide audience. All of the top 25 Web sites in October 2001 may be classified as providing mainstream content for a general audience, and the top 25 Web advertisers reflect these broad interests (see NetRatings.com, 2001). One factor not considered in this list of top web sites or advertisers, of course, is the popularity of sex-related sites as discussed in the previous section.

Gendered Web Sites and Village Sensibilities

Finding mainstream advertising with erotic appeals of the sort commonly used in print versions of *Cosmopolitan* or *GQ* is more difficult. In fact, ads using sexual appeals were completely absent during many visits in 2001 to Cosmopolitan.com, and the circumstances of this magazine's online presence illustrate the potential difficulty of such advertising to a generalized Web audience. Cosmopolitan online is a small part of the women-oriented iVillage.com site, which also showcases other Hearst magazine properties *Country Living*, *Good Housekeeping*, *House Beautiful*, *Marie Claire*, *Redbook*, *Town & Country*, and *Victoria*. Although the iVillage.com site offers original content for its users, it also serves as a marketing vehicle for these magazines, each one appearing within a larger iVillage.com template. On the larger iVillage.com site, the sponsors included GE Appliances, Folgers, Kraft, Dasani water, Astrology.com and iMaternity.com, all using traditional product-oriented advertising in early November 2001. On the particular web pages for Cosmopolitan online, the only sexy image included was the cover model from November's print magazine, used on the web site to identify the *Cosmopolitan* brand and to sell print subscriptions. Even on pages about sex-related topics on the main iVillage.com site, sponsoring

ads usually contained only words or product images for Downy fabric soft-
ener, for a feature film "Life as a House" with images of star Kevin Kline,
and for Depo-Provera birth control. A column titled "Ask the Sex Coach"
featured a banner ad for Fisher-Price toys. The environment of iVillage, created not only for *Cosmopolitan* readers but also for readers of those more
mainstream women's magazines and a generalized female Web audience,
could be seen as a microcosm of the use of sexualized images across
broader Web space. Because a generalized audience uses iVillage, then content and advertising is geared for that wider audience rather than specifically for the *Cosmo* crowd. It seems a mainstream Web site such as iVillage
must play it safer than a gendered space such as *Cosmopolitan* magazine.

GQ online finds itself in a different setting, with its own particular site
design, although a link is offered to CondéNet, a Condé Nast Web site promoting its magazine properties for fashion, cooking, and travel. A
hyperlink is offered for its "men of the year" awards, made in the November 2001 issue of the magazine, and this new page contains sponsor links for
Lexus, Clinique skin supplies for men, and the Discover credit card. All
these ads use logos or product illustrations, much like the iVillage site. Ads
using sexual appeals do appear on this part of the site, however. *GQ*'s online audience is more likely to be a specific demographic, much like its print
magazine, and perhaps not bound by the same limitations as
Cosmpolitan.com, which is embedded in iVillage. One sponsor link led to a
Flash presentation for David Yurman jewelry for women, which featured a
collage of still photography and streaming video of provocatively dressed
women wearing jewelry, two of whom may be coupled possibly as lesbian
partners, an increasingly common strategy for advertising in gendered
women's and men's publications (Reichert, 2001; Reichert, Maly, &
Zavoina, 1999). On *GQ*'s subscription Web page, an ad for Jockey features a
male model wearing only boxers and straddling a bar stool. Other
stand-alone magazine sites, such as Esquire.com and Maximonline.com,
feature sexual appeals in ads, but mostly for their own magazine products
such as subscription sales, books, and newsletters.

Other popular gendered domains may be found as part of the Snow-
ball.com network of properties, and these sites offer insight into how 18- to
35-year-old demographics like those in force at Esquire.com and
Maximonline.com really mean an even younger audience. This reality also
has implications for sex in advertising research. Snowball.com comprises
IGN.com, Chickclick.com, and Highschoolalumni.com, all accompanied
by advertising that mirrors the content at these sites. At IGN.com, which is
an insider videogame review site, a "For Men" link offers content for
so-called "men" ages 12 to 24 years old:

> Fast cars. Faster Women. Movies. Television. Interviews with stars and per-
> sonalities.... These and much more of the finer things in life are served up

daily on the IGN For Men network. Hand-crafted by a gang of highly talented, marauding editorial maniacs, IGN For Men is the ultimate lifestyle destination for America's future: 12-24 year-old men.... Oh, and if you come to IGN For Men and don't find anything of interest, you'd better check your pulse, 'cos (sic) we reckon you're dead. Or getting there... (2001, http://www.ign.com/faq.html)

The "For Men" part of the site offers links to the "babe of the day," to clickable cheerleaders at NFL.com, and to the "For Men" library, which offers "archives of babes, cars, dating, booze, and more" (2001, http://formen.ign.com). Some videogame advertisements at the site feature scantily clad women, who are usually secondary characters (see Fig. 14.2). At Snowball's Chickclick.com site, separate areas exist for teens' (MissClick)

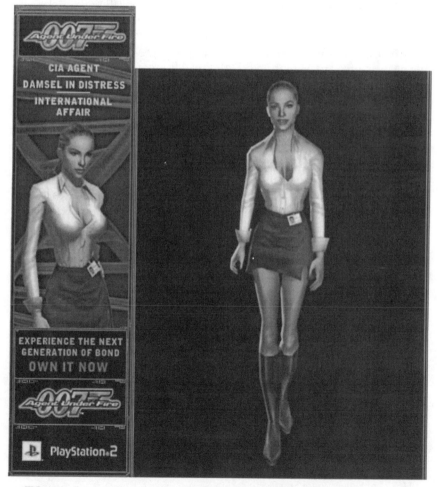

FIG. 14.2. Zoe, a virtual "damsel in distress" from 007: Agent Under Fire.

and women (EstroClick), but content and advertising are not distinguishable between these two areas. Articles about sexually transmitted diseases and ads for birth control exist across both the teens and women's areas, much like booze and babes cohabitate at IGN's "For Men." Snowball.com's properties become a mirror showing an unequal universe in which men have pleasure and women have consequences to consider.

At IGN.com's "For Men" area, photo galleries of "babes" are offered as content that supports macho culture for teenage boys. Both Esquire.com and Maximonline.com also offer photo galleries of women from past covers or feature articles, which may be seen as marketing strategies for driving traffic to their sites. Beyond being a marketing strategy, the photo galleries found at Esquire.com and Maximonline.com (as well as at other sites such as Sportsbetting.com, WWFdivas.com, and Dallascowboys.com) especially mimic soft-core pornography sites, some of which offer free content in exchange for traffic. Sex-related sites that charge most successfully for content, however, are soft-core, "arty" pornography sites, according to one e-commerce analyst (Shreve, 2001), and this content is most similar to photo gallery content offered for free by mainstream Web sites such as Esquire.com, NFL.com, and IGN.com. Another such imitator may be found at Dallascowboys.com, where the cheerleaders are featured in swimsuit calendar poses, as well as individual pictures and personal profiles of cheerleaders that may be found through hyperlinks from a group photo. No such photos are available for football team members; the site offers only mug shots of uniformed players.

Other examples of sexually oriented advertising at gendered sites may be found at Maximonline.com, another stand-alone site that complements its print version. One past banner advertisement from October 2001 depicts two bare-shouldered blond women snuggling with one another. Then, this animated GIF image changes to text over the women's image: "We want a piece of your action!!!" which is then replaced by "Come and play now!!! www.BetOnSports.com." Similar banner advertising on sports sites features a nearly nude women, with "click here" buttons placed on their buttocks or breasts with text that says "Play with me" or "bet now" (see Fig. 14.3). Once a Web user clicks on the banner to visit either BetOnSports.com or SportsBetting.com, he or she is linked to those web sites. At BetOnSports.com's site, there are no images of scantily clad or nude women on the home page. At SportsBetting.com, however, there is a swimsuit gal-

FIG. 14.3. Banner ad for Sportsbetting.com.

lery link and another link for other Webmasters willing to use click-through banners to promote the site (see http://www.sportsbetting.com/partners/banners.html). Among these 23 samples of banners and other ad formats, 17 use nude or scantily dressed women as part of animation that also includes photos of male athletes, and 12 of these banners use images of women exclusively. Because banners are horizontal bars, a reclining body fits their format well; additionally, because Web ads used with editorial content generally are small in size and must communicate their messages economically, much like outdoor advertising, then attention-getting strategies such as depictions of body parts, faces, and provocative words are often used.

Sexually Profiling Users

When Internet users are not visiting gendered domains like Maximonline.com, then ads for gaming, clothing, alcohol, and sports-oriented companies that often feature sexy models are not easy to locate intentionally by surfing to mainstream sites. These kinds of products and web content do use sex in online advertising, with banner, pop-up, pop-under, and interstitial ads for these products responding to user-profiling cues provided by cookies or by information gathered through online surveys completed by Web users. For instance, these cookies or intelligent agents may identify an Internet user as a male between 18 and 35 years old and then target that user for particular advertising, some of which may contain sexual appeals. A progression of sexually explicit advertising is then possible, with ads cued to an Internet user's habits. So, although the editorial content of a Web site may come from its own content server, a separate ad server is used to fill in banners or other ad spaces or to provide pop-up ads when a user with a certain profile visits a web site (Kaye & Medoff, 2001). These same appeals, then, may be virtually invisible to many women and other users not targeted for such online advertising. Users who don't fit the profile of such advertising may visit only mainstream Internet sites designed to serve both genders and all ages, races, ethnicities, belief systems, and/or cultural backgrounds. For users not fitting certain profiles, the absence of sexually oriented advertising may be seen as a benefit of the medium, especially by those who object to such content for a variety of reasons.

These gendered profiling tactics mirror those of gendered magazines such as *Cosmopolitan* and *GQ*, except in more covert fashion. Everyone can buy these magazines, but not everyone can create a surfing profile without going to a lot of trouble that makes herself or himself into a target for particular advertising. It is this covert advertising strategy that may make the Internet as an advertising venue more difficult to study, in terms of how sexually oriented appeals operate in this evolving environment and by whom they are seen. Whereas pull technology tries to attract appropriate audiences for Web content and corollary advertising, push technology is more interesting in terms of sexually oriented appeals. It is used widely on the Web to send content and advertising by email to users who fit demographic profiles or who passively provide clues about their interests through cookies. Then, push technology interprets data from surfing profiles to make users into targets for ads about sites with sexualized content, for ads for sex products, or ads with sexualized content. Sex-tinged ads and messages may then be sent directly to web users' email boxes, although *spamming*—sending unwanted "junk" email—presents its own problems. Allowing users to register at Web sites and to self-select or "opt-in" for certain product information or newsletters are other strategies now used widely (Kaye & Medoff, 2001).

Technology Culture and Ad Sex

Even in niche magazines with specialized audiences that would seem well-suited for profiling, using sex in advertising can go awry. Women working in high technology who subscribe to technology-related publications—but who don't fit the profile of some readers of those magazines—are waging a web-based campaign against ads using sexual appeals. GraceNet.net gives monthly "DisGraceful Awards" to advertisers in high-tech magazines that use sex to sell their products or services (2002). The September 2001 award went to Icon International Group for an ad published in *Competitive Intelligence Magazine* that shows most of a woman's breasts, her head replaced by sheep, a lava lamp, and a printing press. The ad's caption reads: "We keep you abreast of the value chain." Other awards have gone to Compaq/Microsoft, IBM/Lotus, *Wired* magazine, and InfoUSA. GraceNet promotes the "Disgraceful Awards" to raise awareness that women working in technology professions are offended by sexist ads, according to the group's Web site (2002; see www.gracenet.net). Founder Sylvia Paull (personal communication, September 24, 2001) has said the group would like to monitor sexual and sexist appeals on the Web, but simply doesn't have time to search for such ads. Despite women's increasing presence in technology-related fields, many such companies do use sexual and sexist images on Web sites to market products or services, recognizing that technology workers are still predominantly male. One example is a graphic (see Fig. 14.4) used through October 2001 on The-Silo.com, a multimedia company in Australia. The "silo girl," not present on the company's redesigned Web site, is a cartoon dominatrix (see discussion of this sort of imagery, Schroeder & Borgerson, chap. 4, this volume), complete with bullwhip but absent any obvious relationship to the company or its services. Its

FIG. 14.4. The Silo girl.

only relationship would be to the culture of Silo.com's workplace, as established by its owners or webmaster.

Another technology-centered Web site provides an example of the kind of advertising and marketing success that may seen as dependent on sex-tinged appeals. Such advertising by X10.com drove so much traffic to its e-commerce site that it ranked 5th among the top 50 Web sites by Media Metrix for August 2001. A sexually charged ad for X10's "tiny, wireless video camera" was used as a "pop-under" ad for the LATimes.com during summer 2001 ("Basic Instinct," 2001). But the online news site received complaints about the ad and its suggestion that wireless video cameras could be used in the bedroom, so that part of the text was removed (see edited ad, Fig. 14.5). On the left side of the ad, a man's hand holds the technology, which in this ad is a small video camera; it quickly sets a gendered scene of "men of the world" and "women at home" (Winship, 1981; see also Goffman, 1979). In the center, text describes the product, and at right is a photo of a woman in a short black dress sitting with her knees together on a black leather couch; she is looking toward the photo of the product held by a man's hand. The woman may be placed into this ad to attract attention (see Reichert, chap. 2, this volume), but she is also part of the ad's subtle message, which may be a promise to buyers of wireless video cameras that this product enhances one's sex life, sexuality, or sex-esteem (Lambiase & Reichert, in press). If the recipient of this email ad links to X10.com, the camera is touted as a way to safeguard one's home from thieves or to watch babysitters or children when parents are in another room or away from home. Again, another photo illustration links the camera to the young woman on the couch (see Fig. 14.6), suggesting that contrary to the text, the camera has more to do with sex, young women, and videotapes than something as mundane as home security. Another pop-under ad for the same X10.com product appeared during fall 2001, replacing the bedroom surveillance suggestion with "pool" and featuring a bikini-clad woman emerging from a swimming pool (see Fig. 14.7).

On the X10.com Web site, a sexualized message of surveillance is countered by an overall tone of seriousness and wholesomeness—the top of each Web page within the site features a small photo of a man and woman in front of their home, with the words "X10 Home Solutions." When users visit the site for the first time, however, a "tech toys" page is viewed; it has been designed with a photo box that features a different woman each time the page is accessed, in a kind of gallery style. One woman is nude and covered in rose petals; another one of the photos is the woman from the black

FIG. 14.5. Pop-under ad for X10.com.

FIG. 14.6. Illustration from X10.com web site.

leather couch in a new pose, along with a half dozen or so others. A pop-up window that appears over the changing photo says "Capture the Moments!" Other pages of the site contain lists of products (one that's named "Hot Body") that are highlighted in red, with words such as *hot*, *new*, and *free*, in the same style as lists of photos or streaming video made available at sites with sexual content.

Why do some technology-related sites employ sexual appeals, especially those using women's bodies to target men? One response would be that the character of much technological development, including the

FIG. 14.7. Pop-under ad for X10.com.

Internet's own military genesis, has been determined by its male creators. Rakow (1988) and Rothschild (1981) both saw technology itself as gendered, with Rakow suggesting that new questions be asked "about values expressed by technologies and the purposes to which they are put, about the creation and organization of culture, and about the structure of power relationships" (p. 57). Foucault (1977), too, noticed technology's utility for surveillance and knowledge gathering, which are then wielded as tools of power over those people who are the objects of such surveillance (see also Poster, 1990). Haraway (1991) saw things differently by reveling in the coupling of humans and machines, especially the possibilities for women in such networks. To her, the blurring of distinctions between organism and machine, between female and male "cracks the matrices of domination and opens geometric possibilities" (p. 174). Haraway's view notwithstanding, many images circulating on the Internet depend on the virtual coupling of women's bodies with men's eyeballs, making for a lopsided female–male dichotomy within the technology circuit. This time-tested formula of women's bodies displayed for men's eyes seems to be heartily embraced by those developing marketing strategies for the Web, despite egalitarian or postmodern hopes for the medium overall.

Cyber Models Meet Feminists

Depictions of women like those found on Seattle-based X10's site have been debated widely by feminist and mass media scholars for the past 40 years (i.e. Berger, 1972; Bordo, 1988; Friedan, 1963; Goffman, 1979; Kilbourne, 1999; Pingree, Hawkins, Butler, & Paisley, 1976; Steinem, 1990; Williamson, 1978; Wolf, 1991). Twitchell (1996 and chap. 10, this volume), skeptical of the "sex sells" mantra and its harm to women, acknowledged that feminists have produced the "only coherent indictment of Adcult that has ever had a political following, and it has produced real changes in the industry" (p. 142). In the new media of the Web, those pressures still appear to be in place. One example provides evidence of the Web's ability to give power to smaller voices in the global village, with GraceNet.net's pressure of old media through new media tactics. Other scrutiny of sexually charged content or sexist images comes from the Internet's own users against some Web content, such as complaints to Yahoo about sex-related content links and complaints to the LATimes.com about an advertiser's winking hint to use video cameras hidden in bedrooms.

Technology culture, however, has produced another challenge for feminist critics in the development of cyber models for use by Web marketers and retailers. These "virtual women" have become more mainstream versions of computer-generated video game characters, who are highly stereotyped with long hair, long legs, larger-than-average or "balloon" breasts, and often wearing "revealing scraps or sexy tight-fitting pieces of clothing over their super-athletic, unrealistic body shape combinations—slim, very narrow waists and large breasts" (Okorafor & Davenport, 2001, p. 15). One such video game character, CIA agent Zoe Nightshade from "007: Agent Under Fire," is used in a Web advertisement for a game in which James Bond is the main character (see Fig. 14.2).

Female characters in these games are stereotyped in appearance and actions, according to Okorafor & Davenport (2001), and cyber models used to sell products online and off-line are hyper-stereotyped as well, touted as "tireless and cheap" models who "never have a bad day, are eager to please and are great conversationalists" (Genovese, 2001). Virtual model Webbie Tookay is called "perfect" by its creator John Casablancas of Illusion 2K virtual modeling agency because "she never gains weight, and she can be in a number of places at the same time, such as virtual parades, publicity campaigns and electronic games. And most important, she does not abandon her modeling agency for anything" (Illusion 2K, 2000). Cyber or virtual models are being used in a variety of ways online by attracting attention to Web sites, by assisting customers at e-commerce sites and acting as hosts of those sites, and by appearing in print and online advertising. For example, virtual models similar to Webbie Tookay serve as news readers on Web sites such as Ananova.com, where Ananova is a composite of Spice Girl Victoria Beckham and other news anchors (La Ferla, 2001); as fitting assistants on clothing sites such as Landsend.com; as hosts or mascots of sites such as Boo.com, a portal for clothing retailers; and as characters in gaming environments and films, such as "Final Fantasy," which stars computer-animated Aki Ross.

One study raises issues of physical attractiveness and concepts of self when cyber models are used to sell products (Quilty, Solomon, & Englis, 2000). And the Landsend.com site alerts its users to an obvious problem with using virtual models: "Remember, I will look like you as much as you desire. So, if you lie to me, then I'll lie to you too. If I don't quite look like you, then feel free to modify me" (see www.Landsend.com). Manipulating virtual bodies of women simply continues the drive to perfect real female bodies, which have been shrinking in size in depictions in advertising over the past quarter century (Kilbourne, 1999, p. 125). Much like the stereotyped bodies of female video game characters, these virtual models can be used for sex-tinged appeals. Aki Ross of "Final Fantasy" appeared on *Maxim* magazine's Hot 100 list in 2001; a fictional narrative from Boo.com has the site's virtual host, Miss Boo, posing for *The Sun*'s Page Three topless photo in May 2001 (a disclaimer on the site declares that "Timeline listings from Jan. 2001 on are fictional and are in no way intended to reflect the views of boo.com employees or relatives of employees, or anyone in their ancestral line...."). The site's strategy for using Miss Boo has changed since it filed for bankruptcy protection in May 2000 and then was relaunched under new ownership in October 2000; now the cyber host "doesn't dictate products or trends, but encourages the comfortable self-expression of the individual" (see www.boo.com). Clearly, the use of virtual models has been embraced by a few Web sites and in other new media ventures, but their effectiveness has not yet been measured.

CONCLUSIONS FOR FUTURE RESEARCH

One area of future research could focus on determining sex-tinged advertising's suitability for use on the Web. The protests against Yahoo demonstrate the power of mainstream sensibilities to distinguish mainstream space from the Web's abundant soft- and hard-core pornographic content. If a mainstream Web site's advertising uses more explicit sexual appeals, then its mainstream users might categorize that site differently, to the site's benefit or detriment depending on its users' demographics. These investigations could include empirical studies that compare the amount and degree of sexual appeals off-line and online for specific audiences, as well as studies that qualitatively scrutinize entire Web environments for their depictions of sex in advertising and editorial content. These environments and their user habits could be considered through the lens of uses and gratification theory. Other studies could trace the development of gendered Web sites and how these compare to gendered print content and broadcast programming, especially how advertisers in these old and new media environments use sexual appeals to target specific audience types. Finally, many short-term, ongoing studies are needed to assist researchers and advertisers in adapting their methods to an ever-changing online environment. Stempel and Stewart (2000) have outlined general problems for Internet researchers, including depth of use, definitions for an Internet universe, and sampling. All these challenges await those studying advertising and sexual appeals in this new medium.

Also to be considered are international laws, proposals, and filters that seek to control content on the Internet. A California congresswoman introduced legislation in 2001 to protect children from receiving unsolicited email with sexually explicit advertising (Magid, 2001). Another 2001 proposal by the European Union sought to ban hate speech, and it is certain that nations and cultural groups will continue trying to exert controlling influences over Internet content. How might other laws and cultural customs impinge on the use of sexual appeals? In addition to cultural studies research, other analysis concerning accessibility of Web content to teenagers and children might be useful. Because Web content is accessible to anyone of any age with a computer and the knowledge to use a Web browser—unless filters are used—then children and teens may be accessing adult spaces, even mainstream ones such as IGN.com and Maximonline.com, that are supposedly designed for adult audiences but may really be marketing a lifestyle and products to boys as young as 12 years old. "Babes, cars, dating, booze, and more," as offered by IGN.com in its own words (2001, For men archive), hardly seem like suitable topics for younger teens, especially when off-line media and advertisers are working to remove the most obvious appeals targeting young people for alcohol, tobacco, and other products. The use of filters may also have bearing on sexually oriented Web advertising because filters may screen out the content included in such ads.

Interactive technologies on the Web offer much promise for determining how advertising works. Using these future technological capabilities will help researchers studying sexual appeals to determine more accurately just how such advertising affects attention and memory, plus buying habits and lifestyle choices. Audience tracking technology still lacks pinpoint sophistication, but some general data now available could prove useful if researchers can forge relationships with Web-hosting services and their clients. When an ad offers a "click here" button or simply "click-through" capabilities, what percentage of Web users then visits specific sites and completes purchases? Or if no purchase is made, will many people register themselves at these sites to receive marketing newsletter by email? If such an ad features an implicit or explicit sexual appeal, are Web users more likely to "click here" or "click-through"? The success of X10.com's Web campaign for miniature video cameras suggests that sexually oriented ads helped its Web site reach a top-10 ranking, according to Media Metrix (2001). Studies of effectiveness beyond the anecdotal are possible online, in real time and in realistic settings, with much better environments than those usually simulated for studies of print or broadcast advertising. If reliable demographic information is attached to a Web user and her habits, could advertisers track ways that such a user interacts with certain online advertising appeals and then tailor appeals for users fitting that specific sort of profile? This is currently happening in a limited way for a few companies able to afford such technology plus the laborious scrutiny of surfing logs by *bots* and people. More than any other medium, the Web offers the best hope for advertising researchers interested in discovering when, how, and to what degree sexual appeals work, and with what audiences. Also to be studied is how sexual appeals would work in mobile Internet culture, where content appears on hand-held, low-bandwidth devices or where short cell phone messages are paid for by advertisers and have just a few seconds to attract attention or be deleted.

Many advertising executives remain skeptical about the effectiveness of Web advertising, and this, too, must be considered when research is undertaken about sexual appeals on the Web. Are some traditional off-line purveyors of sexually oriented advertising not on the Web because no one yet quite understands how or whether online advertising works, when compared to off-line ads? Does a generalized and international audience make it problematic for such advertisers to repeat strategies honed in narrower off-line media?

The use of cyber or virtual models on e-commerce sites may be studied empirically to determine effectiveness, as suggested by Quilty et al. (2000). Here also is a topic that should interest technology scholars, researchers working in gender studies, and others across many disciplines. If the Internet is gendered as male, then why are most virtual models female? Robots have long been seen as "slaves" that save work for humans, and these online bots are no different. Are they the virtual equivalent of the many pairings of women with machines, which have led to housekeeping drudgery, data-entry tedium, and telemarketing tethers? These virtual models or servants, called "tireless and cheap" by one male creator, may also be seen as places where humans experiment with identities and dream of a nostalgic past when gender was little contested. Scantily clad, unrealistic models may be the technological continuation of the real-world control of women's bodies in media depictions and through legislation and harassment. All these topics deserve testing through vigorous debate, questioning, and research.

The Web is rightly named. It is an enormous tangle of serious and frivolous content—and all that lies in between—and it reveals human desire for connectedness and for acquisition, for exhibitionism and surveillance. Writ across a worldwide medium, these impulses are central to the study of sex on the Internet, as it is used in advertising and marketing efforts. As this new medium develops, researchers of sexual appeals may begin to untangle this Web of relationships, desire, and capitalism to understand advertising culture on the Internet.

REFERENCES

'Adult' sites drive many Web innovations (1999, January 1). *USA Today Tech Report.* Retrieved October 28, 2001, from http://www.marketing.about.com/cs/sexsells

Associated Press. (1999, February 28). Cybersex a big online attraction. *USA Today Tech Report.* Retrieved October 28, 2001, from http://www.marketing.about.com/cs/sexsells

Bartlett, D., and Mitchell, T. (2000, October). *The new media technology revolution in the pornography phenomenon.* Retrieved August 15, 2001, from Queensland University of Technology's School of Media and Journalism web site: http://www.maj.arts.qut.edu.au/units/mjb336/history/2000/dbartlet/

Basic instinct: X10 takes a camera into the bedroom. (2001, July 2). *AdWeek, Southwest Edition, 23,* 26.

Bedell, D. (2001, April 26). Unlikely innovators: Many online technologies were first perfected by the adult industry [Electronic version]. *The Dallas Morning News,* p. 1F.

Berger, J. (1972). *Ways of seeing.* London: Penguin.

Bolter, J. D. (1991). Writing space: The computer, hypertext, and the history of writing. Hillsdale, NJ: Lawrence Erlbaum Associates.

Bordo, S. (1988). Anorexia nervosa: Psychopathology as the crystallization of culture. In I. Diamond & L. Quinby (Eds.), *Feminism & Foucault: Reflections on resistance* (pp. 87–117). Boston: Northeastern University Press.

Carstarphen, M. G., & Lambiase, J. (1998). Domination and democracy in cyberspace: Reports from the majority media and ethnic/gender margins. In B. Ebo (Ed.), *Cyberghetto or cybertopia? Race, class, and gender on the Internet.* Westport, CT: Praeger/Greenwood.

Cherny, L., & Weise, E. R. (Eds.). (1996). *Wired women: Gender and new realities in cyberspace.* Seattle: Seal Press.

For men archive. (n.d.). Retrieved November 10, 2001, from http://formen.ign.com

Foucault, M. (1977). *Discipline and punishment: The birth of the prison* (A. Sheridan, Trans.). New York: Pantheon.

Friedan, B. (1963). *The feminine mystique.* New York: Dell Publishing.

Genovese, D. (2001). *Selling with cybermodels: Will you staff your cyberstore with a cybermodel?* Retrieved October 23, 2001, from http://www.computerbits.com/archive/2001/0700/cybermodels.html

Goffman, E. (1979). *Gender advertisements.* London: Macmillan.

Goldman, D. (2001, April 23). Consumer republic: Yahoo! surrendered: Porn site is out; so is free choice [Eastern edition]. *Adweek, 42,* 17, p. 12.

Gracenet.net's Disgraceful Awards. (2002). Retrieved April 19, 2002, from http://www.gracenet.net

Gruenwedel, E. (2000, November 13). Dude, surf's up [Southwest edition]. *AdWeek, 22,* 94.

Hansell, S. (2001, April 14). After complaints, Yahoo to close access to pornographic sites. *The New York Times,* p. B1.

Haraway, D. (1991). *Simians, cyborgs, and women: The reinvention of nature.* New York: Routledge.

Herring, S. (1993). Gender and democracy in computer-mediated communication [Special issue]. *Electronic Journal of Communication, 3*(2).

Herring, S. (Ed.). (1996). *Computer-mediated communication: Linguistic, social and cross-cultural perspectives.* Philadelphia: John Benjamins Publishing.

IGN.com FAQ. (n.d.). Retrieved November 10, 2001, from http://www.ign.com/faq.html

Illusion 2K. (2000, May 10). *Virtual model worth U.S. $15 million captures the world market.* Retrieved October 15, 2001, from http://www.optidigit.com/press/illusion2K-en-05-00.html

Kaye, B. K., & Medoff, N. J. (2001). *Just a click away: Advertising on the Internet.* Boston: Allyn and Bacon.

Kilbourne, J. (1999). *Can't buy my love: How advertising changes the way we think and feel.* New York: Touchstone.

Klein, M. (1999, August 10). The history and future of sex. *Electronic Journal of Human Sexuality, 2.* Retrieved July 15, 2001, from http://www.ejhs.org

Kopytoff, V. (2000, September 25). Welcome to the world of online ratings. *The San Francisco Chronicle.* Retrieved October 15, 2001 from http://www.sfgate.com/cgibin/article.cgi?file=/chronicle/archive/2000/09/25/BU91280.DTL

La Ferla, R. (2001, August 2). The perfect model: Gorgeous, no complaints, made of pixels. *The Dallas Morning News*, p. 6C.

Lambiase, J. (1999). Internet rhetoric: Redefining an 800-pound Godzilla. In J. Swearingen & D. Pruett (Eds.), *Rhetoric, the polis, and the global village* (pp. 19–21). Mahwah, NJ: Lawrence Erlbaum Associates.

Lambiase, J., & Reichert, T. (in press). Promises, promises: Exploring erotic rhetoric in sexually oriented advertising. In L. Scott & R. Batra (Eds.), *Visual persuasion*. Mahwah, NJ: Lawrence Erlbaum Associates.

Landow, G. (1993). *Hypertext: The convergence of contemporary critical theory and technology*. Baltimore: Johns Hopkins University Press.

Lanham, R. (1993). *The electronic word: Democracy, technology, and the arts*. Chicago: The University of Chicago Pres.

Magid, L. (2001, July 26). *We need a law against smutty spam directed at kids*. Retrieved August 26, 2001, from http://www.larrysworld.com/articles/sjm_spamlaw.htm

McLuhan, M. (1964). *Understanding media: The extensions of man*. New York: Signet Books.

MediaMetrix. (2001, August). *U.S. top 50 web and digital media properties*. Retrieved November 15, 2001, from http://www.jmm.com/xp/jmm/press/mediaMetrixTop50.xml

Needham, K. (2001, July 21). Porn star Danni shows e-businesses her skill. The Sydney Morning Herald. Retrieved August 1, 2001, from http://www.smh.com.au/news/0107/21/national/national17.html

Negroponte, N. (1995). *Being digital*. New York: Knopf.

NetRatings.com. (2001). *Top 25 properties*. Retrieved November 15, 2001, from http://pm.netratings.com/nnpm/owa/NRpublicreports.toppropertiesweekly

Okorafor, N. N., & Davenport, L. (2001, August). *Virtual women: Replacing the real*. Paper presented at the annual conference of the Association for Educators in Journalism and Mass Communication, Washington, D.C.

Pastore, M. (2001). Search engines, browsers still confusing many web users. *Cyberatlas*. Retrieved August 1, 2001 from http://cyberatlas.Internet.com/big_picture/traffic_patterns/article/0,,5931_588851,00.html

Perry, J. (2001, April 23). My Yahoo!?! My, oh my!: Sex sells, sometimes [Electronic version]. *U.S. News & World Report 130*(16), 42.

Pingree, S., Hawkins, R. P., Butler, M., & Paisley, W. (1976). A scale for sexism. *Journal of Communication, 26*(4), 193–200.

Poster, M. (1990). *The mode of information: Poststructuralism and social context*. Chicago: The Unversity of Chicago Press.

Quilty, N., Solomon, M., & Englis, B. (2000, May). *Icons and avatars: Cyber-models and hyper-mediated visual persuasion*. Paper presented at the Advertising and Consumer Psychology Visual Persuasion Conference, Ann Arbor, MI.

Rakow, L. F. (1988). Gendered technology, gendered practice. *Critical Studies in Mass Communication, 5*(1), 57–70.

Reichert, T. (2001). "Lesbian chic" imagery in advertising: Interpretations and insights of female same-sex eroticism. *Journal of Current Issues and Research in Advertising, 23*(2), 9–22.

Reichert, T., Lambiase, J., Morgan, S., Carstarphen, M. G., & Zavoina, S. (1999). Beef-cake and cheesecake: No matter how you slice it, sexually explicit advertising on the rise. *Journalism and Mass Communication Quarterly, 76*(1), 7–20.

Reichert, T., Maly, K. R., & Zavoina, S. (1999). Designed for (male) pleasure: The myth of lesbian chic in mainstream advertising. In M. G. Carstarphen & S. C. Zavoina (Eds.), *Sexual rhetoric: Media perspectives on sexuality, gender, and identity* (pp. 123–132). Westport, CT: Greenwood Press.

Rothschild, J. (1981). A feminist perspective on technology and the future. *Women's Studies International Quarterly, 4*, 65–74.

Salik, S. H. (1995). *Textualizing the body: Electronic colonization of the mind.* Paper presented to the 67th annual convention of the Western States Communication Association.

Sextracker.com. (2001). *What are the impressions, uniques, reloads, etc?* Retrieved on October 30, 2001, from http://www.sextracker.com/about/newmanual/helpsummary.html

Shreve, J. (2001, March 9). Smut glut has porn sites hurting. *Wired.* Retrieved October 3, 2001, from http://www.wired.com/news/business/0,1367,42061,00.html

Stempel, G. H., & Stewart, R. K. (2000, Autumn). The internet provides both opportunities and challenges for mass communication researchers. *Journalism and Mass Communication Quarterly, 77*(3), 541–548.

Steinem, G. (1990, July/August). Sex, lies, and advertising. *Ms.,* 18–28.

Twitchell, J. B. (1996). *Adcult USA: The triumph of advertising in American culture.* New York: Columbia University Press.

Williamson, J. (1978). *Decoding advertisements.* New York: Marion Boyers.

Winship, J. (1981). Handling sex. *Media, Culture and Society, 3*(1), 25–41.

Wolf, N. (1991). *The beauty myth: How images of beauty are used against women.* New York: William Morrow.

PART V

Conclusion

Chapter 15

Future Questions and Challenges: Advertising Research in the Midst of Sex Noise

Jacqueline Lambiase
University of North Texas

Tom Reichert
University of Alabama

The perspectives of this book stake out but a small, sturdy base camp from which to explore sexual appeals in advertising and marketing. As much as one fifth of advertising uses such appeals (Lin, 1998; Reichert, Lambiase, Morgan, Carstarphen, & Zavoina, 1999; Walker, 2000), but sexualized persuasion in the Western landscape looms larger than that because it surrounds us in films, music videos, television programming, Web content, magazine and book covers, and beyond. Among all this visual "sex noise," the most common metaphor for sex is a woman's body, although men's bodies are being commodified as well, as Barbara Stern reminds us in this volume. These appeals to sexual impulses are nothing new, of course; Aristotle discussed them to help speakers connect with particular audiences in *The Rhetoric*. Young men, he said, "are prone to desires and inclined to do whatever they desire. Of the desires of the body they are most inclined to pursue that relating to sex, and they are powerless against this" (1991 translation, p. 165). Aristotle's ideas, of course, are deliberate stereotypes, but that they hold true more than 2,300 years later is proof of their power.

Drive-by, consumable images in contemporary society may be seen as rhetorical commonplaces and sites of overexposure. Annie Lang and her colleagues took this "drive-by" consumption literally in their study of billboard processing, but the drive-by phenomenon is a global one experienced through many media forms. Readers flip magazine pages, Internet users click through Web pages, and television viewers change channels expertly with remote controls. Another perspective about drive-by, consumable images is informed by postmodern writers Don DeLillo and Jean Baudrillard, especially in their focus on dissolving referents and endless simulations. In his novel *White Noise*, DeLillo (1985/1998) imagined the most-photographed barn in America, and two of his main characters visit this drive-by, must-see tourist attraction to discuss its meaning. Their viewing of this overexposed barn is a community experience, "a kind of spiritual surrender. We see only what the others see…. We've agreed to be part of a collective perception" (p. 12).

In an important sense, this drive-by tourist "trap" or white noise as imagined by DeLillo mimics the attraction and repulsion of sexualized images in our society. This "sex noise" becomes apparent only with effort. Once we perceive sex noise, then it is our obligation to look at the spectacle. As Collin Brooke asserts, viewers find it hard to ignore Cindy Crawford as a familiar metaphor for sex. Yet viewers don't linger long, because her particular image is too familiar to the point of saturation, and it is simulated by so many other bodies in a sexualized landscape. Baudrillard (1993) claimed that such images have been "freed from their respective ideas, concepts, essences, values, points of reference, origins and aims" and have begun to "embark upon an endless process of self-reproduction" (p. 6). He continued: "Yet things continue to function long after their ideas have disappeared, and they do so in total indifference to their own content. The paradoxical fact is that they function even better under these circumstances" (p. 6). For Baudrillard, a repetitive visual rhetoric is a rhetoric of disappearance, for "now all we can do is simulate the orgy, simulate liberation" (p. 3). In a postmodern world of erotic images, women are effects, stranded without a cause in a saturated visual landscape. In a world in which "everything is destined to reappear as simulation," especially "women as the sexual scenario" (Baudrillard, 1988, p. 32), women are caught in the same old modernist poses. And men are caught in the same old modernist gazing. But these familiar, simulated dichotomies have been replicated in other ways, because men are posing, too, and women are gazing. Sex noise has brought chaos.

Pornography, too, is a kind of sex noise that is now quickly cloning its off-line presence online through millions of Web images, as discussed by Jacqueline Lambiase in this volume. That the simulation of pornographic poses occurs in advertising is nothing new. Stern (1991) and Wolf (1991) each have written about pornography and sex in advertising from feminist viewpoints, and James Twitchell (1996) asserted ads are produced "in active collusion with the male viewers" (p. 232), with agencies following Aristotle's ancient advice to elicit an emotional response. Twitchell believed "[i]f there were no printed text, we would decode these ads as mild pornography" (p. 233). Baudrillard would say that this relationship between pornography and advertising is more about reproduction than about sex, that in the body's endless replication, symbolic organization and purpose are lost (1993, p. 7).

In this volume, authors of eight chapters address pornography's influence on sexualized images in mainstream ads, and it is one potential research area for scholars, especially in terms of new media. Jonathan Schroeder and Janet Borgerson, Stephen Gould, and Jean Kilbourne all make cases for pornography's influence on sexualized ads. Gould sees pornography as a sexual opinion leader even for advertising images of men, whereas Kilbourne believes pornography—"which is a world of violence, a world of utter disconnection"—is used by advertisers "to shock us into paying attention." Schroeder and Borgerson discuss pornography as a reservoir of "liminal" images that "are often spaces of uncertainly, creativity, danger, and passion," as a "space between—a space to be entered or crossed—(that) can be simultaneously exciting and unnerving." Sexualized advertising itself seems to inhabit a liminal space, where advertisers risk losing mainstream audiences if they push images too close to those associated with hard-core pornography. Lambiase discusses this contested boundary as it exists on the Web, and Gary Hicks notes mainstream advertisers that would never advertise in pornographic publications do appear in highly sexualized magazines for gay and lesbian audiences, much like mainstream advertisers still appear in *Cosmopolitan* and other gendered, sexualized publications. Tom Reichert compares sexual behavior in some advertising to sexual behavior patterns in pornography; Wilson Key briefly discusses pornographic embeds in already sexualized films.

Beyond the connections of pornography among more than half the chapters, other common threads would emerge if chapters could be hyperlinked. Already, Michael LaTour and Tony Henthorne have demonstrated the value of crossing perspectives by using Kilbourne's video *Still Killing Us Softly* in their investigation of whether feminist consciousness-raising translates into women's more critical appraisals of sexy or sexist ads. Future research could test consciousness-raising of men, to test their reactions when viewing advertisements with idealized and/or sexualized male models (Stern's contribution would help to guide this investigation as well). Does media literacy or consciousness-raising research apply to lesbian and gay audiences, now that ads specifically target them using sexual appeals? Although women still are depicted much more often than men in heterosexist and idealized ways, will this always be the case? Now that sexualized stereotyping affects images directed at both men and women, both homosexuals and hetereosexuals (see Hicks' chapter), will these stereotypes raise ire or simply slip into innocuous or insidious sex noise? Juliann Sivulka's backward glance, coupled with contemporary trends, can help researchers in tracking sexual appeals for these diverse audiences and in determining their appropriateness or effectiveness in new settings.

Stephen Gould offers theories for researchers, as well as practical advice for advertising creatives, in his description of advertising lovemaps. He encourages using this lovemap orientation to determine how advertising and sexuality are linked by consumers. His questions—"What products, services, or advertising do you associate with sexuality? What ads enhance your sexual experience?"—might be seen by Kilbourne as just the sort of linkage that is harmful to relationships. She believes advertising's idealized and sanitized version of sex to sell products has no legitimate connection to "real" sexual fulfillment at all. These seemingly counter perspectives could also be used more collaboratively, to determine those symbolic places that advertising does distort or enhance sexual contexts. Schroeder and Borgerson's contribution also would be useful in this investigation, through their discussion of fetishistic imagery and its progression into mainstream advertising. It is the combination of these voices, the intersections of their ideas and disagreements, which make this volume useful for new and long-time scholars studying sexual appeals.

In addition to trying out an advertising lovemap perspective, readers are also invited in another chapter to view the sex noise around us while considering potential subliminal sexual embeds. Wilson Key asserts the existence of images at the edges of our perceptions, brings us up short, and challenges us to look more closely. While Key's viewpoint is challenged in the marketplace of ideas and rejected by many in the academy, as he discusses in his chapter, the sales of his books to the general public are substantial. He seems to be implicitly asking us whether we should dismiss out of hand that "SEX" is placed on Bush's *Time* magazine cover photo, when Bush's own political advertising seemed to use subliminal messages. Scholars and students in the university tradition should continue to engage his ideas, "opposed to all monopolies of knowledge ... in the spirit of open inquiry and debate" (Carey, 2002, p. 15). The research of scholars working with subliminal messages should also be considered in this debate.

Suggestions for research are included in many chapters, most explicitly in the editors' chapters, chapter 2 and chapter 14 that bookend this volume. Reichert encourages academics to share their work with advertising professionals and to study creative environments and pressures that produce sexually oriented advertising. Many viewpoints in this collection are worthy of professionals' attention, if they can be convinced of the usefulness of such information. For instance, Lang and her colleagues raise important questions for those involved in outdoor and others kinds of advertising: Do sexual appeals work when products themselves do not elicit arousal? Should sexual appeals be used with products such as alcohol, which can elicit an arousal response, especially from heavy drinkers? Other contributors raise questions about the Internet economy and new media habits, plus potential saturation. In her discussion of online sexual appeals, Lambiase projects Web-based research models that will be able to discover when, how, and to what degree sexual appeals work—and with what audiences—because Internet users can click through these ads to register interest and even to purchase items, or click away in disinterest or disgust. Online user habits can inform off-line studies, just as off-line norms have been helping researchers begin to scrutinize the Web.

Internet user habits raise important questions about enclave mentalities among the sex noise in general culture. One site of enclaving is a seemingly sex-crazed macho culture, as exhibited by: (a) Web sites such as IGN.com and Maximonline.com (as well as Dallascowboys.com's simulation of *Sports Illustrated*'s swimsuit gallery, only with cheerleaders); (b) new magazines such as *Maxim* and *Stuff*; (c) locker-room talk in sports programming on television and radio; (d) television shows such as "The Man Show." All of these media forms are supported by advertising, some that mimics the style of surrounding programming and editorial content. Are these shows, Web sites, and magazines driven by cultural nostalgia for a certain kind of masculinity? As Stern discusses in her chapter, masculinity is a contested category and is especially ambiguous in advertising, because idealized men often appeal to both heterosexual and homosexual audiences.

Many chapters discuss this ambiguity regarding sexual orientation, and it is another place that advertising reveals both the erasure of categories along with the hardening of categories through sexualized stereotypes, such as the masculine ones described previously. Hicks raises provocative questions of sexual advertising images directed at lesbian audiences, and these are deserving of further study. His study suggests that in ads directed at lesbian audiences in their own publications, women are often fully dressed, with contact limited to embracing. Yet these ads are quite different from so-called "lesbian chic" advertising in mainstream publications, which are often directed at heterosexual women. A follow-up content analysis could focus on sexual appeal advertising in lesbian publications, comparing these depictions with those of female models dressed and posed for heterosexual audiences. One purpose of such research would be to determine to what degree sexual advertising is driven by the heterosexual male gaze, even in women's publications like *Cosmopolitan*, compared to sexual advertising directed at lesbians, which is an audience of women interested in being sexually attractive to women only. Although this advertising exists in an enclave environment, it is an environment without the powerful male gaze and it would be one place potentially to observe its absence.

While Baudrillard (1993) asserted that culture is witnessing "a fading away of sexuality, of sexual beings" (p. 7) in favor of technological simulation and cloning, advertising and other media forms seem to be preserving and reflecting whatever sexuality we can imagine for ourselves in more explicit ways than ever before. Kilbourne, in this present collection, talks about how "unerotic" and "disconnected" some sexual images are in contemporary advertising, and in these characterizations, she seems to be leaning toward Baudrillard's more radical postmodern vision. Whether current advertising is documenting the ascent and ultimate demise of a public sexuality, no one can say. In this environment, however, it seems more important than ever to study advertising appeals among the sex noise and to provide knowledge about its cultural and economic impact.

REFERENCES

Aristotle. (1991). *On rhetoric: A theory of civic discourse* (G.A. Kennedy, Trans.). New York: Oxford University. (Original work published 4th Century B.C.E.)

Baudrillard, J. (1988). *America* (C. Turner, Trans.). New York: Verso. (Original work published in 1986)

Baudrillard, J. (1993). *The transparency of evil: Essays on extreme phenomena* (J. Benedict, Trans.). New York: Verso. (Original work published 1990)

Carey, J. W. (2002). *The engaged discipline.* The Carroll C. Arnold Distinguished Lecture, National Communication Association, November 2000. Boston: Allyn & Bacon.

DeLillo, D. (1998). *White noise.* New York: Penguin Books. (Original work published in 1985)

Lin, C. A. (1998). Uses of sex appeals in prime-time television commercials. *Sex Roles, 38*(5/6), 461–475.

Reichert, T., Lambiase, J., Morgan, S., Carstarphen, M., & Zavoina, S. (1999). Beefcake or cheesecake? No matter how you slice it, sexual explicitness in advertising continues to increase. *Journalism & Mass Communication Quarterly, 76*(1), 7–20.

Stern, B. (1991). Two pornographies: A feminist view of sex in advertising. In R. H. Holman & M. Solomon (Eds.), *Advances in Consumer Research, 18* (pp. 384–391). Provo, UT: Association for Consumer Research.

Twitchell, J. (1996). *Adcult USA: The triumph of advertising in American culture.* New York: Columbia University Press.

Walker, J. R. (2000). Sex and violence in program promotion. In S. T. Eastman (Ed.), *Research in media promotion* (pp. 101–126). Mahwah, NJ: Lawrence Erlbaum Associates.

Wolf, N. (1991). *The beauty myth: How images of beauty are used against women.* New York: William Morrow.

About The Contributors

Janet Borgerson (PhD, University of Wisconsin, Madison) is Visiting Associate Professor in the School of Business at Stockholm University. She is also a research affiliate of the European Center for Art and Management. She is a philosopher who writes on feminist ethical ontology. Her main area of research focuses on concepts of power, agency, and desire in ethical theory, with particular emphasis on how information technology-dependent media influence and interact with ethical, social, cultural, and political institutions.

Collin Gifford Brooke (PhD, University of Texas at Arlington) is Assistant Professor of Rhetoric in the Writing Program at Syracuse University. His research interests include the intersections of rhetoric, critical theory, and technology, with a specific focus on new information and communication technologies. His work has appeared in *JAC: A Journal of Composition Theory*, *PreText Electra (Lite)*, and numerous edited collections.

Xiaomei Cai (PhD, Indiana University) is Assistant Professor in the Department of Communication at the University of Delaware. Her research interests include media message analysis and uses and effects of new media technologies.

Stephen Gould (PhD, The City University of New York) is Professor of Marketing at Baruch College, The City University of New York. He has published more than 40 research articles in such journals as *Psychological Review, Journal of Consumer Research, Journal of Advertising, Journal of Advertising Research, Journal of Current Issues and Research in Advertising*, and *Journal of Marketing Communications*, among others. His current research interests include: consumer lovemaps and sexuality; Internet and technology use by consumers; globally integrated marketing communications; postmodern culture; and cross-cultural research. In addition, he is a frequent research consultant and invited academic speaker.

Tony L. Henthorne (PhD, University of Mississippi) is Professor of Marketing and Director of The Institute for Service Excellence at The University of Southern Mississippi. Dr. Henthorne has been the recipient of the Brant Award for outstanding research in the College of Business and has received the university's Lucas Award to further his research efforts. His works have appeared in such outlets as *Journal of Advertising, Psychology and Marketing, Journal of the Academy of Marketing Science,* and *Journal of Business Ethics.*

Gary R. Hicks (PhD, University of Texas at Austin) is Assistant Professor of mass communications at Southern Illinois University, Edwardsville. He has his PhD in journalism from the University of Texas at Austin, an MA in journalism from the University of Missouri-Columbia, and a BS in broadcast journalism from Texas Christian University. His research focuses on media images of marginalized groups, including the gay/lesbian/transgender community. His work has appeared in the *Journal of Mass Media Ethics.* Prior to getting his doctorate, Hicks worked as an associate producer for public television and as a newspaper reporter.

Wilson Bryan Key (PhD, University of Denver) has authored five books on subliminal communication: *Subliminal Seduction,* 1973; *Media Sexploitation,* 1976; *The Clam-Plate Orgy,* 1980; *The Age of Manipulation,* 1989; and *Subliminal Adventures in Erotic Art,* 1992. Now 76, he lives near Reno, Nevada, and lectures extensively at colleges and universities throughout North America. He has held professorships at Denver, Kansas, Boston, Puerto Rico, and Western Ontario universities. He is currently CEO of Mediaprobe Inc., an international consulting and educational firm, and is writing a new book on media analysis. He is active in Mensa.

Jean Kilbourne (EdD, Boston University) is internationally recognized for her pioneering work on alcohol and tobacco advertising and the image of women in advertising. A widely published writer and speaker who has twice been named Lecturer of the Year by the National Association of Campus Activities, she is best known for her award-winning documentaries *Killing Us Softly, Slim Hopes,* and *Pack of Lies.* She is a visiting scholar at Wellesley College, has served on the National Advisory Council on Alcohol Abuse and Alcoholism, and been an adviser to two surgeons general. She lives in Boston, Massachusetts.

Jacqueline Lambiase (PhD, University of Texas at Arlington) is Assistant Professor in the Mayborn Graduate Institute of Journalism and Department of Journalism at the University of North Texas. Her research interests include media images of women and men, as well as computer-mediated communication. Her work has been published in *Journalism & Mass Communication Quarterly* and in several edited collections.

Annie Lang (PhD, University of Wisconsin, Madison) is a Professor in the Department of Telecommunications at Indiana University. Her research focuses on how people process mediated messages. In particular she is interested in how media structure and content affect emotion and cognition. Her research has appeared in *Communication Research, Journal of Communication, Journal of Broadcasting and Electronic Media, Media Psychology,* and *Communication Yearbook.*

Michael S. LaTour (PhD, University of Mississippi) is the Torchmark Professor of Marketing in the Department of Marketing at Auburn University's College of Business. Dr. LaTour serves on the editorial review boards of *Industrial Marketing Management* and *Psychology and Marketing.* His articles focus on the underpinnings of advertising response and related strategic issues. In addition to works appearing in *Industrial Marketing Management* and *Psychology and Marketing,* his research has appeared in *Journal of Advertising, Journal of Advertising Research,* and *Journal of the Academy of Marketing Science.*

Seungwhan Lee (MA, Korea University) is a doctoral student in the Department of Telecommunications at Indiana University. His research interests include the uses and effects of new communication technologies and designing interactive multimedia.

Tom Reichert (PhD, University of Arizona) is Assistant Professor in the Department of Advertising and Public Relations at the University of Alabama. His research interests include message and advertising effects, images of women and men in the media, and the influence of sexual appeals on persuasion. He authored *The Erotic History of Advertising* (2003) and his research has appeared in *Journal of Advertising, Journal of Communication,* and *Journalism Quarterly.*

Jonathan Schroeder (PhD, University of California, Berkeley) is Associate Professor at Sweden's Royal Institute of Technology in the Department of Industrial Economics and Management. He is also a research affiliate at the European Center for Art and Management in Stockholm. His research focuses on the production and consumption of images, with specific attention to photography as information technology. His book *Visual Consumption* (Routledge, 2002) introduces a theory of visual consumption. Borgerson and Schroeder have published many papers on visual culture together.

Juliann Sivulka (PhD, Bowling Green State University) is Assistant Professor in the College of Journalism and Mass Communications at the University of South Carolina–Columbia, where she teaches courses in creative strategy, campaigns, and history and philosophy of mass media. Sivulka has extensive advertising and marketing experience. She has authored the book *Soap, Sex, and Cigarettes: A Cultural History of American Advertising*.

Barbara B. Stern (PhD, City University of New York) is Professor II in the Department of Marketing at Rutgers, The State University of New Jersey. Her research interests include textual analysis of advertising messages, gender images in advertising, and the influence of message form on marketing communications. Her research has appeared in the *Journal of Consumer Research, Journal of Advertising,* and *Journal of Marketing*. She is the editor of the journal *Marketing Theory* and has won the American Academy of Advertising Outstanding Contribution to Research Award.

James Twitchell (PhD, UNC-Chapel Hill) has been at The University of Florida since 1972 and currently is Alumni Professor of English. He has written *The Living Dead: The Vampire in Romantic Literature* (1980), *Adcult USA: The Triumph of Advertising in America* (1996), *Lead Us Into Temptation: The Triumph of American Materialism* (1999), and *Twenty Ads That Shook The World: The Century's Most Groundbreaking Advertising* (2000). He is currently working on a book about the branding of culture.

Kevin Wise (MA, Indiana University) is a doctoral student in the Department of Communication at Stanford University. His research interests include physiological responses to communication technologies and the ways in which these responses influence how we process mediated messages.

Author Index

A

Alexander, M. W., 16, *34, 35*, 93, *105*
Apter, E., 74, *85*
Aristotle, 273, *278*
Ashmore, R. D., 23, 28, *34, 35, 37*
Atkin, C., 22, *35*
Avery, A. P., 226, *227*

B

Baker, M. J., 22, 23, *34*
Barlow, M., 162, *169*
Barry, T., 12, *34*
Bartlett, D., 251, *266*
Basil, M., 109, 111, *130*
Baudrillard, J., 134, 135, 140, 143, *149*,
        163, *168*, 274, 275, 277, *278*
Bedell, D., 249, *266*
Belch, G. E., 12, 16, 22, 24, *34, 36, 37*, 113,
        130
Belch, M. A., 12, 16, 22, 24, *34, 37*, 113, *130*
Belk, R. W., 162, *168*
Bello, D. C., 18, 23, *34*
Benfield, A., 162, *169*
Benjamin, W., 6, *8*, 134, 135, *149*
Berger, J., 227, 262, *266*
Bhabha, H., 81, *85*
Bly, R., 218, *227*
Boddewyn, J. J., 158, *168*
Bolls, P., 112, 113, 116, *130, 131, 132*
Bolter, J. D., 249, *266*
Borgerson, J., 66, 68, 76, 77, 82, *85, 87*
Bordo, S., 216, 220, 221, 223, 224, *227*, 262,
        267
Borse, J., 109, 110, *130, 131*

Boxer, A., 231, *245*
Bradley, M. M., 110, 111, 112, 116, 122,
        130, 131
Brashers, D. E., 27, 32, *35*
Bristor, J. M., 226, *227*
Brown, D., 14, *34*
Brown, G., 12, *37*, 99, *106*
Brown, S., 166, *168*
Brumbaugh, A. M., 23, *34*
Bryant, B., 12, *37*
Bryant, J., 14, *34*
Bullough, V. L., 1, *8*
Burgess, R. J., 234, *245*
Burgoon, M., 28, *34*
Buss, D. M., 22, *34*
Butler, M., 262, *268*
Byrne, D., 29, *36*, 157, *169*

C

Caballero, M. J., 22, *34*
Cadava, E., 68, *85*
Cain, R. F., 16, 22, *37*
Carey, J. W., 276, *278*
Carstarphen, M., 1, *8*, 11, 18, *36*, 156, *170*,
        244, *246*, 249, 253, *267, 269*, 273,
        278
Carter, A., 76, *85*
Cawelti, J. G., 221, *227*
Caywood, C., 111, *132*
Cherny, L., 249, *267*
Christ, W. G., 111, *132*
Chung, Y., 109, 110, *131*
Churchill, G. A., 22, 23, *34*
Clatterbaugh, K., 217, *227*
Coen, B., 107, *130*
Cohan, S., 217, *227*

Cortese, A. J., 76, *85*
Courtney, A. E., 3, *8*, 32, *34*
Cuthbert, B. N., 110, 111, 112, *131*

D

Dalrymple, H., 42, 47, 54, 58, *62*
Daniel, C., 46, *62*
Davenport, L., 263, *268*
Davison, W. P., 136, *149*
de Beauvoir, S., 215, *227*
D'Emilio, J., 231, 232, *245*
DeLillo, D., 274, *278*
De Mooij, M., 159, *169*
Dempsey, J. M., 15, *35*
Devereaux, G., 154, *169*
Dhillon, K., 109, 111, 112, 116, *131*
Dietz, R., 113, *131*
Dillard, J. P., 33, *35*
Dolliver, M., 11, *35*
Dong, Q., 109, 111, 112, 116, *131*
Dorfman, S., 15, *35*
Dotson, E. W., 225, *227*
Dubin, S. C., 244, *245*
Dudley, S. C., 160, *169*

E

Elliot, R., 68, *86*, 162, *169*
Englis, B. G., 23, 28, *35*, 263, 266, *268*
Etzel, M. J., 23, *34*

F

Fabricant, S.M., 158, *169*
Fanon, F., 84, *85*
Farrell, W., 217, *227*
Fernandez-Collado, C., 22, *35*
Ferrell, O. C., 98, *105*
Fetterley, J., 216, 224, 225, *227*
Fetto, J., *8*, *35*, 156, *169*, 245, *245*
Fischer, E., 226, *227*
Fishburn, K., 47, *62*
Fisher, W. A., 24, *35*, 157, *169*
Fitzsimmons, J. R., 112, *131*
Ford, J. B., 93, 94, 101, *105*
Foucault, M., 158, *169*, 230, *245*, 262, *267*
Fox, S., 44, *62*
Fraedrich, J., 98, *105*
Friedan, B., 59, *62*, 217, *227*, 262, *267*
Friestad, M., 111, *131*

G

Gad, T., 139, *149*
Gangstad, S. W., 18, *37*
Gantz, W., 108, *130*
Gardyn, R., 245, *245*
Geiger, S., 108, *131*
Gelb, B. D., 12, 16, *35*, 216, *228*
Genovese, D., 263, *267*
Giddens, A., 82, *85*
Gilmore, R., 110, 112, *131*
Gobé, M., 139, *149*
Goffman, E., 260, 262, *267*
Goldberg, H., 217, 218, 221, 226, *227*
Goldman, D., 248, 250, *267*
Goldman, R., 76, 84, *86*
Goldstein, R., 109, 111, *132*
Gollwitzer, P. M., 49, *63*
Goodrum, C., 42, 47, 54, 58, *62*
Gordon, L., 67, 81, 84, *86*
Gould, S. J., 25, *35*, 98, 101, *105*, 152, 153,
     154, 156, 157, 158, 159, 163, 164,
     166, *169*, *170*
Graef, D., 22, *35*
Grazer, W. F., 29, *35*
Green, H., 144, *149*
Greenberg, B. S., 15, 22, *35*
Greenwald, M. K., 110, 112, 116, 122, *130*, *131*
Gross, L., 230, 231, *245*
Grosz, E., 76, *86*
Gruenwedel, E., 252, *267*
Gunter, B., 111, *130*

H

Hall, S., 68, 74, *86*, 136, *149*
Hamilton, B., 224, *227*
Hamilton, C., 66, 69, *86*
Hamm, A. O., 110, 116, 122, *131*
Hansell, S., 248, *267*
Haraway, D., 262, *267*
Harris, R. J., 13, *35*
Hartman, T. P., 24, 30, *37*
Hawkins, R. P., 262, *268*
Hay, H., 231, *245*
Heckler, S. E., 13, 22, *36*, 113, *132*
Heeter, C., 15, *35*
Hendler, J., 148, *150*
Henthorne, T. L., 12, 16, 22, 29, *36*, 51, *62*,
     94, 95, 99, 100, 102, 103, 104,
     105, *106*

Herdt, G., 231, *245*
Herring, S., 249, *267*
Hirsch, J., 109, 111, *132*
Hirschman, E. C., 163, *170*
Holgerson, B. E., 16, 22, 24, *34*
Horner, P. M., 23, *35*
Horrocks, R., 221, 222, 223, *227*
Horton, S., 12, *37*
Hunt, S. D., 98, *105*
Hyman, M. R., 99, *106*

I

Irwin, D. G., 219, *227*

J

Jackson, S., 13, 22, 27, 32, 33, *35, 36,* 113, *132*
Jacobellis v. Ohio, 13, *35*
Janello, A., 50, *62*
Jhally, S., 74, *86,* 177, *180*
Johnson, M., 161, 162, *170*
Johnson, S., 147, *150*
Johnston, P., 54, *62*
Jones, A., 162, *169*
Jones, B., 50, *62*
Jones, M. Y., 12, 16, *35,* 216, *228*
Joseph, W. B., 22, 23, *35*
Jourard, S., 226, *228*
Judd, B. B., 16, *34, 35,* 93, *105*

K

Kahle, L. R., 23, *35*
Kaiser, C., 232, *245*
Kaplan, E. A., 78, *86*
Kawahara, K., 112, *130*
Kaye, B. K., 257, 258, *267*
Keesling, G. 29, *35*
Kelley, K., 157, *169*
Kellner, D., 230, *245*
Kerin, R. A., 12, 16, *36*
Kervin, D., 32, *35*
Key, W. B., 7, *8,* 25, *36,* 212
Kibby, M., 216, *228*
Kilbourne, J., 6, *8,* 93, 101, *105, 180,* 262, 263, *267*
Kimmel, M. S., 215, 216, 223, *228*
Klein, M., 249, *267*
Koppman, J., 16, 22, 24, *34*

Kopytoff, V., 250, 251, *267*
Korzenny, F., 22, *35*
Kramer, A., 25, 27, *37*
Kuczynski, A., 167, *170*
Kurzbard, G., 18, *37*

L

Laczniak, G. R., 98, *106*
La Ferla, R., 263, *268*
Lakoff, G., 161, 162, *170*
Lambiase, J., 1, *8,* 11, 18, 30, *36,* 156, *170,* 244, *246,* 247, 253, *267, 268, 269,* 273, *278*
Landow, G., 249, *268*
Lang, A., 108, 109, 110, 111, 112, 113, 115, 116, *130, 131, 132*
Lang, P. J., 110, 111, 112, 116, 122, *130, 131*
Lanham, R., 249, *268*
Lalvani, S., 81, *86*
LaTour, M. S., 12, 16, 22, 28, 29, *36,* 51, *62,* 93, 94, 95, 99, 100, 101, 102, 103, 104, *105, 106*
Lee, S., 109, 110, *131*
Lerman, D. B., 163, *169*
Lévi-Strauss, C., 79, *86*
Levonian-Morgan, B., 104, *105*
Lewis, R., 66, 69, 74, *86*
Lewittes, M., 225, *228*
Lin, C. A., 11, 14, 18, *36,* 273, *278*
Linsangan, R., 15, *35*
Locander, W. R., 161, *170*
Longo, L. C., 23, *34, 37*
Lukenbill, G., 229, *245*
Lutz, R. J., 12, *36*
Lyndon, N., 217, *228*

M

Maclaran, P., 166, *168*
MacKendrick, K., 78, *86*
MacKenzie, S. B., 12, *36*
Magid, L., 264, *268*
Maly, K. R., 254, *269*
Marchand, R., 49, *62*
Mardi, P. M., 232, *245*
McCann, M., 12, *36*
McClintock, A., 78, *86*
McDonald, D., 109, 111, *132*
McGuire, W. J., 12, *36*
McLuhan, M., 248, *268*

Medoff, N. J., 257, 258, *267*
Meijnders, A., 33, *35*
Mercer, K., 80, 81, *86*
Middleton, C., 93, 101, *105*
Miller, C., 101, *105*
Miller, E. G., 42, *62*
Miller, N., 231, *245*
Minowa, Y., 159, *169*
Mirzoeff, N., 68, *86*
Mishkin, M. E., 221, *228*
Mitchell, T., 251, *266*
Money, J., 151, *170*
Montgomery, C., 57, *62*
Moore, N. K., 33, *38*
Morgan, S., 1, *8*, 11, 18, *36*, 156, 161, *170*,
        244, *246*, 253, *269*, 273, *278*
Mormor, J., 232, *245*
Morris, M., 136, 137, *150*
Mosatche, H. S., 25, 27, *37*
Mosher, D. L., 157, *170*
Mosse, G. L., 218, 219, 222, *228*
Moulthrop, S., 146, *150*
Muehling, D. D., 12, *36*
Murphy, P., 98, *106*
Muschamp, H., 185, 186, *193*

N

Nataraajan, R., 94, 95, 104, *105, 106*
Nations, C., 18, *37*
Niebuhr, G., 226, *228*
Nielsen, J., 145, *150*
Needham, K., 249, 251, *268*
Negroponte, N., 248, *268*
Newhagen, J., 109, 111, 112, *131*

O

O'Barr, W. M., 68, *86*
Ogilvy, D., 59, *62*
O'Keefe, D. J., 27, 32, *35*
Okorafor, N. N., 263, *268*
Olsen, B., 159, *170*
O'Neil, S., 230, *245*
Ortner, S. B., 77, *86*
Osgood, C., 111, *132*
Ostrander, G. M., 46, 48, *62*

P

Pagendarm, M., 145, *150*

Paisley, W., 262, *268*
Papson, S., 76, 84, *86*
Pastore, M., 250, *268*
Pechmann, C., 12, *37*
Percy, L., 12, *36*, 113, *132*
Perry, J., 248, *268*
Perry, L., 148, *150*
Peterson, R. A., 12, 16, *36*
Petry, M. C.,112, *130*
Pietz, W., 74, 81, 85, *86*
Pingree, S., 262, *268*
Pitts, P. E., 18, 23, *34*, 94, 95
Poffenberger, A. T., 49, *62*
Pollio, H. R., 161, *170*
Poster, M., 248, 262, *268*
Potter, R. F., 112, 113, 116, *130, 131, 132*
Presbrey, F. S., 43, *63*
Pride, W. M., 22, *34*

Q

Quilty, N., 263, 266, *268*

R

Rakow, L. F., 262, *268*
Ramirez, A., 13, 18, 25, *37*
Ramamurthy, A., 68, *86*
Ratneshwar, S., 12, *37*
Reeves, B., 109, 111, 112, *130, 131, 132*
Reichert, T., 1, *8*, 11, 12, 13, 15, 18, 22, 25,
        30, *35, 36, 37*, 113, *132*, 156, 161,
        170, 244, *246*, 253, 254, *268, 269*,
        273, *278*
Reid, L. N., 1, *8*, 11, 12, 14, 16, 24, 30, *37*,
        38
Reidenbach, R. E., 99, 100, *106*
Richmond, D., 24, 30, *37*
Rickert, T., 139, 148, *150*
Ringberg, T., 216, *228*
Ritson, M., 68, *86*
Robin, D. P., 99, 100, *106*
Rodin, J., 221, *228*
Rosen, D. L., 25, 27, *37*
Ross, M. W., 1, *8*
Rossiter, J. R., 12, *36*, 113, *132*
Rotfeld, H., 93, 95, *105*
Rothschild, J., 262, *269*
Rothschild, M., 109, 111, *132*
Rotundo, A. E., 217, *228*
Rushkoff, D., 133, 134, 139, *150*

Ruth, W. J., 25, 27, *37*

S

Salik, S. H., 249, *269*
Sanders, D., 232, *245*
Sandikci, O., 216, *228*
Sapolsky, B. S., 15, 22, *37*
Sawchuck, K., 138, *150*
Scanlon, J., 49, *63*
Schaumburg, H., 145, *150*
Schneider, E. F., 113, *131*
Schooler, C., 111, *130*
Schroeder, J. E., 66, 67, 68, 69, 76, 77, 81,
    82, 83, *85, 87,* 216, *228*
Schwartz, N., 112, 113, *131*
Schweickart, P. P., 224, *228*
Sciglimpaglia, D., 16, 22, *37*
Scott, J., 112, *131*
Scott, W. D., 43, *63*
Seidler, V. J., 215, 219, *228*
Seidman, S. A., 15, *37*
Severn, J., 16, 22, *37*
Shapiro, E., 1, *8*
Shenk, D., 138, *150*
Shreve, J., 256, *269*
Siemicki, M., 15, *35*
Silberstein, L. R., 221, *228*
Simon, W., 163, *170*
Simpson, J. A., 18, *37*
Simpson, P., 12, 16, *37*
Singh, S. N., 25, 27, *37*
Snook-Luther, D., 94, 95, *105*
Soderman, A., 15, *35*
Soley, L., 1, *8,* 11, 12, 14, 16, 18, *37*
Solomon, M. R., 23, 28, *34, 35, 37,* 263,
    266, *268*
Solomon-Godeau, A., 66, 77, *87*
Stanaland, A., 12, 16, *35,* 216, *228*
Stanley, C., 15, *35*
Steadman, M., 12, 16, *37*
Steinem, G., 262, *269*
Stempel, G. H., 250, 251, 264, *269*
Stern, B. B., 66, 68, 76, 83, *87,* 216, *228,*
    274, *278*
Stevens, L., 166, *168*
Stewart, D. W., 12, *37*
Stewart, R. K., 250, 251, 264, *269*
Strickwerda, M., 109, *131*
Striegel-Moore, R. H., 221, *228*

Strnad, P., 191, *193*
Stroud, J., 12, *37*
Succi, G., 111, *132*
Sumner, J., 109, *131*

T

Tabarlet, J. O., 15, 22, *37*
Taflinger, R., 134, *150*
Tan, A., 111, *132*
Tannenbaum, P., 111, *132*
Tansey, R., 99, *106*
Thayer, R. E., 94, *106*
Theus, K. T., 25, *37*
Thompson, C. J., 161, 163, *170*
Thomson, K., 139, *150*
Thorson, E., 109, 111, *132*
Tinkham, S. F., 24, 30, *37*
Todreas, T., 139, *150*
Trebay, G., 167, *170*
Twitchell, J., 6, *8,* 134, 136, 142, *150,* 262,
    269, 274, *278*

V

Valdivia, A. N., 163, *170*
Villarreal, A., 12, *34,* 113, *130*
Vinikas, V., 48, *63,* 182, 184, *193*
Vitell, S., 98, *105*

W

Wallendorf, M., 162, *168*
Walker, J. R., 15, *38,* 273, *278*
Weininger, O., 220, *228*
Weise, E. R., 249, *267*
Weissberg, L., 66, *87*
Wells, L., 68, *87*
Whipple, T. W., 3, *8,* 32, *34*
White, L. A., 157, *169*
Wicklund, R. A., 49, *63*
Williams, A. J., 102, 103, *105*
Williams, L., 16, *38*
Williamson, J., 72, *87,* 262, *269*
Willis, S., 81, *87*
Wilson, R. D., 33, *38*
Winship, J., 260, *269*
Winsky, J., 91, *106*

Wise, K., 109, *132*
Wolf, N., 244, *246*, 262, *269*, 274, *278*

Y

Yoon, K., 113, *132*

Z

Zavoina, S., 1, *8*, 11, 18, *36*, 156, *170*, 244,
        246, 253, 254, *269*, 273, *278*
Zhao, X., 109, *131*
Zhou, S., 112, 113, *131*
Zizek, S., 138, *150*
Zwick, D., 68, *87*, 216, 228

Subject Index

A

Absolut vodka, 5, 65, 66, 69, 72, 73, 74, 75, 82, 83, 84, 233
Absolut Au Kurant, 66, 69, *70, 71, 72,* 73, *74,* 82, 83, 84
"Absolut Visions" (competition), 69
Ad response
    "feminist consciousness" and, 101–104
    unanticipated audience and, 93, 101, 137
Adbusters (web site), 158
Adcult, 6, 134, 181–193
    gender differences and, 183–184, 188, 191–193
Adolf Coors Company, 7, 234, 237
Advertising Age (trade journal), 91–92
Advertising lovemaps, 6
    characteristics and functions, 153–154
    defined, 152, *156*
    hermeneutic circle and, 160–163, 166–167
    individual differences, 156–157
    overdetermination of, 154–160
    postmodernism and, 163–166
    technological evolution and, 167–168
The Advocate (magazine) 224, 230, 233, 237, 239, 240
Adweek (trade journal), 11
Afrocentrism, 226
The Agency (motion picture), 197
Aguilera, Christina, 137
AIDS, 218, 232, 244
Alcohol, *see also specific brands*
    ads in billboard experiments, 109–111, 113–129

Allen Hosiery, 47
Amazon.com (web site), 146–149, 249, 253
American Men's Studies Association, 226
American Psychiatric Association, 232
Androgeny
    masculine image and, 220–222
Anheuser-Busch, 234, *235,* 237, 240
Anorexia, 188–189, 223
Appeals, *see* Sexual appeals
Aquinas, Thomas, 188–189
Aristotle, 273, 274
Arnott Female Autonomy Inventory, 101–102, 104
Arousal, 5
    ad response and, 91–98
    as dimension of emotion, 111–112
    message encoding and, 121–124
    sexual appeals and, 113–114, 119–120, 122–124, 127–129
    skin conductance and, 114, 116, 118–119
Association of American Soap and Glycerin Producers, 183
Attention
    arousal and, 112–113
    heart rate and, 114–117
    sexual appeals and, 107, 110–111, 113–114, 119–120, 127–129
    valence and, 118
Attention economy, 137–139
Attitude (magazine), 69
Attitude toward the ad, 12, 93, 94, 95, 96, 97, 100, 113, 114
Aura,
    ads and, 134–136, 141–144, 149
AXM (magazine), 240

B

Baileys liqueur, 25, *26*
The Beat Generation, 220
Beckham, Victoria, 263
Bel Ami (magazine), 167
Betty Crocker, 201, *202*, 203–204, *205*, 206
"Bigorexia," 223
Billboards, 5, 107–129
    experiments using, 114–129
Bly, Robert, 218
Boosler, Elayne, 189
Branch Davidian, 210
Bud Light, 7, 234, *235*, 237, 240, *241*, *242*
Bush, George W., 7, 195, 207, *208*, *209*, 210, 211, 276

C

Calvin Klein, 18, 39, 60, 61, 66, 93, 190, 192, 224, 234
Cannon Mills, 52–54
Casablancas, John, 263
Castellanos, Alex, 195, 211
Charlie (perfume), 59, 185
The Cleanliness Institute, 183
Coiner, Charles, 52
Coca-Cola, 60, 137, 139, 141, 187, 189, 190, 223
Coors Light, 234, *236*, 237
Corsets, 39, *40*, 46, 66, 69, *70*, 71–75
Cosmopolitan (magazine), 177, 244, 253, 254, 257, 275, 277
Cousins, Norman, 178
Crawford, Cindy, 6, 140–141, 274
Cyber models, *255*, 262–264, 266

D

Davidoff "Cool Water" ad, *17*
Deontology, 98–99
Disaronno Originale Amaretto, 240, *243*
"DisGraceful Awards," 258
The Dominatrix, 73, 76–77, 192, 258, *259*
Double entendres, 1, 5, 14, 18, 23, 48, 55, 176, see also Sexual referents
Durex condoms, *21*, 28
Dworkin, Andrea, 189

E

E-greetings ad, *24*, 28
The Economy of desire, 158
Elaboration Likelihood Model, 33
Encoding, 12, 108–109
    billboard experiments on, 120–127
Erotic appeals, *see* Sexual appeals
Erotophilia, 156–157
Erotophobia, 156–157
Esquire (magazine), 54, 57, 253
Esquire.com (web site), 254, 256
Evangelista, Linda, 176

F

Faludi, Susan, 189
Farrar, Steve, 226
Farrell, Warren, 217
The Fashion of the Times (magazine), 243
Feminism,
    consumer ad response and, 59–61, 101–104, 189–191
    the masculine dialectic and, 215–217, 226–227
    Men's movement and, 217
Fetishes,
    ads as creating, 162
    corset, 66, *70*, 72, 73
    dominatrix in, 73, 76–77
    explanation of, 65–67, 77
    leather, 67, 77–80
    liminal elements of, 67, 75, 79
    the ontology of, 80–81
    shoes, 77, 82
    stockings, *71*, 72–75
    visual qualities of, 66, 75, 81–82
Fetishism, 65–85, 223
    as lovemap-driven behavior, 152
    the male body and, 223–225
    marketing and, 74–75
    Marxism and, 81
Fireman's Fund ad, 154, *155*
Friedan, Betty, 59, 181, 217
Friedkin, William, 198
Freud, Sigmund, 2, 24, 27, 48, 183
Future Foundation, 225
FX Network, 162

G

Gays
    as contrary to "manly ideal," 220, 222
    "doublespeak" and, 229
    "leather lifestyle" and, 78–79
    marginalization of, 231–232
    media visibility and, 224, 233, 244–245
    sexuality construction and, 230, 233
Gender,
    ad treatment and, 82, 95–101, 191–193,
        253–257
    advertising lovemaps and, 156–157
    billboard results and, 116–118,
        122–123, 128–129
    "gender studies" rubric, 227
    germ theory and, 183–184
    subliminal use and, 204
    web sites and, 253–257
    the workplace and, 185–186
Good Housekeeping (magazine), 42, 46, 54,
    253
Google.com (web site), 146, 149, 250
GraceNet.net, 258, 262
Greenup, Gary, 210
GQ (magazine), 253, 257
GQ.com (web site), 254

H

Hass, Robert, 176
Hay, Harry, 231
Helms, Jessie, 211
Hermeneutic circle,
    advertising and the, 160–163
    postmodernism and the, 163–164, 165
Homosexuals, *see* Gays; Lesbians; Queer
Homoerotic appeals,
    Absolut vodka, *70*, 73–74
    Bud Light, 234, *235*, 237
    Coors Light, 234, *236*, 237
    Disaronno Originale Amaretto, 240,
        243
    Miller Lite, 237, *238*
    Prada, 240, 243
Holeproof Hosiery, 47

I

Illustrated Daily News (tabloid), 49

Iggers, Jeremy, 175
Innuendo, 14, 23, 28, 48, 240, *see also* Sex-
    ual referents
Instinct magazine, 230, 236–237
Interflora company, 240
Internet, banner ads and, 144–146,
    256–257
    information agents and, 147–149
    pornography, 167, 247–248, 250–253,
        256, 274
    popular search terms, 249–250
    sexual profiling on the, 257–258
    as technological marketing agent,
        167–168
    traffic statistics, 250
    web sites and gender, 253–257
Iron John (book), 218
iVillage.com (web site), 253–254
Ivory soap, 47, 182

J

Jacobellis v. Ohio, 13
Jackson, Joe, 144
Jhally, Sut, 177
Johnson, Virginia, 58
The Journal of Men's Health, 226
The Journal of Men's Studies, 216, 226
The Journal of the American Medical Society,
    177
Jovan Musk (perfume), 30, *31*, 175

K

Kanon (cologne), 7, *199*, 200–201, 204
*Killing Us Softly: Advertising's Image of
    Women* (motion picture), 173
Kinsey, Alfred, 58, 231
Kinsey Report, 177
Knutson, Gunilla, 192

L

The Ladies' Home Journal (magazine), 39,
    42, 44, 46, 51, 53, 54
Lambert, Gerald, 182
Lasker, Albert, 183
Laughter and Lust (album), 144
Lears, Jackson, 49

Leather
    as fetish item, 67, 77–80
    Second Skins ad, 164, *165*
Lesbians
    advertising for, 240, 243–244, 277
Lewis, Edith, 45
Liberal Feminist Attitude and Ideology
        Scale, 104
Life (magazine), 52, 231
Limited capacity model of media pro-
        cessing, 5, 108–111, 127–129
Linux Journal (magazine), 1
Listerine, 182
Look (magazine), 11, 52
Lovemaps, *see also* Advertising lovemaps
    consumer, 151–152, 160–163
    cultural consumer, 159, 161, 164
    exercises for finding, 153
    general concept of, 151–152

M

MacKinnon, Catherine, 189
Magazines, *see also specific titles*
    early gay, 233
    mainstream, 233, 253
    sexual appeals in early, 41–62
Maidenform, 59, 190
Marketing,
    as race, 133–134, 139
Marxism, 81, 186, 226
Mapplethorpe, Robert, 76, 80
Masculinisms,
    concept of, 215–219
    research into, 225–226
    masculinities (journal), 216
Masculinity
    definitions, 219–221
    and stereotypes, 221–222
Masters, William, 58
Maxim magazine, 18, *20*, 263, 277
Maximonline.com (web site), 8, 251, *252*,
        254, 256–257, 277
McCarthy, Jenny, 136
McLuhan, Marshall, 164, 186, 201, 211,
        248
Mechanical Brides: Women and Ma-
        chines from Home to Office (ex-
        hibit), 185–186
Media Metrix, 250, 259, 265
Media Watch, 191
Men's studies,
    basis of, 215, 225

    as emerging discipline, 226–227
    masculinist scholarship and, 216
    within gender studies, 227
Men's Studies Association of the Na-
        tional Organization for Men
        Against Sexism, 216
Men's Studies Press, 225, 226
Mencken, H. L., 46
Miller Lite, 237, *238*
Molson Export, 158
Moss, Kate, 188
MTV, 78
Munsey's (magazine), 42

N

1984 (novel), 211
The National Anthem, 162
National Center for Health Statistics, 188
National Gay Newspaper Guild, 229
National Organization of Women, 217
NBC (National Broadcasting Corpora-
        tion), 179
NetRatings.com (web site), 250, 253
The New York Times Magazine, 57, 70, 154,
        164, 243, 251
The New York Times (newspaper), 57
Newsweek, 207, 253
Nike, 176, 190
Nudity, 154
    as sexual information, 13–16
    in early ads, 47, 52–54
    ethics of, in ads, 98–101
    levels of, 16–17, 160
    sexual appeals and, 95–98

O

Ogilvy & Mather, 190
Orienting Responses (ORs), 109–110
Out (magazine), 230

P

Paco Rabanne (cologne), 59–60, 66
Palmolive, 51–52, 182
Paull, Sylvia, 258
Pepe Jeans, 18, *19*
Pepsi, 137, 149
    "Two Kids" ad, 6, 140–144, 147
Perkoff, Shirley, 184

Phallocentric appeals,
  Bud Light, 240, *241, 242*
  Diesel clothing, 237
  Slates clothing, 237, *239*
Photography, 25, 68, 135
  art of the nude, and, 52–54
  fetishism and, 66–67, 74–77, 80–82
Physical attractiveness, 14, 22–23
Playboy (magazine), 55, 61, 191, 253
Poetzle, Otto, 203
Pollock, Linda, 175
Polo Sport ad, *15*
Pornography, 178, 275
  defined, 13, 16
  fashion and, 73,74
  hermeneutic cycle and, 166–167
  Internet, 167, 247–248, 250–253, 256,
      274–275
  objectification and, 173, 176–177, 180,
      191
  subliminals in, 198
Prada (designer), 82, 240, 243
Printer's Ink (trade journal), 48, 50, 57
Promise Keepers, 219, 226
Psychology,
  advertising's early use of, 43–44,
      48–49

Q

Queer Nation, 232
Queer Theory, 226

R

R & G Corsets ad, 39, *40*
Redbook (magazine), 42, 253
Resor, Helen J. Lansdowne, 44, 46, 184
The Rhetoric, 273
Rosen, Raymond C., 178
Ross, Michael, 1
RuPaul, 176

S

S&M (sadomasochism)
  advertising themes, *71*, 76, 163, 166
Safeco Insurance, 233
SAM (Self Assessment Manikin) scale,
    121–122
Saturday Evening Post (magazine), 46, 50, 57
Savage, Dan, 178

Schultz, Robert, 173
Scripps Howard newspapers, 182
Scott, Walter Dill, 43
Second Skins ad, 164, *165*
The "Seven Sisters" (magazines), 42
Sex roles
  consumers and, 46–47, 49–52, 191–193
  manly ideal and, 220
  reversal theory and, 225–226
  paradigm of, 215
Sexing the Media (survey), 225
SexTracker, 250, 259, 265
Sexual appeals, 2–8, *see also* Homoerotic
      appeals; Phallocentric appeals
  ad environment and, 251–253
  billboard experiments using, 113–129
  defined, 13
  early uses of, 39–58
  feminist consciousness and, 101–104
  ethics theory and, 98–101
  lovemaps and, 159–160
  research into Internet, 248, 264–266
  objectification and, 179–180
  satirical study of, 91–92
  sexual brand benefits and, 30, *31*
  sexuality and, 175–177
  technological audiences and, 258–262
Sexual behavior, 14, 16–22
  facial expression and, *19, 20*
  levels of, 18, *21*
Sexual dysfunctions, 177–179, *see also*
      Fetishism
Sexual embeds, 6, 25–27, 206–211
Sexual explicitness,
  defined, *21, 24*, 28–29
Sexual information 13–27, *see also* Nu-
      dity; Sexual behavior; Physical
      attractiveness; Sexual referents;
      Sexual embeds
  defined, 13
  consumer behavior research and, 12
  future research, 27–33
  research types (table), 14
Sexual intensity,
  defined, 28–29
Sexual objectification, 7
  the "gaze" and, 160, 216, 224
  men and, 41, 224–225
  pornography and, 167, 173, 176–177,
      180, 191
  women and, 41, 82, 173–174, 179–180,
      261–262, 273

Sexually explicit ads
    and children, 264–265
Sexual referents, 14, 23, 24, 25
Shields, Brooke, 18, 60, 234
Shepard, Thomas, 11
Silo girl, 258–259
Simonton, Ann, 191
Sisley (designer), 76, 82
Skin
    fetishes and, 79–80
    cleanliness and, 181–182
Sky magazine, 178–179
Snitow, Ann, 176
Snowball.com (web site), 254–256
Society for the Scientific Study of Sexu-
    ality, 1
Soap ads, see also specific brands
    as deodorizer, 181–183
    in romance formula, 44–46, 50–52
Spears, Britney, 137
Spectacle advertising, 6, 134–135, 148–149
Springs Cotton Mills, 5, 55, 56, 57–58, 190
Steichen, Edward, 52–54
Stereotypes,
    fetishism and, 82
    male body and, 221–222
Stewart, Justice Potter, 13
Still Killing Us Softly (motion picture), 93,
    101, 275
Stockings, 47, see also specific brands
    as fetish items 71, 72–75
Stroh's Brewery
    Swedish Bikini Team ad, 103, 191
Stylin (magazine), 222
Subliminals, 134, 195–211
    artistic use of, 197–198, 202, 206, 211
    controversy, 25–27, 198–201
    dissonance and, 203–204
    genitalia in, 25, 197–198, 204, 205
    in motion pictures, 197–198
    prohibitions against, 210
    "RATS," 7, 195, 210–211
    "SEX," 206–208, 209, 276
    synesthesia and, 162, 202

T

Taboo,
    as aura source, 136
    penis as, 223–224
Tantric sex, 164, 167

The "Tease," 54–58
Teleology, 98–99
Tertullian, 188
Thompson, J. Walter, 44
Tide (trade journal), 55, 57
Time (magazine), 7, 207, 208, 209, 233,
    253, 276
Tommy Hilfiger, 229
True Story (magazine), 46, 50, 54
Twiggy, 188

V

Valence
    as dimension of emotion, 111–112
    facial electromyography and 114, 116,
        118
    message encoding and, 121–124
    sexual appeals and, 113–114, 119–120,
        122–124, 128
Venus in furs (novel), 78
Viagra, 1, 143
Victoria's Secret, 61, 66, 251
Virtual models, see Cyber models
Visual consumption, 67–68
    fetishism and, 81–82
Vogue Hommes (magazine), 167

W

Weber, Bruce, 61, 224
Wheel of Retailing model, 167–168
White Noise (novel), 274
Wolf, Naomi, 181, 186–189, 244
Women's studies
    predating Men's studies, 215–216
Woodbury's Facial Soap, 5, 44, 45, 46,
    50–51, 53, 54, 184
World Wide Web, see Internet

X

X10 video camera, 259, 260, 261, 262, 265

Y

Yahoo.com (web site), 140, 248, 250,
    251–252, 262

Z

ZZ Top, 78